American Furniture

AMERICAN FURNITURE 2003

Edited by Luke Beckerdite

Published by the CHIPSTONE FOUNDATION

Distributed by University Press of New England

Hanover and London

Cover Illustration: Detail of the back of a side chair, Baltimore, Maryland, 1803–1805. (Courtesy, Baltimore Museum of Art; photo, Gavin Ashworth.)

Design: Wynne Patterson, Pittsfield, VT
Copyediting: Alice Gilborn, Mt. Tabor, VT
Typesetting: Aardvark Type, Hartford, CT
Printing: Meridian Printing, East Greenwich, RI

Published by the Chipstone Foundation, 7820 North Club Circle, Milwaukee, WI 53217
Distributed by University Press of New England, Hanover, NH 03755
© 2003 by the Chipstone Foundation
All rights reserved
Printed in the United States of America 5 4 3 2 1
ISSN 1069–4188
ISBN 0–9724353–2–8

Contents

Editorial Statement

American Furniture is an interdisciplinary journal dedicated to advancing knowledge of furniture made or used in the Americas from the seventeenth century to the present. Authors are encouraged to submit articles on any aspect of furniture history, essays on conservation and historic technology, reproductions or transcripts of documents, annotated photographs of new furniture discoveries, and book and exhibition reviews. References for compiling an annual bibliography also are welcome.

Manuscripts must be typed, double-spaced, illustrated with black-and-white prints or transparencies, and prepared in accordance with the *Chicago Manual of Style*. Computer disk copy is requested but not required. The Chipstone Foundation will offer significant honoraria for manuscripts accepted for publication and reimburse authors for all photography approved in writing by the editor. Low resolution digital images are not acceptable.

Luke Beckerdite

Introduction

Jonathan Prown

With the publication of *American Furniture 2003*, the Chipstone Foundation continues its institutional mission to promote scholarship in the field of American decorative arts. The current issue offers a rich array of essays that cover many pertinent topics. As in the past, such diversity is by design. Luke Beckerdite, former executive director of Chipstone, first created the journal in 1993 and since then has served as editor. Throughout his tenure, Beckerdite has purposefully merged essays about the more iconic topics in American furniture study with newer analyses and interpretations that have helped to expand the canon of American furniture forms, makers, institutions, and collections. The journal encourages work from established furniture historians and also from younger scholars. Many of the rising figures in the field today got their publishing start in *American Furniture*. The widely acclaimed journal *Ceramics in America,* created in 2001 by Editor Rob Hunter, further demonstrates Chipstone's educational priorities and its support of innovative work in the field.

The year 2004 will see Chipstone's publication of *American Fancy: Exuberance in the Arts, 1790–1840* by decorative arts scholar and dealer Sumpter Priddy. Both in form and content, this groundbreaking study is an exciting addition to the existing body of literature on American furniture. The release of the book parallels the opening of a corresponding exhibit at the Milwaukee Art Museum (April 3–July 3, 2004). The show then will travel to the newly renovated galleries at the Peabody Essex Museum (July 7–October 31, 2004) and to the Maryland Historical Society (December 3, 2004–March 20, 2005). Priddy's study introduces the significant and, to date, curiously overlooked story of Fancy. As much a cultural attitude as a style in the arts, perfectly of its time and place, Fancy stimulated the visual and emotional experience of early Americans and enlivened the look of American homes and public spaces alike. The new book, as well as the exhibit, is informed by many different disciplines— philosophy, art history, aesthetics, gender studies, intellectual history, and economic history—all of which are essential to any informed and well rounded understanding of American Fancy. In this regard, Priddy provides the decorative arts field with an innovative interpretive methodology that necessarily transcends the traditional realms of connoisseurship and quantification, and is customized to meet the needs of his complex topic. *American Fancy: Exuberance in the Arts, 1790–1840* echoes the progressive and transdisciplinary trends that are forwarding work in all other areas of the humanities.

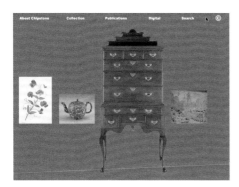

Figure 2   Current publications page from Chipstone.org.

Figure 1   Current home page from Chipstone.org.

Figure 3   A page from the Chipstone website documenting a former Chipstone exhibit at the Milwaukee Art Museum: *If These Pots Could Talk,* an exhibit of the Ivor Noël Hume Collection of Ceramics.

Figure 3   A page from the Chipstone website documenting another former Chipstone exhibit at the Milwaukee Art Museum: *Skin Deep,* an exhibit of inlay furniture.

Chipstone publications of yet another sort enliven the foundation's website, <www.chipstone.org>. Guided by the creative hand of Wynne Patterson, webmaster, this site explores the potential of various digital forms of decorative arts scholarship. To date, the emphasis in many American museum and foundation websites has been to offer an overview of the institution and, in fewer instances, to give partial scholarly access to artifacts in the collections. But new expectations on the part of both the public and younger specialists in the field are sparking more aggressive exploration of the digital realm. A growing number of organizations are actively seeking ways to further their educational programs by making collections available through the creation of more complete visual and information databases, which at last offer scholarly access to information that traditionally has been tucked away in curator work sheets and museum accession files. Chipstone.org now offers fuller access to the foundation's furniture holdings via a searchable and updateable database designed by a team of digital experts at the University of Wisconsin at Madison, and soon the ceramics collection will be online as well. For better or worse, many other organizations are feeling the same pressure to present this type of catalog online instead of on paper—in part because of its ability to be modified and augmented down the road, and also because of the significantly reduced cost and greater public access. Chipstone.org also is investigating the relatively new realm of virtual exhibits, which promise to give longer life to museum installations that in the past disappeared from sight forever after their brief gallery runs. Virtual exhibits effectively preserve the disciplined work of American decorative arts curators and provide a creative teaching alternative for university professors who now can move from conventional slide presentations to online explorations of web-based databases, articles, and exhibits.

In short, Chipstone is pleased to be a part of the evolving character of the American decorative arts world through the support of progressively minded publications and through the investigation of new technological alternatives. Few would argue with the basic fact that over the past several decades the trajectory of cultural studies—including furniture history—has advanced considerably and will undoubtedly continue to do so in the years to come. The role of American decorative arts museums and publishers is to figure out how to contribute to this exciting evolution.

American Furniture

Figure 1   Bishop Roberts, Charleston,
South Carolina, 1735–1739. Watercolor on paper.
15" x 43⅜" (Courtesy, Colonial Williamsburg
Foundation.)

Figure 2   Drayton Hall, Colleton County,
South Carolina, 1738–1742. (Courtesy, Drayton
Hall, National Trust for Historic Preservation;
photo, Ron Blount.)

John Bivins, Jr. *

Early Carving in the South Carolina Low Country: The Career and Work of Henry Burnett

▼ BETWEEN 1690 AND 1775, Charleston grew from a walled town of 800 inhabitants to the fourth largest city in the American colonies with a population of nearly 13,000. During most of the colonial period, the Low Country's society, economy, and culture were intimately linked to cultivation and export of rice and indigo, made possible through the exploitation of slave labor. These valuable commodities gave rise to an immensely powerful class of planters and merchants as well as a prosperous middling society. The scions of the wealthiest families traveled to Europe, had their children educated abroad, and furnished their homes with expensive imported goods as well as those made by local artisans. In 1740 Eliza Lucas noted that Charleston was a "polite agreeable place" where the people "live very Gentile and very much in the English taste (fig. 1)."[1]

As rice culture became entrenched during the second quarter of the eighteenth century, increasing numbers of planters began moving into the city. Drayton Hall, built by John Drayton between 1738 and 1742, was one of the last great plantation houses built outside Charleston (fig. 2). With a double portico derived from a plate in Andrea Palladio's *Quatto Libri* and interior details copied from plate 64 in William Kent's *Designs of Inigo Jones* (1727) (fig. 3), Drayton Hall was one of the most academic expressions of the English taste in Low Country architecture. John Drayton may have purchased these and other design books while in Europe during the 1730s.[2]

Although the artisans who worked on Drayton Hall remain anonymous, one carver was active in the Charleston area during construction of the house. On May 19, 1739, the *South Carolina Gazette* reported "STONE and Wood carving and Carpenters and Joyners Work, done by Richard Baylis, from London." Baylis had arrived in the city by April 13, 1738, when he was described as a "tobacconist" in a mortgage. This was undoubtedly the same man, since Baylis' advertisement also mentioned instruction "in the Art of Curing and Cutting Tobacco." No subsequent references to this carver are known, and it is possible that he returned to England.[3]

Charleston records and surviving furniture suggest that there was minimal demand for the services of professional carvers during the first half of the eighteenth century. The only carver documented in the 1740s is Thomas Watson who left his entire estate to cabinetmaker Thomas Elfe. Not surprisingly, few pieces of Low Country furniture from this period are carved, and those that are tend to have relatively simple ornaments. A tea table that reputedly belonged to Langdon Cheves of Charleston (fig. 4) and a sideboard table that descended in the Ladson family (fig. 5) are typical. Both

Figure 3 View of the chimneypiece in the great hall in Drayton Hall. (Courtesy, Drayton Hall, National Trust for Historic Preservation; photo, Wade Lawrence.)

Figure 4 Tea table, Charleston, South Carolina, 1740–1750. Mahogany with cypress. H. 28½", W. 29¼", D. 19½". (Private collection; photo, Museum of Early Southern Decorative Arts.) The applied edge molding of the top is missing.

Figure 5 Sideboard table, Charleston, South Carolina, 1740–1750. Mahogany with cypress. H. 30¼", W. 40", D. 22¾". (Collection of the Museum of Early Southern Decorative Arts.)

Figure 6   Detail of the knee carving on the tea table illustrated in fig. 4.

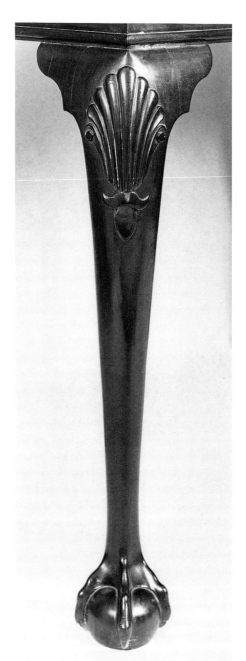

Figure 7   Detail of the knee carving on the sideboard table illustrated in fig. 5.

have simple shells on the knees (figs. 6, 7), although those on the tea table are less conventional in having leaf clusters at the bottom rather than husks. Similar leaves occur on the crest rails of two side chairs (see figs. 8, 9) that appear to be a few years later than the tea table.[4]

The earliest carving that can be attributed to a specific Charleston artisan is from the shop of Henry Burnett. On April 9, 1750, the *South Carolina Gazette* reported: "HENRY BURNETT, House and Ship carver from London, gives Notice to all persons who may be pleased . . . to employ him . . . that their work will be done in the neatest and best manner and on the most reasonable terms." The location of Burnett's shop is not known, but he advised potential customers to "enquire at Mr. Thomas Bentley's on

Figure 8 Side chair, Charleston, South Carolina, 1740–1760. Mahogany with yellow pine and cypress. H. 38¾", W. 22⁵⁄₁₆", D. 18¼". (Collection of the Museum of Early Southern Decorative Arts.)

Figure 9 Detail of the carving on the crest rail of the side chair illustrated in fig. 8.

Elliott's Wharff." Carvers catering to the ship building trade often established their businesses near wharves.[5]

Burnett's largest known commission was for £1000 worth of architectural carving for St. Michael's Church (fig. 10) done between 1754 and 1760. On July 5, 1757, he submitted a bill to the commissioners of the church for £100, which included a variety of moldings and seventy-two modillions for a Corinthian entablature for the facade. Three months later, Burnett charged forty-four pounds for carving "Two Composite Capitals 3 fronts each @ 7.7 for the Steeple." He apparently completed most of his work for the exterior of St. Michael's by November 30, 1758, when he furnished fifty-four double flowers for the portico valued at £108, or forty shillings each.[6]

Most of Burnett's carving was for the interior of the church (fig. 11). A daybook maintained by the commissioners of St. Michael's lists work provided between November 30, 1758, and July 8, 1760. During the winter of 1758, Burnett furnished ornaments for the ceiling including 143 feet of ovolo, eighty-eight trusses, and four large "double flowers" for the ceiling. The following January, he charged seventy pounds for a large "foliage flower" for the middle of the ceiling, £18.15 for fifty feet of ovolo molding for the

front of the galleries, and £338.2 for ten "Ionick Capitals for the Columns that supported the gallerys" (fig. 12). In 1760 Burnett focused most of his efforts on the pulpit, which was extremely elaborate by colonial standards (fig. 13). His work included:

> June 17th. Carved work for the Pulpit: To a Swelling Friese Cut Laurel Leaves 24.—.
> 24 Feet of Ogee carved 5 Leaved grass in the Cornish @ 5/ 6.—.
> 22 Feet Ovolo for the pulpit @ 7/6 8.5.—.
> 1 Large Ogee fully enriched 22 feet @ 10/ 11.—.
> 3/4 Ogee Carved 5 leaved grass 22 Feet @ 5/ £5.10.
> June 17th To 33 feet Ovolo for the Pannels @ 7/6 12.7.6.
> 16 Bracketts for the stairs of the Pulpit @ 40/ 32.—.
> Carving a Swelling Torus cut with Foliage Flowers & cut through & Relieved on the Backside 32.—.
> 40 feet of Ogee on ye Architraves 3/9 7.10.—.
> 1 Pine Apple on the top of the pulpit 12.—.
> 6 Brackets or Supports under the pulpit 9.—.
> July 8th 2 Corinthian Capitals for the Columns that support the Type of the Pulpit @ 29.8 58.16.—.
> 56 Brackets for the Stairs going up into the gallerys @ 20/ 56.—.

Fittingly, the final ornament furnished by Burnett was "a cherebims head & wings cut on the key stone on the upper order of the Steeple" valued at £5.15.[7]

Although the furniture and architectural carving attributed to Burnett's shop indicates that he received the patronage of important Charleston builders and cabinetmakers, he apparently had financial problems. While completing the work in St. Michael's Church, Burnett and his wife Mary had to mortgage three slaves to merchants William Ancrum, Lambert Lance, and Aaron Loocock against a bond for £3,364. On November 25, 1760, Burnett signed over to the merchants £800 of the £1030.15 he received as final payment from the commissioners of the church. The

11   HENRY BURNETT

Figure 14 Detail of a bracket on the stair leading to the gallery in St. Michael's Church. (Photo, Gavin Ashworth.)

Figure 15 Detail of a stair bracket on the pulpit in St. Michael's Church. (Photo, Gavin Ashworth.)

Figure 16 Detail of the Corinthian capital of a column supporting the hood of the pulpit in St. Michael's Church. (Photo, Gavin Ashworth.)

carver died eleven months later with a meager inventory valued at only £118. His effects included "A Lott of Gouges, Hold fast, two saws, one Glue Pott, &c £9—A Lott of New Gouges, thirteen dozen 12— . . . A Drawing Board Square & 3 Books 4— . . . A Carver Bench £1 . . . A Grindstone £2.10 a Lyon Carved & Kings Arms £2." The appraisers of Burnett's estate were builder Samuel Cardy, who certified the carved work in St. Michael's, and cabinetmakers Thomas Elfe and Robert Deans.[8]

The ornament in St. Michael's Church provides a benchmark for attributing other carving to Burnett's shop. Judging from his surviving work, Burnett was reasonably well versed in the late baroque style. His leaves and flowers have a bold, naturalistic quality reminiscent of British carving from

Figure 17 Detail of the carving on one of the supports for the pulpit in St. Michael's Church. (Photo, Gavin Ashworth.)

Figure 18   Benjamin Savage House, 59 Meeting Street, Charleston, South Carolina, 1747–1750. (Photo, Gavin Ashworth.) This residence is commonly referred to as the Branford-Horry House. The piazzas were added by William Branford's son Elias, probably during the second quarter of the nineteenth century.

the second quarter of the eighteenth century. There is no evidence that he was influenced by the rococo style, which became prevalent in the upper echelon of London's carving trade during the late 1740s and early 1750s.

The most complex leaf carving in St. Michael's Church is on the brackets of the stairs leading to the gallery (fig. 14) and pulpit (fig. 15) and the Corinthian capitals supporting the hood (fig. 16). Most of the detail on the gallery brackets is obscured by paint, but it clear that their leaves have distinctive curled ends like those on the supports beneath the pulpit (see fig. 17). The stair brackets for the pulpit were twice as expensive costing forty shillings each. Each has a stippled ground, floral rosette, and overlapping leaves with slightly pointed ends and deep shading cuts.

Burnett also received commissions for architectural carving in at least two residences, the Benjamin Savage House at 59 Meeting Street (fig. 18) and the John Cooper House at 94 Queen Street. Charleston merchant Benjamin Savage purchased the lot from John Allen in 1747 and probably began construction shortly thereafter. In 1750 he left Elizabeth Savage

"the daughter of my brother Thomas . . . my houses and Ground in Charleston . . . with all and singular buildings and appurtenances." Later she married William Branford, a wealthy planter from St. Andrews parish. All of the architectural carving dates from their tenure in the Savage house.[9]

As is the case with many early Charleston dwellings, the most elaborate room in the Savage house is on the second floor (fig. 19). The chimneypiece has bold egg-and-tongue molding, a central tablet with a shell and foliage (fig. 20), and a pulvinated frieze with interlaced strapwork, a diapered

Figure 20   Detail of the tablet appliqué on the chimneypiece illustrated in fig. 19. (Photo, Gavin Ashworth.)

Figure 21   Detail of the pulvinated frieze of the chimneypiece illustrated in fig. 19. (Photo, Gavin Ashworth.)

Figure 22   Detail of one of the floral appliqués of the architrave of the chimneypiece illustrated in fig. 19. (Photo, Gavin Ashworth.)

Figure 23   Detail of the keystone in the principal room on the second floor of the Benjamin Savage House. (Photo, Gavin Ashworth.)

Figure 24   Detail of the keystone in the second floor hall of the Benjamin Savage House. (Photo, Gavin Ashworth.)

background, and either flowers or leaves in the openings (fig. 21). Above the mantle shelf are stop-fluted Doric pilasters framing an architrave with ribbon and leaf moldings, floral appliqués (fig. 22), and a Greek-key inner border. The pilasters flanking the doorway have Corinthian capitals that are less elaborate versions of those supporting the hood of the pulpit in St. Michael's Church (fig. 16). Identical pilasters also frame the door in the hall, but the keystones of the arches are different (figs. 23, 24).

All of the early carving in the Savage House is made of cypress, a diffuse-porous wood that can be difficult to work with edge tools. The appliqué on the tablet of the chimneypiece in the second floor parlor (fig. 20) is the most ambitious carved component in the house, but it is relatively simple when compared with contemporary British work. The large leaves on either side of the central shell have close parallels in other carving associated with Burnett's shop, particularly the leaves on the stair brackets of the pulpit in St. Michael's Church (fig. 15) and the knees of the sideboard table illustrated in figures 43 and 44. Regrettably, early efforts to remove paint from the tablet have obliterated some of the carved detail. The frieze has survived in somewhat better condition. Like most of the leaf carving attributed to Burnett (see figs. 15, 30), the acanthus clusters at the corners of the frieze have lobes that were outlined with relatively flat gouges and deep shading cuts (fig. 21). The carver used the same basic formula of cuts to set in the design of the flowers in the strapwork repeats.

Figure 25 Detail of one of the metopie flowers in the first floor hall of the Benjamin Savage House. (Photo, Gavin Ashworth.)

Figure 26 John Cooper House, 94 Church Street, Charleston, South Carolina, 1745–1755. (Photo, Gavin Ashworth.) This residence is commonly referred to as the Thomas Bee House. The architectural carving on the stair was added a few years after the house was built.

Figure 27 Staircase in the John Cooper House.
(Photo, Gavin Ashworth.)

Figure 28 Detail of a stair bracket in the John
Cooper House. (Photo, Gavin Ashworth.)

Figure 29 Detail of one of the
metopie flowers on the stair frieze
in the John Cooper House.
(Photo, Gavin Ashworth.)

The architectural carving in John Cooper's house (fig. 26) may have
been completed shortly before Burnett's death. Most of his work is on or
near the stair (fig. 27) and includes brackets (fig. 28), newel posts, metopie
flowers (fig. 29), architrave appliqués, and keystones (fig. 30). The metopie

Figure 30 Detail of a keystone over a window in the John Cooper House. (Photo, Gavin Ashworth.)

Figure 31 Detail of a lion head intended for use on the end of an anchor beam. (Courtesy, Old Sturbridge Village). This ornament was never attached.

flowers are virtually identical to those in the first floor hall of the Savage house (fig. 25). These appliqués have five, large overlapping petals with slightly raised centers and fleurons comprised of four, small swirling petals. The most sculptural details in the Cooper house is the lion-head keystone on the arche of the window adjacent to the stair (fig. 30). Burnett carved a comparable keystone with "cherebims head & wings" for the steeple of St. Michael's Church and had "a Lyon Carved & Kings Arms" in his shop when he died in 1761. As a ship carver, Burnett would have been accustomed to producing mastheads and other figural ornaments. Lion's heads similar to those on the keystones in the Cooper house were occasionally attached to the ends of anchor beams (see fig. 31). The leaves descending from the lion's chin are simplified versions of those at the corners of the pulvinated frieze of the chimneypiece in the second floor parlor of the Savage house (fig. 21).

Four pieces of Charleston furniture can be attributed to Burnett's shop based on relationships between their carved details and those in St. Michael's Church and the aforementioned residences. The earliest is a bureau and cabinet (fig. 32) that reportedly descended in the family of Charleston merchant William Laughton Smith (1758–1812). His birth date suggests that he may have inherited the piece from his father Benjamin (1717–1812). Like most British double-case forms made during the second quarter of the eighteenth century, the bureau and cabinet is very architectural. Its pediment has parallels in British design books such as William Salmon's *Palladio Londinensis* (1732) (see fig. 33), and its interior features a writing compartment with a prospect door flanked by stop-fluted pilasters

Figure 32 Bureau and cabinet with carving attributed to Henry Burnett, Charleston, South Carolina, 1750–1755. Mahogany and mahogany veneer with cypress and mahogany. H. 93¼", W. 35⅛", D. 20½". (Collection of the Museum of Early Southern Decorative Arts.)

Figure 33 Design for a door on plate 26 in William Salmon's *Palladio Londinensis* (1732). (Courtesy, Winterthur Museum Library.)

Figure 34 Overall view of the bureau and cabinet illustrated in figure 32, showing the interior of the upper section. The drawers in the cabinet are faced with mahogany veneer and have crossbanded edges that appear to be rosewood.

(fig. 34). The cabinet section is almost completely in the Ionic order, ornamented with a carved pineapple (fig. 35), floral rosettes (fig. 36), a Greek key frieze, and pilasters. Burnett's hand is most evident in the modeling and shading of the rosettes on the pediment, which relate very closely to those on the stair brackets of the pulpit in St. Michael's Church (fig. 15). The rosettes on the pediment are more sculptural, having fleurons comprised of three small petals with a Y-shaped opening (fig. 36) rather than a simple convex element in the center. The small rosettes on the Ionic capitals (fig. 37) are almost identical to those on the pediment. Each of the small petals forming the tiny fleurons has three short shading cuts that converge at the base.[10]

Figure 35　Detail of the pineapple ornament on the pediment of the bureau and cabinet illustrated in fig. 32.

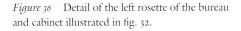

Figure 36　Detail of the left rosette of the bureau and cabinet illustrated in fig. 32.

Figure 37　Detail of the small rosette on the capital of the left, exterior pilaster of the bureau and cabinet illustrated in fig. 32.

The Smith bureau and cabinet is one of the most sophisticated examples of American case furniture from the 1750s. It follows contemporary London practice in having full-bottom dustboards, thin drawer frames and bottoms, delicate dovetail joints, exotic veneers, and moldings that are attached with glue rather than nails. The cabinet section also has details found in the Savage and Cooper houses, including Greek key frets and engaged pilasters. During this period, cabinetmakers and carvers often made their products conform to the specifications of patrons who wanted their furniture to resonate with their interiors.

A desk-and-bookcase that may have descended in the Porcher and Hayward families of Charleston (fig. 38) has engaged pilasters with Ionic capitals that are similar to those on the Smith bureau and cabinet (figs. 37, 39). Both sets of capitals have central rosettes and volutes with small leaves, but the carved details on the bookcase are slightly larger and more clearly

Figure 38 Desk-and-bookcase, Charleston, South Carolina, 1750–1755. Mahogany with cypress and mahogany. H. 97¾", W. 44½", D. 24¼". (Collection of the Museum of Early Southern Decorative Arts.)

Figure 39 Detail of the small rosette on the capital of the left, exterior pilaster of the desk-and-bookcase illustrated in fig. 38.

Figure 40 Detail of the shell ornament on the pediment of the desk-and-bookcase illustrated in fig. 38.

defined. The scallop shell rising from the plinth of the tympanum is one of the most sculptural furniture ornaments attributed to Burnett's shop (fig. 40). Its simple outline and naturalistic convex and concave lobes appear restrained when compared with the deeply modeled, and often gilded,

Figure 41 Dressing chest and cabinet, Charleston, South Carolina, 1755–1760. Mahogany and mahogany veneer with cypress and mahogany. H. 87½", W. 46½", D. 22½". (Private collection; photo, Museum of Early Southern Decorative Arts.)

Figure 42   Detail of the right rosette of the dressing chest and cabinet illustrated in figure 41.

shell ornaments found on contemporary English case pieces. Other than the "leaf grass" molding on the inner edges of the door stiles and rails, none of the carving on the desk-and-bookcase was gilded. The fret on the frieze of the cornice is a smaller version of that on the staircase in the Cooper house. The former was chopped with gouges, whereas the latter was cut with a fret saw. This "figure-eight" pattern is common on Charleston furniture and architecture from the last half of the eighteenth century.[11]

The latest case piece with carving attributed to Burnett's shop is a dressing chest and cabinet that descended in the Custis and Washington families of Fairfax County, Virginia (fig. 41). It has a broken-scroll pediment with a Greek key frieze, and may have had a pineapple ornament like the one on the Smith bureau and bookcase. The original rosette on the right scroll molding (fig. 42) is slightly more complex than those illustrated in figures 15 and 36, but its four-petal fleuron is similar to those on the metopie flowers in the Savage and Cooper houses (figs. 25, 29).[12]

In addition to having carving associated with Burnett, the desk-and-bookcase, bureau and cabinet, and dressing chest and cabinet appear to be from the same cabinet shop. The sequence of moldings comprising their cornices and friezes is virtually identical, and their case construction is very similar. Although the identity of the cabinetmaker remains a mystery, Burnett may have had a business relationship with Robert Deans and Thomas Elfe—the two cabinetmakers that appraised his estate. Deans was a Scot who worked in Charleston from 1750 to 1764 and may have been involved in the construction of St. Michael's Church. Around 1758 he and Charleston

Figure 43   Sideboard table, Charleston, South Carolina, 1750–1760. Mahogany with cypress. H. 27¾", W. 31¼", D. 25½". (Private collection; photo, Museum of Early Southern Decorative Arts.) This table has been reduced in width approximately sixteen inches.

Figure 44 Detail of the knee carving on the sideboard table illustrated in fig. 43.

carpenter Benjamin Baker submitted a proposal to the commissioners of the church for "undertaking and finishing the inside work." Although there is no specific evidence connecting Deans to the aforementioned furniture, the closest parallels to the bureau and cabinet are from Scotland. A similar case piece appears on the engraved billhead used by Edinburgh cabinet-maker Francis Brody. Thomas Elfe was one of the city's most successful cabinetmakers, working from about 1745 to 1775. His account books for the years 1768 to 1775 indicate that he produced elaborate and expensive case forms, but no furniture can be definitively linked to his shop.[13]

A sideboard table altered during the nineteenth century (fig. 43) is the only other piece of Charleston furniture with carving attributed to Burnett. The acanthus leaves on the knees emanate from scroll volutes on the knee blocks (fig. 44) rather than descending from the base of the leg stile as they do on most Low Country tables and chairs. Like the carving on the stair brackets of the pulpit in St. Michael's Church (fig. 15), the foliage on the table stands in high relief. Although different in basic design, the leaves on the table and brackets also have similar outlines, surface contours, and shading cuts. The feet of the table are equally distinctive in having subtly modeled knuckles, no webbing, and relatively tall balls; however, it is impossible to determine whether they represent the work of Burnett or another carver employed by the cabinet shop that made the piece.[14]

Like all of the carvers active in Charleston before him, Burnett had little competition in his trade. The only other carver known to have worked in the city during the 1750s was Henry Hardcastle, who emigrated from New York in 1755 and died the following year. Unlike Hardcastle, Burnett left a strong imprint on the city's material culture. His surviving work documents a developing taste for furniture and architectural carving that eventually reached its peak in the 1760s and early 1770s with the arrival of artisans from the upper echelon of London's carving trade.[15]

*This article is the first in a series that attempts to complete work on Charleston carvers begun by the late John Bivins, Jr. Had he lived a few more months, John would have included this research in his and Bradford Rauschenberg's landmark publication *The Furniture of Charleston, 1680–1820*. The Chipstone Foundation is indebted to Anne McPherson and the Museum of Early Southern Decorative Arts for allowing *American Furniture* to present this material.

1. J. Thomas Savage, "The Low Country," in Ronald L. Hurst and Jonathan Prown, *Southern Furniture, 1680–1730: The Colonial Williamsburg Collection* (New York: Harry N. Abrams, 1997), pp. 23–25; and Bradford L. Rauschenberg and John Bivins, Jr., *The Furniture of Charleston, 1680–1720*, 3 vols. (Winston-Salem, N.C.: Museum of Early Southern Decorative Arts, 2003), 1: 51–52. As quoted in Savage, "The Low Country," p. 24.

2. Savage, "The Low Country," p. 25. For more on Drayton Hall, see Lynne G. Lewis, *Preliminary Archaeological Investigation at a Low Country Plantation* (Charlottesville: University Press of Virginia for the National Trust for Historic Preservation, 1978). Margaret B. Pritchard, "John Drayton's Watercolors," *Antiques* 163, no. 1 (January 2003): 166–73.

3. Rauschenberg and Bivins, *The Furniture of Charleston*, 3: 901–2.

4. Ibid., 3: 1286–87; 1: 263–64, fig. CT-34; 1: 257–59, fig. CT-30. A sideboard table by the same carver and cabinetmaker who produced the Ladson example is illustrated in vol. 1, p. 260, fig. CT-31. It has a history of descent in the Matthews and Peronneau families of Charleston. The other chair, which has carved knees and gadrooned molding attached to the rails, is illustrated in Edward Wenham, *Collectors Guide to Furniture Designs (English and American) from the Gothic to the Nineteenth Century* (New York: Collectors Press, 1928), p. 28.

5. Rauschenberg and Bivins, *The Furniture of Charleston*, 3: 928–29. All of the figures cited are in Charleston currency. From 1758 to 1762 the exchange rate between England and South Carolina was approximately 7:1. John J. McCusker, *How Much is That in Real Money? A Historical Commodity Price Index for Use as a Deflator of Money Values in the Economy of the United States* (Worcester, Mass.: American Antiquarian Society, 2001), p. 69.

6. In 1754 Burnett submitted a bill for unspecified work totaling £200. The Corinthian entablature noted in Burnett's bill of July 5, 1757, included ninety feet of egg-and-tongue bed molding valued at five pence per foot (£22.10), ninety feet of "hanover point" molding at five pence per foot (£22.10), ninety feet of a smaller or less intricate "hanover point" molding at three pence per foot (£16.17.6), and ninety feet of beaded molding at two shillings six pence per foot (£11.5). The seventy-two modillions cost thirty-six pounds, or ten shillings each. (Rauschenberg and Bivins, *The Furniture of Charleston*, 3: 928.)

7. As transcribed in ibid., 3: 928–29.

8. As transcribed in ibid., 3: 929. On January 31, 1774, the *South Carolina Gazette* reported: "The same Day [January 24] died very suddenly, Mr. Samuel Cardy, the ingenious Architect, who undertook and completed the Building of St. Michael's Church" (Beatrice St. Julien Ravenel, *Architects of Charleston* [1945; reprint, Columbia: University of South Carolina Press, 1992], p. 32).

9. Jonathan H. Poston, *The Buildings of Charleston: A Guide to the City's Architecture* (Columbia: University of South Carolina Press for the Historic Charleston Foundation, 1997), pp. 80–81, 236–64. The Savage House is more commonly referred to as the Branford-Horry House, and the Cooper House is more commonly known as the Thomas Bee House. Bee was an attorney, planter, delegate to the Continental Congress, and judge. He owned the house from 1771 to 1799. The author thanks J. Thomas Savage for these references.

10. Rauschenberg and Bivins, *The Furniture of Charleston*, 1: 84–88.

11. Ibid., 1: 88–92.

12. Ibid., 1: 92–95.

13. Ibid., 3: 963–65 (Deans); 3: 995–1003 (Elfe); 1: 84–88.

14. Ibid., 1:272–74, fig. CT-40.

15. For more on Hardcastle, see Luke Beckerdite, "Origins of the Rococo Style in New York Furniture and Interior Architecture," in *American Furniture*, edited by Luke Beckerdite (Hanover, N.H.: University Press of New England for the Chipstone Foundation, 1993), pp. 15–39.

Nancy Goyne Evans

Everyday Things: From Rolling Pins to Trundle Bedsteads

▼ THROUGH THE YEARS scholars have paid little more than minor attention to the ordinary products and activities of the furniture craftsman, aside from the body of material interpreted as folk art. Formal furniture and objects crafted from fine cabinet woods have dominated the pages of published works. Nevertheless, original documents that illuminate the period of handcraftsmanship in America before 1850 are filled with references to the objects, implements, and fixtures of everyday life in the domestic setting. Because of the wealth of material available, this study will explore only a limited number of selected topics, some more broadly than others. Principal among these are wooden objects associated with the kitchen and adjacent facilities, furniture for sleeping, boxes and selected storage furniture, and equipment used in the fabrication of cloth and other household textiles.[1]

Kitchen Furniture and Equipment

Two of the most common pieces of furniture associated with the kitchen during the period covered by this study are the table and the rush-bottom slat-back side chair, both identified in craftsmen's accounts by their intended place of use. At least one written reference and a variety of visual images hone in on a critical feature associated with the kitchen table, the absence of stretchers. In October 1802 Silas Cheney, a cabinetmaker and chair maker of Litchfield, Connecticut, made special note of a customer's order for a "Citchen table with Crecher." The request suggests that bracing of this type was unusual in kitchen tables (fig. 1), a circumstance borne

Figure 1   Kitchen table, southern New England, 1780–1810. Maple with pine top. H. 27½", W. 42½", D. 30½". (Private collection; photo, Winterthur Museum.)

Figure 2 Kitchen, or common, side chair, Bergen County, New Jersey, 1800–1830. Maple and ash. H. 40¼", W. 19⅜", D. 18". (Courtesy, Winterthur Museum, gift of Charles van Ravenswaay.)

out by illustrations of the period that focus on this area of the home. One particularly relevant visual reference is John Lewis Krimmel's sketch of a young woman ironing (fig. 6). The absence of stretchers on tables that served as stand-up work surfaces offered convenience for the feet and protection for the shins.[2]

Prices for kitchen tables were modest, the dimensions and choice of material determining the exact cost. Of the documents used in this study that itemize kitchen tables, approximately one-third name the construction material. The records range in date from the late eighteenth century to the late 1830s and in geographic origin from northern New England to the

Middle Atlantic region. Pine was the popular choice. One example was combined with "whitewood," probably yellow poplar. Cherry was the second most popular choice, with maple named occasionally. An account entry for September 9, 1822, in the records of Job E. Townsend of Newport, Rhode Island, describes another selection: "a Kitchen Table Burch frame and a Pine Top." The same year Silas Rice of Middletown, Connecticut, acquired a kitchen table with a butternut top from Elizur Barnes. Decades earlier in 1770, Samuel Williams built the wealthy Philadelphian John Cadwalader a sturdy "Oak Top Kitchen Tabble."[3]

In terms of size, more kitchen tables are identified as "large" than as "small." Actual dimensions, given only occasionally, range from two feet, three inches, in the bed to "5½ feet long." The working surface and/or storage function of a table was enhanced by the addition of a fall leaf and a drawer. The single leaf, also called a "flap" or "wing," was relatively common; two leaves were rare. When the leaf was not in use, the table often was positioned with the closed board at the back.[4]

Aside from providing a working surface to pursue household chores, the kitchen table served at times as a family dining center, especially in the cold winter months when the kitchen frequently was the warmest room in the house. A notation of 1830 in the accounts of Elisha H. Holmes of Essex, Connecticut, to a "Kitcheon dining table" serves to confirm this function. Although many kitchen tables likely were painted, there is little mention of finish in period records. A few documents identify stain and varnish as a protective surface.[5]

A group of seating pieces, designated "kitchen chairs" in records, can be identified from their unit costs as slat-back side chairs (fig. 2). In general, valuations range from three shillings to 4s.6d. Major General Henry Knox paid Stephen Badlam, Jr., of Dorchester Lower Mills (Boston) 3s.8d. in 1784 for each of six kitchen chairs ordered at the shop. By comparison, other woven-bottom chairs, namely those in the banister-back and fiddle-back (vase-back) patterns, cost consumers an additional 1s.6d. or more. A Windsor side chair was priced still higher. For orientation purposes, it is well to note that the decimal-based currency system adopted by the new United States in the late eighteenth century usually equated the dollar with six shillings in the old-style currency of the country. Many craftsmen, however, continued to use the pound as the monetary unit in their records well into the nineteenth century.[6]

A small group of kitchen chairs whose valuations exceeded 4s.6d. or five shillings was embellished. Customers may have requested the addition of another "back," or slat, to the basic three-slat structure, ordered turnings of more ornamental character than standard (fig. 2), or contracted for something more than a common stained or colored finish. When Erastus Holcomb ordered "six citching chairs painted green and varnished" in 1820 at Oliver Moore's shop in East Granby, Connecticut, he paid six shillings (one dollar) per chair. Conversely, low prices in kitchen chairs sometimes reflected the lack of finish on the wood or the absence of the woven bottom, the work left to the customer or a handy neighbor. The quality of rushwork in a woven seat was another factor that influenced cost. William Barker's work for Jabez Bowen, Jr., at Providence in the 1760s indicates that a "fine bottom" cost two-thirds more than a standard one. It was a fact of life that rush-bottom chairs had to be returned to the local chairmaker or bottomer on a regular basis for seat repair or replacement. This circumstance more than any other gave the plank-seat Windsor an advantage, permitting the new construction to sweep the vernacular seating market by the American Revolution.[7]

Special kitchen seating appears in records from time to time. In January 1822 True Currier of Deerfield, New Hampshire, sold an area resident "a kitchen chair with rockers & arms" for one dollar. A customer of Philadelphia cabinetmaker David Evans also made an unusual request. Shortly after the end of the Revolution, George Bringhurst ordered "a Pine Bench for [the] Kitchen 2 or 3 Seats." The long form probably was backless with board ends cut out in an ornamental pattern to form feet (see fig. 21).[8]

Closets, shelves, and storage furniture, such as cupboards and dressers, were critical in the colonial and federal kitchen to hold equipment for meal preparation and dining and the paraphernalia associated with other activity in the area. Storage furniture had open shelves or enclosed compartments, or combinations of the two features. When Joel Bartlet made alterations to his house in Newbury, Massachusetts, in 1749, Skipper Lunt charged him five pounds for "making [a] cuberd in ye new kit[c]hen." The price was a pound less than Lunt's charge for a chest of drawers or a set of cane-back chairs. The exact purpose of Abigail Bursley's storage unit purchased almost ninety years later from Moses Parkhurst of Paxton is noted in the craftsman's accounts: "To one crockery cupboard."[9]

With the kitchen in constant use, the need for furniture repair was inevitable. Moses Ingersol was indebted to Elisha Hawley of Ridgefield, Connecticut, in 1794 for making a cleat (probably a foot) for his cupboard. In Barre, Massachusetts, Luke Houghton responded to customer needs in the 1820s by putting a back on a cupboard for the widow Abigail Wheeler and two "turns" for doors on a similar storage piece for Doctor Anson Bates. At about the same date Miles Benjamin, a cabinetmaker of Cooperstown, New York, made a new cupboard turn for one of his customers.[10]

The accounts of five craftsmen who worked in central and eastern Pennsylvania sometime during the fifty-year period between 1790 and 1840 shed considerable light on the popularity of the kitchen cupboard, or dresser, in a region inhabited by individuals of both English and German background. Among them Jacob Bachman, Friedrich Bastian, John Ellinger, Abraham Overholt, and Peter Ranck produced dozens of examples. Collectively, their records add dimension to the study of the form.[11]

The records identify a few cupboards with glazed doors in the top section. Overholt produced an eighteen-dollar "dish cupboard with 24 panes" in 1827 for Magdelena Gross. A related Pennsylvania cupboard is in the left background of figure 17. Rather than hinged to swing out, the doors were made to slide. The interior shelves hold china cups, pewter plates, glassware, and crockery. Many dressers were of open construction, as indicated

in the modest pricing of some examples. Lewis Miller's sketch of an incident that occurred in 1809 in York, Pennsylvania, illustrates the general form of the open dresser (fig. 3). As explained by Miller, members of the Rupp family of butchers were driving a young steer through the streets when it bolted and charged through the open door of Jacob Laumaster's kitchen knocking over the dresser. The visual account of the calamity provides an unusual opportunity to examine the contents of the furniture form: a row of spoons secured in slots at the front edge of a shelf probably was made of pewter; lighting devices, comprising a candlestick and a dish-type lamp, were stored on the flat top of the projecting cornice; earthenware for everyday use located on the open shelves consisted of plates, cups, bowls, a cream pot, and a covered sugar bowl; two-tined forks and knives may have had bone or wooden handles; a coffee mill still pitching through the air probably rested on the deep top surface of the lower cupboard along with the large crock at the left, which may have held preserves.[12]

Many dressers were painted. Overholt mentioned brown and red (reddish brown). Although he did not specify the wood used for his painted cupboards, many of his contemporaries relied on yellow poplar, the wood identified in Bachman's account with Evans. Overholt also produced many "walnut kitchen dresser[s]" and charged substantially more for them than the painted cupboards.[13]

Mention of two special-purpose cupboard forms occurs in the accounts of both Pennsylvania and New England craftsmen. Householders who purchased milk or cheese cupboards may have placed them in a buttery, or dairy room, located in a cool part of the house. The cupboards likely were deep, with open fronts and shelves of shallow vertical depth to accommodate the large milk pans used to separate cream from fresh milk or to store and cure the large cylinders of cheese the housewife and family members made from milk curds. Overholt noted in 1804 that he "made a milk cupboard for Christian Gross and painted it brown" at a charge of £2.12.6.[14]

Several records mention bench-mounted food-processing equipment. In 1834 William Clark of Lebanon County, Pennsylvania, purchased a "Sasuage

Figure 4 Stave bucket, eastern United States, 1790–1830. Pine. H. 11¾", Diam. 9¼". (Courtesy, Winterthur Museum, gift of H. Rodney Sharp.) The bail handle is missing.

Bench" from John Ellinger for $1.50. William Rawson of Killingly, Connecticut, filled a customer order in 1840 by making an "Apple paring Bench." When Israel Houghton provided a similar piece of equipment at Petersham, Massachusetts, he described it as an "aple paring masheen." "Machine" was a word applied to a range of simple hand-operated mechanical devices in an era before other power sources were employed.[15]

Laundry Equipment

The two principal domestic activities centered in the kitchen and adjacent areas were laundry and food preparation. Either could employ considerable equipment, as identified in early records.

Doing the household laundry required a substantial amount of water, which had to be carried from a well or other water source to a stove or hearth where it was heated. Pails, or buckets, of stave construction bound around with wooden hoops and fitted with carrying bails attached at opposite sides to the tops of staves of extended length were the common vessels for this task (see fig. 4). Other pails held a general supply of household water or were used as scrub buckets.

Cabinetmakers as well as handymen-carpenters supplied householders with pails, some purchased in pairs. Families also called upon local woodworkers for repairs when bails and bottoms required replacement. Other pails were repainted. Joseph Griswold of Buckland, Massachusetts, recorded in 1818 that he painted several pails blue and another red. Red also was the color requested by a customer of Allen Holcomb a few years later in central New York, with the further instruction that the interior be painted white. Another customer paid Holcomb fifty cents for "painting 2 pails yellow & inside white."[16]

The actual process of washing clothes required tubs, vessels larger than pails and also of stave construction. The word "trough" was an alternative term. Cedar is mentioned specifically as the material of some tubs. F. Andrew Michaux, Jr., in extensive observations made from 1806 to 1809 when studying the forest trees of North America and their uses, commented on the "superior fitness of this wood for various household utensils," principally pails, wash tubs, and churns. He further noted that "the hoops are made of young cedars stripped of the bark and split into two parts."[17]

Most wash tubs were elevated above floor or ground level for convenience of use. The usual support was the wash bench, a piece of equipment mentioned frequently in craftsmen's accounts. The substantial range in price suggests that material, size, and construction method could vary considerably. David Evans, a cabinetmaker of Philadelphia, made the family of Charles Shoemaker a "Large Wash bench 6 foot Long" in 1791 and charged the head of the household 7s.6d., a price that exceeded a day's pay for a journeyman woodworker at the top of his trade. Another woodworker identified the support for a wash tub as "a washing Stuell."[18]

Soaping, soaking, scrubbing, rinsing, and, frequently, boiling in a kettle were tasks associated with the laundry. Laundresses frequently had both hard and soft soap available for the job. The "Soap Tub made of white pine" purchased in 1823 by a customer of Samuel Douglas near Canton, Connecticut, apparently stored soft soap. When Abraham Overholt of Pennsylvania noted in 1822 "I made a washboard for Jacob Lederman," he identified a critical piece of equipment used in most households to scrub clothes. His charge was fifty cents, the common price recorded from New England to Pennsylvania. Clothes heavily soiled might require the assistance of a pounder, precisely identified by Job Danforth of Providence as a "pounder to pound Cloaths." An alternative term was "wash pounder." Both Silas Cheney of Connecticut and Daniel and Samuel Proud of Providence pinpointed the usual fabrication method of the implement as turning.[19]

A popular item from the beginning of the nineteenth century was a piece of equipment identified in craftsmen's records as a washing machine. Some accounts note repairs; other modest charges appear to identify simple attachments to be mounted on standard equipment. When the price of a new machine approached or exceeded ten dollars, something out of the ordinary was indicated. In general, the form was that of a tub or box, open or closed at the top and fitted with some type of manual mechanism to introduce agitation. In 1800 Philip Filer of upstate New York priced his eleven-dollar "woshin mill" the same as his best bedsteads. Several years later in Connecticut Oliver Moore sold a "washing Mashine" for as low as $5.75, although he sold it "without irons," that is, without the metalwork that was part of the operating mechanism. As Nicholas Low, a New York City merchant, developed his upstate property at Ballston Spa in the early 1800s, his on-site agent contracted with local craftsmen to furnish a new hotel. In a letter to Low dated November 6, 1803, George White noted that Elihu Alvord, one of the artisans employed on the job, "also has a patent for making Washing Machines @ $10. each Sayd to answer very Well."[20]

Once the clothes were washed, rinsed, and wrung, they were ready to be dried. In good weather they could be placed out of doors, where they were hung on clotheslines, draped on bushes, and/or spread on the grass. Clothespins are named in many craft records, although the term can be ambiguous, as indicated in the records of several woodworkers. Two separate entries in the account book of Allen Holcomb of New York state describe the dual meaning of the term "clothespin." On October 26, 1824, he sold Doctor Hailman "45 Close pins to hold Close on a line" at two cents apiece. There is little question that these were small turned or shaved cleft sticks of the type illustrated in figure 5. A decade earlier Holcomb turned "24 Nubs for Clothes hangings" for another customer. These were pins turned with round tenons at one end for insertion into a pinboard mounted on the wall to store cloaks and other garments. Further clarification of the use of pins on the wall occurs in two accounts: Jonathan Gavit of Salem, Massachusetts, described nubs as "pins . . . to hang Cloaths on"; Joel Mount of Juliustown, New Jersey, spent part of a day in 1846 "putting up close pines."[21]

Of all the accouterments for the laundry, the one mentioned most frequently is the "clotheshorse," or "frame," also referred to occasionally as a

Figure 5 Clothespin, a Shaker community in eastern United States, 1800–1860. Wood. L. 6¾". (Courtesy, Winterthur Museum, gift of Mrs. Edward Deming Andrews.)

"clothes screen." The lone reference to a "clothes ladder," which appears in the accounts of James Francis of Connecticut for March 17, 1797, probably identified a similar piece of furniture, since stiles and rails of open construction are common to both clothes frames and ladders. The function of this piece of equipment, regardless of the terminology, is described succinctly in an item dated August 26, 1766, on a sheet of accounts drawn by Nathaniel Kinsman of Massachusetts: "To a hors to dry Cloths." During periods of inclement or severely cold weather, the laundry was dried indoors, at which times folding frames for drying were a necessity. Frequently wet laundry was scattered from the kitchen to the attic. A highly specialized type of clothing frame mentioned by David Hall of Connecticut is represented by a group of four "Stocking boards" sold in 1793 for two shillings.[22]

The incidence of clothes frames in craftsmen's accounts describes a broad geographic spread. In Portsmouth, New Hampshire, Dolly Wendell paid Joseph Cotton nine shillings ($1.50) in 1800 for "a Close horse & Hinges." At two dollars, Humberston Skipwith of Mecklenburg County, Virginia, paid slightly more for his clotheshorse in 1819. Although records identify some clotheshorses of small size, of greater interest are the frames that consisted of three or four panels, described as "folds," "falls," or "wings." The term "folds" was the most popular. The accounts of Miles Benjamin, of Cooperstown, New York, mention a "double clothes Horse." Whether the folds were of larger size or greater number than usual is unclear, although at three dollars this was the most expensive frame listed anywhere.[23]

Records list painted clothes frames, and when a color is named, it is usually white. Silas Cheney of Connecticut sold a horse of this finish to Oliver Wolcott in 1802 for six shillings (one dollar). At Hartford Daniel Wadsworth paid more than two times that amount to Benoni A. Shepherd for his white frame. When requested, both cabinetmakers also produced cherrywood clothes frames. The only other cabinet wood associated in records with this frame is birch. Job E. Townsend of Rhode Island made one in 1823 for seventy-five cents. In New York state Philip Filer sold "Stuf for [a] Closehorse" for twenty-five cents, a savings to the consumer of $1.75 over the framed price.[24]

Ironing followed washing during the week, preferably when the hearth or stove was in use for another purpose, such as baking, so that the flatirons could be heated at the same time. The critical piece of furniture for this task was the "ironing bench," "table," "board," or "folding board." In December 1800 Reubin Loomis of Connecticut made note of "puting up a bench to iron on" at the small charge of 2s.6d. (forty-one cents). Later in Maine, Paul Jenkins recorded a job of making an "ironing tabel 2 drass" (drawers) for Captain George Lord. The price at $2.84 reflected the cost of constructing a frame with four legs and providing drawers for storage. Illustrating this type of table are the plain examples visible in figure 6, a drawing made by John Lewis Krimmel in the Delaware Valley near Philadelphia. Whether the extended ironing surface at the left represents the

Figure 6   John Lewis Krimmel, *Woman Pressing and Folding Laundry,* Philadelphia, Pennsylvania, or vicinity, ca. 1819–1820. Watercolor over pencil. Dimensions not recorded. (Courtesy, Winterthur Library: Joseph Downs Collection of Manuscripts and Printed Ephemera.)

table top or a long board laid over the top is unclear. The extended table top in the right background probably is a loose board.[25]

The laundress shown in figure 6 is using a flatiron. A trivet to support the hot iron is at the right and a flatiron grown cold at the left. The tables are covered with old blankets or flannel and a top sheet. Many housewives reserved a set of table covers especially for ironing. The wooden laundry basket on the floor is made of angled, butted boards with handholds at the ends. Another drawing by Krimmel clearly delineates a row of flatirons stored on a kitchen shelf high above the hearth. Some flatirons had cast metal handles; others had wooden grips. Abner Haven of Framingham, Massachusetts, replaced two wooden flatiron handles in 1820 for the family of Captain John J. Clark, charging seventeen cents for each.[26]

References to the ironing board identify various forms, from a large board to lay on another flat surface to a large board fixed or hinged to a table. The variety is described in Philadelphia records, where no less than five leading cabinetmakers active in the late eighteenth century recorded this form in their accounts. Both William Wayne and Thomas Tufft produced a "large Ironing Board." David Evans gave the dimensions of a similar board in 1787 as "6 foot by 3 foot 8." Earlier he had described "an Ironing Board & Pine table" made for another customer. A further indication of a board and table combination occurs in Daniel Trotter's work for Stephen Girard, a merchant prince of the city. Although Trotter billed the two items separately, they were posted together under the same date. An order to William Savery in 1771 from Philadelphian John Cadwalader describes the most complex unit, and again the cabinetmaker priced the two units separately: "To a Kitchen Table 4 foot by 2 f[oot] 6 I[nches] with a Drawer 1.0.0 / And fixing the Ironing Board to it 0.2.6."[27]

The folding board, its physical appearance not further described, appears in several accounts from northeastern Massachusetts. The price, which varied from five shillings to nine shillings, was modest. Elias Hasket Derby, the leading merchant of Salem, bought his board in 1784 from Samuel

Cheever. Daniel Ross sold a board a few years later at Ipswich. In 1799 Isaac Floyd of Medford provided Boston merchant Benjamin H. Hathorne with a folding board at the same time he supplied a kitchen table.[28]

Baking Equipment

Perhaps no piece of household equipment is mentioned as frequently in craftsmen's accounts as the trough for making bread. Of four terms that emerge from records, "bread trough" is the most common by far. That name was used in more than sixty percent of the fifty documents in the study that list this equipment. "Dough trough" was next in popularity, representing twenty-eight percent of the sample. "Kneading trough" accounted for a modest twelve percent of the sample, and one document identified a "baking trough." In terms of regional preference, "bread trough," "kneading trough," and "baking trough" were found almost exclusively in New England and New York state records, whereas "dough trough" was the choice in the greater Delaware Valley, comprising eastern Pennsylvania, New Jersey, and Delaware.

Most bread troughs appear to have been simple boxes with steep canted sides, frequently made of butted boards, and designed to stand on a table. Prices ranged from less than fifty cents to about two dollars, suggesting that size, material, and construction method could vary substantially. A small group of troughs was priced higher. Abraham Overholt of Bucks County, Pennsylvania, described one of these as "a dough tray table . . . painted . . . red" and charged three dollars. He used brown paint on other examples. Friedrich Bastian of Dauphin County identified the same equipment as a "Doe troft with feet" priced at four dollars. Even more expensive was Hiram Taylor's "Dotraugh l[a]rge size at five dollars" sold in 1836 in Chester County.[29]

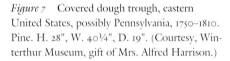

Figure 7 Covered dough trough, eastern United States, possibly Pennsylvania, 1750–1810. Pine. H. 28", W. 40¼", D. 19". (Courtesy, Winterthur Museum, gift of Mrs. Alfred Harrison.)

The supported bread trough illustrated in figure 7 would appear to fit Taylor's description. Remnants of reddish brown paint remain on the dovetailed box, frame, and lid. Among other references to the bread trough are several that mention a "cover" or "top." One had a stained finish. A customer of John Austin in Methuen, Massachusetts, purchased a "meal Chest" in 1772 when he acquired his "Bead tropp." William Mather of Whately sold a "sifting stick" together with a bread trough.[30]

The "process of making household bread" was described succinctly in the early nineteenth century in the first American edition of Abraham Rees' *Cyclopaedia*: "To a peck of meal . . . add a handful of salt, a pint of yeast [or other leavening agent], and three quarts of water . . . ; the whole being kneaded in a bowl or trough . . . will rise in about an hour; . . . then mould it into loaves, and put it into an oven to bake." For forming the dough into loaves, the housewife might find "a Bord to roal Bread on" a convenient piece of equipment. Many householders had a large brick oven constructed as part of the fireplace. Other ovens were located in a separate building out of doors.[31]

The large size and high temperature of the bake oven necessitated the use of a long-handled implement called a "peel" to insert and remove baked goods. An alternative term for this equipment was described by Elizur Barnes of Middletown, Connecticut: "To peal (or b[r]ead shovel)." The example with arched head illustrated in figure 8 is more ornate than common. The complete furnishing for a bakehouse, possibly for commercial use, is itemized in the accounts of Daniel and Samuel Proud of Providence under the date 1779. Charles Boller purchased four bread peels, including a large one. He then paid the Proud brothers for "putting on a lock to bake house," supplemented by "making a Lage Led [large lid] to a Chest for the Bake house" and "an Oven led for [the] bake house."[32]

To store baked bread householders purchased a plain, utilitarian "bread box," or "bread chest," for a modest sum. More popular was the "bread tray" used in serving. Although some references to a tray likely identify the bread trough, others refer to a low open box (see figure 12). Dovetailed and butted construction was available. In 1821 Titus Preston of Connecticut sold a "bread trey without dovetailing" for four shillings (sixty-six cents). Handymen could purchase "Stuff for [a] Bread tray" for self assembly.[33]

On February 15, 1813, Oliver Moore of East Granby, Connecticut, recorded the sale of a bread tray to "The state of Connecticut" for $1.50. As East Granby was the site of the Newgate Prison, the tray appears to have been purchased for use at that facility, more likely by the warden than by the inmates. An alternative term and form for this serving piece, as recorded by Allen Holcomb in central New York, was "Bread Boat." The cost was a modest fifty cents.[34]

A piece of baking equipment mentioned with some frequency in craftsmen's records is the gingerbread board, also called a gingerbread "mold" or "print." Use of this accessory was reserved for the ginger-flavored confection rolled on a board rather than the cakelike variety. Rees' *Cyclopaedia* describes typical ingredients as flour, sugar, pounded almonds, ginger, licorice, powdered aniseed, and rose water. When mixed to a paste, the cook was directed to "roll it, print it, and dry it in a stove."[35]

The cost of a gingerbread board varied, depending on size, material, and degree of incised or carved decoration on the printing face. Unfortunately, craftsmen's accounts reveal nothing about the nature of the decoration. A "Cake board" purchased for twelve cents in 1819 from Nathan Cleaveland of Franklin, Massachusetts, was a simple affair compared to the "gingerbread mould" acquired in 1802 by a customer of Daniel Ross in Ipswich for more than four dollars. A few years earlier a client of Job E. Townsend of Newport, Rhode Island, ordered a "Dubble Gingerbread Print" for which he paid only 1s.6d. (twenty-five cents).[36]

The rolling pin was an essential piece of equipment for rolling out paste for sweets and dough for pies. The form was a cylinder, sometimes swelled slightly through the center and formed into small handles at the ends. Early pins (see fig. 9) have short thick knoblike handles. Before ball bearings were introduced to this implement, the palms of the hands conveyed motion to the pin. Eighteenth-century European prints illustrating the kitchen sometimes include this activity. Several craft records identify the fabrication method. In 1825 Increase Pote of Maine charged a customer twenty-five cents for "turning one Roleing pinn." Some customers purchased "a Roleing Board" with their rolling pin.[37]

Pie making is little mentioned in woodworking accounts, primarily because the fabrication of baking dishes was the province of the potter. On two occasions, however, the papers of the Norris family of Philadelphia describe the rolling board as a "Pye Board," and one is identified as "large." Thomas Tufft, a cabinetmaker of the city, supplied the equipment along with a rolling pin. Pies in great quantity and variety—fruit, vegetable, custard, and meat—were a diet staple of the American family, assuring that the rolling pin and board were in constant use. Harriet Beecher Stowe described how at baking time, and especially at the Thanksgiving holiday, "butteries and dressers and shelves and pantries were literally crowded with [a] jostling abundance" of baked pies and cakes.[38]

Figure 9   Rolling pin, eastern United States, 1750–1800. Walnut. L. 18¾", Diam. 2⅜". (Courtesy, Winterthur Museum.)

Butter and Cheesemaking Equipment

Many families, even those living in close proximity to an urban area, kept one or two cows to provide fresh milk for family use and to convert the surplus into butter and cheese. Milking was a twice-a-day chore. Milking stools, often three-legged, and milk pails were kept handy by the back door or in an adjacent milk house, which also might be furnished with a "milke hows tabl." Alexander Low of Freehold, New Jersey, constructed a table of this description in 1806 and charged his customer sixteen shillings ($2.66). In southern New England Elisha H. Holmes, Job E. Townsend, and Philip Deland produced milking stools for twenty-five cents or less in the early nineteenth century.[39]

Fresh milk was placed in low, broad milk pans to allow the cream to rise for skimming to make butter. The remaining curds were used for making cheese. Although many documents mention the butter churn, repairs to

Figure 10 Lewis Miller, detail of *Claus Huf-schmit at the Butter*, York, Pennsylvania, 1814 or later, depicting an incident of 1810. Watercolor. (Courtesy, York County Heritage Trust, Pennsylvania.)

used churns were more common than new equipment. Two Massachusetts craftsmen, Philip Deland and Samuel Davison, priced their churns from $1.50 to three dollars. Deland described his two-dollar churn as "first rat[e]." A typical churn of the colonial and federal periods is illustrated in figure 10. It is an upright tapered cylinder constructed of staves bound with hoops. Although making butter was a relatively simple task, a poorly made churn could produce disastrous results. Martin Weiser of York, Pennsylvania, bought butter from Claus Hufschmit after his wife gave up and concluded that her churn was "bewitcht."[40]

From time to time householders called upon a local woodworker to freshen the appearance of their churn with a new coat of paint, a job that cost between ten cents and twenty-five cents as recorded by Josiah P. Wilder and Gaius Perkins in northern New England and John Ellinger in Pennsylvania. The most common repair was replacement of the "dasher," or "dash" as it often was denominated. This interior mechanism creates the agitation necessary to obtain butter. When in 1794 Job Danforth of Providence made a new dasher for a customer's churn, he also supplied a "cover," sometimes called a "top." A further request directed to woodworkers, particularly by householders in Pennsylvania, was for boxes and molds to form, store, and print butter. For example, Abraham Overholt of Bucks County recorded on January 19, 1804: "I made a pair of walnut butter boxes and a butter mold for Henrich Kindig."[41]

Cheesemaking often went hand-in-hand with processing butter if a family had sufficient milk. Records occasionally mention the sale of a cheese tub, as for example the one supplied for $1.25 in 1816 by Chapman Lee of Massachusetts. The usual request was for a cheese press or repairs to one already in use. The cost of a press varied broadly—from as little as sixty-two cents to $3.50—suggesting that the mechanism could be relatively simple or complex. Several craftsmen calculated their charge for a cheese press based on actual working time, although it is unclear who supplied the materials, the craftsman or the consumer. In 1774 Samuel Hall, a cabinetmaker, house carpenter, glazier, and farmer of Connecticut made a charge of 1s.9d. (twenty-nine cents) for "half a days work making a chees press." Twelve years later John Paine, a jack-of-all-trades on Long Island, calculated a full day's labor for making a press at only 2s.6d. (forty-one cents).[42]

Sophisticated presses were available by the early nineteenth century. In 1807 Robert Whitelaw of Vermont made his first ledger entry for the sale of "a patent Cheese press" priced at a substantial six dollars. Whether he was the patentee or purchased the rights to manufacture the press is not indicated.[43]

Utensils for Food Storage, Preparation, and Serving

Salt and sugar for cooking, baking, and preserving were available from merchants and shopkeepers. Although a family might have a significant quantity on hand in a storeroom or other location for butchering and preparing foods for winter use, having small containers of both salt and sugar in the kitchen was more convenient for day to day use. Craftsmen

Figure 11 Salt box, probably decorated by John
Drissel, upper Bucks County, Pennsylvania, 1796.
Wood. H. 9⅞", W. 6⅛", D. 7". (Courtesy, Win-
terthur Museum.)

from New England to Pennsylvania made salt boxes. At seventy-five cents,
a container made by Peter Ranck of Lebanon County, Pennsylvania, was
priced somewhat higher than those acquired from other craftsmen, including Philadelphia cabinetmaker Samuel Ashton. Most boxes probably
were plain painted, and some were made to hang on the wall. A few examples from the German-settled regions of eastern Pennsylvania bear striking
ornament (fig. 11).[44]

The hinged-lid, hanging salt box made in 1796 for Margaret Miller
(fig. 11) is part of a small group of ornamented wooden objects associated
by signature or motif with decorator John Drissel of upper Bucks County.
A woodworker of the region provided structural interest by fashioning an
ornamental backboard and lid. The undecorated box likely sold for less
than one dollar. In rural Pennsylvania few craftsmen earned that much for
a day's labor, which usually extended to ten or twelve hours, more than
enough time to complete a box of this type.

Sugar was available in large quantities in granular form, although most
householders made do with loaves of sugar molded in hard cones. Records

describe both sugar boxes and "suger boles." The bowls were turned and may have had a lid to protect the contents from flies and other insects, as the use of window screens was rare. To remove chunks of sugar from the cone to pulverize it for use, a householder needed a special implement easily fabricated in most woodworking shops. In Rhode Island, where sugar refining was a substantial business, William Barker, Daniel and Samuel Proud, and Job E. Townsend all sold sugar "mallets." In New York state Philip Filer referred to the same implement as a sugar "pounder," and in Chester County, Pennsylvania, Hiram Taylor sold sugar "mashers."[45]

Craft records list more pestles than mortars, suggesting that the pestle was more susceptible to damage or easily misplaced. Accounts identify turning as the fabrication method, and most prices fell between ten cents and twenty cents. A "pestle for Morter" priced in 1788 at two shillings (thirty-three cents) by Samuel Wayne of Philadelphia appears to have been made of a costly wood, such as lignum vitae. Both lignum vitae and maple mortars were available in 1798 at the Providence estate sale of William Barker. The business records of Philip Deland of West Brookfield, Massachusetts, indicate that the mortar and pestle met several needs in the kitchen. In 1834 the craftsman sold a "spice mortar and pestle." Seven years later another customer called for a "salt mortar and pestle." One craftsman produced a cover for a mortar.[46]

A somewhat unusual piece of kitchen equipment listed in craft records from Maine to Philadelphia is a chopping box, also termed a "trough," "tray," or "board." David Evans of Philadelphia identified at least one use for this item in a day book entry dated 1782: "a chopping Box for mincing meat." Records mention both cherry and oak as the construction material. John Cadwalader of Philadelphia appears to have purchased his oak board as an accessory to his oak-top kitchen table purchased at the same time.[47]

Two entries in the accounts of Elisha H. Holmes of Essex, Connecticut, suggest that little in the routine of daily life escaped the purview of one's neighbors. On October 9, 1826, a Mrs. Hill purchased a chopping box for fifty cents from Holmes. One month later to the day William Williams visited Holmes' shop and bought his wife "1 chopping Box like Mrs Hills." Holmes still sold chopping boxes for fifty cents in 1829.[48]

Lime or lemon juice was an ingredient in punch, a popular drink that also contained citrus zest, sugar, water, and either rum or brandy. To extract juice easily from the fruit the preparer needed a pair of squeezers, variously called "lemon," "lime," or "squash squeezers." Several references to squeezers dating to the 1740s occur in the accounts of Solomon Fussell of Philadelphia. Turning was the common fabrication method, and the price was low—about one shilling or slightly more—for a long period. Daniel Ross, a craftsman of Ipswich, Massachusetts, made a "Lemmon press" for a customer. "Press" may have been an alternative term or the description of a squeezer mounted on a low stationary frame to accommodate a bowl to catch the juice.[49]

Although coffee was not as popular a beverage as tea, it was common enough that the coffee mill, used for grinding coffee beans, occurs with regularity in the visual and written documents used in this study. The calamity that occurred in York, Pennsylvania, when a steer bounded into the Laumaster kitchen upsetting the dresser, as sketched by Lewis Miller (fig. 3), reveals the presence of a coffee mill in the household. Miller sketched another mill, complete with handle, hopper, and box, on the mantelpiece of the kitchen in the York Hotel. Still another mill appears in the right foreground of John Lewis Krimmel's painting, *Quilting Frolic* (fig. 17).[50]

References to coffee mills in craft documents focus almost exclusively on repairs because many new mills used in America through the mid-nineteenth century were imported from England. Several notations cover general repairs. During the 1790s Daniel Ross of Massachusetts supplied a new handle for a mill, and Job Danforth of Rhode Island replaced a box bottom. One day in August 1799 Isaac Floyd of Medford, Massachusetts, was busy "Making wood for [a] Coffee mill" for a local customer.[51]

References to miscellaneous appliances for kitchen use serve to broaden an understanding of the equipment and gadgetry available to householders before factory production made these and related items commonplace. The appearance and mechanism of some items are more easily perceived than those of others. "Sticks to stur toddy" are identified in the accounts of Daniel and Samuel Proud of Providence and Elizur Barnes of Middletown, Connecticut, the price in the six to eight cent range. Toddy is a drink made of spirits and hot water sweetened. Stirring sticks probably took varied forms. One privately owned seven-inch example that by tradition was used for toddy is made of ash. The slender cylindrical shaft flares at either end to form a small bonelike protuberance.[52]

The "Stick to fill Sasages" in the accounts of the Proud brothers of Providence perhaps approximated the form of the toddy stick, the bulges at the ends serving as tampers. At seventy-five cents, the "egg beating machine" sold by Thomas Boynton of Windsor, Vermont, possibly had some moving parts. Considerably more expensive was the "Cage to press Currens in . . . $1.75" made in 1814 by Nathan Lukens in or near Philadelphia for a member of the Richardson family. The word "currant," as used here, is unclear. It may identify a fresh or dried grape, although it more likely refers to the edible berries of a shrub of the genus *Ribes* whose juice was used for making jelly and jam.[53]

Perhaps more easily identified is the "Cabbage box" purchased in 1835 from the shop of John Ellinger of Lebanon County, Pennsylvania, by Daniel Ulrich. Sauerkraut, or finely cut cabbage fermented in brine, was a favorite vegetable among the Pennsylvania Germans. Ulrich's cabbage box may have served to receive the shredded vegetable for transfer to a large fermentation tub. The process calls to mind an incident recorded at York, Pennsylvania, in 1806 by Lewis Miller in his sketch book. Anthony Ritz and his wife were in the cellar of their home tending to a batch of sauerkraut near a small window with an open grate. Passing by in the street above was John Lohman who "through the little window made his water in the tub, without knowing it."[54]

Records identify a container for storing knives and other flatware as a "knife box" or "tray." Of the two terms, box was the more common. When two expensive mahogany examples are eliminated from the survey, the price range extends from thirty-three cents to $1.38. Moses Parkhurst of Massachusetts made the box valued at thirty-three cents in 1819, possibly spending less than half a day because his next posting for the same customer is a charge of $2.50 for "2½ Days work." The box valued at $1.38 was made by Isaac Ashton of Philadelphia in 1793. Because the majority of boxes and trays recorded in documents cost one dollar or less, it appears that all were of the same open form (see fig. 12), the cheaper ones of butted construction, those of higher price dovetailed and possibly divided by a central arched partition with a hand slot. A box of this description stands on the table at the left in figure 17, part of its flatware already laid on the cloth. By contrast, the brown-painted pine example illustrated in figure 12 has a high back with a central hole for hanging on a wall or other flat surface.[55]

As early as 1732 a turner from London advertised hardwood bowls at Philadelphia. Turning was an alternative to the laborious task of hand whittling. The turned applewood bowl illustrated in figure 13 is attributed to Felix Dominy and descended in his family of East Hampton, Long Island. Although the bowl measures about nine inches in diameter, it probably is smaller than the "large Wooden bowl" listed in the accounts of both Robert Whitelaw of Vermont and Philip Deland of Massachusetts, priced at thirty-four cents and fifty cents, respectively. At sixteen shillings ($2.66), John Sanders of upstate New York paid a premium price in 1820 for his "knot bowl" (burl wood). Bowls made of common wood could be painted, as indicated in the accounts of Allen Holcomb of Otsego County.[56]

In an era before matched cooking ware or even stamped metal lids were available, cooking vessels were covered with inexpensive turned disks of

Figure 12   Knife box, eastern United States, 1790–1850. Pine. H. 4½", W. 12¾", D. 6¾". (Courtesy, Winterthur Museum, gift of H. Rodney Sharp.)

Figure 13   Bowl attributed to Felix Dominy, East Hampton, Long Island, 1820–1835. Burl apple (by microanalysis). H. 5", Diam. 9⅜". (Courtesy, Winterthur Museum, gift of Mrs. Carl Mason [Phoebe Dominy]).

wood, usually identified as "pot lids" or "pot covers." In 1818 Abner Haven of Framingham, Massachusetts, priced "a lid to an Iron kittle" at six cents. Similar equipment identified as "Tops for Kettles for Kitchen" cost Samuel Larned considerably more while he was serving as a diplomat at Lima, Peru, in 1832. Another use for wooden lids, as noted in 1834 by Moyers and Rich of Wythe Court House, Virginia, was as "Milk covers." Complementing the array of lids available were wooden spoons and sets of measures.[57]

For serving prepared foods or beverages household members could use a "Tea Bord" or "Tea Waiter." Dimensions are specified occasionally, as for example in 1789 when Jonathan Kettell of Massachusetts sold a "Tea Board 2 feet 1 Inch." In a 1751 public notice John Tremain of New York suggested that customers might want to "find their own Stuff" (material) when ordering tea boards or other cabinetwork from his shop. Serving trays are depicted in both figures 17 and 28, although their oval form suggests they could have been fabricated of japanned sheet iron, a popular alternative.[58]

With utensils and vessels in constant use, repairs were an ongoing concern in most households. Wooden handles were particularly vulnerable. Those for beverage pots—coffee and especially tea—top the list. Most replacement handles cost one shilling to three shillings, except for those placed on silver vessels, which often cost more. New handles for silver tea and coffee pots in two Virginia families in 1790–1791 cost six shillings apiece. A "kink teapot handle," possibly one with a reverse-curve profile, cost even more when purchased from Joshua Delaplaine by Doctor Brown-john of New York City in 1741. A complement to a new teapot handle purchased in Newport, Rhode Island, just before the Revolutionary War, was a "Nub for the Top." Ephraim Haines of Philadelphia turned pot handles, whereas some other artisans made them by shaving and shaping blanks.[59]

Caution should be exercised when interpreting references to knife handles because some identify a knife used as a tool rather than as a table utensil. An account book entry made in 1812 by Alexander Low of Freehold, New Jersey, is straightforward: "to 10 handels for knives & forkes" at three shillings the lot. Elisha Hawley of Ridgefield, Connecticut, identified the fabrication method when he recorded "turnin five nife handles" in 1793. Occasionally a craftsman produced a "knife handle with ferel." There also are references to repairs to a special knife identified as a "Chopin Knife Handle" in several accounts, including that of Lemuel Tobey of Dartmouth, Massachusetts.[60]

Craftsmen also made handles for utensils employed directly in cooking. References to the chafing dish, a type of double boiler, occur with frequency in accounts. In 1758 Joseph Symonds of Massachusetts replaced a "chafn desh handel" for a customer at a charge of 2s.6d. (forty-one cents). Sometimes a wood turner produced a batch of handles to meet the needs of a metalworker or hardware merchant. Other records identify several long-handled kitchen tools. Most common is the "dipper," occasionally referred to as a "ladle." The work varied from "putting [a] handle on [a] dipper" to producing an all "wooden dipper," such as the "first rate" one that Philip Deland sold for twenty-five cents. A related tool is the skimmer, whose bowl is more shallow than that of the dipper. A member of the Almy and Brown firm at Providence was indebted to William and John Richmond in 1799 for providing a "Scimmer handle" at thirty-seven cents. In 1827 Nathaniel Knowlton of Maine recorded "toaster handles."[61]

A boon to the housewife in daily household activity, especially the preparation of meals, was a clock, whether it stood on a shelf or on the floor near the kitchen. In the immediate work area a simpler time gauge for monitoring short tasks was the double glass filled with sand (see fig. 14). Although this device measures prescribed periods of time, usually an hour, the experienced housewife could identify shorter periods by observing the level of sand in the top or bottom glass. A cage, frequently of turned wood, protected the glass from damage. A device of this type is identified in the accounts of George Short of Newburyport, Massachusetts, in 1815 as "a time glass frame"; the charge was seventeen cents.[62]

The nature of activity in the colonial and federal kitchen and its adjacent storerooms assured there would be problems with rodents. Compounding the situation during the warm months was the necessity of leaving the windows and doors standing open without benefit of screens, which still were uncommon. Although household cats performed good service, inexpensive wire traps would have been a welcomed addition. In at least one instance a local woodworker was called upon to build a better mousetrap. Doctor Hazard of Newport, Rhode Island, engaged Job E. Townsend in January 1819 to provide "a Mohogony Mouse Trap with 12 holes & springs" for which he paid two dollars.[63]

Figure 14 Hour glass in frame, New England, possibly southeastern Massachusetts, 1780–1820. Maple, glass, leather, and sand. H. 6⅞", Diam. 3¾". (Private collection; photo, Winterthur Museum.) The glass has a history of use in the Lafayette Masonic Lodge of Charleton, Massachusetts, which was chartered in 1796 and disbanded ca. 1827.

The water bench identified in the accounts of several craftsmen may have been indistinguishable from the wash bench, a common piece of laundry equipment. Use of the term may focus on the alternative function of the furniture as a stand to hold buckets of water to fill general household needs—drinking, cooking, hand washing, dishwashing, scrubbing, and the like. John Ellinger of Lebanon County, Pennsylvania, charged from two dollars to three dollars for his water benches. In Bucks County Abraham Overholt painted a bench brown. The buckets used to store water probably were no different from those in the laundry (see fig. 4). A sketch of a "Scrub Woman," made by the Baroness Hyde de Neuville during a residency in the United States with her husband in the early 1800s, clearly delineates a stave bucket bound with hoops supporting at the rim a scrubbing brush of flatiron form. At Philadelphia Solomon Fussell kept a supply of hog bristles, which he used to make the scrubbing brushes he sold during the 1740s for 2*s*.6*d*. apiece.[64]

References to brooms and mops occur with frequency in craft records. The material of the broom head is identified as broom corn. In 1821 Luke Houghton of central Massachusetts charged thirteen cents for a "corn broom." The price was higher in some shops. A decade earlier in Connecticut James Gere sold a corn broom for twenty-five cents. The common form of broom at the time was a cylindrical pole with the sweeping material wrapped around one end and tied to form a cylindrical head (see fig. 17). By contrast, mops often were purchased incomplete. A woodworker provided the turned handle, sometimes called a "stick," and the purchaser completed the mop by attaching woolen scraps or yarn. Albert Greene purchased mop handles at two different times during the 1820s from John Proud of Rhode Island.[65]

Although craftsmen list brushes as items of trade, few identify their specific function. Like the mop, some handles were sold separately. Elizur Barnes of Connecticut produced "2 Brush handles 6 feet Long" for a business customer in 1822. Purchases made in 1834 by Peter Gansevoort in Albany from Stephen Van Schanck included several cleaning utensils: "1 Sweeping Brush" for one dollar, "2 Dusting Brushes" for seventy-five cents, and "2 Dust Pans" for fifty cents. At Beverly, Massachusetts, Isaac Flagg supplied Robert Rantoul with a pair of shoe brushes a few years earlier. The Providence business accounts of Almy and Brown identify a "wisk Broem" purchased from William Barker.[66]

One use for water stored on the water bench was dishwashing. Three times a day water for this task was heated on the hearth. Families, usually large already, often were extended at mealtime by the presence of apprentices and hired help. Tubs for washing and rinsing dishes probably were commonplace. Other equipment seldom is identified. In 1789 Stephen Collins, a Philadelphia merchant, paid Robert Mullen, a carpenter, fifteen shillings for "making a Bottel and Plait Drenor." Equipment of this general description still met the needs of the domestic household some thirty years later when Elizur Barnes charged a Connecticut customer twenty-five cents for "putting Leggs to [a] Bottle Drainer."[67]

The lone reference to a soap dish and wash bowl, which Philip Deland supplied a family in Massachusetts in the early 1840s, appears to identify objects made of wood. By contrast, a common entry in woodworker's records is the "towel roller." The price was modest. In the early nineteenth century David Alling charged thirty-one cents at Newark, New Jersey, George Landon recorded 31¼¢ at Erie, Pennsylvania, and Robert Whitelaw asked only seventeen cents at Ryegate, Vermont. Perhaps more expensive than any recorded towel roller is the relatively ornate example with scalloped top in figure 15. In place of the usual turned cylinder, or roller, this rack has a roll shaped to paneled form through the use of a drawknife. John Lewis Krimmel, a Delaware Valley painter, delineated a different roller pattern in one of his early nineteenth-century sketches. Two shaped vertical boards with sweeping ends top and bottom support

Figure 15 Towel roller, eastern United States, 1780–1840. Walnut. H. 9¼", W. 19¾", D. 5". (Courtesy, Winterthur Museum.)

between them a roller that is removable via an open slot in one of the vertical panels.[68]

Spinning, Quilting, Weaving, and Related Equipment
Although imported textiles were available in abundance throughout the period covered by this study, records indicate that woodworking craftsmen fabricated a substantial amount of equipment used in the production of domestic cloth and needlework into the second quarter of the nineteenth century. As early as the 1720s Jacob Hinsdale built "Great," or wool, wheels for his rural neighbors in Harwinton, Connecticut. By the 1750s Robert Crage could offer residents in the vicinity of Leicester, Massachusetts, a range of equipment for home spinning. John Green's purchases of February 9, 1757, included "a foot wheel" (also known as a "spinning," "flax," or "linen" wheel), "a woollen wheel," and "a Clock Reel," a device used to wind spun fibers into skeins for storage or ease in handling.[69]

During the dark uncertain days preceding the Revolution, urban craftsmen also offered spinning and related equipment. Wright and McAllister of New York City, located "at the Spinning-Wheel, nearly opposite St. Paul's Church, Broad-Way," encouraged the public to support American manufactures. In 1775, Philadelphia cabinetmaker Francis Trumble advertised to hire several journeymen spinning-wheel makers and solicited suppliers for "500 setts of stocks and rims for spinning wheels."[70]

John Lewis Krimmel sketched some of the apparatus of spinning in the early nineteenth century (fig. 16). Clearly delineated from the front and side is a flax wheel, also called a "foot wheel" because the treadle mounted between the three legs activates the wheel by means of foot action and a cord. Mounted on the plank, or table, immediately behind the wheel is

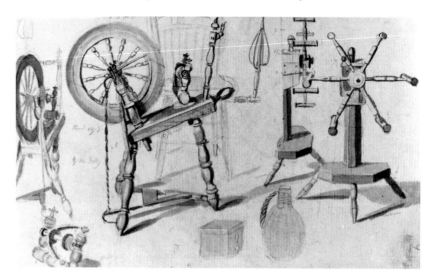

the low spinning mechanism consisting of a U-shaped flyer, a slender cylindrical bobbin, and a multi-disk-turned whorl, all drawn in detail at the lower left. As the flyer revolves it twists the thread being spun and leads it to the bobbin where it is wound. The flyer is set in motion by means of a continuous cord that forms a loop around the wheel rim and the whorl of the spinning mechanism. The tall turned pole next to the spinning mechanism is part of the distaff. It supports near the top the distaff cage, an apparatus wound around with unspun fiber, which the artist has sketched separately. Two views of a winding wheel appear at the right in the sketch. The size of the box supporting the wheel and the vague suggestion of a dial below the nave appear to identify the apparatus as a clock reel. Spun fiber to be measured into skeins was wound around the outside of the cylinders at the arm tips as the wheel was rotated. The clock recorded the revolutions.

As late as 1820 the United States census of manufactures pinpoints pockets of settlement where spinning was still firmly entrenched in the economy of the home: central New York state, north central Pennsylvania, south New Jersey, south central and western Virginia, central Georgia, and various locations in the newly settled regions of Kentucky, Tennessee, Ohio, and Indiana. Although the country was experiencing a nationwide recession at this date and many craftsmen reported that business was dull, there were a few bright spots. James W. Moore, a wheelwright who constructed flax and cotton wheels, reels, swifts, and bedsteads in Rutherford County, Tennessee, stated that "there has been a greater demand for articles in my business than heretofore [and] sales have generally been productive." Uzziel Church produced a comparable line of equipment in his two-man shop in Union County, Indiana. He reported that sales were "verry good and Ready." Artisans in all areas also responded to a steady demand for repairs to equipment already in use.[71]

Although the wool wheel is considerably larger than that used to spin flax or cotton, the mechanism is simpler and the cost was more modest. The accounts of Jonathan Dart of New London County, Connecticut, are revealing on this point. Large and small wheels made in his shop in 1796–1797 were priced at eleven shillings to thirteen shillings and twenty-one shillings, respectively. In a Massachusetts record the material of the wheel, large or small, is identified as oak. At Boston, painter Daniel Rea, Jr., noted on several occasions that he had painted a spinning wheel "mehogony Colour." When householders ordered a new wheel from the local wood-worker the charge, like those for other products, was posted to his account, the balance satisfied periodically by payment in cash, services, labor, barter goods, and the like. In 1818 George Landon noted a special arrangement with one of his customers in Erie, Pennsylvania: "Ebenezer Graham . . . is to have a big wheel Maid by the last of february for wich he is to Give 3½ Bushels of weete or $4:50 in Cash." Amos Purinton of Weare, New Hampshire, sold many spinning wheels to peddlers, who carried them disassembled to eager consumers throughout the state.[72]

Two other pieces of spinning equipment, the swift and the quill wheel, filled critical needs when converting skeins of yarn to manageable form as balls or wound bobbins for use in knitting and weaving. The common swift had a collapsible horizontal reel mounted on a short vertical shaft with a screw base for clamping to the edge of a table or other flat surface. Householders often purchased their swifts in pairs. Elisha H. Holmes sold "1 pr of winding swifts" in Connecticut in 1827 for fifty cents. In a letter dated at London in 1766, Benjamin Franklin wrote to his wife in Philadelphia saying that he was sending their daughter "two little Reels," and he explained further: "The Reels are to screw on the edge of a Table, when she would wind Silk or Thread. The Skein is to be put over them and winds better than if held in two Hands." The quill wheel looks like a large spinning wheel; however, the simple mechanism at the front holds a bobbin, or quill, to be filled with yarn for weaving. The price usually was slightly more than that of a clock reel. In 1813 Abner Haven of Massachusetts sold "a quil wheel" for $1.50, the same price charged by James Whitelaw in Vermont a few years earlier.[73]

The records of a few craftsmen identify frames for executing needlework as well as small looms for weaving tapes. The accounts of Jeduthern Avery of Bolton, Connecticut, and Philemon Robbins of Hartford list a "Lace fraim," each priced low at twenty-five cents and fifty cents, respectively. Of more frequent mention is the embroidery frame, also identified by Robbins as a "Tabourret frame" and by others as a "tambour frame." At Litchfield Silas Cheney supplied Sarah (Sally) Pierce, proprietress of a successful girl's school, with a number of embroidery frames, including one fitted with a stand priced at eight shillings ($1.33). Cheney identified another frame as cherrywood. Philadelphia records name mahogany as the material of some frames and Daniel Trotter and Thomas Affleck as two cabinet-makers who produced them.[74]

Small hand or table looms appear to have been uncommon. A reference to a "Garter Loom for Miss Salie" (probably a member of the Taliaferro family) in an unidentified Virginia account book of the 1760s and 1770s is the only one to specify a function other than tapemaking. The modest price was 1s.6d. (twenty-five cents). A turned tape loom made by the Proud brothers of Providence a few years later was priced about the same. Tape looms made by Jacob Hinsdale and John Wheeler Geer of Connecticut for about five shillings appear to have been more elaborate, perhaps open boxes formed of butted boards.[75]

An item rarely mentioned in records is the "thread stand." Nathan Cleaveland of Franklin, Massachusetts, listed one in 1828 priced at sixty-two cents. The notation calls to mind several journal entries made by Edward Jenner Carpenter while serving an apprenticeship in Greenfield. On September 18, 1844, he noted: "Mr. Buzzell was up here tonight & turned some ivory feet for a spool stand that he is making for the Mechanics Fair, it is going to be a nice one." Further entries followed during the course of a week. Finally on Friday evening, September 27, following the fair, Carpenter wrote: "the spool stand that Buzzell made sold for five dollars. W. F. Davis bought it."[76]

Evidence of the purchase of quilting frames and repairs to equipment in use covers a broad area extending from Vermont to the Delaware Valley and likely beyond. Just as broad was the pricing of the equipment, from as little as 16½¢ to well over two dollars. The accounts of Jacob Bachman of rural Pennsylvania, which record the sale of new frames during the seven years from 1830 to 1837, list three price levels—fifty cents, one dollar, and $1.50. Obviously, size, finish, material, and the fabrication of a special support structure had a bearing on the cost. Other records provide confirmation. Job Danforth of Providence sold a frame in 1806 for 8s.3d. ($1.36), although he priced another described as "Small" at only fifty-eight cents.[77]

Of particular interest is an entry in the accounts of Ezekiel Smith of Massachusetts for repairs to a quilting frame accompanied by the notation "mending your Chears [chairs] Backs." The two items were priced together, offering a strong suggestion that use of the frame was interconnected with the chairs. Frames not fitted with their own supports sometimes were balanced on the backs of chairs when in use. Either the lengthwise or crosswise bars could be made longer for this purpose. By contrast, the quilting frame illustrated in figure 17 was constructed to rest on its own supports. Neither the lengthwise or crosswise bar extends far enough beyond the corner joint to provide adequate support on a chair back. In addition, two holes pierce the tip of the short crosswise bar, indicating that when the frame was used the tips of the short bars were placed over slim extension pieces at the tops of four standards. The accounts of Thomas Boynton of Vermont confirm that the individual pieces of quilting frames were referred to as "Bars." The records of an anonymous Boston woodworker also identify special seating purchased for use around a frame in June 1758, when John Avery acquired "a quilting fram[e]" and "2 stulles" for four shillings.[78]

Figure 17 John Lewis Krimmel, *Quilting Frolic,* Philadelphia, Pennsylvania, or vicinity, 1813. Oil on canvas. 16⅞" x 22⅜". (Courtesy, Winterthur Museum.)

The happy scene depicted in figure 17 apparently is true to common practice of the late eighteenth and early nineteenth centuries. A frolic, or general merrymaking, attended by neighbors, friends, and family often was the climax of a group working session for spinning or knitting fibers, processing harvested foodstuffs, or completing a task, such as making a quilt. Refreshments, music, and dancing were common accompaniments. Jacob Hiltzheimer, a businessman and street commissioner of Philadelphia in the late eighteenth century, noted in his diary that he attended at least two frolics. One was a "cider frolic," the other a celebration associated with a house raising in Market Street.[79]

Weaving equipment was large, bulky, and expensive, and beyond the means of many families. Nevertheless, craftsmen's accounts provide good evidence of the construction and repair of looms for domestic use. The records of four craftsmen in locations extending from Maine to Pennsylvania describe a price range of $6.50 to nine dollars for the loom. James Geer of Groton, Connecticut, was explicit in identifying the construction material of his looms as chestnut. Thomas Boynton of Windsor, Vermont, recorded making "a bench for a loom," a simple affair for which he charged twenty-five cents. Many other business accounts record repairs to looms and the supply of small accessories essential to the weaving process.[80]

Householders set up their looms in any of several areas in the home or on the property, depending on family size and availability of space: the attic, a spare room, an ell or attached shed, and even a freestanding building. The probate records of Ebenezer Tracy, Sr., a cabinetmaker and chairmaker of eastern Connecticut, describe a "weaving house" in the estate division. The estate inventory further lists a loom and accessories along with a quill wheel, five wool wheels, three linen wheels, and a clock reel. Raw material on hand included fifty pounds of flax and three pounds of wool.[81]

Bedsteads, Children's Furniture, and Low Stools

A majority of documents consulted for this study contain references to furniture built for repose and sleep. The discussion is limited to bedsteads of moderate cost, thus eliminating frames of higher price made to accommodate expensive hangings or constructed of fine cabinet wood. As explained by Thomas Sheraton in *The Cabinet Dictionary* (1803), the term "bed" in a general sense "includes the bedstead and other necessary articles incident to this most useful of all pieces of furniture," namely the mattress, linens, blankets, outer covers, and pillows. Like the bedstead, mattresses varied widely in quality, from cases filled with straw to those made of flock (fabric fragments, frequently wool, cut up and used for stuffing), feathers, and curled horsehair. Although it was expensive, Sheraton endorsed the hair mattress because of its "elastic nature, which prevents from sinking so as to perspire." He also had some special words of wisdom often repeated today: "And all such persons, who by a relaxed habit have contracted weaknesses in the back, should be particular in avoiding soft beds."[82]

A popular design was the low-post bedstead (see fig. 18), its corner supports often formed with a combination of blocked and turned elements. An alternative term for this frame—"common bedstead"—was used less frequently. Probably deriving directly from British terminology was the name "stump bedstead," as found in the accounts of William Rawson of

Figure 18   Low-post, or common, bedstead, Massachusetts, 1740–1790. Ash. H. 34¾", L. 80", W. 48⅜". (Courtesy, Winterthur Museum, gift of Joseph Downs.)

Killingly, Connecticut, and in a bill prepared by James Linacre of Albany. A rarer term is "short-post bedstead," which appears in the accounts of Peter Ranck of Lebanon County, Pennsylvania. Also belonging to the low-post group is the frame identified as a "toad back bedstead" in the accounts of Reubin Loomis of Connecticut in 1806. The name derives from the particular design of the headboard, which has an arch across the top and deep U-shaped cutouts forming long fingers at the joints with the head posts. The profile appears to have been duplicated several decades later in the backs of painted fancy chairs, where it is termed a "frog back."[83]

The cost of a low-post bedstead varied substantially—from less than one dollar to well over seven dollars. Several factors influenced price. Many, if not all, higher priced bedsteads came equipped with a sacking bottom, as suggested in several records of Philadelphia origin. For instance, Nathan Trotter paid six dollars for a "Low-post Bedstead & bottom &c." in 1821. When acquiring low-post bedsteads several decades earlier, John Cadwalader and William Wallis paid eighteen shillings ($2.97) and nineteen shillings ($3.13), respectively, for "Sacken & Lacing" and a "Bottom & line." A sacking bottom served in place of bed slats to support the mattress and bedding. It consisted of a stout, coarse cloth attached by means of lacing, or cord, to small, turned, regularly-spaced "pins" (also called "knobs," "nubs," and "buttons") mounted upright on a ledge inside the frame. An alternative support structure is illustrated in figure 18, which has a drilled frame to receive a rope bottom. The rope lacing was drawn taut by means of a T-shaped wooden implement with a cleft shaft called a "bed key." Several appear in craftsmen's records. In the 1820s Elisha H. Holmes of eastern Connecticut and Miles Benjamin of central New York supplied customers with inexpensive bed keys.[84]

Choice of wood also influenced the price of a bedstead. In 1798 a customer of Daniel Ross in Massachusetts chose birch and paid $2.33 for his "Common" frame. A "best curled maple" low bedstead purchased in 1822 from William Jones in Delaware cost five dollars. Although James Gere identified a "common bedstead 2nd Quality" priced at two dollars in 1826, the Connecticut record provides no indication of how quality was determined: choice of wood, simplicity of design, or another factor? Paint was the finish on many bedsteads, and a range of colors was available. Two are listed in Connecticut records. In 1800 Silas Cheney made a low bedstead painted red (reddish brown); five years later Solomon Cole painted a similar frame green. Both cost fourteen shillings ($2.31). Size and headboard design were other factors that determined price. The pointed-top panel in figure 18 took less time to saw to form than a headboard with curves.[85]

A frame only slightly less popular than the low-post bedstead was one built with a joint in the long side rails near the headboard and supported at that point by an extra pair of feet and a cross brace. The popular name for this frame was "turn-up bedstead." A few woodworkers in Connecticut used the alternative term "joint bedstead." As its name implies, the turn-up bedstead was built to fold up against a wall to clear floor space for other activity. Two of its basic components, the corner posts and the headboard, were similar to those in the low-post bedstead. Unlike the press bedstead, which also is jointed, the frame usually did not fold into a wall closet or box. It could be concealed from view, however, through the use of a cover made of fabric or other material.[86]

The price range and average cost of the turn-up bedstead was similar to that of the low frame. The picture can be enlarged somewhat based on craftsmen's accounts. A few frames had high posts at the head. In 1825 Elisha H. Holmes made one at Essex, Connecticut, for $4.50. A similar bedstead made by Elizur Barnes in 1822 for a customer in Middletown also had "Buttons," identifying it as a frame to be fitted with a sacking bottom rather than a rope support. Oliver Moore's "joint bedstead with he[a]d posts turned" may have had high posts. When charging another customer for "helping your Father to turn bed posts," the East Granby craftsman noted that the task required "one days work in my shop in ye labour."[87]

The turn-up bedstead, like other frames, could be made in single or double widths. Philemon Robbins produced a single one at Hartford in 1834. A rare account entry was penned at Northampton, Massachusetts, in 1805 by Harris Beckwith: "to A turn up Bedsted and Box." The low charge of three dollars indicates the furniture was made of common wood to be painted. Abner Taylor of Lee noted an alternative finish a decade later with an account entry for "a Bedstead to turn up Stained." Space requirements in the home changed from time to time, leading one customer of Job E. Townsend in Rhode Island to pay him for "Altering a Bedsted to turn up." When not used for sleeping, the bed could be folded out of the way. This convenience may have been foremost in the mind of a consumer billed by Job Danforth at Providence in 1803 for "a Turnup Beadstead for one of your men." Hired men and journeymen commonly occupied quarters on the premises of their masters—in the attic, in a shop loft or shed, or in another outbuilding. Wherever bedded, economy of space likely was critical.[88]

Trundle bedsteads appear with frequency in craftsmen's records—as many as the combined total for low-post and turn-up frames. Although the price range was broader than that for the other two bedsteads, the average cost of the trundle bedstead at $2.60 was still only seventy-seven to eighty percent that of the larger frames. The term "trundle" actually identifies the small wheels at the bottom of the posts, which are part of the furniture's basic construction (see fig. 19). Dictionaries cite "truckle" as an alternative term for both the wheels and the bedstead and pinpoint the unique feature of this frame: "a low bed on wheels, that may be pushed under another bed." Reubin Loomis of Connecticut and Charles C. Robinson of Philadelphia were two of a small number of craftsmen who used the word truckle instead of trundle. Abner Taylor of Massachusetts described the frame as "a Bunk or trundle bed stead."[89]

Eighteenth- and nineteenth-century diaries, letters, and journals often describe the trundle bedstead as a sleeping place for children, although the earlier function of this piece of furniture was broader. In the Middle Ages and later students often occupied trundle frames in the chambers of

their tutors. The inexpensive frame also provided a place to bed servants, who in early practice frequently slept in the same chamber with their master.[90]

A few accounts identify special features or unusual circumstances connected with the purchase of the trundle bedstead, as for instance Philemon Robbins's record of a "trundle bedstead with sides" made in 1834 at Hartford. Another Connecticut craftsman, Titus Preston of Wallingford, billed Jared Allen ten shillings ($1.65) in 1804 when he "finished a trundle bedsted of your timber." Other documents and extant frames address the support structure for the mattress. Hiram Taylor of Chester County, Pennsylvania, and Samuel Douglas of near Canton, Connecticut, described trundle bedsteads with "board bottoms." Figure 19 illustrates an alternative support system with rails drilled to accommodate a rope grid. The accounts of David Evans of Philadelphia and the Waters family of Salem, Massachusetts, document the use of the more expensive sacking bottom, with its cords for lacing a stout cloth to the frame.[91]

Occasionally, records identify the construction material and finish of the trundle bedstead. In 1811 Saint George Tucker of Williamsburg, Virginia, paid John Hockaday for a "Colourd poplar Trunnell Bedstead." Expenses for a set of casters, seven yards of cord, three yards of sail duck, thread, and labor for making the sacking bottom supplemented the charge. Several accounts identify painted surfaces. Those of Boston ornamental painter Daniel Rea, Jr., and Middletown, New Jersey, cabinetmaker Fenwick Lyell name green paint specifically. Customers of Silas Cheney in Connecticut and Abner Taylor in Massachusetts chose a stained finish for their trundle bedsteads.[92]

Furniture repairs accounted for a substantial amount of a craftsman's working time. In the case of the trundle bedstead one of the repetitive tasks was the replacement of the wheels, or trundles. Two early references from the 1750s appear in the Massachusetts accounts of Robert Crage of Leicester and Peter Emerson of Reading. Samuel Hall provided "trundles for a Bidsted" in Middletown, Connecticut, preceding the Revolutionary War. Use of the trundle bedstead continued during the early nineteenth century, when Alexander Low of Freehold, New Jersey, and other craftsmen continued to supply new wheels to these frames. Some bedsteads sustained more extensive wear and damage. Perez Austin of Canterbury, Connecticut, provided new timber for a bedstead he repaired, and Isaiah Tiffany of Norwich added two braces to strengthen a frame.[93]

Until the Windsor took over the market in children's seating following the Revolution, "little" chairs with rush or, more rarely, board bottoms were the choices available to consumers. "Little" was the preferred term for the child's chair in craftsmen's accounts, and notations such as that made by Robert Crage of Leicester, Massachusetts, confirm that the two words were synonymous: "To a Childs Little Chare 0.1.4." The low price of Crage's chair suggests that it was purchased as an open frame without the woven bottom and possibly without any surface finish.[94]

The business records of Solomon Fussell of Philadelphia provide a comprehensive account of early seating for children. The price of side chairs varied from 2s.6d. to 3s.6d., three shillings being the usual charge. Included in this range were a few chairs described by color: white, brown, and black. Two special designs were priced slightly higher. Fussell identified one as a "4 Slat" chair, which suggests that the standard back had three slats or possibly only two. At 4s.6s. the "rake back" chair was the most expensive. The raked design introduced a bend to the cylindrical back posts just above the seat to create an inclined back for greater comfort. To produce the rake Fussell employed two-axis turning, a labor-intensive procedure reflected in the cost.[95]

Fussell offered another piece of seating furniture to his customers described as a "Childs Table chair" priced at five shillings to 5s.6d. The modern term is "highchair." In the late eighteenth century "dining chair" became the common name for this tall seat, especially as Windsor construction began to dominate the market. As descriptive terms, the words dining and table focus on the chair's place of use rather than the now common tray, which was a later, nineteenth-century innovation along with the foot rest. The tall chair was built to the appropriate height to permit the child to join family members around the dining table at mealtime, as confirmed in an account entry made by Samuel Durand of Milford, Connecticut, dated January 24, 1815: "To 1 Chair for Child to Sit at table." The charge was six shillings.[96]

A few documents identify rush-bottom rocking chairs for children. Some chairs were built to form originally; others were converted for rocking at a later date. After the Revolution when the Windsor began to dominate the vernacular seating market, open-frame construction is identified in records through price (usually in the range of four shillings), terminology, or other internal evidence. At Hartford in 1834 Philemon Robbins described his product: "To 1 flagg seat childs chair with Rockers." The cost was sixty-eight cents (four shillings).[97]

The seats in children's rush-bottom furniture required refurbishing or replacement periodically. The replacement cost with material and labor was about nine pence (twelve cents). Although the charge was modest, the recurring maintenance in rush-bottom seating gave the plank-bottom Windsor a decided edge with consumers. Paint helped stabilize a woven seat, although few householders appear to have opted for the extra expense. One of Oliver Moore's customers in Connecticut decided on a positive course of action in 1820 and paid the craftsman for "puting a bottom in [a] small Chair and painting it twice over." Sometimes the seats of new chairs were painted at purchase. Elizur Barnes charged seventy-five cents for "a Little Cheir Seat Painted." The replacement of a chair seat sometimes prompted other repairs, as in 1758 when Isaiah Tiffany saw "to puting an Arm & bottom to a little Chair."[98]

The "Small bord chair for child" or, as also described, "little chair with board bottom," was salable well into the nineteenth century. The price varied from as little as fifty cents to just over one dollar. The most popular design was the "childs wood seat ch[ai]r with hole." The geographic range of this form was broad— from Newark, New Jersey, to New Ipswich, New Hampshire. Extending the variety of board seating is the rare identification of a "Childs Banch" priced at 7s.6d. ($1.16) in the accounts of Silas Cheney of Connecticut. This simple piece of furniture may have had shaped board ends of the type illustrated in figure 21. The gocart was another special form requested occasionally. In the colonial and federal periods the word referred to a framework to support a child when learning to walk. Robert Crage of Massachusetts built "a goe Cart for a Child" in 1758 and charged 2s.8d. In Connecticut Samuel Hall repaired a gocart in 1789 by providing three new "trundles," or wheels.[99]

Because most families were large in the colonial and federal periods, the cradle was an important form, as amply demonstrated in craftsmen's accounts. Records offer little particular description of the open box on rockers, although many examples were of board construction, either butted (see fig. 20) or dovetailed. The "Post cradle" described in 1826 by Elisha H. Holmes of Connecticut was joined with mortises-and-tenons. Holmes also identified a "Round end cradle." The accounts of two other craftsmen itemize a "Cradle with a Head," or hood. Abner Taylor of Massachusetts substituted the word "top." The only mention of a "swing," or suspended, cradle is that in the accounts of Solomon Cole of Connecticut, and it was expensive at £1.14.6 ($5.69). The average price of a cradle on rockers, excluding two expensive examples, was two dollars to $2.50.[100]

Records provide a greater amount of information about the materials of cradle construction, identifying six basic woods—pine, yellow poplar, birch, gum, walnut, and cherry. Mahogany and cedar cradles priced at twelve dollars and ten dollars, respectively, hardly qualify as "everyday things." A common price for a pine cradle was two dollars; yellow poplar was slightly more expensive. Jonathan Kettell of Massachusetts sold a birch cradle in 1790 for one pound ($3.30). David Evans made a gumwood cradle in Philadelphia shortly after the Revolutionary War. The walnut cradles in the sample originated in eastern Pennsylvania, whereas cherrywood construction was fairly broad, covering southern New England, New York state, and southeastern Pennsylvania.[101]

Figure 20 Miniature cradle, probably eastern Massachusetts, 1810–1840. Pine. H. 6", L. 12⅝", W. 5". (Private collection; photo, Winterthur Museum.) In design and construction this example is similar to a full-size cradle.

Stain and paint were common finishes on cradles. One stained example was made of "whitewood" (yellow poplar). Pine is identified as a painted wood, and records list several paint colors. The blue mentioned in three accounts dating between 1799 and 1802 probably was made from the pigment Prussian blue, which produced a vivid medium-light shade. The account books of two painters, William Gray of Salem, Massachusetts, and Daniel Rea, Jr., of Boston identify "Seder Colour" and "mehogony Colour," both likely executed in imitation of wood grain. The only cradle repair work identified in records used in this study is rocker replacement. The need was widespread, as recorded from Freehold, New Jersey, to Dartmouth, Massachusetts.[102]

Cribs appear in craftsmen's records in fewer numbers than cradles, and for the most part they were priced consistently higher. When an infant outgrew the cradle, there was the crib or the trundle bed. The tall crib could be drawn close to a mother's bed. If one side were constructed to lift out or fall down, the mother had access to her child during the night without getting out of bed.[103]

Particular information about the crib's appearance is sparse in records. Cherrywood is named as the material of construction in the accounts of Elisha H. Holmes of Essex, Connecticut, and Job Danforth of Providence. Daniel Rea, Jr., painted several cribs, one identified as green, an indication that less costly woods also were used in the construction of such forms. The addition of casters provided ease of movement within the bed chamber and other areas. One family purchased a "Double crib bedstead" from Holmes, although whether to hold twins or to serve another purpose is unknown. Modifications to a crib could extend its useful life, as in 1823 when the Ward family of Middletown, Connecticut, sought the services of Elizur Barnes to lengthen a crib. Perhaps the ultimate in pre-Victorian crib design was one built at Hartford in 1835 for Charles Goodwin by Philemon Robbins. The small bedstead had a sacking bottom and a "sett of hooks for vallance roods."[104]

Crickets and footstools frequently are distinguished one from the other in records, although a close relationship is suggested in the item "a Cricket or foot stool" in the accounts of Abner Taylor of Massachusetts. Randle Holmes's definition of a stool in the *Academie of Armory & Blazon* (1688) further notes the interchangeability of the two terms: "a kind of low footed stool, or Cricket as some call it." Nevertheless, colonial and federal craftsmen appear to have made distinctions between the two, as confirmed in account entries and recorded prices. A tabulation of cost indicates that the average price of the cricket was about thirty percent less than that of the footstool, and the figure drops to about fifty percent when the price extremes in both categories are eliminated from the tabulation. Clearly, the cricket was simpler in design and likely smaller in size than the footstool.[105]

Even within their individual categories the cricket and the footstool could vary in appearance, as indicated by brief descriptions that accompany some account entries. Either stool could have a solid wooden top or an open frame for upholstery. The wooden top also could be concealed by

stuffing. Carpeting, and more specifically Brussels carpeting, is identified in records as an appropriate cover. Not all tops were rectangular; oval is mentioned in at least one document. Paint, and in particular green paint, covered some surfaces. The varnish coat mentioned in other records probably covered woods such as birds-eye maple, curled maple, and mahogany, all of which are named in the records.[106]

Evidence suggests that crickets usually had turned legs. The casualty rate appears to have been relatively high, given the number of leg repairs mentioned in records. One unusual variation was the "Cricket with wheels" made by Philemon Robbins in 1835 for a Hartford resident. An alternative support to the turned leg was the panel end with an arch cut out at the bottom to form feet. The cricket shown in figure 21, which is representative of this group, is a particularly fine example because the cyma arches of the end panels are repeated in the apron at each long side. The construction is simple. Both aprons abut the side faces of the end panels at rabbets and are nailed in place; the panel ends are set at a slight cant. The top board is nailed to the top edge of the panels, the nails visible in single rows on the board top near either end. A plainer example appears in the right foreground of figure 17.[107]

Crickets and footstools, or "low stools," functioned in various ways. Women used low stools to elevate their feet above floor drafts, and a mother could support a nursing child on the knee of a leg elevated on a low stool. The foot support also was a boon to the elderly. As early as 1718 John Gaines II of Ipswich, Massachusetts, charged a customer two shillings (thirty-three) for "a cricket for yr mother." The low stool was synonymous with childhood as well. Children sat on crickets to pursue their lessons, work on their sewing, participate in devotions, or to listen to stories. The same stools were used for standing at the knee of a parent or teacher to recite or read aloud a lesson. The limited surface area of the stool discouraged fidgeting. In 1816 Job E. Townsend of Newport, Rhode Island, recorded that a Mrs. Kindel paid him one dollar for "making 4 Creekets for her Children."[108]

Low stools served an expanded function in churches and meeting-houses. Parishioners often purchased low stools for use in their private pews. At Providence John G. Hopkins sold Albert C. Greene, Esq., "one pare of Crickets for pew." Fenwick Lyell made "7 foot Stools for Pews" for the family of John J. Post at Middletown, New Jersey. A longer support was the foot bench, which could serve two occupants of a pew seated side by side. In 1837, George Merrifield of Albany constructed a pair for one dollar. The "pair [of] foot benches" purchased by the wealthy New Yorker Arthur Bronson in 1832 were out of the ordinary at seven dollars. Perhaps they were for use with his two eighty-dollar sofas acquired a few months earlier.[109]

Storage Furniture and Boxes

Adequate, convenient storage that was part of the built structure of the house was uncommon in the colonial and federal periods. Householders met this need in part by engaging local woodworkers to build any of a variety of cupboards and shelves where they would serve to advantage. Descriptions usually are brief, and few specific locations are identified.

Records name only the corner cupboard, or buffet, as a recognizable form. Presumably other units were rectangular. Common locations for corner cupboards were front and back parlors, where they held dishes and other equipment used in dining, tea service, and related activities. The "cupboard for your fire place" built by Titus Preston for a Connecticut customer also appears to have been located in a principal space, such as the parlor or kitchen. The "cellar" cupboard named by Enos Reynolds of Massachusetts may have stored preserved foods. An addition to a house provided a convenient opportunity to increase both living and storage space. In 1805 Robert Whitelaw of Vermont charged James Whitelaw seventy-five cents after spending "one day making a Cupboard in your New room."[110]

Features noted occasionally in descriptions of cupboards are paneled doors, shelves, and locks. When Jonathan Loomis built a book cupboard for Captain Lucius Graves at Whately, Massachusetts, in 1815, he charged extra for the "trimming for Do." The material of the common cupboard is seldom mentioned, and size usually is expressed as "large" or "small," when identified at all. An exception is the "pine Corner Cupboard" built by William Savery of Philadelphia for John Cadwalader in 1771. The storage piece stood five feet, six inches high and measured two feet deep from the center front. The cost was £2.10. A common cupboard repair was rehanging the doors.[111]

Hanging cupboards are difficult to discern in craftsmen's accounts. Only in notations such as "a job of work putting up Cupboard" is this form distinguished from others. Perez Austin of Canterbury, Connecticut, provided a few additional particulars in his accounts for February 1831. The craftsman spent half a day "making a paniel Cubboard Dore." This was followed by almost another "half Days work Caseing & han[g]ing [the] Cubboard."[112]

Bookshelves and bookracks are about equally represented in craftsmen's accounts of the early nineteenth century. Prices ranged from under one dollar to over three dollars, although most racks were higher priced than shelves. Bookcases were still more expensive. The form of the bookrack is speculative. Given its price, it was more than a simple table-top unit and different from a standard set of shelves. Early in 1832 the Boston firm of Samuel Chamberlain and Son purchased both a set of shelves and a rack for seventy-five cents and two dollars, respectively. An entry "To Putting up Book Rack" in the accounts of Elizur Barnes of Connecticut indicates the storage unit hung on a wall. Perhaps it was a shelf-like framework with horizontal bars across the front similar to a plate rack to house books with the front covers visible.[113]

Housing books was just one of several named functions of hanging and wall shelves. Next in importance was a shelf to support a clock. References "to putting up clock shelve" range in origin from New Jersey to northern New England, demonstrating the widespread incidence of this practice. Paul Jenkins of Maine provided a "mahoganey shelf for [a] time piece," and William Hook of Massachusetts supplied a "Brackit." A patron of Thomas Boynton's Vermont shop in 1841 commissioned "a flower pot shelf" and paid seventy-five cents. Decades earlier Nathaniel Kinsman of Massachusetts responded to a request for "a Bord for [a] mantle." Whether the board replaced a damaged one or created a shelf where none had existed is unknown. The mantle shelf illustrated in figure 17 supports a pitcher, two books, and a vase of flowers.[114]

Other references describe the nature of the shelving or the place of installation. In accounts dating to 1792 Isaac Ashton of Philadelphia described a job of installing three corner shelves and two long shelves priced by the shelf at 82½¢ and $1.23½, respectively. A year earlier Job Danforth of Providence charged a householder for "puting Shelfs in your closet," and a New York City resident sought the services of Peter Oldershaw to install kitchen shelves at seven shillings for the work and materials.[115]

References to the low chest with hinged lid and bracket feet occur in almost half the documents consulted for this study (see fig. 22). Based on

Figure 22 Low chest, Pennsylvania, 1765–1810. Pine and yellow poplar. H. 28⅛", W. 49⅛", D. 23¼". (Courtesy, Winterthur Museum, gift of H. Rodney Sharp.)

the evidence, it appears that the low chest was the most common piece of movable storage furniture in the American home in the late colonial and federal periods. Descriptive information that accompanies many accounts permits insight into the function, materials, structural embellishment, paint colors, and general size of the low chest.

The basic purpose of this furniture was to store textiles, both personal apparel and bedding (also called bed linens). Records identify the low box without drawers as the most common form of lidded chest. Of the 143 chests tabulated in the sample, fifty-three percent appear to have been of this form. One- and two-drawer chests were of about equal popularity, representing twenty-one percent and twenty percent of the sample, respectively. Three-drawer chests accounted for about 3.5% of the total. At one dollar to six dollars, the price range of the lidded chest was broad. The few examples below and above that range were eliminated from the calculation as being of simpler form or of expensive wood. The average cost of 124 priced chests was $3.20; however, the greatest concentration of examples (fifty-eight percent) was in the $1.50 to three dollar price range.

The purchaser of a lidded chest could choose from a variety of other structural options. One individual ordered a "fast," or sham, drawer, a feature that simulated a more costly construction while maintaining adequate interior storage space. A customer of Elisha H. Holmes in Connecticut called for a "Pine chest secret draw" and paid $2.75. The interior till, a small lidded box or drawer mounted high on an end board, was a feature of some chests. In 1831 Mrs. Nancy Barnes of Preston commissioned an elaborate example—"one large pine Chest with 2 drawers & till with 3 Small Drawers &c."—valued at six dollars and paid with "seamstress work." Exterior trim was another option (see fig. 22), whether a belt molding on the case or an ornamental drop centered in the base. A lock positioned at the center top of the case was a regular request. Although brasses are seldom mentioned, this hardware was more common than apparent, as many cases were built with drawers.[116]

Records that identify the material of the low chest indicate that pine was the principal choice, and the number built was greater than that of the other selections combined. New England was a center of pine chest construction, and Elisha H. Holmes of Connecticut filled many orders. As an alternative choice some of his customers requested chests made of butternut, a wood of the walnut family (*Juglans cinerea*) that had some currency in cabinetmaking in eastern Connecticut and Rhode Island. Two other named woods appear in Pennsylvania work, yellow poplar and black walnut (*Juglans nigra*). Abraham Overholt of Bucks County built low chests of either material. The original selection was still broader, as indicated in documents such as probate inventories.[117]

Records identify stain and varnish as the finish for some low chests. Elisha H. Holmes stained at least one butternut chest. At Middletown, Connecticut, in 1822 Elizur Barnes recorded making a "Cloths Chest Staind & varnished," although he did not name the wood. The more common finish was paint. Of twenty-nine references in the sample, nineteen name a specific color. Brown and green each are mentioned once. "Red" probably identifies a brownish color. On at least two occasions Oliver Moore of East Granby made "a low Chest painted Mahorony" (mahogany). The paint may have duplicated the brown shade of the wood or simulated the actual grain of the material.[118]

A popular color among consumers was blue, sometimes identified as Prussian blue. In 1809 James Chase built a plain "four foot Chest painted Blue" in New Hampshire and charged his customer $1.83. Blue-painted chests appear to have been in demand in eastern Connecticut where Amos Denison Allen, among others, finished a more elaborate example in 1802 described as a "Chest with 1 draw blue with lock." The $3.05 price reflects the greater amount of work involved in making a drawer and providing a lock. Of unusual appearance was the "poplar chest with three drawers and blue speckled" made in 1791 by Abraham Overholt for Martin Oberholtzer (Overholt) of Pennsylvania. At $6.19 this was one of the higher priced chests in the survey. The cost reflects the labor-intensive task of building a dovetailed case and drawers and creating a special finish. Overholt was the only craftsman to note that he painted a chest with contrasting trim: "I made a chest with three drawers, I painted it blue and the mouldings red."[119]

Some accounts give the specifics of chest dimensions. The shortest length recorded is two feet, ten inches; the longest, four feet. Notations of size usually elicited other particulars. In 1816 Titus Preston of Connecticut penned one of the most complete descriptions located: "a chest with a till & a fast draw the chest about 3f. 6 I[n]. long & 1f. 5 I[n]. square / also the draw under the till & fastning it / the lock & screws was ⅓." At $2.90 the price was within the popular range.[120]

A number of accounts identify sea chests by name. The craftsmen who produced these specialized containers usually lived at urban or regional centers of waterborne commerce. In a detailed notice of the mid-1770s, Francis Trumble of Philadelphia offered a wide range of cabinetware and common products, including the sea chest. The postwar years brought increased demand for this specialized gear box as the new American nation expanded its commercial base and established an independent economy.[121]

The records of Amos Denison Allen provide insight into the appearance and special features of the sea chest. From his location in eastern Connecticut, Allen had access to New London and Long Island Sound via Norwich and the Thames River. In July 1799 Gideon Hoxey paid sixteen shillings for "1 Chest for sea 3 [ft]-9 Ins long—19 or 20 wide with a case." In November another customer ordered "1 sea Chest 3-10 long &c" with a "small draw" priced at fifteen shillings. Not every chest was purchased by the person who used it. James Francis of Wethersfield, a trading town below Hartford on the Connecticut River, charged Captain Francis Bulkley twelve shillings in 1797 for "a Sea Chest for your Son Will'm." Then, as today, parents often assisted their sons in establishing a career that would sustain them in their adulthood.[122]

Information on containers known as trunks, although limited, describes the basic options. Pricing and other data indicate that the term identified both small personal boxes and large receptacles used for travel, shipping, and storage. The small "Cherry trunk" made in 1789 by Elisha Hawley of Connecticut for seventy-five cents and the eighteen-inch mahogany container purchased for fifty cents from George Short of Massachusetts a quarter-century later were of suitable size to hold papers, personal effects, and other small items that might come to hand. Either George or Joseph Short also penned a series of account entries in 1815–1816 that sheds further light on form and pricing. One customer purchased three groups of small trunks for a total of twenty-four items, probably for resale. The cheapest group contained twelve "15 in[ch] trunks flat top at 2 cts." The individual box cost of thirty cents suggests that the craftsmen priced the containers by size at two cents per inch. This assumption is borne out by the twenty-one-inch and twenty-four-inch trunks, which cost sixty-three cents and seventy-two cents, respectively, or three cents per inch. What accounted for the difference in price? The logical conclusion is that the larger boxes had domed lids, which required more time to construct.[123]

In an 1828 edition of his dictionary, Noah Webster defined the trunk as "a box or chest covered with skin." Entries in several accounts confirm the general use of protective covers on the exterior of these containers. The 1785 household inventory of William Rhinelander, a shopkeeper of New York City, itemizes both leather-covered and hair-covered trunks. A new "Trunk Coverd with Leather" could cost as much as £2.10 ($8.25), the price paid by Saint George Tucker in Virginia a few years earlier. A fellow Virginian, Richard Blow, bought a "Traveling Trunk" for a client later in the century, although the cover is not identified. Another choice was described in 1835 at Hartford by Philemon Robbins as a "traveling box coverd with oil cloth" priced at $3.50.[124]

A cluster of small drawers contained within a common open-front case suitable for placing on a table or other flat surface usually was termed a "nest of drawers" in early records. A horizontal or vertical rectangle is the common case form, although triangular stacks appear on occasion. The cost was variable, depending on size, number of drawers, construction method, material, and embellishment. Alternative terms for the nest of drawers include "box of draws," used by Reubin Loomis of Connecticut, and "case with 14 drawers," a description employed by George Short of Massachusetts. All three terms—"nest," "box," and "case"—also appear in Chester County, Pennsylvania, inventories dating to the 1750s. When Amos Denison Allen of Connecticut noted that he made "6 Small Draws for Tacks" on June 22, 1802, he also described a nest, as these receptacles would have been impractical for use outside a common container.[125]

Records occasionally identify other uses for collections of small drawers. During the 1760s the Charles Norris family of Philadelphia acquired a "Nest of Seed Draws [for the] Garden." A "Neast of draws" purchased by Doctor Knowles from Benjamin Baker at Newport, Rhode Island, in 1788 may have been for use in his medical practice. Popular in Chester County, Pennsylvania, was the "nest of spice boxes," although other names also describe this specialized case. A bill prepared in 1771 at Carlisle by William

Denny identifies one type of construction material: "one Walnut Nest with 7 Drawrs." Another document indicates that painted wood served on occasion. One householder, Jonah E. Latimer of Essex, Connecticut, ordered a "Nest of draws lock in top draw."[126]

Boxes of personal size are often mentioned in craftsmen's accounts, whether purchased new or brought to a shop for repairs or alteration. Although little description accompanies most business entries, extant boxes provide insights on construction and design. Hinged lids were common, sliding lids less so. The rectangular shape prevailed, although a vertical versus a horizontal orientation introduced variation. Other options included finish and ornament, flat versus curved surfaces (an arched lid, for example), flat or footed bases, and the addition of handles, knobs, and locks. Butted boards or dovetailed corners were construction options. Drawers and interior partitions were available. Joseph Symonds of Massachusetts made "a box with pertions" (partitions) in 1750 followed later by "a box with a Draw."[127]

Records provide insights into the woods used in box construction, but finishes—paint, stain, and varnish—are seldom mentioned. The basswood box purchased in 1829 in Massachusetts by Henry W. Miller and the pine box made later in Connecticut by James Francis were probably painted. A step up in quality although not necessarily in price, which was determined by size and the nature of the work, were a cherrywood box with a drawer made at Middletown by Elizur Barnes and a "Birch Box 10 in Long 5½ wide & 4½ high" from the shop of George Short in Massachusetts. Walnut boxes were common in eastern Pennsylvania. A comprehensive study of Chester County estate inventories recorded before 1850 identifies 130 examples, which comprise seventy-eight percent of all boxes identified by material in those documents. The use of mahogany was widespread, some boxes framed cheaply from shop scraps. George Short charged one customer only fifty cents for making an eighteen-inch mahogany trunk. In New Jersey John Sager's price was considerably higher at 18s.9d. ($3.09).[128]

The candle was the principal source of artificial light in the American home until well into the nineteenth century. The considerable amount of work involved in making tallow candles at home and the substantial cost of buying "manufactured" spermaceti candles dictated that householders used either sparingly. The incidence of candleboxes in craftsmen's accounts is considerable, although some references identify large packing cases used to transport spermaceti candles in bulk. Householders sometimes used other large boxes to store a supply of newly dipped candles. A cool cellar was best; however, care was needed to protect the precious contents against rodent damage. Small finished boxes held modest supplies of candles for daily use (see fig. 23). The usual price in New England and the Middle Atlantic region was less than one dollar and sometimes as low as twenty cents. Documents provide little description of material or form. Boxes were made to stand on a flat surface or to hang on a wall away from the heat of the hearth. The candlebox illustrated in figure 23, which is made of butted pine boards painted, has a sliding lid with a raised panel created by deep

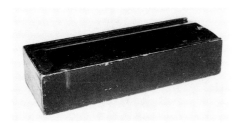

Figure 23 Candlebox, eastern United States, 1750–1830. Pine. H. 2⅞", L. 14", W. 5¼". (Courtesy, Winterthur Museum, gift of H. Rodney Sharp.)

chamfers and a finger notch for access at the front edge. A candlebox bought near Rome, New York, in 1799 from Philip Filer had "36 Candil Rods." These were short sticks to be tied with wicks and used in candle dipping.[129]

Boxes made to contain head gear include those for wigs, hats, and bonnets. Except for ceremonial purposes, the use of wigs began to fade after the Revolution. Thus most references to wig boxes and their repair date before the war. Again, source materials provide little description, although the low cost of new boxes suggests they were basic utilitarian forms. Woodworkers provided both hat and bonnet boxes in some numbers, yet except for "two Chesnut hatboxes" made in 1820 by Perez Austin of Connecticut for seventy-five cents apiece, records provide no identification of material or feature. At sixty cents to eighty-five cents apiece, hat boxes were more expensive than bonnet boxes, which ranged from thirty cents to fifty cents apiece. An alternative term for the hat box was "hat case," although the latter was used infrequently. Woodworkers and others also repaired and refurbished boxes for head gear. Silas Cheney made a new bonnet-box lid in 1800 for the family of Tapping Reeve, the eminent proprietor of the Litchfield Law School. From time to time customers called upon Daniel Rea, Jr., of Boston to repaint their hat boxes. Abraham Overholt of Bucks County, Pennsylvania, recorded a related request in 1799: "I painted five paper hat boxes blue for Martin Oberholtzer."[130]

Specialized boxes made for women center on the container used to hold sewing equipment, also called a "work box" or "fancy box." The price range indicates that this item could be a simple painted box or a receptacle fashioned from fine cabinet wood. Notes about work box repairs identify varnishing, painting, and a new top. Of related function was the "pin box with drawer" purchased in 1834 at Hartford from Philemon Robbins by the Reverend Joel Howes. The mahogany work stand purchased at the same time was perhaps for the same family member. On July 31, 1844, Edward Jenner Carpenter, a Massachusetts apprentice, commented in his journal: "I finished the work box that I agreed to make when I was at home . . . all but varnishing. I have been at work putting on the lock all the evening." Two other boxes for women are notable because their function is identified. On May 10, 1775, Charles Norris' widow Mary bought "a box for Stays and sundreys" for three shillings from Philadelphia cabinetmaker Thomas Tufft. A female member of the Charles Lee household was the recipient of a "box for jewels" acquired in 1831 from Luke Houghton in Massachusetts. At sixty-seven cents this was a relatively basic container.[131]

Boxes constructed for men describe two principal activities, grooming and relaxation. Entries for shaving boxes in craftsmen's accounts provide little additional information aside from identifying one mahogany example that cost two dollars in 1828 at the Connecticut shop of Elisha H. Holmes. A few craftsmen supplied boxes priced well under fifty cents, which probably identifies butted construction and painted surfaces. Howard Smith of New Haven priced a razor case at $1.25. The second group of boxes made for men relates to smoking. The construction material again ranges from mahogany to painted wood. In 1775 Edmund Townsend of Newport,

Rhode Island, fabricated a "mahogany Pipe box." Pipe boxes are slim, vertical containers with an open bin at the top and a drawer, when present, at the bottom. A complement to the pipe box was the tobacco box, its modest cost again reflecting its utilitarian character. John Wheeler Geer of Connecticut sold one in 1779 for as little as one shilling.[132]

A significant item in craftsmen's accounts, as reflected in the number of references, is the spit, or spitting box, the precursor of the cuspidor. In use the low, square box was filled with sand, which gave rise to the alternative name "sand box." Notably, all references from New Jersey and Pennsylvania in the sample use the present participle "spitting" to identify this container, whereas New England references, which are four times as numerous, almost always use the term "spit box."[133]

The disagreeable habit of spitting appears to have been firmly entrenched in American society before 1744 when the Tuesday Club of Annapolis, Maryland, required that "each member . . . provide his own sand-box as a spittoon in order to spare the floors at members' houses." Touring the new United States in 1783 Francisco de Miranda, a Spanish American visitor, noted the continued widespread use of tobacco in pipes and for chewing, and visitors who followed invariably commented on the "loathsome spitting" that accompanied chewing. Traveling by American steamboat in the 1840s, Englishman James Dixon discovered that the practice of chewing tobacco and spitting was "almost general." He found "nearly the whole deck soon became coloured and almost impassable." Apprentice Edward Jenner Carpenter was one of those caught up in the habit. He tried giving up chewing several times without success. In August 1844 he wrote: "I concluded to quit chewing tobacco, but I don't believe I shall hold out, for the habit has got pretty well fastened on to me."[134]

The nature of its use precluded that the spit box was anything more than utilitarian in material and construction. References suggest that most boxes were painted, and green is mentioned in the accounts of Elizur Barnes of Connecticut. Some boxes appear to have been fixed in place where they were used, as suggested by Fenwick Lyell of New Jersey who in 1808 supplied "1 Spiting Box and 4 Brackets." The cost was six shillings (one dollar), although the usual price for the box alone was twenty-five cents to forty cents. The presence of spit boxes in places of business and assembly was universal: Grove Catlin, an innkeeper of Litchfield, Connecticut, bought spit boxes from Silas Cheney; the firm of Ebenezer and George Merriam, bookbinders and stationers, purchased sand boxes from Philip Deland of West Brookfield, Massachusetts; Gershom Jones, a Providence pewterer acquired a box from Job Danforth, Sr.; another Providence resident, businessman Richard W. Green, patronized the partners Church and Sweet for office furnishings that included "2 Spit Boxes." When the seat of national government moved from New York City to Philadelphia in 1790, David Evans recorded an order to supply "50 spitting Boxes for Congress."[135]

More than a dozen references to medical boxes of one type or another occur in documents assembled for this study. Seven identify purchases made by doctors, and two record orders placed by Robert Rantoul, a druggist of Beverly, Massachusetts. In 1834 Philemon Robbins of Hartford named a "Capt E Flower" as the purchaser of a "Medicine chest" for three dollars. Perhaps Flower was a ship captain and purchased the box for use on board his vessel.[136]

The terms "medicine box," "medicine chest," and "medicine case" all appear in records and at times may have been used interchangeably. "Case" also may identify a stationary piece of furniture. Items designated "boxes" in the sample were priced the lowest at under one dollar. The most expensive item recorded was a "Walnut Medicine Chest" priced at $18.48 and made in 1786 by Philadelphia cabinetmaker David Evans for a Doctor Bass. At three pounds ($9.90), another high-priced container was the "Case for your Drugs" made in Connecticut by John Durand for Doctor Charles Carinton in 1775. One doctor in Maine ordered his chest with a lock. Other notable items include the "six boxes for Salts at 25 Cts a piece" made in Connecticut for Doctor Richard Ely and the four "Pill Boxes" painted at Boston by Daniel Rea, Jr., for Doctor William Jackson.[137]

Quadrant cases and compass boxes identified in craftsmen's accounts were receptacles for nautical instruments. Daniel Rea, Jr., refurbished a quadrant case in 1790 with a fresh coat of paint. Two craftsmen located on the lower Connecticut River, navigable by ocean-sailing vessels, noted the construction of new quadrant cases. Elizur Barnes of Middletown priced his case at one dollar. The two-dollar case made by Elisha H. Holmes of Essex was probably constructed better or made of more expensive materials. Compass boxes were cheaper. Newburyport, Massachusetts, cabinetmaker George Short produced one for twenty-five cents in 1814.[138]

Hearth-related Equipment

A convenient piece of fireplace equipment during the late eighteenth and nineteenth centuries was the small hand bellows used to fan a fire on the hearth (see fig. 24). Woodworkers supplied the front and back boards, complete with handles, and leatherworkers provided the fittings for the metal nozzle and the flexible sides that created an interior chamber, or air cavity. In recording the sale of boards for bellows, a craftsman usually identified the transaction as "a pair of Bellows woods," although Jonathan Kettell of Newburyport, Massachusetts, also used the term "set" of bellows woods.[139]

Before painted and ornamented bellows became popular in the early nineteenth century, craftsmen made boards from fine cabinet woods finished in stain and varnish. Oliver Avery of Connecticut listed cherry-wood in his records, a wood also supplied by Daniel Ross in Massachusetts. Ross' records identify maple and mahogany as other choices. Material status is reflected in the prices of individual pairs of boards: maple, forty cents; cherrywood, forty-five cents; mahogany, 83½¢. On one occasion Ross supplied "Birch Bellows woods [and] Brass nose" for fifty cents. Repairs noted by Job E. Townsend of Rhode Island in 1783 describe "a new top to a mohogony Bellosses." Sometimes a consumer acquired a

Figure 24 Hand bellows by Bulkley and Austin, New Haven, Connecticut, 1800–1830. Probably cherry. H. 2¼", L. 21⅞", W. 8⅝". (Courtesy, Winterthur Museum, bequest of Henry Francis du Pont.)

"Bellows & Hearth Brush" as a set, as itemized in an 1837 bill from Pells and Company to Arthur Bronson of New York City. The stained boards of the bellows illustrated in figure 24 appear to be cherrywood, and the decorative focus of the object is its turned ornament rather than paint. The bold pattern of concentric circles is centered by a large boss. On the back-board a central, circular depression bears a small paper label of the manufacturers: "BULKLEY & AUSTINS / Factory / NEW HAVEN" enclosed within a chain of bellflowers.[140]

The fireboard, a wooden panel used to conceal a fireplace opening during the months of warm weather, was an item of some consequence in craftsmen's records (see fig. 25). A few artisans, including Benjamin Baker of Rhode Island and Isaac Ashton of Philadelphia, used the alternative term "chimney board" to identify this screen. In Maine Paul Jenkins expanded the nomenclature when describing a board he made as a "fire Blind." Other evidence suggests that Jenkins referred to the appearance of the board rather than the form itself. An entry in the accounts of Elisha H. Holmes of Connecticut for "1 Fire board window blind style" provides an explanation. The boards probably were louvered like many exterior window shutters, also referred to in records as "blinds." The cost of the boards

Figure 25   Fireboard, New England, possibly Sutton, Massachusetts, 1820–1850. White pine. H. 26½", W. 39½". (Courtesy, Winterthur Museum.)

at $1.75 and $1.25, respectively, adds support to the explanation, as many other examples in the records were priced well below one dollar. An advantage of louvered-board construction was the protection it gave from the intrusion of birds and small animals via the unused chimney, while permitting the circulation of outside air.[141]

Several other references to fireboards expand the picture. In 1822–1823 Elizur Barnes was called upon at Middletown, Connecticut, for several tasks of note. One customer wanted "a fire Board and sheat Iron lining." Another job found Barnes "Sawing [a] Fire board for handiron." Once after supplying a fireboard to a householder, Barnes spent time "Fiting it in." Other boards were free standing. A few records refer specifically to fireboards of framed construction. One frame appears to have housed a solid wood panel. Another frame may have been open to receive a different material, perhaps black muslin ornamented with pasted decoration cut from wallpaper, as suggested by Catherine Beecher.[142]

Few records elaborate on the finish of the fireboard and then only in basic terms. Thomas Boynton of Vermont, among others, recorded the use of varnish and paint. Allen Holcomb identified green paint as the choice of one customer in central New York. The records are silent on the subject of painted ornament, although some of the more expensive boards must have been finished in this manner. Many survive today with the original decoration intact. The trompe l'oeil design of the fireboard illustrated in figure 25 creates the illusion of an open fireplace complete with the tin-glazed earthenware tiles popular among prosperous American householders. Other decorative choices include a "large paperd fire board" purchased in 1815 in Massachusetts from Abner Taylor. Similar, perhaps, was the "Bordering for [a] Fire Board" ordered in New York City by Robert L. Livingston in 1832 from upholsteress Rebecca Williamson, proprietress of a "Fring & Ornamental Factory" at 120 William Street.[143]

Woodworkers, especially those working in the eighteenth century, received regular calls for long wooden handles for warming pans. Oliver Wickes of Rhode Island described the fabrication method: "To Turning one wormingpan handle." His charge in 1801 was seventeen cents. Both the design of the pan and its method of use insured the need for repairs from time to time. The wooden handle fits into a cylindrical metal sleeve projecting from one side of a large, lidded, circular metal pan. Householders or their hired help filled the pan with hot coals from the hearth and then passed it "hastily and sharply all over the bed" to warm the bedding and draw out the dampness, taking care to avoid scorching the sheets or setting the bed on fire. The weight of the filled pan and the fragile joint between pan and handle led many a craftsmen to record his work at "putting a handle into a warming pan."[144]

The foot stove was a second piece of early equipment that required hot coals to function (see fig. 26). A removable interior pan held the coals within a small metal chamber with perforated sides and top and an access door at the front. A wooden framework with corner posts supported the chamber, or box. Oftentimes the corner posts were turned in the popular

Figure 26 Foot stove, eastern United States, 1790–1830. Walnut and tinned sheet metal. H. 5¾", W. 9", D. 7¾". (Courtesy, Winterthur Museum, gift of H. Rodney Sharp.)

double-baluster profile of the hourglass (see fig. 14). A wire bail handle at the top provided portability.

Foot stoves, considered the province of women, were especially popular in Dutch-American communities. Like the bed warmer, foot stoves frequently were stored in or near the kitchen where they could be filled conveniently with hot coals from the kitchen hearth for use in parlors and bed chambers or any place in the home where comfort from the cold was required. Because foot stoves were portable, they could be carried outside the home for use in carriages, church pews, and other large interior spaces with little or no artificial heat.[145]

In April 1827 Catherine Gansevoort, widow of Peter, Jr. (1749–1812), of Albany paid a fee of one dollar to Henry A. Guardinien, sexton of the North Dutch Church, for "Fireing Your foot Stoves." These warming devices probably were the "two Cherry foot stoves" the widow had purchased in 1816 from Peter M. Hench for two dollars. Beyond the spiritual center, foot stoves were useful in spaces devoted to secular pursuit. The November 19, 1750, issue of the *New-York Gazette* carried a theater notice that is pertinent: "The House being now floor'd, is made warm and comfortable; besides which Gentlemen and Ladies may cause their stoves to be brought."[146]

Aside from the cherrywood stoves purchased by Catharine Gansevoort, records identify a "Whitewood Stove" (probably yellow poplar) purchased in 1806 at Middletown, New Jersey, from Fenwick Lyell. Broadening the selection is the walnut stove illustrated in figure 26. Several documents that identify repairs to foot stoves extend the geographic range of the form, including those of Silas Cheney of Litchfield, Connecticut, and Samuel Fithian Ware of Cape May County, New Jersey.[147]

Picture and Other Frames

Frames for pictures, mirrored glass, and other materials were requested everywhere—from the Maine shop of William H. Reed to that of Moyers and Rich in southwestern Virginia. A few picture frames are identified specifically as frames for portraits, or likenesses. Silas Cheney used both terms at his shop in Connecticut. In 1828 Increase Pote of Maine exchanged a "Portrait frame" priced at six dollars for 12½ pounds of coffee. Three years earlier Joseph G. Waters of Salem, Massachusetts, paid K. H. Shaw $2.50 for "Framing a Portrait of John Q Adams." The "portrait" probably was a print. The reverse of the bill identifies Shaw as a gilder. Another type of picture noted only rarely in records is the landscape. Chapman Lee of Massachusetts produced a "Landscape [frame]" in 1822 priced low at twenty-five cents. Some frames listed anonymously in other records likely were intended for the same purpose.[148]

General references to "picture frames" broaden the inquiry. Many name the surface finish, paint being the most common. Elisha H. Holmes of Connecticut recorded black-painted and yellow-painted frames. William Barker "color[ed] 27 picter fraims" at Providence in 1763, a process that may have been synonymous with staining. In Virginia, Saint George Tucker

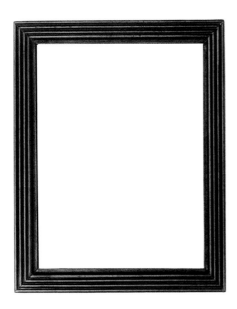

Figure 27   Picture frame, eastern United States, 1790–1830. Wood. H. 10", W. 8". (Courtesy, Winterthur Museum.)

paid the sum of twelve shillings in 1791 for "blacking and varnishing Six picture frames." The blacking probably was a composition material that employed lampblack. Artisans created more lustrous surfaces through gilding and bronzing. Charges posted by Paul Jenkins in Maine for making a "Large picter frame" in 1837 include fifty cents for "cutting glass for the same" and twenty-five cents for "⅔ book gold Leef." Veneering capitalized on the grained patterns of various woods. The Massachusetts apprentice Edward Jenner Carpenter reported in August 1844 that he had sawed "some stuff . . . for some frames to a couple of pictures . . . my grandfather brought down here the other day." A day later he veneered the frames: "I put mahogany on to one & zebra wood on to the other."[149]

When Elisha H. Holmes charged a customer two dollars for twelve picture frames in 1830, he debited the account another forty-two cents for "Triming . . . the same." A possible explanation of this charge is that Holmes attached strips of composition beading to the molded surfaces. One of the most common methods of ornamenting a frame was molding wood with a plane or other tool. The multiple rows of flat beading on the face of the frame illustrated in figure 27 were formed in this manner, and the general use of the technique is underscored by Jonathan Kettell of Newburyport, Massachusetts, who supplied "Mouldings for pictures frames." A more costly ornamental technique is cited in the business papers of William Beekman, a New York City resident. The reference also provides a general summary of the framing process. In 1795 Cornelius Roosevelt supplied Beekman with four picture frames at a basic charge of five shillings apiece. Carving and gilding added another five shillings to the individual price. Roosevelt completed the order with four panes of glass, two priced together at sixteen shillings and two priced together at twelve shillings. Although the frames likely were identical in pattern, two sizes were represented, as indicated in the dual pricing of the glass. When making picture frames at Salem, Massachusetts, for the Orne family in 1763, Jonathan Gavit figured his charge by the amount of material used rather than the number of frames made: "To frameing 54 foot of Pictures."[150]

The woods craftsmen used in framemaking were varied, although the present sample identifies only oak and mahogany. Most surfaces, regardless of material or ornamental technique, received a finish coat of varnish. The addition of a metal ring placed at the top of a small frame provided a convenient hanging device. B. A. Norton and Company supplied brass rings for pictures hung for Samuel Larned of Providence. Picture hanging was a service also requested in 1836 by Arthur Bronson of New York City. A further task performed by Elizur Barnes in 1821 for a customer in Connecticut is described as "Painting & Varnishing 17 Picture Fraimes & Putting in Pictures at house." The charge was $1.25. Household mishaps required the attention of the woodworker from time to time. The Proud brothers of Providence glued a picture frame for a customer, charging only six cents. A patron of Newport cabinetmaker Job E. Townsend had a different, although relatively common, problem: "To framing one Pickter Broking Glass."[151]

References to looking glass frames provide less information than those for pictures. The standard maintenance calls were for mending, varnishing, and gilding. A broader look at repairs and alterations occurs in account entries made by Job Danforth of Providence. In 1801 he charged six shillings for "putting a back to a looking glass to finding screws to putting up & gluing frame." A day later another customer approached him with a request for "cutting a looking glass frame." Whether the alteration was due to a broken glass or changing household needs is not indicated. An alternative to the rectangular-bordered glass was the "oval looking glass frame." Philemon Robbins of Hartford recorded an example in 1834.[152]

Maps varied widely in size, from those that fit neatly into small frames to others of large size hung without benefit of a standard wooden support. Maps, like prints, often were framed unglazed, as glass was expensive. To protect the fragile paper from smoke, dust, vermin, and tears, the surface often was varnished. This practice had its own set of problems, however, because the coating material was unstable, causing discoloration and in some cases crackling. Craftsmen's accounts identify the two methods of map framing. Both Elisha H. Holmes of Essex, Connecticut, and Thomas Boynton of Windsor, Vermont, posted charges for "framing and varnishing a map." The alternative procedure is highlighted in the accounts of William Beesley of Salem, New Jersey: "to a map frame & glass.[153]

Two other references to framed maps identify the subjects. A 1794 entry in the accounts of Job E. Townsend of Newport, Rhode Island, describes "framing a Map of Dublin." Several decades later Elisha H. Holmes of Essex, Connecticut, charged seventy-five cents for "Frameing & varnishing United States chart." If Holmes used the term chart properly, this was a map focusing on coastal navigation.[154]

Large maps generally were left unframed but varnished. To provide a support for hanging and a weight to keep the sheet from curling, many maps were fitted with rollers, or "sticks" (see fig. 28). Consumers purchased maps already fitted with rollers or employed a local woodworker to turn the requisite supports. Some customers may have attached the maps

Figure 28 Joseph S. Russell, *Dining Room of Dr. Whitridge,* Tiverton, Rhode Island, ca. 1848–1853, depicting a scene of 1814–1815. Watercolor. 7 1/16" x 9 1/2". (Courtesy, New Bedford Whaling Museum.)

themselves, as suggested by Joseph Griswold of Massachusetts, who supplied "two map rollers" for forty cents in 1820. The meaning of Titus Preston's account of "puting rollers to a map" is clear, and the Connecticut craftsman's charge of four shillings (sixty-six cents) indicates that he also supplied the rollers. The map on rollers visible in figure 28 probably depicts the New England coast. It occupies a prominent place in the dining room of Doctor Whitridge of Tiverton, Rhode Island, and provides information on the placement of similar maps in eighteenth- and nineteenth-century homes.[155]

Framed slates for school children are itemized in craftsmen's accounts with some frequency from the late eighteenth century through the early nineteenth century. Both New England and the Middle Atlantic region are represented. The cost was modest, varying from 12½¢ to just over forty cents, the exact figure probably a direct reflection of the size and material of the frame. Account entries for this work show little variation. Nathan Topping Cook of Long Island recorded making a "Slate frame," whereas Nathaniel Sterling of Wilton, Connecticut, described the task as "puting A frame on A slate."[156]

Miscellaneous items housed in frames constitute a diverse group. Needlework (usually described as samplers) forms the largest assemblage. Charges were in the fifty cents to one dollar range. Records sometimes identify the family member responsible for the handiwork, as noted by James Gere of Connecticut who charged William Walker fifty-eight cents for "framing sampler for [your] Daughter." Next in popularity were frames for profiles, or silhouettes. The small size of these pictures kept the frame cost low—sometimes as little as 4½¢ apiece. Thomas Boynton of Vermont recorded a series of pertinent transactions, some reflecting quantity purchases, as for instance the "25 profile frames" priced at 16½¢ apiece acquired in 1834 by Lyman Cowdry. Another customer borrowed equipment for taking images. When the apparatus was not returned after many months, Boynton charged the customer four dollars for "a profile machine lent last Spring."[157]

Another item sought by householders was a frame to house a family register, described by Elizur Barnes of Middletown, Connecticut, as "a Fraim For [a] Family Record." The charge was seventy-five cents. Farther down the Connecticut River at Essex, Elisha H. Holmes's price for "Frameing & glaseing [a] Family Regester" was one dollar. In 1799 Job Danforth produced "a fraim for [a] Diaplomia" for two different customers at Providence. One of them also paid for "pa[i]nting & gilden Dito" and a "glas for Dito." Of more uncertain identification is Stephanus Knight's work in "fraiming a Chart of history" done a few years later at Enfield, Connecticut.[158]

The painting illustrated in figure 17 provides visual documentation of picture placement in the home. The large, multi-functional room that serves for dining, socializing, and a family gathering place has as its principal focus the chimneypiece. Both the arrangement and subject matter of the pictures are of interest. The centerpiece is a medium-size framed print of George Washington. The naval prints flanking the portrait probably are scenes from the War of 1812. The pair of profiles in gilt frames flanking the vase of flowers are recognizable as hollow-cut images produced at Peale's Museum in Philadelphia.

Equipment for Games, Sports, and Pastimes

Craftsmen's accounts identify three board games popular in the colonial and federal periods—checkers, chess, and backgammon. Of these, checkers appears to have been the most common. The equipment then, as now, consisted of a board and a set of checkermen. Although citations are brief, consumers could choose from two finishes when purchasing a board, paint or inlay. Daniel Rea, Jr., of Boston painted checkerboards for two shillings or three shillings (thirty-three cents or fifty cents). A ship chandler purchased one, possibly for resale at his chandlery to a mariner. At Kennebunk, Maine, Paul Jenkins charged $1.50 for a "mahoganey chequar bord," probably made of light and dark wood. Some craftsmen may have supplied plain boards for customers to take to an ornamental painter, who provided the playing surface. The method of fabricating the checkermen is described in several accounts, including that of Increase Pote of Portland, Maine: "To Turning one Seet Checker men @ 2/3" (37½¢).[159]

The equipment for chess was similar to that for checkers, except the men usually were more elaborate, a circumstance reflected in the price. Thomas Boynton of Windsor, Vermont, charged $1.50 for "a Sett of Chessmen" in 1822. Shortly after the Revolutionary War Thomas Jefferson paid Philadelphia cabinetmaker Thomas Affleck the substantial sum of nine dollars for a board and set of men. The convertible, hinged game board illustrated in figure 29 is marked on the obverse for chess or checkers. The plain, turned men are for playing checkers.[160]

Backgammon was another board game that required turned pieces, or men, for play, although the use of dice and turned dice cups (see fig. 29) introduced an element of chance that may have made the game more appealing to some individuals. In 1780 Daniel and Samuel Proud of Providence

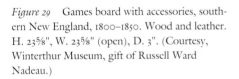
Figure 29 Games board with accessories, southern New England, 1800–1850. Wood and leather. H. 23⅝", W. 23⅝" (open), D. 3". (Courtesy, Winterthur Museum, gift of Russell Ward Nadeau.)

reported "turning 2 Back gammon Cups." Several decades later Increase Pote turned a number of sets of backgammon men for a local firm in Portland, Maine, probably for resale. The reverse, or interior, of the board shown in figure 29 is painted to accommodate the game of backgammon. The terms "backgammon board" and "backgammon box" probably were interchangeable, as suggested by similar five-dollar charges recorded by Thomas Boynton of Vermont for the first named and by Samuel Silliman of Duanesburg, New York, for the second. Apprentice Edward Jenner Carpenter mentioned this game in a journal entry for February 11, 1845: "I have been a making me a backgammon board for 2 or 3 nights back. George Gillagan [a painter] said he would paint it if I would make him a box." In a list of disbursements for outfitting the sloop *Fame* at Newport, Rhode Island, in 1799 is a charge from Stephen Goddard of the well-known family of cabinetmakers to Captain Thomas Dennis for "2 Bacgammon Boards," probably for use on shipboard.[161]

References to making equipment for billiards are uncommon in craftsmen's accounts, probably because the table required for playing the game was expensive. A few individuals may have had access to a private table, and others possibly frequented local taverns so equipped. Members of the Townsend family of Newport, Rhode Island, recorded the sale of billiard equipment in the 1770s. Job Townsend, Jr., made "two Billard Bols," and Job E. Townsend supplied "2 Billiards Sticks."[162]

Outdoor sports required other types of equipment. Ice skating was a winter diversion in the North and parts of the South. Merchants sometimes imported skates from England. At other times local craftsmen met customer requests. In Vermont Thomas Boynton made several account entries for "wooding skates" at charges ranging from twenty-five cents to fifty cents. The wooden platforms supported the feet and secured the metal runners; leather straps attached the skates to the feet. In Providence and Philadelphia craftsmen made particular note of parental largesse: "to wooding a pair of skates for your Son."[163]

Manifestations of parental affection extended beyond a pair of ice skates. In 1806 Massachusetts artisan Harris Beckwith noted the production of "A Hand Sled for your Boy." The term "hand sled" is an important distinction because most references to sleds in craftsmen's accounts refer to horse-drawn pleasure or work vehicles. A younger child would have owned the hobby horse Joseph Pemberton sent to the Philadelphia shop of William Savery for repairs in 1774. The purchase of a "fishing Box Compleate" by Thomas Osborn in 1828 from Thomas Timpson of New York probably represented personal equipment, although the "complete" nature of the gear suggests that a son or sons may have shared their father's enjoyment of the sport.[164]

Another popular outdoor adult sport among individuals of both Dutch and British background was ninepins, a game in which the pins were set in three rows forming a square. Ideally the playing alley, or green, was perfectly level, although most courses probably were "make do," laid out on ground as flat as available in community or private locations. Some inns maintained an alley for the accommodation of patrons. Evidence of the game appears in European prints and in several American records. The accounts of Josiah P. Wilder of New Hampshire record a charge of seventy-five cents in June 1838 for "Turning [a] set of Nine pins." Three decades earlier Robert Whitelaw of Vermont helped a customer "turn balls to play ninepins" for the sum of twenty-five cents, an indication that Whitelaw spent approximately a quarter of a working day on the task.[165]

Although not sporting equipment in the usual sense, the walking stick, or cane, served as a companion for a leisurely stroll and an item of fashionable dress during the period covered by this study. The interchangeable nature of the terminology is demonstrated in the accounts of Robert Whitelaw: "To mending a walking Cane." Ornamental examples abound today, although many are machine products of later date. Those in the sample were principally utilitarian in nature, as reflected in their low cost. Philadelphia cabinetmaker Francis Trumble advertised "walking sticks" and

Figure 30   Walking stick, eastern United States, possibly southeastern New England, 1800–1830. Curled maple. L. 40½", Diam. 1½" (at head). (Courtesy, Winterthur Museum.)

a selection of utilitarian wares in 1775. Turning was a common method of fabrication, as identified in 1815 by the Proud brothers of Providence and Allen Holcomb in New York state. The walking stick illustrated in figure 30 is a fine specimen of the turner's art. Its simulated bamboo work executed in curled maple has close parallels in Windsor chair making. Careful study reveals the subtle styling of the graduated segments, rounded at the top and flaring at the base, complemented at the head by a spherical knob that fits into the palm of the hand. A metal ferrel protected some cane tips from wear and mud. The Proud brothers added one to a stick made in 1782.[166]

Eighteenth- and early nineteenth-century records indicate that householders were fascinated with birds, which they kept indoors in cages or sheltered out of doors in appropriate houses. Many wire-formed cages were imported into North America from metal manufacturing centers in England. The example visible in figure 17 may fit this description. Some cages were made by the craftsmen who sold them, although the same individuals sometimes imported goods for sale. Probably representative of the latter practice was the "Birds Cage with 2 Apartments" sold by Annapolis Maryland cabinetmakers John Shaw and Archibald Chisholm in 1772. There is no mistaking the meaning of a July 26, 1809, entry in the account book of Silas Cheney of Connecticut: "to makeing [a] Bird Cage" for $1.50. Some craftsmen also repaired or refurbished bird cages. In 1792, Boston painter Daniel Rea, Jr., billed John Codman for "Gilding and Varnish'g a Bird Cage."[167]

Records occasionally identify the intended occupant of a new cage. The accounts of Philadelphia merchant Stephen Girard are particularly informative. Twice in 1826 Girard patronized the shop of wireworkers Joseph and John Needles. During one visit he paid $2.50 for a "mocking Bird Cage." By the early 1800s this little creature had been a prized household pet in America for well over a hundred years. A century earlier, a European traveler in Virginia noted that mocking birds were being sent to England for sale. Girard's other purchase from the Needles firm was a "mahogany Canary Cage / 2 Fountains," the price slightly more at $2.62½. Originally, this songbird inhabited the Canary Islands in the Atlantic Ocean off the coast of Africa, although Girard may have acquired his pet elsewhere.

Figure 31 Martin box, or house, Kankakee, Illinois, ca. 1917. Illustrated in Joseph H. Dodson, *Your Bird Friends and How to Win Them* (Kankakee, Ill.: Joseph H. Dodson, 1917), p. 17. (Courtesy, Winterthur Library: Printed Book and Periodical Collection.)

Girard's brother and occasional partner, John, also had an interest in birds. Several decades earlier he had visited the cabinet shop of Daniel Trotter and ordered "a Board for a parrot Stand." The brightly-colored, exotic pet was a favorite with bird fanciers, from retired mariners to spinsters.[168]

For outdoor accommodation of birds one structure dominates the records—the "martin box," also called a "martin house" (see fig. 31). The purple martin, a member of the swallow family, is noted for its colonizing habit. Thus, from the colonial period to the present its built accommodation has been a multi-compartment facility. From New England to Pennsylvania householders cheerfully accommodated these aerial feeders. The highest-priced martin box recorded was made in 1817 by Thomas Boynton of Vermont for three dollars and described as "a painted martin house and a pole to set it on." In Connecticut Stephanus Knight assisted one of his customers in housing several colonies of martins: "To Painting Martin-boxes finding stuf and helping put them up." Peter Ranck of Pennsylvania charged a customer 3s.9d. for a martin box, considerably less than the eight shillings paid in Massachusetts by Elias Hasket Derby for "mending [a] martin box." Records identify one other avian structure, a "Wren hous" built in 1785 by Benjamin Baker in Rhode Island for merchant Jacob Rodriguez Rivera. Baker's charge of seven shillings ($1.16) reflected "1 Day work."[169]

Beyond the Door

The woodworker's sphere of activity extended beyond the interior of the home to the exterior environment encountered when members of the household stepped through the door. The stoop, veranda, and yard all offered many reminders of the regular interaction between the two groups. The domestic scene illustrated in figure 32, which captures the essence of family life, serves as an appropriate vehicle to conclude a discussion of everyday things.

Figure 32 Anne-Marguerite, Baroness Hyde de Neuville, *The Cottage*, New Brunswick, New Jersey, 1813. Watercolor and graphite. 6¾" x 8¼". (Collection of the New-York Historical Society.)

The cottage yard at the small farm in New Brunswick, New Jersey, purchased by the Baron and Baroness Hyde de Neuville (fig. 32) and occupied during two sojourns in America in the early nineteenth century, is alive with activity, both visible and perceived. The porch, or veranda, is filled with potted plants placed there on a bench, shelf, or stand by the mistress of the house, who stands in the doorway. The number of containers for flowers listed in woodworkers' accounts indicates that this item was not the exclusive province of the potter. Records from New Hampshire to Pennsylvania identify flower pots and boxes fabricated in both rural and urban locations. Luke Houghton of Massachusetts and Miles Benjamin of New York state sold flower boxes for fifty cents or less. Mary Norris paid considerably more for boxes acquired from Philadelphia cabinetmaker Thomas Tufft.[170]

Craftsmen's accounts provide little insight into the appearance of these receptacles. An unusual notation is that for "a Flower Pot Picketed" recorded in 1824 by Elizur Barnes of Connecticut. The term "picketed" appears to describe stave construction, which was common in the fabrication of pails and buckets (see fig. 4). Two years earlier Barnes produced a "large Green Flowerpot." Paint, and green paint in particular, was a common finish for flower pots. In northeastern Massachusetts painters William Gray and Daniel Rea, Jr., each recorded a job of painting flower pots in the early 1790s for customers who were physicians. If a consumer were prepared to supply his own labor, he could purchase the necessary "green paint for flower pots" from a woodworker, as recorded in 1823 by Thomas Boynton of Vermont.[171]

The porch of the Hyde de Neuville farm cottage provided several options for plant display. A shelf fixed to the railing of the balustrade held the greatest number of flower pots. The small platform for plants at either end of the porch recalls an account entry made at Albany by George Merrifield for "a plant stand." Benches for plants occur in several New England records, including a "Green Bench for flower pots" made by Elizur Barnes of Middletown, Connecticut, in 1824. Although primarily for sitting, the long bench on the porch of the Hyde de Neuville cottage could have held plants as well. Another stand for indoor or outdoor use was the "ladder for flowers" acquired in the 1830s by Albert C. Greene of Providence. This structure likely was of rectangular or semicircular, stepped form.[172]

Two items to the right of the Hyde de Neuville cottage enlarge upon the contribution of the woodworker to the botanical interests of a household. The large watering can relates to a credit entry posted by John E. Mehargue in central Pennsylvania when a customer provided a "bottom in [a] Water Can." The portability of the tree next to the can is addressed in an item recorded by Friedrich Bastian in a neighboring town on the Susquehanna River: "to a Box for to Plant in a Tree." As drawn, the container appears to be a stave tub with hoops. Nor are these references isolated examples of the practice. James Skerrett of Philadelphia paid a craftsman for making "2 Tree Boxes." In Vermont, Thomas Boynton described the product as "a Box for a tree to grow in." Unit prices ranged from over one dollar to about fifty cents.[173]

Without the image of the dog house in the Hyde de Neuville yard, it would be difficult to ascertain the appearance of this shelter as constructed before the mid-nineteenth century. Few early dog houses survive because of their utilitarian function and use outdoors. The design, as might be expected, is a simple gable end with a tall arch for an entrance. In 1789 Robert Mullen, a Philadelphia carpenter, built a dog house for the family of Stephen Collins, a prominent Quaker merchant of the city. In the Hyde de Neuville drawing, one of the family's pets naps comfortably in its private lodging and another rests in the cool shade beneath the porch. On at least two occasions craftsmen noted the sale of a puppy. John Durand provided one in 1766 for a customer in coastal Connecticut, and Silas Cheney made a similar sale several decades later in western Connecticut. The price was modest—between fifty cents and seventy-five cents.[174]

A simple picket-type fence surrounds the Hyde de Neuville cottage and yard, the entrance via a gate with a hand latch. Exterior structures of this type were particularly subject to wear and the elements. In April 1800 Silas Cheney posted a charge of six shillings (one dollar) for "making fence one day," the sum equal to his price for two crickets. Stephanus Knight of Enfield devoted less than a day to the same task a few years later, charging a customer 3s.9d. for "Work on the fences about the hous." At Providence, Job Danforth identified a regular call from householders when debiting an account for "hanging your gate."[175]

Inside the yard children play in front of the cottage porch. The records of several craftsmen identify small wheeled vehicles for children. In 1803 Silas Cheney charged as little as nine shillings ($1.50) for a "Childrens wagon." The form, as drawn by the baroness, is a cradlelike box on wheels (see fig. 20). Use on rough, uneven ground insured that these small conveyances would require the attention of a woodworker periodically. In Windsor, Vermont, Thomas Boynton charged a patron twenty-five cents for "fixing [a] childs waggon" in 1822. Another customer requested the same service some years later.[176]

In the lower yard a young girl with a pitcher draws water for household use at a well capped by a pump fitted with a hand lever. At least two craftsmen identified the fabrication method of the lever. In 1777 William Gray of Salem, Massachusetts, posted a charge to a customer's account for "Turning a handle for well." Silas Cheney identified the same job as "turning [a] pump handle." Both charges were less than twenty cents. At the base of the pump a large stave tub, not unlike the container supporting the tree near the cottage door, caught the overflow. The contents of the tub were suitable for watering the dogs and the plants. In the pursuit of everyday life, the water of the well, like the products and activity of the woodworker, represented a substantial support inside and outside the home.[177]

1. This study is based on information drawn from more than 230 original documents, comprising principally account sheets and books, and collections of family and business papers. The records extend in date from the late colonial period to about 1850 and range in place of origin from Maine to Virginia.

2. Silas Ellis Cheney Daybook, Litchfield, Connecticut, 1802–1807, account with Charles Cilbern, Oct. 18, 1802, Litchfield Historical Society, Litchfield, Connecticut (hereafter cited LHS); Jane C. Nylander, *Our Own Snug Fireside: Images of the New England Home, 1760–1860* (New Haven, Conn.: Yale University Press, 1994), figs. 119, 124, 127: Elisabeth Donaghy Garrett, *At Home: The American Family, 1750–1870* (New York: Harry N. Abrams, Inc., 1990), pp. 97, 107, 170.

3. References to kitchen tables appear in 67 documents used in this study. Pine and whitewood table in Elisha Harlow Holmes Daybook, Essex, Connecticut, 1825–1850, account with Abby Parker, October 10, 1828, Connecticut State Library, Hartford (hereafter cited CSL). Job E. Townsend Account Book, Newport, Rhode Island, 1803–1828, account with Mary Ann Marble, September 9, 1822, Newport Historical Society, Newport, Rhode Island, (hereafter cited NHS); Elizur Barnes Account Book, Middletown, Connecticut, 1821–1825, account with Silas Rice, February 5, 1822, Middlesex Historical Society, Middletown, Connecticut; Samuel Williams Bill to John Cadwalader, Philadelphia, March 14–23, 1770, Gen. John Cadwalader Papers, Cadwalader Collection, Historical Society of Pennsylvania, Philadelphia (hereafter cited HSP).

4. Philemon Robbins Account Book, Hartford, Connecticut, 1833–1836, account with Ebenezer Allen, May 15, 1834, Connecticut Historical Society, Hartford (hereafter cited CHS); Titus Preston Ledger, Wallingford, Connecticut, 1795–1817, account with Elias Gaylord, March 23, 1805, Sterling Library, Yale University, New Haven, Connecticut (hereafter cited Yale).

5. Garrett, *At Home,* p. 96; Holmes Daybook, account with Mason H. Post, March 6, 1830.

6. Stephen Badlam, Jr., Bill to Maj. Gen. Henry Knox, Boston, September–November 1784, Henry Knox Papers, New England Historic Genealogical Society, Boston, Massachusetts.

7. Oliver Moore Account Book, East Granby, Connecticut, 1808–1821, account with Erastus Holcomb, May 15, 1820, CHS; William Barker Account Book, Providence, Rhode Island, 1750–1772, account with Jabez Bowen, Jr., 1767, Rhode Island Historical Society, Providence (hereafter cited RIHS).

8. True Currier Account Book, Deerfield, New Hampshire, 1815–1838, account with David Prescott, January 1822, Joseph Downs Collection of Manuscripts and Printed Ephemera, Winterthur Library, Winterthur, Delaware (hereafter cited DCM); David Evans Daybook, Philadelphia, 1774–1782, account with George Bringhurst, 1782, HSP.

9. Skipper Lunt Account Book, Newbury, Massachusetts, 1736–1772, accounts with Joel Bartlet, May 1749, Benjamin Tucker, January 1744, and Isaac Merrill, January 1745, Peabody Essex Museum, Salem, Massachusetts (hereafter cited PE); Moses Parkhurst Account Book, Paxton, Massachusetts, 1814–1861, account with Abigail Bursley, December 30, 1837, Old Sturbridge Village, Sturbridge, Massachusetts (hereafter cited OSV).

10. Elisha Hawley Account Book, Ridgefield, Connecticut, 1781–1805, account with Moses Ingersol, August 14, 1794, CHS; Luke Houghton Ledger A, Barre, Massachusetts, 1816–1827, accounts with Abigail Wheeler, July 14, 1824, and Dr. Anson Bates, September 15, 1820, Barre Historical Society, Barre, Massachusetts (hereafter cited Barre); Miles Benjamin Daybook and Ledger, Cooperstown, New York, 1821–1829, account with H. Luce and Company, June 13, 1825, New York State Historical Association, Cooperstown (hereafter cited NYSHA).

11. Jacob Bachman Account Book and Daybook, Lancaster County, Pennsylvania, 1816–1837 and 1822–1861, and Friedrich Bastian Account Book, Bethel Township, Dauphin County, Pennsylvania, 1802–1829, DCM; John Ellinger Account Book, Palmyra, Lebanon County, Pennsylvania, 1832–1845, Pennsylvania Farm Museum, Landis Valley; Abraham Overholt Account Book, Plumstead Township, Bucks County, Pennsylvania, 1790–1833, and Peter Ranck Account Book, Jonestown, Lebanon County, Pennsylvania, 1794–1817, in *The Accounts of Two Pennsylvania German Furniture Makers, Sources and Documents of the Pennsylvania Germans, III,* edited and translated by Alan G. Keyser, Larry M. Neff, and Frederick Weiser (Breinigsville, Pa.: The Pennsylvania German Society, 1978).

12. Overholt Account Book, account with Magdelena Gross, April 14, 1827, in Keyser et al., *Accounts,* p. 19; *Lewis Miller, Sketches and Chronicles* (York, Pa.: Historical Society of York County, 1966), p. 72.

13. Overholt Account Book, accounts with Jacob Holdman, August 31, 1792, and Johannes Detweiler, March 17, 1802 (brown paint), and Magdelena Gross, April 14, 1827 (red paint), in Keyser et al., *Accounts,* pp. 7, 12, 19; Bachman Account Book, account with Martin Farry, August 10, 1819, and Daybook, accounts with Jacob Rohrer, April 18, 1823, and Adam Kindig, April 9, 1836.

14. Nylander, *Snug Fireside,* pp. 199–202; Overholt Account Book, account with Christian Gross, March 31, 1804, in Keyser et al., *Accounts,* p. 13.

15. Ellinger Account Book, account with William Clark, November 1834; William Rawson Account Book, Killingly, Connecticut, 1835–1853, account with Mr. Payson, August 23, 1840, OSV; Israel Houghton Account Book, Petersham, Massachusetts, 1811–1847, account with Gardner Stevens, September 9, 1811, DCM.

16. Pairs of buckets are recorded in the following: Daniel and Samuel Proud, Daybook and Ledger, Providence, Rhode Island, 1810–1834, account with Harvey Robinson, January 22, 1819, RIHS; Ebenezer Smith, Jr., Bill to Robert Rantoul, Beverly, Massachusetts, October 1796–June 1797, Papers of Robert Rantoul, Beverly Historical Society, Beverly, Massachusetts. Pail bail in Barnes Account Book, account with Sage and Button, December 23, 1821; bucket bottoms in John E. Mehargue Ledger, probably Halifax, Pennsylvania, 1825–1860, credit account with John Barry, May 24, 1844, DCM. Joseph Griswold Account Book, Buckland, Massachusetts, 1816–1844, account with Josiah Spaulding, April 1818, and Daybook, 1816–1843, accounts with Josiah Spaulding and Asa Nichols, March 25, 1818, Private collection (microfilm, DCM); Allen Holcomb Account Book, New Lisbon, New York, 1809–1828,

accounts with Jacob Tull, March 24, 1824, and Aaron Wing, July 1, 1822, Metropolitan Museum of Art, New York.

17. Wash trough in Bachman Daybook, accounts with Christian Bachman, April 8, 1824, and Jacob Brackbill, April 23, 1825; cedar tub in Barker Account Book, 1750–1772, account with William Proud, July 17, 1763. F. Andrew Michaux, Jr., *The North American Sylva*, 3 vols. (Philadelphia: J. Dobson, 1842), 3: 186.

18. David Evans Daybook, Philadelphia, 1784–1806, account with Charles Shoemaker, April 9, 1791, HSP; Unidentified Woodworker's Daybook, York, Maine, ca. 1761–1781, account with Capt. Joseph Havies, May 2, 1773, PE (moved from Boston, ca. 1761; see note 78).

19. Nylander, *Snug Fireside*, pp. 130–40; Samuel Douglas Account Book, near Canton, Connecticut, 1810–1858, account with Isaac Williams, May 3, 1823, CSL; Overholt Account Book, account with Jacob Lederman, March 4, 1822, in Keyser et al., *Accounts*, p. 18; Job Danforth Ledger, Providence, Rhode Island, 1788–1818, account with Amos Throop, December 12, 1791, RIHS. Wash pounder in David Alling Ledger, Newark, New Jersey, 1803–1853, account with Pruden Alling, November 8, 1832, New Jersey Historical Society, Newark. Silas Ellis Cheney Daybook, Litchfield, Connecticut, 1813–1846, account with Orman Marsh, May 15, 1817, LHS; Daniel and Samuel Proud Ledger, Providence, Rhode Island, 1770–1825, account with Duty Roberts, February 10, 1803, RIHS.

20. Phillip Filer Account Book, near Rome, New York, 1798–1839, account with Mr. Hathaway, June 20, 1800, DCM; Moore Account Book, account with B. Philips, January 5, 1811; George White Letter to Nicholas Low, Ballston Spa, New York, to New York City, November 6, 1803, Nicholas Low Papers, Library of Congress, Washington, D.C. (hereafter cited LC); Nylander, *Snug Fireside*, pp. 130–40.

21. Holcomb Account Book, accounts with Dr. Hailman, October 26, 1824, and Dan Smith, March 30, 1813; Jonathan Gavit Bill to Timothy Orne, Salem, Massachusetts, May–June 1763, Timothy Orne Papers, PE; Joel Mount Ledger, Juliustown, New Jersey, 1829–1865, account with Samuel Ellis, November 19, 1846, HSP.

22. James Francis Account Book, Wethersfield, Connecticut, 1797–1835, account with Thomas Mygate, March 17, 1797, CHS; Nathaniel Kinsman Bill to Josiah Brown, Gloucester, Massachusetts, January 1763–July 1768, Nathaniel Kinsman Papers, PE; Nylander, *Snug Fireside*, p. 139; David Hall Daybook, Chatham, Connecticut, 1785–1812, account with Capt. Seth Overton, December 12, 1793, CHS.

23. Joseph Cotton Bill to Miss Dolly Wendell, Portsmouth, New Hampshire, January–February 1800, Wendell Papers, Baker Library, Harvard University, Cambridge, Massachusetts (hereafter cited BL); Smith and Ghiselin Bill to Humberston Skipwith, Mecklenburg County, Virginia, October 30, 1819, Swem Library, College of William and Mary, Williamsburg, Virginia (hereafter cited SL); Benjamin Daybook and Ledger, account with Richard Cooley, December 21, 1825.

24. Cheney Daybook, 1802–1807, account with Oliver Wolcott, December 3, 1802; Benoni A. Shepherd Bill to Daniel Wadsworth, Hartford, Connecticut, July–August 1829, Daniel Wadsworth Papers, CHS; Silas Ellis Cheney Ledger, Litchfield, Connecticut, 1799–1817, account with Oliver Wolcott, May 9, 1801, LHS; J. E. Townsend Account Book, account with William E. Williams, May 24, 1823; Filer Account Book, account with George Huntington, May 24, 1799.

25. Nylander, *Snug Fireside*, pp. 140–42; Reubin Loomis Account Book, Windsor-Suffield, Connecticut, 1796–1836, account with Almeron Gillot, December 1800, CHS; Paul Jenkins Daybook, Kennebunk, Maine, 1836–1841, account with Capt. George Lord, September 26, 1839, DCM.

26. The Krimmel drawing showing flatirons stored above the hearth is illustrated in Garrett, *At Home*, p. 166; Abner Haven Account Book, Framingham, Massachusetts, 1809–1830, accounts with Capt. John J. Clark, July, September, 1820, DCM.

27. William Wayne Bill to Samuel Wallis, Philadelphia, February 18, 1770, photostat of unknown origin, DCM; Thomas Tufft Bill to Mrs. Mary Norris, Philadelphia, March–October 1783, Harrold E. Gillingham Collection, HSP; Evans Daybook, 1784–1806, account with Benjamin Poltney, March 3, 1787, and Daybook, 1774–1782, account with William Lane, May 23, 1776; Daniel Trotter Bill to Stephen Girard, Philadelphia, January–August 1786, Girard Papers, Girard College, Philadelphia (microfilm, American Philosophical Society, Philadelphia); William Savery Bill to John Cadwalader, Philadelphia, August 1770–March 1771, Gen. John Cadwalader Papers, Cadwalader Collection, HSP.

28. Samuel Cheever Bill to Elias Hasket Derby, Salem, Massachusetts, February 1784–November 1785, Derby Papers, vol. 1, PE; Daniel Ross Account Book, Ipswich, Massachusetts,

1781–1804, account with Robert Farley, April 6, 1793, PE; Isaac Floyd Bill to Benjamin H. Hathorne, Medford, Massachusetts, August 31, 1799, Ward Family Manuscripts, PE.

29. For an illustration of bread making and a bread trough see Nylander, *Snug Fireside,* p. 197. Overholt Account Book, accounts with Magdelena Gross, April 14, 1827, Johannes Detweiler, March 30, 1796, and Henrich Kindig, March 26, 1803, in Keyser et al., *Accounts,* pp. 9, 12, 19; Bastian Account Book, account with John Smith, March 15, 1819; Hiram Taylor Account Book, Chester County, Pennsylvania, 1828–1855, account with David Wilson, March 29, 1836, DCM.

30. Joseph Griswold Ledger, Buckland, Massachusetts, 1804–1836, account with Joshua Welden, April 10, 1804, Private collection (microfilm, DCM), and Daybook, Accounts with Levi White, April 20, 1817, and Josiah Spaulding, May 1, 1822; Nathan Lukens Bill to Nathaniel Richardson, vicinity of Philadelphia, March–June 1814, Richardson Papers, Friends Historical Library, Swarthmore College, Swarthmore, Pennsylvania; John Austin Account Book, Massachusetts and New Hampshire, 1766–1803, account with Daniel Kusel, Methuen, Massachusetts, 1772, DCM; William Mather Account Book, Whately, Massachusetts, 1808–1825, account with Seth Clark, January 7, 1809, Historic Deerfield, Deerfield, Massachusetts.

31. Abraham Rees, *The Cyclopaedia, or Universal Dictionary of Arts, Sciences, and Literature* (Philadelphia: Samuel F. Bradford, 1810–1824), s.v. "bread"; Danforth Ledger, account with Rufus Waterman, January 17, 1807.

32. Barnes Account Book, account with Ephraim Bound, April 24, 1824; D. and S. Proud Ledger, account with Charles Boller, January–July 1779.

33. Bread box in R. Loomis Account Book, account with Jarusha Mather, May 1802; bread chest in Philemon Hinman Account Book, Plymouth, Connecticut, 1804–1817, account with Dudley Roberts, October 18, 1812, CHS. Titus Preston Ledger, Wallingford, Connecticut, 1811–1842, account with Merit Tuttle, October 2, 1821, Yale; Barnes Account Book, account with Samuel Starr, January 15, 1824.

34. Moore Account Book, account with State of Connecticut, February 15, 1813; Holcomb Account Book, account with Cornelius Janey, January 15, 1828.

35. Rees, *Cyclopaedia,* s.v. "gingerbread."

36. Nathan Cleaveland Ledger, Franklin, Massachusetts, 1810–1828, account with Sanford Ware, February 1819, OSV; Ross Account Book, account with Asa Baker, February 1, 1802: Job E. Townsend Ledger, Newport, Rhode Island, 1794–1802, account with William Beebe, February 2, 1796, NHS.

37. A Dutch kitchen is illustrated in Louise Conway Belden, *The Festive Tradition: Table Decoration and Desserts in America, 1650–1900* (New York: W. W. Norton for the Winterthur Museum, 1983), p. 191. Increase Pote Account Book, Portland, Maine, 1824–1830, account with William Capen, July 19, 1825, Maine Historical Society, Portland (hereafter cited MeHS); Ebenezer Porter Bill to Robert Manning, Salem, Massachusetts, December 16, 1824, Papers of Robert Manning, PE.

38. Thomas Tufft Bills to Mrs. Mary Norris, February 10, 1775, and March–October 1783, Norris Family Accounts, Gillingham Collection; Harriet Beecher Stowe, *Oldtown Folks* (Boston: Fields, Osgood, 1869), as quoted in Nylander, *Snug Fireside,* p. 271.

39. Milk pails in William Barker Account Book, Providence, Rhode Island, 1784–1787, account with Jethro Lapham, ca. 1785, RIHS. Alexander Low Account Book, Freehold, New Jersey, 1784–1826, account with Lowes Thomson, May 30, 1806, Monmouth County Historical Association, Freehold, New Jersey (hereafter cited MHA); Elisha Harlow Holmes Ledger, Essex, Connecticut, 1825–1830, account with Samuel Ingham, November 7, 1829, CHS; J. E. Townsend Ledger, account with John Taylor, February 6, 1806; Philip Deland Account Book, West Brookfield, Massachusetts, 1812–1846, account with Cheeny Dewing, May 4, 1844, OSV.

40. Nylander, *Snug Fireside,* pp. 199–202; Deland Account Book, account with Benjamin Babbit, August 25, 1835; Samuel Davison Ledger, Plainfield, Massachusetts, 1795–1824, account with Steven Worner, August 1801, Pocumtuck Valley Memorial Association, Deerfield, Massachusetts.

41. Josiah P. Wilder Daybook and Ledger, New Ipswich, New Hampshire, 1837–1861, accounts with Aaron Davis, June 22, 1837, and Cooper I. Blood, May 6, 1841, Private collection (typescript, Visual Resources Library, Winterthur; hereafter cited VRL); Gaius Perkins Ledger, Woodstock, Vermont, 1804–1824, credit account with Artemas Lawrence, February 1818, Vermont Historical Society, Montpelier (hereafter cited VHS); Ellinger Account Book, account with John Bixler, October 5, 1833; Danforth Ledger, account with Andrew Dexter,

December 3, 1794; Overholt Account Book, account with Henrich Kindig, January 19, 1804, in Keyser et al., *Accounts,* p. 13.

42. Tub and press in Chapman Lee Ledger, Charlton, Massachusetts, 1799–1850, accounts with David Crage, May 1816, and Thomas Foskett, March 6, 1810, OSV; a press in Joseph Fairchild Account Book, Watertown, Connecticut, 1754–1806 and later, account with David Johnson, June 27, 1757, CHS. Samuel Hall Ledger, Middletown, Connecticut, 1754–1795, account with David Sage, June 21, 1774, CHS; John Paine Account Book, Southold, New York, 1761–1815, account with Ezra L'Hommedieu, June 1, 1786, Institute for Colonial Studies, State University of New York, Stony Brook, New York.

43. Robert Whitelaw Ledger, Ryegate, Vermont, 1804–1831, accounts with James Whitelaw, Alexander Miller, and William Burroughs, 1807–1810, VHS.

44. Ranck Account Book, account with Christopher Rickert, May 23, 1799, in Keyser et al., *Accounts,* p. 87; Samuel Ashton Account Book, Philadelphia, 1794–1803, credit account with George Sower, March 11, 1803, DCM.

45. Sugar boxes in William Barker Account Book, Providence, Rhode Island, 1787–1798, estate account, July 1, 1798, RIHS; bowls in Oliver Avery Account Book, North Stonington, Connecticut, 1789–1813, account with Nathaniel Hewitt, June 19, 1794, DCM. Barker Account Book, 1750–1772, account with Deborah Rogers, May 4, 1772; D. and S. Proud Ledger, account with Gershom Jones, August 16, 1790; Job E. Townsend Account Book and Ledger, Newport, Rhode Island, 1778–1794, account with Sarah Lake, May 21, 1779, NHS; Filer Account Book, account with Matthew Brown, January 10, 1802; H. Taylor Account Book, account with Gen. Joshua Evans, November 14, 1835.

46. Samuel Wayne Bill to Samuel Coates, Philadelphia, June 12, 1788, Reynell and Coates Collection, BL; Barker Account Book, 1787–1798, estate account, July 1, 1798; Deland Account Book, accounts with Ebenezer and George Merriam, March 24, 1834, and Jacob Dupee, June 7, 1841; Benjamin Baker Account Book, Newport, Rhode Island, 1760–1792, account with Dr. Knowles, March 13, 1788, NHS.

47. Chopping trough in Jenkins Daybook, account with Mark Prime, November 26, 1836; chopping tray in Alexander H. Gilbert Account Book, Chester, Connecticut, 1831–1852, account with George H. Abernethy, March 8, 1839, CHS. Evans Daybook, 1774–1782, account with George Bringhurst, 1782; Williams Bill to Cadwalader, March 14–23, 1770.

48. Holmes Daybook, accounts with Mrs. Hill, October 9, 1826, William Williams, November 9, 1826, and Calvin Williams, September 17, 1829.

49. Belden, *Festive Tradition,* pp. 237–39; Solomon Fussell Account Book, Philadelphia, 1738–1748, accounts with John Naylor, August 21, 1742, and William Whitebread, June 2, 1747, Stephen Collins Papers, LC. "Sqush squesers" in Danforth Ledger, accounts with Gershom Jones, August 11, 1789, Richard Jackson, July 7, 1795, and Jabez Bowen, August 4, 1806; turning mentioned in D. and S. Proud Ledger, account with Jonathan W. Coy, July 23, 1799. Ross Account Book, account with Dr. John Manning, May 1783.

50. Kitchen of York Hotel illustrated in *Lewis Miller,* p. 24.

51. Ross Account Book, account with John Heard, December 7, 1793; Danforth Ledger, account with Amos Throop, February 13, 1798; Floyd Bill to Hathorne, August 31, 1799.

52. D. and S. Proud Ledger, account with Jonathan W. Coy, December 11, 1798; Barnes Account Book, account with William R. Swarthel, February 4, 1824.

53. D. and S. Proud ledger, account with Rufus Warren Kemball, December 9, 1820 (?); Thomas Boynton Ledger, Windsor, Vermont, 1810–1817, account with Stephen Conant, December 11, 1815, Dartmouth College, Hanover, New Hampshire (hereafter cited DC); Lukens Bill to Richardson, March–June 1814.

54. Ellinger Account Book, account with Daniel Ulrich, October 16, 1835; Ritz cellar illustrated in *Lewis Miller,* p. 50.

55. Parkhurst Account Book, accounts with Jonathan Frost, December 13, 1819, and August 31, 1820; Isaac Ashton Account Book, Philadelphia, 1777–1794, account with C. Davis, February 20, 1793, DCM.

56. Advertisement of William Morgan, *Pennsylvania Gazette* (Philadelphia), November 9–16, 1732; Whitelaw Ledger, account with Robert Scott, March 1811; Deland Account Book, account with Jacob Dupee, December 30, 1840; George Cooper Bill to John Sanders, probably Schenectady, New York, May 20, 1820, Sanders Papers, New-York Historical Society, New York (hereafter cited NYHS); Holcomb Account Book, account with Joshua Weaver, July 1821.

57. Pot covers in Ross Account Book, account with Asa Baker, January 5, 1791. Haven Account Book, account with Abner Mellen, October 10, 1818; Hodghton and Company Bill

to Samuel Larned, Lima, Peru, September 27, 1832, A. C. and R. W. Greene Collection, RIHS; Thomas J. Moyers and Fleming K. Rich Account Book, Wythe Court House, Virginia, 1834–1840, account with John Mayre, May 6, 1834, DCM.

58. Tea board in Baker Account Book, account with William Potter, March 7, 1792; tea waiters in Henry Potter Account Book, Newport, Rhode Island, 1771–1802, credit accounts with Edmund Townsend, March 27 and July 23, 1773, NHS. Jonathan Kettell Account Book, Newburyport, Massachusetts, 1781–1794, account with Capt. William Noyes, September 1789, PE; advertisement of John Tremain, *New-York Gazette Revived in the Weekly Post-Boy* (New York), August 26, 1751, as quoted in *The Arts and Crafts in New York, 1726–1776*, compiled by Rita S. Gottesman (1938; reprint, New York: Da Capa Press, 1970), pp. 118–19.

59. Robert Borland Bill to Richard Blow, Portsmouth, Virginia, April 29, 1791, Richard Blow Papers, SL; Henry Mann Bill to Maj. Thomas Jones, Richmond, Virginia, September 1789–January 1790, Papers of the Jones Family of Northumberland County, Virginia, LC; Joshua Delaplaine Account Book, New York, 1720s–1770s, account with Dr. Brownjohn, September (?) 12, 1741, NYHS; Job Townsend, Jr., Ledger, Newport, Rhode Island, 1750–1778, account with Job Howland, May 14, 1769, NHS; Ephraim Haines Bill to Stephen Girard, Philadelphia, October 1806–November 1807, Girard Papers.

60. Low Account Book, account with John Craig, Jr., August 24, 1812; Hawley Account Book, account with John Watrons, October 16, 1793; Holcomb Account Book, account with Eliakim How, December 23, 1815; Lemuel Tobey Daybook, Dartmouth, Massachusetts, 1786–1792, account with Simpson Hart, October 20, 1791, OSV.

61. Joseph Symonds Account Book, Salem, Massachusetts, 1738–1766, account with Benjamin Osgood, November 12, 1753, PE. Batch of handles in Ross Account Book, account with Aaron Smith, January 27, 1792; ladles and dippers in Barker Account Books, 1750–1772 and 1787–1798, accounts with Jabez Bowen, Jr., September 9, 1768, and Barker estate, July 1, 1798; dipper repair in Barnes Account Book, account with Josiah Williams, May 17, 1824. Deland Account Book, account with E. and L. Merriam, June 23, 1840; William and John Richmond Bill to Almy and Brown, Providence, Rhode Island, July 3, 1799, Almy and Brown Papers, RIHS; Nathaniel Knowlton Account Book, Eliot, Maine, 1812–1859, account with John Raitt, 3d, March 28, 1827, MeHS.

62. George Short Account Book, Newburyport, Massachusetts, ca. 1807–1821, account with Thomas H. Balch, May 23, 1815, PE.

63. J. E. Townsend Account Book, account with Dr. Hazard, January 27, 1819.

64. Ellinger Account Book, accounts with Henry Garman, August 11, 1833, and William Yarkey, January 2, 1836; Overholt Account Book, account with Henrich Kindig, March 26, 1803, in Keyser et al., *Accounts,* p. 12; Hyde de Neuville sketch illustrated in Jadviga M. da Costa Nunes, *Baroness Hyde de Neuville: Sketches of America, 1807–1822* (New Brunswick, N.J.: Rutgers University, 1984), p. 20; Fussell Account Book, accounts with Robert Moore Taylor, January 2, 1741, Joseph Marshall, January 15, 1742, and (for hog bristles) Michael Hilton, April 23, 1741.

65. L. Houghton Ledger A, account with John Bacon, June 25, 1821; James Gere Ledger, Groton, Connecticut, 1809–1829, account with Richard Stroud, May 1, 1810, CSL; Nylander, *Snug Fireside,* p. 118; John Proud Bills to Albert C. Greene, East Greenwich, Rhode Island, 1820, 1827, Greene Collection.

66. Barnes Account Book, account with Josiah Williams and Company, May 2, 1822; Stephen Van Schanck Bill to Peter Gansevoort, Albany, New York, August 1834, Papers of Peter Gansevoort, Gansevoort-Lansing Collection, New York Public Library, New York (hereafter cited NYPL); Isaac Flagg Bill to Robert Rantoul, Beverly, Massachusetts, 1823, Papers of Robert Rantoul; William Barker Bill to Almy and Brown, Providence, Rhode Island, February 1793–September 1795, Almy and Brown Papers, RIHS.

67. Robert Mullen Bill to Stephen Collins, Philadelphia, July 21, 1789, Stephen Collins Papers, LC; Barnes Account Book, account with Samuel Eells, April 16, 1822.

68. Deland Account Book, accounts with Jacob Dupee, April 13, 1842, and November 9, 1843; Alling Ledger, account with Peter Jacobus, July 20, 1835; George Landon Account Book, Erie, Pennsylvania, 1813–1832, account with John Morris, January 1, 1825, DCM; Whitelaw Ledger, account with Andrew Warden, September 16, 1807; Krimmel sketch illustrated in Garrett, *At Home,* p. 104.

69. Jacob Hinsdale Ledger, Harwinton, Connecticut, 1723–1774, account with Nathaniel Smith, December 1727, Yale; Robert Crage Ledger, Leicester, Massachusetts, 1757–1781, account with John Green, February 9, 1757, OSV.

70. Advertisement of Wright and McAllister, *New-York Packet and the American Advertiser* (New York), June 13, 1776, as quoted in Gottesman, *Arts and Crafts,* p. 256; advertisement of Francis Trumble, *Pennsylvania Gazette,* December 27, 1775.

71. Records of the 1820 United States Census of Manufactures, including James W. Moore, Rutherford County, Tennessee, and Uzziel Church, Brownsville, Union County, Indiana, National Archives, Washington, D.C. (microfilm, DCM).

72. Jonathan Dart Account Book, New London, Connecticut, 1793–1800, account with Ephraim Browning, March 11, 1796, and list of sales, March 1797, CHS; Crage Ledger, credit accounts with Samuel Richardson, May 4, 1768, and Thomas Green, 1777; Daniel Rea, Jr., Daybook, Boston, 1789–1793, account with Simon Hall, May 30, 1791, BL (microfilm, DCM); Landon Account Book, account with Ebenezer Graham, January 16, 1818; Amos Purinton (1777–1843), Weare, New Hampshire, as listed in Charles S. Parsons, "New Hampshire Notes" (typescript, VRL).

73. Holmes Daybook, account with Henry Sandford, December 17, 1827; Franklin letter, April 6, 1766, as quoted in Francis Phipps, *The Collector's Complete Dictionary of American Antiques* (Garden City, N.Y.: Doubleday, 1974), p. 549; Haven Account Book, account with William Clark, April 1813; Whitelaw Ledger, account with Samuel Clough, Jr., September 3, 1807.

74. Jeduthern Avery Account Book, Bolton-Coventry, Connecticut, 1811–1855, account with Joseph Talcott, October 1828, CHS; Robbins Account Book, accounts with Henry Hudson, December 28, 1835, and unidentified customer, November 3, 1834; Cheney Daybook, 1802–1807, accounts with Sally Pierce, June 11 and 16, 1807; Silas Ellis Cheney Daybook, Litchfield, Connecticut, 1807–1813, account with Mrs. Adams, February 13, 1808, LHS; Daniel Trotter Bill of Accounts with Benjamin Thaw, Philadelphia, 1785–1798, DCM; Thomas Affleck Bill to John Cadwalader, Philadelphia, January–June 1775, Gen. John Cadwalader Papers, Cadwalader Collection.

75. Unidentified Cabinetmaker's Account Book, vicinity of Fredericksburg, Virginia, 1767–1777, account with Capt. Lawrence Taliaferro, October 10, 1775, DCM; D. and S. Proud Ledger, account with Elisha Peck, August 26, 1789; Hinsdale Ledger, account with unidentified customer (page torn), February 1728; John Wheeler Geer Account Book, Preston, Connecticut, 1774–1818, account with Charles Phelps, June 13, 1777, CHS.

76. Cleaveland Ledger, account with Daniel Thurston, 1828; Christopher Clark, "The Diary of an Apprentice Cabinetmaker: Edward Jenner Carpenter's 'Journal,' 1844–45," in *Proceedings of the American Antiquarian Society,* vol. 98, pt. 2 (Worcester, Mass.: by the society, 1989), pp. 358–60.

77. Bachman Daybook, accounts with Isaac McCalester, September 13, 1830, Francis Herr, September 19, 1832, and Benjamin Brackbill, August 9, 1837; Danforth Ledger, accounts with Thomas Jackson, October 20, 1791, and Isaac Pearce, November 23, 1806.

78. Ezekiel Smith Account Book, Taunton, Massachusetts, 1773–1831, account with Jonathan Bliss, April 24, 1778, DCM; Boynton Ledger, 1810–1817, account with William Leverett, October 22, 1816; Unidentified Woodworker's Daybook, Boston, 1756–1761, account with John Avery, June 13, 1758, PE (moved to York, Maine, ca. 1761; see note 18).

79. Nylander, *Snug Fireside,* pp. 225–28; *Extracts from the Diary of Jacob Hiltzheimer, of Philadelphia, 1765–1798,* edited by Jacob Cox Parsons (Philadelphia: William F. Fell, 1893), pp. 10, 83.

80. Knowlton Account Book, account with Benjamin Lamson, August 30, 1814; O. Avery Account Book, accounts with Samuel Chapman, April 1815, and Cyrus Williams, July 16, 1815; Bastian Account Book, accounts with Martin Peck, April 5 and May 1, 1823; J. Gere Ledger, accounts with Henry F. Lamb, January 20 and April 3, 1815; Boynton Ledger, 1810–1817, account with William Ayers, May 21, 1816.

81. Nylander, *Snug Fireside,* pp. 177–78; Ebenezer Tracy, Sr., Inventory and Estate Division, Lisbon Township, New London County, Connecticut, 1803–1805, Genealogical Section, CSL.

82. Thomas Sheraton, *The Cabinet Dictionary,* 2 vols. (1803; reprint, New York: Praeger, 1970), 1: 42–44.

83. Christopher Gilbert, *An Exhibition of Common Furniture* (Leeds, England: Temple Newsam, 1982), fig. 7; Rawson Account Book, account with Mr. Carder, October 27, 1838; James Linacre Bill to Mr. Elmendorf, Albany, New York, June 12, 1794, Sanders Papers; Ranck Account Book, account with George Merk, January 21, 1811, in Keyser et al., *Accounts,* p. 171; R. Loomis Account Book, account with Dr. G. Wilks Hanchet, February 1806. A frog-back chair is illustrated in Nancy Goyne Evans, "Frog Backs and Turkey Legs: The Nomenclature of Vernacular Seating Furniture, 1740–1850," in *American Furniture,* edited by Luke

Beckerdite (Hanover, N.H.: University Press of New England for the Chipstone Foundation, 1996), p. 49, fig. 33.

84. Jacob Super Bill to Nathan Trotter, Philadelphia, December 27, 1821, Trotter Family Papers, BL; Samuel Williams Bill to John Cadwalader, Philadelphia, July 18, 1771, Cadwalader Collection; W. Wayne Bill to Wallis, February 18, 1770; Holmes Daybook, account with Richard W. Hart, October 22, 1828; Benjamin Daybook and Ledger, account with Daniel Huson, May 14, 1823.

85. Ross Account Book, account with John Lummas, April 1798; William G. Jones Bill to Sarah Ann Baily, Wilmington, Delaware, June 3, 1822, Latimer Papers, DCM; James Gere Ledger, Groton, Connecticut, 1809–1839, account with James Fanning, Jr., April 1826, CSL; Cheney Ledger, 1799–1817, account with Caleb Bacon, January 10, 1800; Solomon Cole Account Book, Glastonbury, Connecticut, 1794–1809, account with John Caswell, November 29, 1805, CHS.

86. Turn-up bedsteads are illustrated in Barry A. Greenlaw, *New England Furniture at Williamsburg* (Williamsburg, Va.: Colonial Williamsburg Foundation, 1974), cats. 19–21.

87. Holmes Daybook, account with Ansel Pratt, September 2, 1825; Barnes Account Book, account with Elisha Birdsey, March 21, 1822; Moore Account Book, accounts with Calvin Barber, January 28, 1818, and Phineas Newton, Jr., February 27, 1815.

88. Robbins Account Book, account with William G. Comstock, July 21, 1834; Harris Beckwith Ledger, Northampton, Massachusetts, 1803–1807, account with Asahel Pomeroy, February 6, 1805 (?), Forbes Library, Northampton, Massachusetts; Abner Taylor Account Book, Lee, Massachusetts, 1806–1832, account with Asahel Foot, July 29, 1815, DCM; J. E. Townsend Ledger, account with Gilbert Chase, January 25, 1800; Danforth Ledger, account with Stephen Abbott, 1803.

89. R. Loomis Account Book, account with Amos Curtis, November 1821; Charles C. Robinson Daybook, Philadelphia, 1809–1825, account with David Sheldrake, January 28, 1817, HSP; A. Taylor Account Book, account with Elisha Foot, ca. 1811.

90. Garrett, *At Home*, pp. 52, 121–23; Nylander, *Snug Fireside*, pp. 31, 93; Percy Macquoid and Ralph Edwards, *The Dictionary of English Furniture*, 3 vols. (1924–1927; reprint 2d ed., Woodbridge, England: Baron Publishing for Barra Books, 1983), 1: 69.

91. Robbins Account Book, account with Taylor and Miller, January 8, 1834; Preston Ledger, 1795–1817, account with Jared Allen, August 20, 1804; H. Taylor Account Book, account with John Tucker, October 11, 1835; Douglas Account Book, account with Isaac Barnes, October 22, 1813; Evans Daybook, 1774–1782, account with Clement Biddle, May 27, 1776; William Webb Bill to Joseph G. Waters, Salem, Massachusetts, February 28, 1831, Waters Family Papers, PE.

92. John Hockaday Bill to St. George Tucker, Williamsburg, Virginia, April 13, 1811, Tucker-Coleman Collection, SL; Rea Daybook, 1789–1793, account with Stephen Codman, July 25, 1793, and Daniel Rea, Jr., Daybook, Boston, 1794–1797, account with John Coffin Jones, October 12, 1794, BL (microfilm, DCM); Fenwick Lyell Account Book, Middletown, New Jersey, 1800–1813, account with John Hilliker, December 6, 1807, MHA; Cheney Daybook, 1802–1807, account with Moses Seymour, Jr., November 28, 1804; A. Taylor Account Book, account with Oliver Ives, September 14, 1816.

93. Crage Ledger, account with Nathaniel Tolman, May 9, 1759; Peter Emerson Daybook, Reading, Massachusetts, 1749–1759, account with Joseph Smith, March 2, 1756, Boston Public Library, Boston, Massachusetts; S. Hall Ledger, account with Joseph Blake, October 31, 1769; Low Account Book, account with William Bennett, December 11, 1816; Perez Austin Account Book, Canterbury, Connecticut, 1811–1832, account with Joseph Safford, March 6, 1832, CHS; Isaiah Tiffany Account Book, Norwich, Connecticut, 1746–1767, account with Urian Hosmer, January–May 1755, CHS.

94. Crage Ledger, account with Asa Baldwin, January 1759.

95. Fussell Account Book, accounts with John Knowles, Jr., May 25, 1744, Jacob Durbrow, November 16, 1738, Jeremiah Elfreth, February 12, 1742, John Naylor, May 8, 1744, and Thomas Robinson, August 10, 1742.

96. Fussell Account Book, accounts with Robert Wood, February 6, 1740, and Benjamin Franklin, January 24, 1744; Samuel Durand Daybook, Milford, Connecticut, 1806–1838, account with Davis Smith, Jr., January 24, 1815, Milford Historical Society, Milford, Connecticut (hereafter cited MiHS).

97. Robbins Account Book, account with Dr. Kissum, March 29, 1834.

98. Moore Account Book, account with Erastus Holcomb, May 26, 1820; Barnes Account

Book, account with William Scranton, April 16, 1822; Tiffany Account Book, account with Nathaniel Backus, Jr., August 2, 1758.

99. Jenkins Daybook, account with George Perkins, December 15, 1837; Griswold Account Book, account with Horace Wells, May 25, 1817; Alling Ledger, account with S. S. Morris, January 25, 1839; Wilder Daybook and Ledger, account with Capt. Luke Cram, January 7, 1851; Cheney Daybook, 1802–1807, account with Moses Seymour, Jr., July 24, 1805; Crage Ledger, account with Jonathan Pudney, March 14, 1758; S. Hall Ledger, account with Joseph Willcocks, November 23, 1789.

100. Holmes Ledger, accounts with Alford Worthington, October 15, 1826, and Stephen W. Starkey, December 16, 1826; S. Hall Ledger, account with Giles Goodrich, February 27, 1781; Timothy Loomis Account Book, Windsor, Connecticut, 1768–1804, account with Simeon Loomis, January 1771, CHS; A. Taylor Account Book, account with Robert M. Ashley, April 1817; Cole Account Book, account with Dr. Harris Reed, August 2, 1804.

101. Mahogany cradle in Robbins Account Book, account with E. B. Stedman, June 13, 1835; cedar cradle in Elijah and Jacob Sanderson Bill to Nathan Reed, Salem, Massachusetts, May 2, 1798, Papers of Nathan Reed, PE. Kettell Account Book, account with Capt. Richard S. Noyes, July 1790; Evans Daybook, 1774–1782, account with Benjamin Saixes, December 6, 1781. Walnut cradles in Overholt Account Book, account with Daniel Kraut, January 20, 1801, in Keyser et al., *Accounts,* p.12, and George Claypoole Bill to Samuel Meredith, Philadelphia, April–October 1773, Clymer-Meredith-Read Papers, NYPL; cherrywood cradles in Danforth Ledger, account with Holcroyd and Tillinghast, May 18, 1804, and Samuel Silliman Account Book, New York state and Connecticut, 1804–1807, account with shop (Duanesburg, New York), December 1804, NYSHA, and David Evans Daybook, Philadelphia, 1796–1812, account with Joseph Shea, March 27, 1798, HSP.

102. Stained whitewood cradle in Holmes Daybook, account with Russell H. Post, September 10, 1827; painted pine cradle in Ross Account Book, account with John Fitz, November 3, 1792; red cradle and blue cradle in Cole Account Book, accounts with Howell Holmes, June 9, 1804, and Roger Holister, August 8, 1800; other blue cradles in Jacob Merrill, Jr., Ledger, Plymouth, New Hampshire, 1784–1812, account with Samuel Derbon, October 18, 1803, New Hampshire Historical Society, Concord, New Hampshire, as transcribed in Parsons, "New Hampshire Notes," and Amos Denison Allen Memorandum Book, Windham, Connecticut, 1796–1803, account with Col. Swift, November 18, 1799, CHS. William Gray Ledger, Salem, Massachusetts, 1774–1814, account with John Chipman, June 8, 1794, PE; Daniel Rea, Jr., Daybook, Boston, 1778–1789, account with Thomas Wells, March 18, 1785, and Ledger, Boston, 1764–1799, account with Thomas Clement, May 31, 1771, and Ledger, Boston, 1789–1797, account with Campbell and Ward, December 1, 1792, BL (microfilm, DCM); Low Account Book, account with John Lloyd, April 7, 1797; Lemuel Tobey Daybook, Dartmouth, Massachusetts, 1773–1777, account with Silas Swift, October 22, 1774, OSV.

103. Garrett, *At Home,* p. 122; Nylander, *Snug Fireside,* p. 31.

104. Holmes Daybook, accounts with Capt. Champlin, July 25, 1825, and Russell Doane, April 6, 1829 (double crib); Danforth Ledger, account with Samuel Ames, June 15, 1807; Rea Daybook, 1789–1793, accounts with Dr. Bulfinch, April 28, 1790, and Cabot Clay, August 16, 1791; Barnes Account Book, account with William B. Ward, August 12, 1823; Robbins Account Book, account with Charles Goodwin, April 4, 1835.

105. A. Taylor Account Book, account with Dr. Hubbard Bartlett, October 9, 1812; Randle Holme, *Academie or Store-House of Armory & Blazon* (1688), as quoted in *Oxford English Dictionary,* s.v. "cricket."

106. Wooden-top stool in Currier Account Book, account with Moses Prescott, January 1822; open-frame stool in Holmes Daybook, account with Miss Hotchkiss, May 1, 1826; carpet-covered stools in Holmes Daybook, account with Sidney Morgan, September 1, 1825, and Robbins Account Book, account with Wildman and Hamilton, July 24, 1834; oval-top stool in Lyell Account Book, account with John J. Post, February 27, 1808; painted stools in Daniel Rea, Jr., Daybook, Boston, 1789–1802, account with Arnold Wells, October 12, 1801, BL (microfilm, DCM), and Filer Account Book, account with Benjamin Wright, October 10, 1809; varnished stool in Holmes Ledger, account with Charles Conklin, March 1826; maple or mahogany stools in Boynton Ledger, 1810–1817, account with William Leverett, April 28, 1817, and Holmes Daybook, account with Charles E. Fisk, February 7, 1828.

107. Turned legs in Pote Account Book, account with Nathaniel Elsworth, December 8, 1824, and Currier Account Book, account with Peter Jenness, November 1834. Robbins Account Book, account with Charles Brainard, June 17, 1835.

108. John Gaines II Account Book, Ipswich, Massachusetts, 1712–1749, account with Phillip Fowler, July 29, 1718, DCM; J. E. Townsend Account Book, account with Mrs. Kindel, January 26, 1816. Crickets in use by a child and a mother with baby are illustrated in Nylander, *Snug Fireside,* p. 175; other crickets in use are illustrated in Garrett, *At Home,* pp. 63, 72.

109. John G. Hopkins Bill to Albert C. Greene, Providence, Rhode Island, September 1834–December 1835, Greene Collection; Lyell Account Book, account with John J. Post, November 16, 1808; George Merrifield Account Book, Albany, New York, 1831–1847, account with Mr. Kelso, March 11, 1837, DCM; H. Moricet Bill to Arthur Bronson, New York, May–August 1836, Bronson Family Papers, NYPL.

110. Corner cupboard in Mount Ledger, account with Samuel J. Lewis, April 1, 1837. Preston Ledger, 1795–1817, account with Billious Cook, December 9, 1805; Enos Reynolds Daybook, Boxford, Massachusetts, 1793–1840, account with Samuel Heath, September 18, 1810, PE; Whitelaw Ledger, account with James Whitelaw, October 24, 1805.

111. Jonathan C. Loomis Account Book, Whately, Massachusetts, 1808–1828, account with Capt. Lucius Graves, March 29, 1815, DCM; William Savery Bill to John Cadwalader, August 1770–March 1771.

112. William Rowell Account Book, Amesbury, Massachusetts, 1832–1852, account with John T. Stickney, May 16, 1839, OSV; P. Austin Account Book, account with Walter Eaton, February 1831.

113. Unidentified Cabinetmaker's Ledger, probably Salem, Massachusetts, 1824–1840, account with Samuel Chamberlain and Son, February–April 1832, PE; Barnes Account Book, account with Thomas McDonough, September 30, 1822.

114. Mount Ledger, account with Samuel J. Lewis, February 22, 1837; Jenkins Daybook, account with Capt. Ivory Lord, October 9, 1838; William Hook Bill to Benjamin H. Hathorne, Salem, Massachusetts, June 1812, Ward Family Manuscripts; Thomas Boynton Ledger, Windsor, Vermont, 1817–1847, account with Horace Everett, February 13, 1841, DC; Kinsman Bill to Brown, January 1763–July 1768.

115. I. Ashton Account Book, account with Mr. Fernant, January 7, 1792; Danforth Ledger, account with Rufus Waterman, March 15, 1791; Peter Oldershaw Bill to Walter Livingston, New York, December 3, 1791, Robert R. Livingston Papers, NYHS.

116. Preston Ledger, 1811–1842, account with Phineas Stevens, October 3, 1816; Holmes Daybook, accounts with Gamaliel Conklin, March 27, 1829; James Gere Ledger, Groton, Connecticut, 1822–1852, account with Mrs. Nancy Barnes, September 30, 1831, CSL.

117. Holmes Ledger, accounts with Jabez Southmayd (?), January 28, 1826 (pine), and Russell Doane, October 24, 1828 (butternut); Overholt Account Book, accounts with Carl Zelner, March 17, 1791 (yellow poplar), and Michael Walder, May 25, 1792 (walnut), in Keyser et al., *Accounts,* pp. 4, 6.

118. Holmes Ledger, account with Russell Doane, May 14, 1830; Barnes Account Book, account with Samuel Kirby, April 3, 1822; Moore Account Book, accounts with Silvy Clark, March 10, 1809, and Veranus St (?) , March 27, 1813.

119. Prussian blue in Rea Daybook, 1794–1797, account with Daniel Rea Tert[iarie]s (?), September 15, 1794. James Chase Account Book, Gilmanton, New Hampshire, 1807–1812, account with Ezekiel Rowe, February 13, 1809, as transcribed in Parsons, "New Hampshire Notes"; Allen Memorandum Book, account with Daniel Ladd, March 13, 1802; Overholt Account Book, accounts with Martin Oberholtzer, March 31, 1791, and Maria Sturd, March 28, 1797, in Keyser et al., *Accounts,* pp. 4, 10.

120. Preston Ledger, 1811–1842, account with Phineas Stevens, October 3, 1816.

121. Trumble advertisement in *Pennsylvania Gazette.*

122. Allen Memorandum Book, accounts with Gideon Hoxey, July 5, 1799, and Mr. Selden, November 15, 1799; Francis Account Book, account with Capt. Francis Bulkley, November 15, 1797.

123. Hawley Account Book, account with Thomas Rockwell, August 16, 1789; Short Account Book, accounts with Richard Drown, November 11, 1814, and Ebenezer Stedman, December 30, 1815, January 6 and 13, 1816.

124. Webster, *Dictionary* (1828), s.v. "trunk," as quoted in Margaret B. Schiffer, *Chester County, Pennsylvania, Inventories, 1684–1850* (Atglen, Pa.: Schiffer Publishing, 1974), p. 129; William Rhinelander Estate Inventory, New York, November 9, 1785, NYPL; Richard Booker Bill to St. George Tucker, Williamsburg, Virginia, 1777, Tucker-Coleman Collection; Hales Richardson Bill to Richard Blow, Norfolk, Virginia, October 25, 1794, Richard Blow Papers; Robbins Account Book, account with Thomas Day, July 3, 1835.

125. R. Loomis Account Book, account with Thaddeus Lyman, August 1816; Short Account Book, account with Charles Short, March 1, 1816; Daniel Davis, Mary Chamberlain, and William Melchoir Estate Inventories, 1754, 1752, and 1755, as quoted in Schiffer, *Chester County Inventories,* p. 118; Allen Memorandum Book, account with Charles Clark, June 22, 1802.

126. Charles Norris Cash Book, Philadelphia, 1760–1761, Norris Family Accounts, HSP; Baker Account Book, account with Dr. Knowles, March 13, 1788; Joseph Reynolds Estate Inventory, 1735, as quoted in Schiffer, *Chester County Inventories,* p. 121; William Denny Bill to Stewart Rowan, Carlisle, Pennsylvania, June 29, 1771, DCM; R. Loomis Account Book, account with Dr. G. Wilks Hanchet, 1808; Holmes Ledger, account with Jonah E. Latimer, May 1828.

127. Symonds Account Book, accounts with H. Higginson, February 3, 1750, and Mr. Hallack (?), February 18, 1756.

128. E. G. and A. Partridge Bill to Henry W. Miller, Worcester, Massachusetts, July–December 1829, DCM; Francis Account Book, account with Thomas Griswold, January 21, 1833; Barnes Account Book, account with Giles S. Cotton, August 6, 1821; Short Account Book, accounts with Frederick Strong, January 25, 1816, and Richard Drown, November 11, 1814; Schiffer, *Chester County Inventories,* p. 102; John Sager Daybook, Bordentown, New Jersey, 1805–1817, account with Samuel Clayton (?), October 10, 1805, HSP.

129. Nylander, *Snug Fireside,* pp. 106–7, 109–11; Filer Account Book, account with George Huntington, March 20, 1799.

130. P. Austin Account Book, account with Joseph Simms, March 26, 1820. Hat case in Ross Account Book, account with Richard Lakeman, November 24, 1788. Cheney Ledger, 1799–1817, account with Tapping Reeve, February 1, 1800; Rea Daybook, 1794–1797, account with Charles Smith, April 1, 1794; Overholt Account Book, account with Martin Oberholtzer, April 18, 1791, in Keyser et al., *Accounts,* p. 4.

131. Sewing box in William Crout Bill to Charles Wistar, probably Philadelphia, June 2, ca. 1830s, Charles Wister Papers, DCM; work box in Boynton Ledger, 1810–1817, account with William Leverett, October 6, 1815, and repairs in account with Thomas Leverett and Son, March 20, 1817; other repairs in Boynton Ledger, 1817–1847, account with Jonathan H. Hubbard, June 22, 1837; fancy box in Thomas Safford Ledger, Canterbury, Connecticut, 1807–1835, account with James Burnap, September 27, 1810, CSL. Robbins Account Book, account with Joel Howes, February 1, 1834; Clark, "Diary of Edward Jenner Carpenter," pp. 344, 348; Thomas Tufft Bill to Mrs. Mary Norris, Philadelphia, May 10, 1775, Norris Family Accounts, Gillingham Collection; Luke Houghton Ledger B, Barre, Massachusetts, 1824–1851, account with Charles Lee, June 5, 1831, Barre.

132. Holmes Ledger, account with Jonah E. Latimer, December 12, 1828; Howard Smith Account Book, New Haven, Connecticut, 1844–1849, account with Lewis A. Northrup, February 24, 1846, CHS; Potter Account Book, credit account with Edmund Townsend, April 18, 1775; J. W. Geer Account Book, account with George Palmer, January 12, 1779.

133. Sand boxes in Deland Account Book, account with Washington Walker, September 6, 1826, and O. Avery Account Book, account with Elias Hewitt, September 1816.

134. *Gentleman's Progress: The Itinerarium of Alexander Hamilton, 1744,* edited by Carl Bridenbaugh (Chapel Hill, N.C.: University of North Carolina Press, 1948), p. xvii; *The New Democracy in America: Travels of Francisco de Miranda in the United States, 1783–84,* translated by Judson P. Wood, edited by John S. Ezell (Norman, Okla.: University of Oklahoma Press, 1963), p. 6; Frances M. Trollope, *Domestic Manners of the Americans,* 2 vols. (London: Whittaker, Treacher, 1832), 1: 24; James Nixon, *Personal Narratives of a Tour through a Part of the United States and Canada* (New York, 1849), pp. 33–34, as quoted in Eleanore H. Gustafson, "Clues and Footnotes," *Antiques* 114, no. 5 (November 1978): 958; Clark, "Diary of Edward Jenner Carpenter," p. 349.

135. Barnes Account Book, account with Reuben Chaffee, June 11, 1822; Lyell Account Book, account with John J. Post, November 16, 1808; Cheney Daybook, 1813–1846, account with Grove Catlin, June 24, 1814; Deland Account Book, account with Ebenezer and George Merrium, June 25, 1834; Danforth Ledger, account with Gershom Jones, June 6, 1800; Church and Sweet Bill to Richard W. Greene, Providence, Rhode Island, May 1829–December 1831, Greene Collection; Evans Daybook, 1784–1806, account with Philadelphia County Commissioners (for the United States Congress), December 9, 1790.

136. E. Smith, Jr., Bill to Robert Rantoul, and Ebenezer Smith, Jr., Bill to Robert Rantoul, Beverly, Massachusetts, April 1811–July 1812, Papers of Robert Rantoul; Robbins Account Book, account with Capt. E. Flower, August 26, 1834.

137. Evans Daybook, 1784–1806, account with Dr. Bass, January 9, 1786; John Durand Account Book, Milford, Connecticut, 1760–1783, account with Dr. Charles Carinton, February 11, 1775, MiHS; Jenkins Daybook, account with Dr. Burleigh Smart, December 22, 1836; Silliman Account Book, account with Dr. Richard Ely (probably East Haddam, Connecticut), May 20, 1807; Rea Daybook, 1789–1793, account with Dr. William Jackson, January 30, 1792.

138. Rea Daybook, 1789–1793, account with William Williams, July 27, 1790; Barnes Account Book, account with Sage and Russell, August 12, 1824; Holmes Daybook, account with C. U. Hayden, July 1826; Short Account Book, account with Thomas H. Balch, August 27, 1814.

139. Kettell Account Book, accounts with Joshua Greenleaf, May 1791 (pair) and February 14, 1792 (set).

140. O. Avery Account Book, account with Randall Wells, June 20, 1809; Ross Account Book, accounts with Thomas Ross, December 1803–January 1804 (cherry, maple, mahogany) and Aaron Smith. October 28, 1799 (with nose); J. E. Townsend Account Book and Ledger, account with John Bass, January 13, 1783; Pells and Company Bill to Arthur Bronson, New York, April 11, 1837, Bronson Family Papers.

141. Baker Account Book, account with William Potter, August 26, 1791; I. Ashton Account Book, account with Cornell Wiles, December 20, 1791; Jenkins Daybook, account with Joseph Dane, July 6, 1838; Holmes Ledger, account with Samuel Ingham, June 30, 1828.

142. Barnes Account Book, accounts with Jonathan Barnes, December 18, 1822, Dr. Charles Dyer, May 21, 1823, and Thomas McDonough, December 18, 1822. Framed board in James Linacre Bill to Mr. Elmendorf, Albany, New York, December 8, 1806, Sanders Papers; open frame in Rowell Account Book, account with Moses Goodrich, June 22, 1840. Catherine Beecher, *A Treatise on Domestic Economy* (Boston: Marsh, Capen, Lyon, and Webb, 1841), p. 349, as quoted in Nylander, *Snug Fireside*, p. 127.

143. Boynton Ledger, 1810–1817, accounts with Frederick Pettes, October 8, 1813, and Alden Spooner, August 9, 1813, and Ledger, 1817–1847, account with Mrs. Sarah Townsend, August 29, 1817; Holcomb Account Book, account with V. P. Van Renssalear, June 22, 1822; A. Taylor Account Book, account with Jenner Foot, December 13, 1815; Rebecca Williamson Bill to Robert L. Livingston, New York, July 21, 1832, Livingston Papers.

144. Oliver Wickes Bill to William Arnold, East Greenwich, Rhode Island, December 1799–February 1804, Greene Collection; *Book of the Household,* 2 vols. (London: London Printing and Publishing Company, ca. 1870), 2: 551, as quoted in Donald L. Fennimore, *Metalwork in Early America* (Winterthur, Del.: Winterthur Museum, 1996), p. 175; see also pp. 176–79 for turned wooden handles. Handle repair in J. Durand Account Book, account with Samuel Sanford, September 23, 1762.

145. Garrett, *At Home,* pp. 190–91, 214.

146. Henry A. Guardinien Bill and Peter M. Hench Bill to Catherine Gansevoort, Albany, New York, April 7, 1827, and March 14, 1816, Papers of Catherine Gansevoort, Gansevoort-Lansing Collection; theater notice in *New-York Gazette Revived in the Weekly Post-Boy,* November 19, 1750, as quoted in Gottesman, *Arts and Crafts,* p. 122.

147. Lyell Account Book, account with William Popham, December 3, 1806; Silas Ellis Cheney Ledger, Litchfield, Connecticut, 1816–1822, account with James Winship, January 2, 1821, LHS; Samuel Fithian Ware Account Book, Lower Township, Cape May County, New Jersey, 1826–1849, account with James R. Hughes, November 14, 1830, DCM.

148. William H. Reed Account Book, Hampden, Maine, 1803–1848, account with Jedediah Merrick, May 17, 1808, DCM; Moyers and Rich Account Book, credit account with E. M. D. Reed, July 12, 1837; Cheney Ledger, 1799–1817, account with Dan Huntington, October 1801, and daybook, 1802–1807, account with Amos Doolittle, July 9, 1806; Pote Account Book, account with James Mountfort, May 7, 1828; K. H. Shaw Bill to Joseph G. Waters, Salem, Massachusetts, March 31, 1825, Waters Family Papers; Lee Ledger, account with Harvey Dresser, April 1822.

149. Holmes Ledger, account with Asa P. Williams, July 1826, and Daybook, account with Heman Starkey, October 15, 1827; Barker Account Book, 1750–1772, account with Samuel Maye, November 4, 1763; Samuel Abell Bill to St. George Tucker, probably Williamsburg, Virginia, August 9, 1791, Tucker Coleman Collection. Gilding and painting in Boynton Ledger, 1817–1847, accounts with Joseph Flood, June 1, 1825, and Dr. E. E. Phelps, December 2, 1840; bronzing, painting, and veneering in Robbins Account Book, accounts with Ludlow and Oakley, August 19, 1834, and Mr. Sperry, October 28, 1835. Jenkins Daybook, account with Capt. Edmand Wise, December 16, 1837; Clark, "Diary of Edward Jenner Carpenter," p. 351.

150. Holmes Ledger, account with Samuel C. Burt, February 9, 1830; Kettell Account Book, account with Edward Bass, November 2, 1784; Cornelius Roosevelt Bill to William Beekman, New York, July–August 1795, White-Beekman Papers, NYHS; Gavit Bill to Orne, May–June 1763.

151. Oak in Robbins Account Book, account with Dr. Barry, February 20, 1835; mahogany in Holmes Daybook, account with Calvin Williams, January 13, 1826, and Isaac Wright Account Book, Hartford, Connecticut, 1834–1837, account with Winship and Work, February 1, 1834, CSL. B. A. Norton and Company Bill to Samuel Larned, Providence, Rhode Island, January–June 1844, Greene Collection; Matthew Marshall Bill to Arthur Bronson, New York, December 29, 1836, Bronson Family Papers; Barnes Account Book, account with John L. Lewis, August 17, 1821; D. and S. Proud Daybook and Ledger, account with Phillip Lewis, July 11, 1828; J. E. Townsend Account Book and Ledger, account with Henry Barber, January 11, 1793.

152. Danforth Ledger, accounts with Jabez Bowen, August 17, 1801, and Thomas Jackson, August 18, 1801; Robbins Account Book, account with Charles H. Dickinson, May 23, 1834.

153. Map framing discussed in E. McSherry Fowble, *Two Centuries of Prints in America, 1680–1880* (Charlottesville, Va.: University Press of Virginia for the Winterthur Museum, 1987), pp. 22–23. Holmes Daybook, account with Richard Hayden, September 26, 1827; Boynton Ledger, 1810–1817, account with Curtis and Coolidge, September 6, 1813; William G. Beesley Daybook, Salem, New Jersey, 1828–1836, account with William Carpenter, February 16, 1829, Salem County Historical Society, Salem, New Jersey.

154. J. E. Townsend Ledger, account with Joshua Crandel, August 7, 1794; Holmes Ledger, account with Asa P. Williams, July 1826.

155. Map sticks in Cheney Daybook, 1813–1846, account with Orman Marsh, May 15, 1817. Griswold Daybook, account with Joseph Allen, April 8, 1820; Preston Ledger, 1795–1817, account with Nicholas Jones, December 30, 1803.

156. Nathan Topping Cook Account Book, Bridgehampton, New York, 1792–1823, account with Samuel Brown, February 1806, DCM; Nathaniel Sterling Account book, Wilton, Connecticut, 1801–1809, account with Ebenezer Bennett, January 22, 1803, CHS.

157. J. Gere Ledger, 1822–1852, account with William A. Walker, April 28, 1834; Boynton Ledger, 1810–1817, accounts with Lemuel Hedge, March 16, 1812 (4½¢ profile frames), and Benjamin Tuells, November 22, 1815 (profile machine lent), and Ledger, 1817–1847, account with Lyman Cowdry, May 4, 1834.

158. Barnes Account Book, account with Joel Jacobs, January 23, 1824; Holmes Ledger, account with David Williams 2nd, April 1827; Danforth Ledger, accounts with Samuel Clark, August 5, 1799, and Stephen Abbott, August 9, 1799; Stephanus Knight Account Book, Enfield, Connecticut, 1795–1809, account with Nehemiah Pruddan, April 7, 1803, CHS.

159. Daniel Rea, Jr., Daybook, Boston, 1772–1800, account with Thomas Brattle, January 28, 1773, BL (microfilm, DCM), and Daybook, 1789–1793, account with Joseph Callender, February 23, 1791; Jenkins Daybook, account with William Adams, February 1, 1838; Pote Account Book, account with George Clark, November 29, 1824.

160. Boynton Ledger, 1817–1847, account with Simeon Ide, April 17, 1822; Thomas Jefferson Account Book, eastern United States, 1783–1790, account with Thomas Affleck, Philadelphia, January 14, 1783, Massachusetts Historical Society, Boston (hereafter cited MHS).

161. The popularity of backgammon in Virginia is discussed in Jane Carson, *Colonial Virginians at Play,* Williamsburg Research Studies (Williamsburg, Va.: Colonial Williamsburg, 1965), pp. 75–76. D. and S. Proud Ledger, account with Jonathan W. Coy, August 30, 1780; Pote Account Book, account with Pearson Little and Robertson, November 25, 1826; Boynton Ledger, 1817–1847, account with Dr. Daniel Jenison, December 25, 1818; Silliman Account Book, account of shop work, January 1805; Clark, "Diary of Edward Jenner Carpenter," p. 378; Account of Disbursements for Sloop *Fame,* Newport, Rhode Island, 1799, account with Stephen Goddard, Wetmore Papers, MHS.

162. J. Townsend, Jr., Ledger, account with James Sisson, March 26, 1770; J. E. Townsend Account Book and Ledger, account with John Goddard, September 29, 1779.

163. Carson, *Colonial Virginians at Play,* pp. 190–92; Boynton Ledger, 1810–1817, accounts with Benjamin S. Pilsbury, December 24, 1813, and Curtis and Coolidge, November 6, 1814; Danforth Ledger, account with Charles Holden, January 6, 1792; Thomas Tufft Bill to Mrs. Mary Norris, Philadelphia, 1775 or later, Norris Family Accounts, Gillingham Collection.

164. Beckwith Ledger, account with Isaac Geer, January 23, 1806; William Savery Bill to Joseph Pemberton, Philadelphia, January 1774–November 1775, Pemberton Papers, HSP;

Thomas Osborn Receipt Book, New York, 1823–1846, receipt of Thomas Timpson, July 28, 1828, NYPL.

165. The sport of bowling is discussed in Carson, *Colonial Virginians at Play,* pp. 171–80. Carson also illustrates an unidentified European (probably Dutch) print dating to the late seventeenth or early eighteenth century that shows a game of ninepins in progress outside an inn. The pins are arranged in three rows. Wilder Daybook and Ledger, account with Joseph A. Spear, June 4, 1838; Whitelaw Ledger, account with Samuel Clough, Jr., May 4, 1808.

166. Catherine Dike, *Walking Sticks,* Shire Album 256 (Haverfordwest, Wales: C. I. Thomas and Sons for Shire Publications, 1990), pp. 3–6; Whitelaw Ledger, account with Robert Scott, September 5, 1811; Trumble Advertisement; D. and S. Proud Ledger, accounts with Calvin Dean, June 16, 1815, and Christopher Whipple, January 5, 1782 (with ferrel); Holcomb Account Book, account with Eliakim How, December 1, 1815.

167. Bill of John Shaw and Archibald Chisholm to James Brice, Annapolis, Maryland, November 1772–May 1775, Brice-Jennings Papers, Maryland Historical Society, Baltimore; Cheney Daybook, 1807–1813, account with Isaac Baldwin, July 26, 1809; Rea Daybook, 1789–1793, account with John Codman, March 10, 1792.

168. Joseph and John Needles Bills to Stephen Girard, Philadelphia, September 5, 1826, and March 5, 1826, Girard Papers; Carson, *Colonial Virginians at Play,* p. 101; Daniel Trotter Bill to John Girard, Philadelphia, November 1787–February 1788, Girard Papers; Garrett, *At Home,* pp. 73, 106.

169. Jacobs Bird-House Company, *Seventh Annual Birdhouse Booklet* (Waynesburg, Pa.: Jacobs Bird-House Co., 1915); Joseph H. Dodson, *Your Bird Friends and How to Win Them* (Kankakee, Ill.: Joseph H. Dodson, 1917); Boynton Ledger, 1810–1817, account with Horace Everett, April 19, 1817; Knight Account Book, account with Ephraim P. Potter, April 8, 1801; Ranck Account Book, account with Martin Meily, ca. 1798, in Keyser et al., *Accounts,* p. 209; Samuel Cheever Bill to Elias Hasket Derby, Salem, Massachusetts, January 1792–October 1793, Derby Papers; Baker Account Book, account with Jacob Rodrigues Rivera, May 20, 1785.

170. Nunes, *Hyde de Neuville,* pp. 16, 17, 33; Daniel Bixby Account Book, Francestown, New Hampshire, 1839–1849, unidentified account, November 1840, DCM; Bachman Daybook, account with Elizabeth Houser, April 7, 1828; L. Houghton Ledger A, account with Seth Lee, May 28, 1821; Benjamin Daybook and Ledger, account with George A. Starkweather, May 26, 1828; Thomas Tufft Bill to Mrs. Mary Norris, Philadelphia, June 2, 1775, Norris Family Accounts, Gillingham Collection.

171. Barnes Account Book, accounts with Selden and Hurd, May 4, 1824, and William Williams, October 3, 1822; Gray Ledger, account with Dr. Edward A. Holyoke, July 8, 1793; Rea Daybook, 1789–1793, account with Dr. Bulfinch, April 28, 1790; Boynton Ledger, 1817–1847, account with Capt. David Smith, January 1, 1823.

172. Merrifield Account Book, account with H. B. Haswell, November 19, 1840; Barnes Account Book, account with William Williams, November 1, 1824; Hopkins Bill to Greene, September 1834–December 1835.

173. Mehargue Ledger, credit account with John Barry, June 11, 1844; Bastian Account Book, account with George Remley, July 18, 1825; Isaac H. Madera Bill to James Skerrett, Philadelphia, March 18, 1833, Papers of James J. Skerrett, Loudoun Papers, HSP; Boynton Ledger, 1810–1817, account with Alden Spooner, August 9, 1813.

174. Robert Mullen Bill to Stephen Collins, Philadelphia, November 1789, Collins Papers; J. Durand Account Book, account with Samuel Sanford, May 15, 1766; Cheney Daybook, 1807–1813, account with Abraham Knowlton, September 15, 1809.

175. Cheney Ledger, 1799–1817, accounts with Caleb Bacon, April 24, 1800, and Oliver Wolcott, December 29, 1801; Knight Account Book, account with Stephen Root, May 17, 1807; Danforth Ledger, account with Timothy Gladding, June 28, 1804.

176. Cheney Daybook, 1802–1807, account with Ebenezer Boles, April 1803; Boynton Ledger, 1817–1847, accounts with Edward R. Campbell, August 1, 1822, and Samuel Patrick, April 7, 1841.

177. Gray Ledger, account with Capt. Josiah Batchelder, Jr., May 1777; Cheney Daybook, 1807–1813, credit account with Charles T. West, March 5, 1812.

Sarah Neale Fayen

Tilt-Top Tables and Eighteenth-Century Consumerism

▼ PERHAPS NO SINGLE PIECE *of American cabinetware of the Georgian period is so universally admired, so eagerly sought after by collectors . . . as a tripod tea table fabricated of rich grained wood, skillfully elaborated with a scalloped top cut from an individual part of solid crotch mahogany, ball-and-claw feet, and . . . various ornamentations on the pedestal and legs.*

William McPherson Hornor, Jr.

Few American furniture forms are more iconic than the tilt-top tea table. Over the years, antique dealers, curators, and collectors adopted their own language for the features of these tables that were most valued in the modern marketplace. Circular tops with carved edges—usually called "scallop'd" in the eighteenth century—acquired the name "piecrust," and the mechanism that allowed the tops of some tables to tilt up into a vertical position, rotate, and be removed entirely—referred to as a "box" by many colonial tradesmen—became known as a "birdcage." These and other stylistic and structural features attracted some collectors, while large tops made of highly figured mahogany or tables with histories of ownership in prominent colonial families captivated others. Today, tilt-top tea tables are in virtually every major collection of eighteenth-century American furniture, and they remain in great demand. Indeed, in 1986, a Philadelphia tilt-top tea table was the first piece of American furniture to exceed $1,000,000 at auction.[1]

Despite this long-standing admiration of tilt-top tea tables, their initial development in the eighteenth century, their subsequent rise to popularity, and their importance as cultural texts remains largely unexplored. Documentary sources and surviving tables suggest that the arrival and proliferation of this new form were inextricably linked to changes in the economy, increased Atlantic trade, and accelerating consumerism that emerged among the middle ranks of English society. By the mid-1730s, middle-market tilt-top tables like those made in London and the outlying provinces began appearing in well-to-do American homes. Associated from the start with genteel social interactions—especially tea drinking—tilt-top tables became indispensable components of fashionable parlors and symbols of status and refinement for politicians and planters as well as artisans and laborers. Furniture historians have traditionally studied tilt-top tea tables as landmarks of eighteenth-century cabinetmaking. In contrast, this article will address the tilt-top tea table in cultural context by investigating the circumstances that propelled it to the forefront of fashion and exploring the effects of its arrival on consumer behavior and social life.

New Tables

From the outset, tilt-top tables looked very different from conventional tables (fig. 1). Dining tables, dressing tables, and rectangular tea tables have joined frames, fixed tops, and four or more legs, whereas tilt-top tables typically feature a single pillar supported by three legs. Although people generally invent new types of furniture to accommodate changing needs, this novel table form gained popularity more for its appearance than its utility. Undeniably, tilt-top tables were versatile and useful. Their tops tilted up and down on battens (see fig. 2), and many had castors making them easier to move and store. Also, tables with box mechanisms could be oriented so the tripod feet either fit into the corner of a room or along a wall. Tables that changed shape to save space, however, were by no means a new invention. For centuries Europeans had been making tables with falling leaves, foldable frames, and removable tops. A tripod table with a tilting top did not offer considerably more convenience. It was simply a new solution to the old problem of spatial efficiency. Why did English colonists in the 1730s want a new type of table? What social, psychological, economic, or aesthetic needs did tables with central pillars, tripod legs, and tilting tops fulfill? How did their success change the way people interacted or experienced life inside their houses?[2]

To answer these types of questions, scholars from several fields have demonstrated the benefits of studying both production and consumption. Consumption has been a popular topic of inquiry since 1982 when social historians Neil McKendrick, John Brewer, and J. H. Plumb used the phrase

Figure 1 Tea table attributed to William Savery, Philadelphia, Pennsylvania, 1745–1755. Walnut. H. 29⅝"; Diam. of top: 34¾". (Courtesy, Philadelphia Museum of Art; purchased with the Haas Community Fund and the J. Stodgell Stokes Fund.)

Figure 2   Tea table, eastern Virginia, 1750–1770.
Mahogany. H. 27⅛"; Diam. of top: 32¾".
(Courtesy, Colonial Williamsburg Foundation.)

"consumer revolution" to describe the increased demand for a growing variety of goods among eighteenth-century residents of the British Atlantic world. Starting in 1675, ownership of domestic goods increased dramatically in England. Scholars have shown that middling artisans and farmers owned goods that their grandparents would have considered luxuries: forks, table knives, linens, mirrors, books, and of course, tea cups and tea tables. Many factors contributed to this increase, including cheaper production due to technological advances, improved transportation, and less hierarchical political climates. As historian Gloria Main has written, "a major change did take place during the eighteenth century [among] ordinary people—in their *style* of life as well as their standard of living."[3]

Objects experts and material culture scholars who traditionally focus on modes of production have also emphasized in recent years the need for studying consumption. Social historian Cary Carson's memorable mantra, "Demand came first!" has inspired innovative rethinking about the hand-in-hand development of consumer desire and new production. Other scholars have emphasized the importance of studying all the parties who create an object and assign it cultural meaning. In these studies, exploring human motivation rather than quantifying artifactual evidence becomes the intellectual goal.[4]

The tea table occupied a potent position in the imagination of eighteenth-century consumers. The social ritual of tea drinking, made popular by the English elite beginning in the 1680s, was increasingly affordable and widespread in the colonies after the turn of the century. It became a venue for a new genteel code of conduct that spread throughout the middling social ranks over the course of the eighteenth century. This set of polite manners emphasized physical cleanliness, graceful deportment, and pleasant conversation. It was a model of how people should treat one another that allowed individuals from different social backgrounds to comfortably interact according to a shared set of rules. In the common imagination, the ritual of tea drinking was frequently identified by the tea table itself. For instance, a Philadelphia advertisement for "so very neat" pewter tea wares began "To all Lovers of Decency, Neatness and Tea-Table DECORUM." Here, "tea table" functioned as a metonym that succinctly denoted politeness. Rather than using the words "refined" or "fashionable," this retailer and many others used the tea table to associate their products with the genteel lifestyle.[5]

Other advertisements further demonstrate the centrality of the tea table in the imaginations of refined consumers. Retailers selling imported stoneware and porcelain teawares suggested that customers purchase "blue and white tea table setts" or "a genteel tea table sett." Rather than being identified as "tea sets" or "tea drinking vessels," the ceramic wares were described as being of the table. The tea table, more than the teapot or the tea cup that rested on its surface, was the object by which the ritual gained recognition and acceptance. In other words, the piece of furniture around which people gathered to entertain each other with wit and flirtation became the signifier of that particular mode of interaction. The tea table was as much an idea as a particular piece of furniture. As luxurious dining equipage previously

Figure 3 Joseph Highmore, *Mr. B. Finds Pamela Writing,* England, 1743–1744. Oil on canvas. 25⅝" x 29⅞". (Courtesy, Tate Gallery, London/Art Resource, N.Y.) This scene is based on Samuel Richardson's popular novel, *Pamela* (1740). According to Charles Saumarez Smith, "Pamela is shown in a space which she is clearly able to treat as her own with writing implements on the table in front of her; but her private space is invaded by Mr. B." The tilt-top table is clearly the central fixture in Pamela's specifically feminine space.

restricted to the wealthy and powerful became increasingly affordable, all the excitement of fashionable social gatherings became bound up in one item—the tea table.[6]

In addition to being a primary signifier of gentility, the tea table also connoted a "new female gentility" (see fig. 3). As historian David S. Shields has demonstrated, women brought social tea drinking into the home in the first decades of the eighteenth century. Originally, tea drinking and its associated rituals of visits and lively conversation provided the wives of socially prominent husbands an entré into the public sphere. The "brash honesty" that characterized tea table discussions constituted a sort of circumspection that effectively policed the actions of the powerful and elite by threatening to expose scandal and subject any wrong-doers to ridicule. Critics of the ladies' new power used the tea table much like advertisers to succinctly identify a mode of interaction—in this case, frivolous gossip between women. "Tea table chat" was frequently disparaged in newspapers, books, and private accounts by men whose authority felt threatened.[7]

Open criticism of gossip did not hinder the widespread embrace of tea table interactions by either gender. Through the eighteenth century, more and more people learned the ins and outs of the tea drinking ritual, which existed in countless variations in different towns and cities. The tilt-top tea table probably contributed to tea's popularity because it facilitated lively interactions among guests while maximizing opportunities to display refinement. A circular table—effectively the social stage—provided spatial parity to all players. No one dominated from the head of the table and no one "sat below the salt." In addition, a table with a central pillar rather than traditionally joined legs created open spaces for ladies to display their silk brocaded skirts, and for men to elegantly cross their legs and show off their

Figure 4 Gawen Hamilton, *Family Group,* England, ca. 1730. Oil on canvas. 28½" x 35½". (Courtesy, Colonial Williamsburg Foundation.)

stockinged calves. No vertical table legs obscured a person's clothing or posture, both primary means for display in the eighteenth century (fig. 4).[8]

Of course, early Americans owned several different kinds of tea tables. In addition to the circular tilt-top tables there were joined rectangular examples with molded tops. Both versions were frequently called "tea tables" in documents, making their relative popularity and use difficult to decipher. Rodris Roth suggested that the circular tea tables enjoyed greater popularity than rectangular versions. Roth based her statement on the frequent appearance of tilt-top tables in prints and paintings from the era. An equally subjective piece of evidence is the much greater number of circular tea tables that survive in comparison to rectangular versions. Though impossible to pin-point, the popularity of the tilt-top table probably stemmed in part from its unusual form that departed dramatically from traditional table construction. This novelty makes it an informative cultural text carrying significant meaning for the historian.[9]

Inception and Arrival
During the 1680s, European joiners began mounting tea trays imported from the Far East on joined frames. This probably led to the production of rectangular tea tables, the earliest of which had turned (see fig. 5) or scrolled legs. London joiners probably began making examples with cabriole legs (see fig. 6) by the late 1710s, but the earliest American examples appear to

Figure 5 Tea table, probably Williamsburg, Virginia, 1710–1720. Walnut. H. 27½", W. 26½", D. 21½". (Courtesy, Colonial Williamsburg Foundation.) This is one of the earliest tea tables from the colonial period. It has finely turned columnar legs and an edge molding nailed to the top rather than being set into a rabbet.

Figure 6 Joseph van Aken, *An English Family at Tea*, ca. 1720. Oil on canvas. 39" x 45¾". (Courtesy, Tate Gallery.) The rectangular tea table illustrated in this painting has an applied edge molding, shaped skirt, and angular cabriole legs.

date from the 1720s (see fig. 7). Tilt-top tables probably developed as a hybrid of different forms. Candle stands with central pillars and fixed tops were popular in Europe during the seventeenth century. Elaborate versions with carved and gilded surfaces were often made in pairs. In court or other elite settings, they typically flanked a central table and mirror in the French-inspired ensemble sometimes called the "triad." The inventory of James Brydges, first Duke of Chandos, listed a "large Tea Table cover'd with silver" with a pair of stands to match valued at £750. British craftsmen may have modified their stand designs by adding round, table-sized tops during the early eighteenth century. Dutch artisans began producing tables with central pillars and relatively large, oval tilting tops somewhat earlier (see fig. 8). These distinctive forms were conceptual forerunners of the British tilt-top tea table. Given the considerable amount of travel and stylistic exchange between Holland and England during the late seventeenth and early eighteenth centuries, it is conceivable that British artisans borrowed the idea of

Figure 7   Tea table, possibly from the shop of Peter Scott, Williamsburg, Virginia, 1725–1740. Mahogany. H. 26¾", W. 29½", D. 17⅜". (Courtesy, Colonial Williamsburg Foundation.)

Figure 8   Nicolaas Verkolje (1673–1746), *Two Ladies and a Gentleman at Tea*, 1715–1720. Dimensions not recorded. (Courtesy, Victoria and Albert Museum, London.) Art historian Peter Thornton notes that small oval tables like the one depicted in this scene were very popular in Holland. "Such forms often had a painted top which was hinged on a tripod pillar, so that when not in use, it could be placed close to the wall where it provided colorful decoration" (*Authentic Décor: The Domestic Interior, 1720–1920* [New York: Viking, 1984], p. 79, no. 95).

Figure 9 Tea table, Philadelphia area of Pennsylvania, ca. 1720. Walnut and cherry. H. 27⅛"; Diam. of top: 31⅝". (Private collection; photo, Gavin Ashworth.)

Figure 10 Candle stand, Philadelphia, 1710–1720. Walnut. H. 28⅞", W. 17¾", D. 16¾". (Private collection; photo, Gavin Ashworth.)

a tilting top from Netherlandish sources and adapted it to their own stand or table forms.[10]

Most English appraisers, merchants, and tradesmen used the term "pillar and claw" to describe tilt-top tea tables (the word "claw" designated the three legs). Other common nomenclature included "claw table" and "snap table," an onomatopoetic name inspired by the catch that held the top in a horizontal position. One of the earliest American references to this form is in the probate inventory of Captain George Uriell (d. 1739) of Anne Arundel County, Maryland. His household possessions included "two Mohogany Claw Tables" worth £3.3. Documentary references increased during the following decades. The inventory of a Charleston man taken in 1740 listed "one round mahogany claw foot table." Five years later, Philadelphia cabinetmakers Joseph Hall and Henry Rigby advertised a "Pillar and Claw table" and an "old Pillar & Claw Mahogy Table." The qualifier "old" implies that the table was made well before 1745.[11]

Some colonists struggled to describe this new furniture form. In 1749 appraisers for the estate of John Calder of Wethersfield, Connecticut, referred to his tilt-top tea table as a "stand" with a "fashion swivel leaf." In this context "fashion" probably meant "modish" or "stylish." "Stand table" was used throughout the colonies, most consistently in Wethersfield and Rhode Island. Many appraisers alluded to the kinetic action of the top in describing these tables. The 1757 estate inventory of Boston merchant Peter Minot, for example, listed a "Mahogany Turn up Table."[12]

"Tea table" with no qualifier was the most common name for the tilt-top variety in British North America. References to "tea tables" occur in advertisements and inventories from the first quarter of the eighteenth century, but they probably denoted rectangular forms. During the 1730s, the term became more ambiguous as it was increasingly applied to circular as well as rectangular tea tables. This shift is evident in merchant advertisements that offer iron and brass "tea table ketches." Occasionally appraisers, merchants, and artisans differentiated between circular and rectangular tea tables. An inventory taken in Savannah, Georgia, in 1768 lists "1 Mahogany Tea Table Round" valued at one pound. Some regions adopted consistent habits of nomenclature. People in Philadelphia tended to call rectangular tea tables "square." A lack of descriptive language generally implied a tilt-top form in that city. The fact that Americans consistently used "tea table" rather than "pillar and claw table" or other English terms may suggest a more common association among colonists between tilt-top tables and tea drinking.[13]

The earliest surviving American tilt-top tea table was made in the Philadelphia vicinity and probably dates from the 1720s (fig. 9). Its pillar turnings, faceted base block, and flat-sided cabriole legs appear to be just one step removed from the baroque stand illustrated in figure 10. Moreover, the use of a wrought iron catch rather than an imported brass one suggests that the latter hardware was not readily available when the table was made. Another tea table with a faceted base block survives (fig. 11), but it was probably made a decade later. Its rounded legs, pad feet, and columnar

Figure 11 Tea table, Philadelphia, 1730–1740. Mahogany. H. 28"; Diam. of top: 29¼". (Courtesy, Philadelphia Museum of Art; gift of Lydia Thompson Morris.)

pillar illustrate the transition in Philadelphia from baroque Netherlandish designs toward the tilt-top table form that became popular among English consumers. By the early 1740s, at least one Philadelphia shop was producing relatively uniform tilt-top tables (see fig. 12). Examples in this group typically have complex tops with up to twelve repeats, inverted balusters, and battens with short cross pieces that fit snugly around the top board of the box.

The production of tilt-top tea tables increased during the following decades throughout the colonies. Some colonial cabinetmakers made examples that rivaled those of their London counterparts. Williamsburg, Virginia, cabinetmaker Peter Scott began producing highly sophisticated tilt-top tables about 1745. An elaborate example that descended in the Lee

Figure 12   Tea table with carving attributed to the shop of Samuel Harding, Philadelphia, Pennsylvania, 1735–1745. Mahogany. H. 27"; Diam. of top: 31". (Courtesy, Diplomatic Reception Rooms, U. S. Department of State.)

family of Stratford Hall (fig. 13) may have served as a model for tables that he made for other prominent Virginia families. A walnut tilt-top tea table labeled by Philadelphia cabinetmaker William Savery (fig. 1) is roughly contemporary with Scott's but has no carving on the top or pillar. This pair illustrates that elaborately carved and relatively plain tilt-top tables were being made simultaneously in the 1740s.[14]

Production

The patterns of production and distribution of tilt-top tables within the colonies indicate that they were being built inexpensively for a mid-level market. Making a tilt-top table required turning skills and the ability to perform simple joinery. In addition to the pillar, the turned components

Figure 13 Tea table attributed to Peter Scott, Williamsburg, Virginia, 1740–1750. Mahogany. H. 28¾"; Diam. of top: 32¹³⁄₁₆". (Courtesy, Robert E. Lee Memorial Association; photo, Gavin Ashworth.)

Figure 14 View of the Dominy shop showing a table top mounted on a lathe. (Courtesy, Winterthur Museum.) The Dominy family shop was located in East Hampton, Long Island.

on a tilt-top table could include colonettes or miniature balusters if the object had a box and the top if it had a scalloped or molded edge. Because such tops were too large to be turned over the bed of the lathe, they were typically mounted on an arbor and cross (fig. 14). Some tables represent the work of a single artisan whereas others are the products of several tradesmen (see fig. 15).[15]

Growing demand in this era encouraged specialization and collaboration between artisans. In the seventeenth century, English craftsmen and traders challenged Dutch dominance of the Atlantic market by espousing mercantilism, a system of commercial trade that took advantage of English holdings in America and the Caribbean. The success of this carrying trade convinced English tradesmen as well as the Crown that making and marketing goods efficiently and selling them inexpensively to middle range consumers could yield substantial profits. Glenn Adamson has demonstrated that caned chairs made first in London and later in Boston between 1700 and 1730 pioneered a mercantilist production strategy in America. Caned chair makers imitated the carved crests and front stretchers that were fashionable among the late seventeenth-century elite. They could sell them inexpensively, however, by buying the stretchers and stiles in large number from specialist turners who made them quickly and efficiently. Merchants then sold the caned chairs throughout the Atlantic rim to consumers hoping to ally themselves with their fashionable counterparts in London.[16]

Artisans on both sides of the Atlantic recognized that focusing production and cooperating with other specialists made all of their jobs easier, reduced their costs, and raised their profits. Tilt-top tables, whose parts

Figure 15 Tea table, probably Norfolk, Virginia, 1760–1775. Mahogany. H. 28¾"; Diam. of top: 29¾". (Collection of the Museum of Early Southern Decorative Arts.) This tea table probably represents the work of a cabinetmaker, a turner, and a carver.

required distinct sets of skills and tools, lent themselves to collaborative production. Documentary records indicate that turners sold and traded tilt-top table pillars and tops on the open market much like caned chair makers had traded stiles and stretchers in previous decades. In the May 30, 1751, issue of the *Pennsylvania Gazette,* Joseph Pattison, "Turner from London," directed his advertisement for "tea table tops, and tea boards, pillars, balusters" to other artisans. In 1754 Joshua Delaplaine, a New York carpenter, joiner, and merchant, bought three "pillers of Mahogany" from John Paston and sold "a mahogany round tea table" to Samuel Nottingham, Jr. The account book of Charleston cabinetmaker Thomas Elfe documents a similar business relationship with turner William Wayne. In September 1771 Elfe paid Wayne £1.10 for "2 tea table pillars & turning."[17]

Some craftsmen traded tilt-top table parts over considerable distances. Beginning in 1766 Samuel Williams repeatedly advertised "mahogany and walnut tea table columns" and "mahogany tea table tops" for local use or for "exportation." This suggests that he sold components to merchants engaged in the venture cargo trade. On June 10, 1784, Solomon Lathrop, a joiner in Springfield, Massachusetts, recorded "carrying 8 tea table pillars to Windsor," about fifteen miles away. By the second half of the eighteenth century, the demand for tilt-top tea tables and other furniture forms had become sufficient to sustain specialization and collaboration in rural areas.[18]

Most artisans who routinely produced tilt-top tables probably kept parts on hand to be assembled on short notice. Large cabinet shops in Britain often stockpiled sizable quantities of standard components. The 1763 inventory of London carver, cabinetmaker, and upholsterer William Linnell listed "38 setts of claws for pillar and claw tables" and "4 setts of carved table claws Do." Similarly, Philadelphia joiner Joshua Moore had "13 tea table pillars" and "1 Tea Table top" at his death in 1778.[19]

Some turners sustained their businesses by making pillars for uses other than tilt-top tables. At least two baluster-shaped tilt-top table pillars have been connected to craftsmen involved in architectural construction. In 1787 Thomas Hayden of Windsor, Connecticut, rendered a cross-section drawing of a baluster-and-ring pillar for a tilt-top table on the same page as plans for architectural cornice moldings (fig. 16). William Hosley and Philip Zea have attributed one table with an identical pillar to Hayden and suggest that he may have made the drawing as a guide to local craftsmen producing similar tables. Patricia E. Kane and Wallace Gusler have established more tangible links between furniture and architectural turnings. Kane has shown that the pillar on one Newport tilt-top table (fig. 17) matches the balusters on the second floor of Touro Synagogue (built 1763) (fig. 18), and Gusler has demonstrated that the pendant on the Peter Scott table illustrated in figure 13 is similar to those in the George Wythe and Galt houses in Williamsburg, Virginia (fig. 19).[20]

Some artisans who produced tilt-top table parts began their careers in the chair making trade. William Savery apprenticed with Solomon Fussell, a Philadelphia chair maker who maintained a large shop that produced seating in competition with Boston exports. Fussell made both joined and

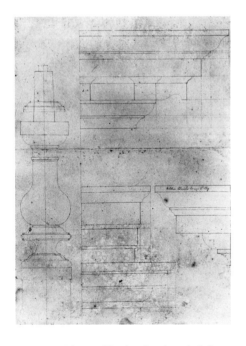

Figure 16 Thomas Hayden drawing of a baluster for a tilt-top tea table, Windsor, Connecticut, 1787. Dimensions not recorded. Ink on paper. *The Great River: Art and Society of the Connecticut Valley, 1635–1820*, edited by Gerald W. R. Ward and William N. Hosley, Jr. (Hartford, Conn.: Wadsworth Atheneum, 1985), p. 225.

Figure 17   Tea table, Newport, Rhode Island, 1760–1770. Mahogany. H. 26⅝"; Diam. of top: 31⅞". (Photo, Israel Sack, Inc.)

Figure 18   Detail of three balusters in Touro Synagogue, Newport, Rhode Island, ca. 1763. (Courtesy, Touro Synagogue; photo, Gavin Ashworth.)

Figure 19   Detail of a pendant in the George Wythe House, Williamsburg, Virginia, 1750–1755. (Redrawn from an original by Singleton Peabody Moorehead; courtesy, Colonial Williamsburg Foundation.)

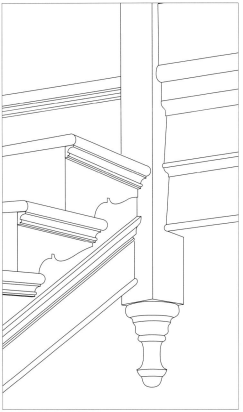

turned chairs and bought seat lists and slats from specialists outside his shop. By the time Savery completed his apprenticeship in 1741, he would have known how to assemble chairs using parts obtained from other craftsmen. Even though he continued to work at the "Sign of the Chair," Savery broadened his repertoire by making tables and case furniture. Tilt-top tables may have been one of the first new forms he produced since they could be made quickly and easily using piecework, possibly pillars and tops furnished by the same turners who sold him and his master chair components. The requisite hardware was readily available from Fussel who advertised "brass tea table catches" in 1755.[21]

Carved tables required additional collaboration. Some large cabinet shops had workforces that included cabinetmakers, turners, carvers, and other specialists. Regrettably, cabinetmakers' account books rarely specify whether a tradesman was a shop employee or an independent contractor. For instance, Thomas Elfe paid Thomas Burton seven pounds "for Carving a Pillar and Claws" in 1771, but the nature of their business relationship remains unclear. Evidence suggests, however, that cabinetmakers making tables and other furniture for wealthy customers went to great lengths to secure skilled carvers. In the May 31, 1762, issue of the *New York Mercury*, immigrant "Cabinet and Chair-Maker" John Brinner reported that he had "brought over from London six Artificers" and offered:

Figure 20   Tea table, New York, 1760–1770. Mahogany. H. 29"; Diam. of top: 29". (Chipstone Foundation; photo, Gavin Ashworth.)

all sorts of Architectural, Gothic, and Chinese, Chimney Pieces, Glass and Picture Frames, Slab Frames, Gerondoles, Chandaliers, and all kinds of Mouldings and Frontispieces, &c. &c. Desk and Book-Cases, Library Book-Cases, Writing and Reading Tables, Commode and Bureau Dressing Tables, Study Tables, China Shelves and Cases, Commode and Plain Chest of Drawers, Gothic and Chinese Chairs; all Sorts of plain or ornamental Chairs, Sofa Beds, Sofa Settees, Couch and easy Chair Frames, all Kinds of Field Bedsteads.

Philadelphia cabinetmaker Benjamin Randolph also imported labor from England. His principal carvers—John Pollard and Hercules Courtenay—trained in major London shops, signed indentures to pay for their passage to the colonies, and established their own businesses after their terms had expired. It is unlikely that either Randolph or Brinner required much outside labor when their shops were fully staffed.[22]

Luke Beckerdite has identified a group of four New York tilt-top tables that were made in one large cabinet shop but carved by four different artisans. Two of the tables (figs. 20–23) were clearly carved in the same shop because the tradesmen who decorated each of them collaborated on a chimneypiece in Van Cortlandt Manor. Although Beckerdite theorized that all four tables may have been produced and carved under the same roof, it is also possible that they are the products of a single cabinet shop and three independent carving firms, one of which employed two hands.[23]

Figure 21 Tea table, New York, 1760–1770. Mahogany. H. 29"; Diam. of top: 29". (Private collection; photo, Gavin Ashworth.)

Figure 22 Detail of the pillar of the tea table illustrated in fig. 20.

Figure 23 Detail of the pillar of the table illustrated in fig. 21.

Figure 24 Tea table with carving attributed to the shop of James Reynolds, Philadelphia, Pennsylvania, 1766–1775. Mahogany. Dimensions not recorded. (Private collection; photo, Christie's.)

Even the largest cabinet shops occasionally required piecework or services from specialists. Randolph's competitor Thomas Affleck commissioned carving from independent artisans, particularly James Reynolds (see fig. 24) and the firm Bernard and Jugiez. The tea table illustrated in figure 25 has

carving attributed to Bernard and Jugiez, and its pillar has details that relate to those on firescreens that Affleck made for Philadelphia merchant John Cadwalader.[24]

Dispersal

Between 1740 and 1790 tilt-top tea tables became nearly ubiquitous fixtures in American parlors and drawing rooms. Their increased production coincided with a substantial escalation of travel and trade throughout the British Empire in the 1740s and economic prosperity in the Americas. Historians John J. McCusker and Russel R. Menard have argued that the colonial economy grew in two spurts. The first spurt directly followed initial settlement in the seventeenth century. The second spurt, which began in the 1740s and continued until the Revolutionary War, coincides with the spreading popularity of tilt-top tea tables. After almost a century of "stagnation," the colonial economy began offering people more opportunity for financial gain than the English economy. More people in the colonies became involved in harvesting, transporting, and selling foodstuffs and raw materials from America to Europe. As their assets grew, these colonists developed a desire for fashionable household goods including new forms like the tilt-top table.[25]

The economic boom lured not only merchants but also ambitious craftsmen prepared to profit from increased demand. Among these were cabinetmakers, joiners, turners, and carvers trained in British urban centers and in the provinces. Immigrant artisans arrived with distinctive stylistic

Figure 26   Tea table, probably Boston, Massachusetts, 1750–1765. Mahogany. H. 27½"; Diam. of top: 36". (Courtesy, Winterthur Museum.)

Figure 27   Detail showing the pillars on (from left to right): tea table, Boston or Salem, Massachusetts, 1760–1770; tea table, Newport, Rhode Island, 1760–1780; tea table, eastern Virginia, 1750–1770. (Courtesy, Winterthur Museum; John Nicholas Brown Center for the Study of American Civilization; private collection, photo, Colonial Williamsburg Foundation.)

vocabularies and work habits. This led to the dispersal of leg profiles, pillar shapes, and construction details characteristic of many British shop, town, city, and regional furniture making traditions. For example, pillars with spiral-fluted urns occur on tables made in eastern Massachusetts, Newport, Rhode Island, and eastern Virginia (see figs. 26, 27). This motif crossed the ocean with English furniture makers who frequently turned spiral-fluted urns on pillars for tilt-top tables as well as bedposts and other forms. Newport absorbed large numbers of English immigrants after the Seven Years' War ended in 1763, and Norfolk was a much larger city where

Figure 28 Detail showing the pillars on (from left to right): tea table, Massachusetts, 1750–1770; tea table, Newport, Rhode Island, 1755–1775; tea table, Philadelphia, Pennsylvania, 1740–1755; tea table, eastern Virginia, 1750–1770. (Courtesy, Winterthur Museum; Society for the Preservation of New England Antiquities, gift of Mrs. H. K. Estabrook, photo, David Bohl; Philadelphia Museum of Art; Colonial Williamsburg Foundation.)

Figure 29 Detail showing the pillars on (from left to right): tea table by Theodosius Parsons, Windham, Connecticut, 1787–1793; tea table, Pennsylvania, 1760–1780; tea table, Norfolk, Virginia, 1765–1775. (Courtesy, Mabel Brady Garvan Collection, Yale University Art Gallery; Winterthur Museum; Museum of Early Southern Decorative Arts.)

the majority of craftsmen either had trained in England or with an English master. It is equally plausible that British tilt-top tables themselves inspired the design for spiral-fluted urns, particularly in the Boston-Salem area where imported furniture had a strong influence on local production.

Similarly, tilt-top tea tables with plain columnar pillars and baluster shaped pillars survive from nearly every port city in America (see figs. 28, 29). Both of these ubiquitous turnings have clear British precedents (see figs. 3, 4, 41), but, like the spiral-fluted urn pattern, they display considerable variety in shape, proportion, and molded detail (see figs. 1, 11, 30, 31).[26]

As a result of furniture importation and immigration, many generic tilt-top tables made in the North American colonies looked more alike than different. Not only did similar turned pillars appear hundreds of miles from each other, but tables made throughout the colonies also shared the same basic top and leg designs. Tables with plain tops, turned tops, and scalloped tops (see fig. 32) were made from New England to Charleston. Most artisans who produced tilt-top tea tables used dovetails to attach the

a

b

c

d

Figure 31 Tea table by Theodosius Parsons, Windham, Conecticut, 1787–1793. Cherry. H. 27⅜"; Diam. of top: 36¼". (Courtesy, Mabel Brady Garvan Collection, Yale University Art Gallery.)

Figure 32 Detail showing the scalloped tops on (a) tea table, probably Connecticut, 1765–1785; (b) tea table, New York, 1765–1785; (c) tea table, Philadelphia, 1765–1775; (d) tea table, Charleston, South Carolina, 1760–1770. (Courtesy, Milwaukee Art Museum, Layton Art Collection; Chipstone Foundation; Winterthur Museum; Museum of Early Southern Decorative Arts.)

legs to the pillar rather than to a base block like the examples shown in figures 9 and 11. Although the legs on tilt-top tea tables display considerable variation in shape, arch, and splay, most fall into two basic categories: those with strong cyma shapes and high arched knees, and those with weaker cyma shapes and relatively flat knees (see fig. 33).

Of course, variations from shop to shop and region to region do exist. Some Charleston tables (fig. 34) resemble English examples more closely than those from other American cities, whereas many Connecticut tables combine designs commonly found in Philadelphia (fig. 35), New York, and

Figure 33 Detail showing the legs of (from left to right): tea table, Philadelphia, 1765–1775; tea table, Virginia, 1750–1770. (Courtesy, Winterthur Museum; Museum of Early Southern Decorative Arts.)

Figure 34 Tea table, Charleston, South Carolina, 1760–1770. Mahogany. H. 28½"; Diam. of top: 31¼". (Collection of the Museum of Early Southern Decorative Arts.)

Figure 35   Tea table attributed to a member of the Chapin family, Hartford or East Windsor, Connecticut, 1775–1790. Cherry. H. 29¼"; Diam. of top: 31¼". (Chipstone Foundation; photo, Gavin Ashworth.) Eliphalet Chapin (1741–1807) worked as a journeyman in Philadelphia in the 1760s. When he returned to his native Connecticut, he continued to use construction features, proportions, and decorative details common in Philadelphia. His work influenced his cabinet-maker family members, Amzi (1768–1835) and Aaron (1753–1838).

Boston. A small group of Newport tables even deviates from the standard pillar and claw design by incorporating multiple pillars or a cabinet with drawers (see fig. 36). Despite these decorative differences, tilt-top tables of the same basic type were available to those who could afford them in all the American cities in the mid-eighteenth century.

The suggestion that similar tilt-top tables were made throughout the colonies challenges the regional differences traditionally catalogued by furniture historians. In "Regionalism in Early American Tea Tables," furniture scholar Albert Sack suggested that artisans in each colony made pillar forms specific to their location. To some degree, Sack is correct. Tables similar to the ones he illustrated certainly do survive from the regions he indicated; however, more specific information is usually needed to pinpoint a table's place of origin. More importantly, the pillars, tops, and legs shown in figures 27–29, 32 and 33, point out that reality often defies regional categorization. An approach focused on the people who made and used tilt-top tables—rather than the tables themselves—yields a more complex story of trans-Atlantic migration and trade.[27]

Like chairs, which could be produced quickly and economically using specialized labor and piecework, tilt-top tables were perfectly suited for the furniture export trade. Following the model established by Boston

Figure 37 Tea table, Newport, Rhode Island, 1760–1780. Mahogany. H. 27½"; Diam. of top: 33⅝". (Private collection; photo, Museum of Early Southern Decorative Arts.) Most Newport tea tables that appear to have been exported are relatively plain. It is doubtful that venture cargo shipments included elaborate examples like those occasionally made for Rhode Island patrons.

Figure 38 Desk, Newport, Rhode Island, 1760–1770. Maple with chestnut and tulip poplar. H. 40⅞", W. 38⅜", D. 20⅞6 ". (Private collection; photo, Museum of Early Southern Decorative Arts.)

tradesmen, merchants, and ship captains during the 1720s, sea-faring entrepreneurs increasingly carried raw materials and finished goods between ports in England, North America, and the West Indies. A Rhode Island tea table that descended in the family of Wilmington, North Carolina, Judge Joshua Grainger Wright (fig. 37) may have been exported by a Newport Quaker merchant who maintained business ties with Friends communities in North Carolina. A similar Newport table was probably carried to Berwick, Maine, around mid-century and sold to the father or grandfather of Ichabod Goodwin.[28]

The Wright and Goodwin tables resemble examples with plain columnar pillars from England, Newport, Norfolk, and elsewhere. Patricia E. Kane has argued that some Newport furniture makers developed standardized models exclusively for the export market. Some Newport tradesmen referred to tilt-top tea tables as "fly tables." In 1758 Job Townsend, Jr., charged Isaac Elizer forty-five pounds for "a Mohogony Fly Table with a Turned Top." Over the next two years Elizer bought two additional fly tables and four tea boards, which suggests that he may have acquired them for export. "Fly tables" appear frequently in other Newport records, especially in the early 1760s when merchant activity was at its height in that city.[29]

Historians have demonstrated that Newport artisans such as John Cahoone and John Townsend made plain furniture—primarily desks, chests of drawers, and tables—to ship with merchants trading along the Atlantic coast and with the West Indies. The tilt-top tables that Kane identified as "standard models" fit in with this genre of work. Like the desk illustrated in figure 38, they were sturdy forms that could be assembled

Figure 39   Tea table, Chester County, Pennsylvania, 1788. Walnut, maple, ash, and lightwood inlay. H. 27"; Diam. of top: 23¾". (Courtesy, Winterthur Museum.)

quickly and inexpensively through the use of piecework, patterns, and collaborative arrangements. The frequent appearance of tilt-top tables in venture cargo shipments also attests to the form's popularity with mid-level consumers throughout the colonies.[30]

The correlation between increased production of tilt-top tables and economic growth in the colonies after 1740 may explain why tilt-top tables from Massachusetts survive in much lower numbers than those from more southerly areas. New England never took full advantage of the "burgeoning Atlantic economy" in part because the markets for their products grew much slower than the region's rapidly increasing population. Agricultural land was becoming scarce, towns more crowded, and people in northern New England lived under constant threat of attack from the French and Native Americans who launched violent assaults on British settlements during King George's War (1739–1748) and the Seven Years' War (1756–1763). These factors may have discouraged artisans from immigrating to the region and impeded the importation and local production of certain luxury goods including tilt-top tea tables.[31]

By the last quarter of the eighteenth century, artisans in rural areas and in non-English communities made tilt-top tables that mimicked mainstream urban versions. Were it not for the chip carved ring and unusually deep cove at the top of its pillar, a table with the label of Windham, Connecticut, furniture maker Theodosius Parsons could be attributed to almost any city or town (fig. 31). By contrast, the artisan responsible for the unusual form illustrated in figure 39 made an Anglo-American tilt-top table using Pennsylvania German construction and design sensibilities. The top is inlaid in traditional Pennsylvania German fashion with the owners' initials

Figure 40 Epergne by William Cripps, London, 1759/60. Silver. H. 15¾", L. 26¼", W. 26". (Courtesy, Colonial Wiliamsburg Foundation.)

and the date in lightwood stringing. The top tilts on hinged iron straps that are screwed to a large wooden cube at the top of the plain turned pillar, a creative interpretation of the conventional block or box. The tilt-top table had become sufficiently widespread among the rural populace that it crossed cultural boundaries.[32]

Consumer Choices

Timothy H. Breen has argued that the "challenge of the eighteenth-century world of goods was its unprecedented size and fluidity, its openness, its myriad opportunities for individual choice, that subverted traditional assumptions and problematized customary social relations." As part of this world of goods, the novelty of the tilt-top table form and the choices it offered consumers suggest shifting needs, tastes, and buying habits.[33]

At its inception, the tilt-top table was a new aesthetic choice. When covered with a cloth, the tops of tilt-top tables almost seemed to float in space. Other domestic objects from the second and third quarters of the eighteenth century reflected similar aesthetic sensibilities. Delicate arms and feet (fig. 40) supported the center sections and cups of silver epergnes, and wineglasses and goblets rested on thin stems with double-helix twists.[34]

The tilt-top table form might be viewed as a quintessential anglo-American interpretation of the rococo, defined by Jonathan Prown and Richard Miller as a combination of "rational thought" and the "public articulation of unorthodox, hedonistic, and erotic forms of expression." In some ways, the tilt-top tea table was symmetrical and ordered. Even when the top was tilted up, the table's façade was visually balanced. On the other hand, the form communicated a degree of precariousness. A heavy item placed too close to the edge of the top could topple the whole structure to the floor. Judging from the number of tables with broken tops, pentil blocks, and boxes, this happened with considerable frequency. The tilt-top

Figure 41 Robert West, *Thomas Smith and His Family*, Britain, 1733. Oil on canvas. 35⅛" x 23⅜". (Courtesy, National Trust Photographic Library/ Upton House, Beardstead Collection; photo, Angelo Hornak.)

table's simultaneous embodiment of order and unpredictability and its strong association with women potentially locate it in "rococo culture." Certainly less expensive and more widely owned than the pedimented and carved high chests studied by Prown and Miller, the tilt-top table probably contributed to the spreading enthusiasm for a mainstream expression of imaginative forms.[35]

The tilt-top table retained its imaginative form through the eighteenth-century, but consumer preferences in decoration shifted. The tastes of some early American consumers were similar to those of their English counterparts. Many upper-class British patrons commissioned relatively simple tilt-top tea tables as the paintings illustrated in figures 3 and 4 suggest. Robert West's painting of Thomas Smith and his family (fig. 41) depicts a tea table of the same basic design as the Savery one (fig. 1). Both objects have circular tops that are about as wide as the tables are high, boxes, simple columnar pillars, and graceful cabriole legs. Neither exhibit carving or any other significant decoration.

In the 1750s more wealthy American patrons commissioned elaborately carved tilt-top tables. An example that descended in the Wharton family of

Philadelphia is one of the earliest with carved ornament (fig. 12). The shells and husks on its knees are associated with Samuel Harding, a prominent tradesman whose shop furnished much of the architectural carving in the Pennsylvania State House (Independence Hall). Although Harding's birthplace is unknown, many of the carvers whose work is represented on existing tilt-top tea tables immigrated to the colonies during the third quarter of the eighteenth century. A large percentage arrived during the 1760s, attracted by the growth in America's economy after the Seven Years' War.[36]

English design books, including William Ince and John Mayhew's *The Universal System of Household Furniture* (1759) and the Society of Upholsterers' *Genteel Household Furniture in the Present Taste* (1760), illustrated "Claw Tables," but the engravings bear little resemblance to American work (fig. 42). The bases of the English tables are extremely sculptural and

Figure 42 Designs for "Claw Tables" illustrated on plate 13 of the 1762 edition of William Ince and John Mayhew's *The Universal System of Household Furniture*. (Courtesy, Winterthur Library: Printed Book and Periodical Collection.)

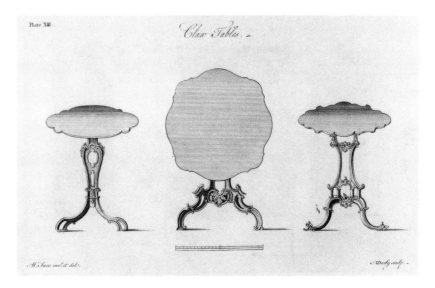

organic, whereas those on most American examples simply have carved details overlaid on an otherwise conventional form. Some of the most elaborate English tables may have been constructed and decorated by carvers. American tables, in contrast, were usually made by cabinetmakers and carved by professionals working in the same shop or independently.

A tilt-top tea table that descended in the Eyre family of Philadelphia is one of the most refined examples made in the colonies (fig. 43). It has well-drawn and finely executed cabochons and leaves on the knees, a flower-and-ribbon motif on the astragal at the base of the pillar, and expressive foliage on the compressed ball above (fig. 44). Although the carving contributed greatly to the rich appearance of the table, it did not challenge the basic design formula. The shape of the legs, their attachment to the pillar, and the pillar design—a compressed ball surmounted by a slightly tapering column—have precise parallels in uncarved tea tables from the Philadelphia area. The same relationship between carved and uncarved forms can be observed on Philadelphia case furniture from the 1730s through the 1780s.[37]

The makers and sellers of tilt-top tables offered consumers several options, all of which affected price. The 1756 and 1757 price agreements from

Figure 43 Tea table, Philadelphia, 1765–1775. Mahogany. H. 28½"; Diam. of top: 36¼". (Chipstone Foundation; photo Gavin Ashworth.)

Providence, Rhode Island, listed "stand tables" in three woods. Mahogany tilt-top tables cost one and a quarter times more than walnut, which cost one and a quarter times more than maple. A similar ratio appears in the Philadelphia cabinetmaker's price list of 1772.[38]

Size also influenced price. The Providence agreements indicated that "stand tables" were more expensive than "candlestands." Similarly, the "tea table" section of the Philadelphia price list included a lower priced "folding stand," which had a top less than twenty-two inches in diameter and could be made with or without a box. Thomas Elfe offered tops in five sizes priced from ten pounds to fourteen pounds at increments of one pound. He generally referred to the most expensive tilt-top examples as "large tea tables."[39]

The idea that some craftsmen conceived of turned tops in incremental sizes with incremental prices is supported by entries in the account book of Job Townsend, Jr. He sold tea boards ranging from six to twenty inches in diameter, priced from £1.15 to twenty pounds. Townsend's customers paid from ten shillings to several pounds extra for each additional inch. Although he did not sell turned tops individually, he owned a lathe and undoubtedly made them for the tilt-top tables he sold.[40]

Repetitive production and demand allowed furniture makers to establish standard prices for generic ornamental details such as "Leaves on the Knees" and "Claw feet." Even elaborate carving like that on Peter Scott's tea tables and kettle stands (see figs. 13, 45–47) could be offered as an option

Figure 44　Detail of the carving on the pillar of the tea table illustrated in fig. 43.

Figure 45   Tea table attributed to the shop of Peter
Scott, Williamsburg, Virginia, 1765–1775. Mahogany.
H. 28"; Diam. of top: 31¼". (Collection of the
Museum of Early Southern Decorative Arts.)

with a set price. This was especially true of objects constructed and carved in the same shop or made and decorated by tradesmen who collaborated regularly. In many instances, cabinetmakers simply added on charges for the carver's labor. Thomas Affleck's bill to John Cadwalader for eighteen major pieces of furniture made between October 13, 1770, and January 14, 1771, included references "To Mr. Reynolds Bill for Carving the Above £37" and "To Bernard & Jugiex for Ditto £24."[41]

Figure 46 Kettle stand attributed to the shop of Peter Scott, Williamsburg, Virginia, 1765–1775. Mahogany. H. 31¼"; Diam. of top: 21". (Private collection; photo, Gavin Ashworth.)

Figure 47 Detail of the top of the kettle stand illustrated in fig. 46.

A tea table that reputedly belonged to Michael and Miriam Gratz of Philadelphia has legs with enormous C-scrolls and carving attributed to Bernard and Jugiez (fig. 48). The maker had to saw the legs from unusually thick stock to accommodate the scroll volutes, and the carver had to decorate the sides of the legs rather than just the top (fig. 49). This extra material and labor would have increased the price of this table significantly. In contrast, the C-scrolls on the legs of the South Carolina table illustrated in figures 50 and 51 may have been a standard option since they required minimal work.[42]

The fact that tilt-top tables were sold at different price levels locates them among other commodities that revolutionized the way people of middling wealth acquired stylish goods. Textiles were the first luxury household goods that came within reach of the non-elite. Over the course of the seventeenth century, laborers, artisans, and tradesmen who formerly could afford only woolens suddenly found themselves choosing between a bewildering array of weaves, colors, and decorative combinations. After textiles,

Figure 48   Tea table with carving attributed to
Bernard and Jugiez, ca. 1765. Mahogany. H. 28⅜";
Diam. of top: 36". (Collection of Mrs. George
M. Kaufman; photo, Gavin Ashworth.)

Figure 49 Detail of a leg on the tea table illustrated in fig. 48.

other fashionable commodities began to follow this pattern. Stylish but relatively inexpensive leather chairs and caned chairs became available to members of the middle class, tin-glazed earthenware and refined stoneware emerged as alternatives to porcelain, and importers began selling green tea at cheaper prices to compete with Bohea tea in the 1710s. Although not widely popular in the colonies before the 1740s, the tilt-top table may have been the furniture form most successfully marketed to the middle class.[43]

Because of its distinct role as a consumer commodity affiliated with female gentility, the tilt-top table might be considered in the category of teaware rather than furniture. When choosing a tea table, consumers probably considered how it would complement their teapot, salver, spoons, and ceramics rather than other furniture they owned. Few tilt-top tables were made en suite with other furniture forms, with the possible exception of the Philadelphia examples that descended in the Stevenson family. Tilt-top tea tables, however, often have details that relate to those on teawares (see figs. 46, 47). Consumers may have purchased tables with scalloped tops that complemented the edge treatment of salvers and tea boards or vice versa. Even the more modest dished tops had visual cognates in silver and brass trays and tazza.[44]

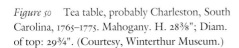

Figure 50 Tea table, probably Charleston, South Carolina, 1765–1775. Mahogany. H. 28⅜"; Diam. of top: 29¾". (Courtesy, Winterthur Museum.)

Figure 51 Detail of a leg on the tea table illustrated in fig. 50.

It is difficult to generalize at which point in their acquisition of requisite tea-related objects consumers chose to buy tea tables. Historians and archaeologists examining several geographic areas have suggested that colonists bought refined artifacts little by little as their funds allowed. Fittingly, it seems that middling consumers tended first to acquire the equipment required for brewing and consuming tea. Owning a few tea cups or a tea pot, however, did not necessarily indicate a full shift toward the genteel lifestyle. In contrast, buying a tea table—whose very name signified refinement—may have been a more meaningful choice. By all accounts, tilt-top tea tables cost more than ceramic tea wares. On the other hand, they tended to cost much less than silver teapots, kettles, and salvers. Many consumers were willing to spend more for their teawares than their tablewares. Evidence from the Chesapeake region suggests that some consumers bought porcelain teawares but could only afford creamware for their tables. By extension, middling families who may not have been able to afford a set of carved chairs or a looking glass may have purchased a tea table.[45]

The popularity of tilt-top tea tables may have helped spread the consumerist impulse that made possible later increases in stylish goods, most notably Wedgwood's successful creamware. Creamware introduced a much less expensive type of polite ware to the ceramic market and also offered different types of decoration at varied prices (fig. 52). Consuming fashionable goods in considerable number was a new activity for the British middling ranks in the eighteenth century. It required a change in attitude and often a change in the patterns of daily life. When creamware appeared on the market in the late 1760s, the appetites of middle-class consumers were already whetted for tea-related objects that signified status but fell within their financial reaches. Within a decade, wealthy Americans as well as those with less financial wherewithal had replaced their old tea and table wares with the new type. The attitudes and infrastructure necessary for this rapid and total change in ceramic consumption patterns had been generated over the previous decades by a wide range of fashionable goods—calicos, forks, mirrors, and many others. Among these goods was the tilt-top tea table.[46]

Ironically, the success of creamware probably contributed to the eventual demise of the tilt-top tea table's status. Craftsmen continued to make tripod tables through the Federal era (often with attenuated, neo-classical style legs and pillars) but they did not carry the same connotations. The tables that often signified wealth and status in the early nineteenth century were long segmented dining tables that filled large dining rooms and entertaining halls. Tilt-top tables may have lost their ability to communicate status when tea drinking and ownership of teawares—particularly creamware—became nearly ubiquitous after 1770. In the stores of Chesapeake retailers, creamware plates represented 73.3 percent of all plates sold in the 1770s, and 96.2 percent in the 1780s.[47]

In 1774 several colonial newspapers published rhymes titled "A Ladies' Adieu to her Tea Table." The poems all differed somewhat, but shared the patriotic fervor that led men and women throughout the colonies to boycott tea in protest of England's high taxes. The abandonment of tea seemed

Figure 52 Similar creamware plates with different decorative treatment. (Left) probably Staffordshire, ca. 1775–1785; (right) possibly Leeds, ca. 1780–1790. (Courtesy, Audrey and Ivor Noël Hume; photo, Gavin Ashworth.)

to accompany a heavy heart, not for want of the drink but rather for the tea table accoutrements. "Farewell the Tea Board, with its gaudy Equipage, / Of Cups and Saucers, Cream Bucket, Sugar Tongs, / The pretty Tea Chest also, lately stor / With Hyson, Congo and best Double Fine." By making these tea-related goods more widely available, the consumer revolution had engendered a desire for material objects among middling people faster than ever before. The tilt-top tea table was the product of its particular historical moment. Its production relied on the commercial trade networks that characterize the mid-eighteenth century, and its function and appearance not only facilitated but came to symbolize the fashionable modes of social interaction that changed daily life for so many. With changes in society and taste after the American Revolution, the tilt-top table lost its potency in the imaginations of American consumers.[48]

ACKNOWLEDGMENTS For their generous assistance and encouragement, the author thanks Glenn Adamson, Luke Beckerdite, Eleanore Gadsden, J. Ritchie Garrison, Dudley and Constance Godfrey, Wallace B. Gusler, Charles F. Hummel, Jack Lindsey, Ann Smart Martin, and Jonathan Prown.

1. William McPherson Hornor, Jr., "A Study of American Piecrust Tables," *International Studio* 99, no. 411 (November 1931), 38–40, 78–79; Christie's, New York, January 25, 1986.

2. For a discussion of tables that change shape, see Peter Thornton, *Seventeenth-Century Interior Decoration in England, France & Holland* (New Haven, Conn.: Yale University Press, 1978), pp. 226–30; and Adam Bowett, *English Furniture, 1660–1714 From Charles II to Queen Anne* (Woodbridge, Eng.: Antique Collectors' Club, 2002), pp. 106–7.

3. Neil McKendrick, John Brewer, and J. H. Plumb, *The Birth of a Consumer Society: The Commercialization of Eighteenth-Century England* (Bloomington: Indiana University Press, 1982). Lorna Weatherill, *Consumer Behavior and Material Culture in Britain, 1660–1760* (New York: Routledge, 1988), pp. 25–42. Lois Green Carr and Lorena S. Walsh, "Changing Lifestyles and Consumer Behavior in the Colonial Chesapeake," in *Of Consuming Interests: The Style of Life in the Eighteenth Century,* edited by Cary Carson, Ronald Hoffman, and Peter J. Albert (Charlottesville: University Press of Virginia, 1994), pp. 59–166. Gloria L. Main, "The Standard of Living in Southern New England, 1640–1773," *William and Mary Quarterly* 45, no. 1 (January 1988), p. 127. Other recent volumes that address eighteenth-century consumerism include *Consumption and the World of Goods,* edited by John Brewer and Roy Porter (New York: Routledge, 1993); *The Consumption of Culture, 1600–1800: Image, Object, Text,* edited by Ann Bermingham and John Brewer (New York: Routledge, 1997); Richard Bushman, *Refinement of America: Persons, Houses, Cities* (New York: Vintage, 1992), p. 184.

4. Cary Carson, "The Consumer Revolution in British North America: Why Demand?," in *Of Consuming Interests,* p. 486; Ann Smart Martin, "Makers, Buyers, and Users: Consumerism as a Material Culture Framework," *Winterthur Portfolio* 28, nos. 2/3 (summer/autumn 1993), pp. 141–57.

5. *Pennsylvania Gazette,* March 15, 1733, Accessible Archives, item 1225. Unless otherwise noted, all further references to this newspaper are from Accessible Archives and only the date and item number will be cited. For a succinct discussion of politeness, see John Styles, "Georgian Britain, 1714–1837, Introduction," in *Design and the Decorative Arts, Britain 1500–1900,* edited by Michael Snodin and John Styles (London: V&A Publications, 2001), p. 183. For a more in-depth discussion of politeness, see Norbert Elias, *The Civilizing Process: The Development of Manners,* translated by Edmund Jephcott (New York: Urizen Books, 1978). For histories of tea drinking in Britain and America, see William H. Ukers, *All about Tea* (New York: Tea and Coffee Trade Journal Company, 1935); William H. Ukers, *The Romance of Tea: An Outline History of Tea and Tea-Drinking Through Sixteen Hundred Years* (New York: Alfred A. Knopf, 1936); and Rodris Roth, "Tea Drinking in 18th-Century America: Its Etiquette and Equipage," in *Material Life in America, 1600–1860,* edited by Robert Blair St. George (Boston: Northeastern University Press, 1988), pp. 439–62.

6. *Pennsylvania Gazette*, April 18, 1771, item 48630; and May 25, 1769, item 44688.

7. David S. Shields, *Civil Tongues and Polite Letters in British America* (Chapel Hill: University of North Carolina Press for the Omohundro Institute of Early American History and Culture, 1997), pp. 99–140.

8. Carson, "The Consumer Revolution in British North America: Why Demand?," pp. 586–92.

9. Roth, "Tea Drinking in 18th-Century America," p. 447.

10. Thornton, *Seventeenth-Century Decoration in England, France & Holland*, pp. 229–30. See p. 229, fig. 216, for a Javaese laquer tea table mounted on a circa 1680 English base. Also see Bowett, *English Furniture*, p. 25. London chair maker Thomas Phil sold chairs with sawn cabriole legs, described as "frames of ye newest fashion," to Edward Dryen of Canons Ashby in Northamptonshire in 1714 (see Nancy E. Richards and Nancy Goyne Evans, *New England Furniture at Winterthur: Queen Anne and Chippendale Periods* [Hanover, N.H.: University Press of New England for the Winterthur Museum, 1997], p. 27). Wallace B. Gusler was the first furniture scholar to suggest that the tea table illustrated in fig. 7 could be by Peter Scott. See Wallace B. Gusler, "The Tea Tables of Eastern Virginia," *Antiques* 135, no. 5 (May 1989): 1247. A dining table with related feet reputedly came from Robert Carter's house Corotomin, which burned in 1729 (the author thanks Luke Beckerdite for this information which is based on Carter family tradition). Bowett, *English Furniture*, p. 14. Ralph Edwards and Percy Macquoid, *The Dictionary of English Furniture from the Middle Ages to the Late Georgian Period*, 3 vols. (1924–1927; reprint and rev., London: Barra Books Ltd., 1983), 3:145–54. Ralph Edwards, *The Shorter Dictionary of English Furniture from the Middle Ages to the Late Georgian Period* (London: Country Life, Ltd., 1964), p. 528. For more on the possible Netherlandish influences on the development of the tilt-top tea table, see Thornton, *Seventeenth-Century Decoration in England, France & Holland*, p. 230; and Peter Thornton, *Authentic Décor: The Domestic Interior, 1720–1920* (New York: Viking, 1984), p. 79, no. 95.

11. For a succinct discussion of English names for tilt-top tables, see Richards and Evans, *New England Furniture at Winterthur*, p. 274, nt. 1. For Uriell's inventory, see card file, Museum of Early Southern Decorative Arts (hereafter cited MESDA), Winston-Salem, North Carolina. E. Milby Burton, *Charleston Furniture, 1700–1825* (Narberth, Pa.: Livingston Publishing Company for the Charleston Museum, 1955), p. 49. Jack L. Lindsey, *Worldly Goods: The Arts of Early Pennsylvania, 1680–1758* (Philadelphia: Philadelphia Museum of Art, 1999), p. 151. Among these unusual descriptors, English terms continued to appear in American records through the eighteenth century. The 1767 probate inventory of George Johnson of Fairfax County, Virginia, listed a "Moho Snap Table" valued at £1.1.0 (MESDA card file).

12. Kevin M. Sweeney, "Furniture and the Domestic Environment in Wethersfield, Connecticut, 1639–1800," in St. George, ed., *Material Life in America, 1600–1860*, p. 277. *Providence Price Agreement, 1757*, Crawford Papers, Rhode Island Historical Society, reprinted in Michael Moses, *Master Craftsmen of Newport* (Tenafly, N.J.: MMI Americana Press, 1984), p. 357. David L. Barquist, *American Tables and Looking Glasses in the Mabel Brady Garvan and Other Collections at Yale University* (New Haven, Conn.: Yale University Art Gallery, 1992), p. 233.

13. For early references to tea tables, see David B. Warren, Michael K. Brown, Elizabeth Ann Coleman, and Emily Ballew Neff, *American Decorative Arts and Paintings in the Bayou Bend Collection* (Princeton, N.J.: Princeton University Press for the Museum of Fine Arts, Houston, 1998), p. 36; and Barquist, *American Tables and Looking Glasses*, p. 90. The earliest known advertisement for "tea table ketches" appeared in the *Pennsylvania Gazette* in 1741 (Barquist, *American Tables and Looking Glasses*, p. 232; and William McPherson Hornor, Jr., *Blue Book, Philadelphia Furniture, William Penn to George Washington*, [Philadelphia: privately printed, 1935], p. 143).

14. The tea tables and stand shown in figures 9–11 are illustrated and discussed in Jack Lindsey, *Worldly Goods*, pp. 150–54, nos. 82, 83, 85, 99. Lindsey dated the earliest table (fig. 9) 1715–1735 and suggested that the faceted base block may be a transitional feature linking it stylistically to the stand (fig. 10) and tea table shown in figure 11. Although his proposal may be correct in this instance, faceted base blocks occur much later on furniture from Newport, Rhode Island. (See *Antiques* 94, no. 6 [December 1968]: 827; and Richards and Evans, *New England Furniture*, pp. 278–79, 287–88.) For more on the table illustrated in fig. 12, see Clement E. Conger and Alexandra W. Rollins, *Treasures of State: Fine and Decorative Arts in the Diplomatic Reception Rooms of the U.S. Department of State* (New York: Harry N. Abrams, 1991), p. 81. Gusler, "The Tea Tables of Eastern Virginia," pp. 1245–46; the example shown in fig. 9 of Gusler's article is not of the period.

15. Evidence regarding this type of turning is scant because no seventeenth- or eighteenth-century encyclopedias illustrate the process. Craftsmen probably used a lathe attachment similar to the "Arbor & Cross for Turning Stands," which survived in the workshop of the Dominy family of cabinetmakers in East Hampton, Long Island (see Charles F. Hummel, *With Hammer in Hand* [Charlottesville: University of Virginia Press for the Winterthur Museum, 1968], p. 90). Similar to modern day face-plates, the attachment had an iron cross with four holes for screws that engaged the stock. This allowed the workpiece to spin on a vertical plane. Many tabletops have four holes in the undersides measuring equal distances from the center point and from each other (see Patricia E. Kane, "The Palladian Style in Rhode Island Furniture: Fly Tea Tables," in *American Furniture*, edited by Luke Beckerdite [Hanover, N.H.: University Press of New England for the Chipstone Foundation, 1999], pp. 14–15, nt. 8). Even tops without such holes may have been turned. Some craftsman may have glued the top to a board that was attached the cross. The author thanks Michael S. Podmaniczky for his insights on these processes.

16. Glenn Adamson, "The Politics of the Caned Chair," in *American Furniture*, edited by Luke Beckerdite (Hanover, N.H.: University Press of New England for the Chipstone Foundation, 2002), pp. 175–206. For more on caned chair makers trading chair parts, see Benno Forman, *American Seating Furniture, 1630–1730, An Interpretive Catalog* (New York: W. W. Norton, 1988), pp. 248–49.

17. *Pennsylvania Gazette,* May 30, 1751, item 13033. J. Stewart Johnson, "New York Cabinetmaking prior to the Revolution" (master's thesis, University of Delaware, 1964), p. 28. Barquist, *American Tables and Looking Glasses,* pp. 232–23. "The Thomas Elfe Account Book," *South Carolina Historical and Genealogical Magazine* 36, no. 2 (April 1936): 57, 61.

18. *Pennsylvania Gazette,* December 19, 1771, item 50175. Also see an earlier version of the same advertisement on May 15, 1766, item 37944. *The Great River: Art and Society of the Connecticut Valley, 1635–1820,* edited by Gerald W. R. Ward and William N. Hosley, Jr. (Hartford, Conn.: Wadsworth Atheneum, 1985), p. 226, nt. 3. For a discussion of how craftsmen negotiated their exchange relationships in individual social economies, see Edward S. Cooke, Jr., *Making Furniture in Preindustrial America: The Social Economy of Newtown and Woodbury, Connecticut* (Baltimore, Md.: Johns Hopkins University Press, 1996), p. 5. For examples of the relationships between less specialized rural artisans in North Carolina, see John Bivins, Jr., *The Furniture of Coastal North Carolina, 1700–1820* (Chapel Hill: University of North Carolina Press for MESDA, 1985), pp. 60–63.

19. Helena Hayward and Pat Kirkham, *William and John Linnell: Eighteenth-Century London Furniture Makers,* 2 vols. (New York: Rizzoli International, 1980), 1:171. Nancy Ann Goyne, "Furniture Craftsmen in Philadelphia, 1760–1780. Their Role in Mercantile Society" (master's thesis, University of Delaware, 1963), p. 215.

20. Ward and Hosley eds., *The Great River,* pp. 225–26. Kane, "The Palladian Style in Rhode Island Furniture," pp. 7–9. The author thanks Wallace Gusler for this information.

21. Benno M. Forman, "Delaware Valley 'Crookt Foot' and Slat-Back Chairs: The Fussell-Savery Connection," *Winterthur Portfolio* 15, no. 1 (spring 1980): 46. For Savery labels, see Hornor, *Blue Book,* pls. 88–93. *Pennsylvania Gazette,* September 25, 1755, item 18764.

22. "The Thomas Elfe Account Book, 1765–1775," *South Carolina Historical and Genealogical Magazine,* 36, no. 2 (April 1935): 57, 61. Luke Beckerdite, "Immigrant Carvers and the Development of the Rococo Style in New York, 1750–70," in *American Furniture,* edited by Luke Beckerdite (Hanover, N.H.: University Press of New England for the Chipstone Foundation, 1996), pp. 246–47. Luke Beckerdite, "Philadelphia Carving Shops, Part III: Hercules Courtenay and His School," *Antiques* 131, no. 5 (May 1987): 1046. Leroy Graves and Luke Beckerdite, "New Insights on John Cadwalader's Commode-Seat Side Chairs," in *American Furniture,* edited by Luke Beckerdite (Hanover, N.H.: University Press of New England for the Chipstone Foundation, 2000), pp. 153–60.

23. Beckerdite, "Immigrant Carvers," pp. 249–55.

24. The author thanks Alan Miller and Luke Beckerdite for the information on the table illustrated in figure 24. Luke Beckerdite, "Philadelphia Carving Shops, Part II: Bernard and Jugiez," *Antiques* 128, no. 9 (September 1985): 505.

25. John J. McCusker and Russell R. Menard, *The Economy of British North America, 1607–1789* (Chapel Hill: University of North Carolina Press for the Omohundro Institute of Early American History and Culture, 1985), pp. 60–68, 268–69. Carson, "The Consumer Revolution in British North America: Why Demand?," p. 617.

26. Ronald L. Hurst and Jonathan Prown, *Southern Furniture 1680–1830, The Colonial Williamsburg Collection* (New York: Harry N. Abrams, 1997), p. 318. Ronald L. Hurst,

"Cabinetmakers and Related Tradesmen in Norfolk, Virginia, 1770–1820" (master's thesis, College of William and Mary, 1989), pp. 10, 15. Margaretta M. Lovell, "'Such Furniture as Will Be Most Profitable,' The Business of Cabinetmaking in Eighteenth-Century Newport," *Winterthur Portfolio* 26, no. 1 (spring 1991): 29–30. Hurst discusses the transfer of furniture-making traditions between American cities in "Cabinetmakers and Related Tradesmen in Norfolk," pp. 19–20. For more about the influence of London commerce and production on the rural Chesapeake, see Lois Green Carr and Lorena S. Walsh, "The Standard of Living in the Colonial Chesapeake," *William and Mary Quarterly* 45, no. 1 (January 1988): 139.

27. Albert Sack, "Regionalism in Early American Tea Tables," *Antiques* 131, no. 1 (January 1987): 248–63.

28. David Hancock, *Citizens of the World: London Merchants and Integration of the British Atlantic Community, 1735–1785* (Cambridge, Eng.: Cambridge University Press, 1995). John Bivins, Jr., "A Catalog of Northern Furniture with Southern Provenances," *Journal of Early Southern Decorative Arts* 15, no. 2 (May 1989): 61. John Bivins, Jr., "Rhode Island Influence in the Work of Two North Carolina Cabinetmakers," in *American Furniture,* edited by Luke Beckerdite (Hanover, N.H.: University Press of New England for the Chipstone Foundation, 1999), pp. 79–80. For Goodwin's table, see Brock Jobe and Myrna Kaye, *New England Furniture: The Colonial Era* (Boston: Houghton Mifflin Company, 1984), pp. 298–99.

29. Kane, "The Palladian Style in Rhode Island Furniture," pp. 1–2. In England the term "fly table" typically referred to a breakfast table with short leaf supports or "flys" (Christopher Gilbert, *The Life and Work of Thomas Chippendale,* 2 vols. [New York: Macmillan Publishing, Co., 1978], 1:302). Martha H. Willoughby, "The Accounts of Job Townsend, Jr.," in *American Furniture,* edited by Luke Beckerdite (Hanover, N.H: University Press of New England for the Chipstone Foundation, 1999), p. 131.

30. Jeanne Vibert Sloane, "John Cahoone and the Newport Furniture Industry," in *New England Furniture, Essays in Memory of Benno M. Forman,* edited by Brock Jobe (Boston: Society for the Preservation of New England Antiquities, 1987), pp. 88–112. Lovell, "'Such Furniture as Will Be Most Profitable,'" pp. 27–62. For more on the desk illustrated in fig. 38, see Luke Beckerdite, "The Early Furniture of Christopher and Job Townsend," in *American Furniture,* edited by Luke Beckerdite (Hanover, N.H.: University Press of New England for the Chipstone Foundation, 2000), p. 47. Beckerdite argues that many aspects of Newport case design and construction were developed to facilitate the furniture export trade.

31. McCusker and Menard, *The Economy of British North America,* p. 102; John J. McCusker, *Money and Exchange in Europe and America, 1600–1775, a Handbook* (Chapel Hill: University of North Carolina Press for the Omohundro Institute of Early American History and Culture, 1978), p. 133. Main, "The Standard of Living in Southern New England," p. 127. Kerry A. Trask, *In the Pursuit of Shadows: Massachusetts Millenialism and the Seven Years War* (New York: Garland Publishing, Inc., 1989), pp. 2–3. Kenneth Lockridge, "Land, Population, and the Evolution of New England Society 1630–1790," *Past and Present* 39 (April 1968): 68–69.

32. For a discussion about how some Pennsylvania German communities adopted and adapted Anglo-American designs, see Cynthia G. Falk, "Symbols of Assimilation or Status? The Meanings of Eighteenth-Century Houses in Coventry Township, Chester County, Pennsylvania," *Winterthur Portfolio* 33, no. 2/3 (summer 1998): 107–34.

33. T. H. Breen, "The Meanings of Things: Interpreting the Consumer Economy in the Eighteenth Century," in Brewer and Porter eds., *Consumption and the World of Goods,* p. 251.

34. For further discussion of the growing choices available to eighteenth-century consumers, see Martin, "Makers, Buyers, and Users," p. 155; and Breen, "'The Baubles of Britain': The American and Consumer Revolutions of the Eighteenth Century," in Carson, Hoffman, and Albert eds., *Of Consuming Interests,* p. 452; and Breen, "The Meanings of Things," p. 251.

35. Jonathan Prown and Richard Miller, "The Rococo, the Grotto, and the Philadelphia High Chest," in *American Furniture,* edited by Luke Beckerdite (Hanover, N.H.: University Press of New England for the Chipstone Foundation, 1996), p. 108.

36. For more on Harding, see Luke Beckerdite, "An Identity Crisis: Philadelphia and Baltimore Furniture Styles of the Mid-Eighteenth Century," in *Shaping a National Culture: The Philadelphia Experience, 1750–1800,* edited by Catherine E. Hutchins (Winterthur, Del.: Winterthur Museum, 1994), pp. 243–81. For more on furniture carving, see Luke Beckerdite, "Philadelphia Carving Shops, Part I: James Reynolds," *Antiques* 124, no. 5 (May 1984): 1120–33; and Beckerdite, "Philadelphia Carving Shops, Part II: Bernard and Jugiez," pp. 498–513; and Beckerdite, "Philadelphia Carving Shops, Part III: Hercules Courtenay and His School," pp. 1044–63; and Beckerdite, "Carving Practices in Eighteenth Century

Boston," in *New England Furniture: Essays In Memory of Benno M. Forman,* pp. 123–62; and Beckerdite, "Immigrant Carvers," pp. 233–65.

37. Christie's, "The Collection of Mr. and Mrs. James L. Britton," New York, January 16, 1999, lot 592. Prown and Miller, "The Rococo, the Grotto, and the Philadelphia High Chest," p. 105.

38. For the Providence price list, see Moses, *Master Craftsmen of Newport,* p. 357. For the Philadelphia price list, see Martin Eli Weil, "A Cabinetmaker's Price Book," *American Furniture and Its Makers,* edited by Ian M. G. Quimby (Chicago, Ill.: University of Chicago Press for the Winterthur Museum, 1979), p. 187. The 1772 Philadelphia price list only includes mahogany and walnut, but maple was an option available throughout the region.

39. Weil, "A Cabinetmaker's Price Book," p. 187. "The Thomas Elfe Account Book, 1765–1775," *South Carolina Historical and Genealogical Magazine* 37, no. 4 (October 1936): 151.

40. Willoughby, "The Accounts of Job Townsend, Jr.," pp. 109–61.

41. For more on the Scott tea tables and stand, see Gusler, "The Tea Tables of Eastern Virginia," pp. 1246–51. Affleck's bill to Cadwalader is transcribed in Nicholas B. Wainwright, *The House and Furniture of General John Cadwalader* (Philadelphia: Historical Society of Pennsylvania, 1964), p. 44.

42. Several Charleston tables with pierced C-scrolls on the undersides of the legs are known, the most elaborate of which is in the collection of the Chipstone Foundation.

43. Carole Shammas, "The Decline of Textile Prices in England and British America prior to the Revolution," *Economic History Review,* n.s., 47, no. 3 (August 1994): 483–507 (JSTOR, University of Michigan, <http://links.jstor.org/sici?sici>, p. 402). Adamson, "The Politics of the Caned Chair," pp. 174–206.

44. The Stevenson tables are on view at the Philadelphia Museum of Art.

45. Several authors discuss the piecemeal acquisition of consumer goods. See Carr and Walsh, "The Standard of Living in the Colonial Chesapeake," p. 141; and Main, "The Standard of Living in Southern New England," p. 128; and Sweeney, "Furniture and the Domestic Environment in Wethersfield," p. 288. In *Consumer Behavior and Material Culture in Britain,* p. 28, Lorna Weatherill demonstrated that between 1690 and 1725 middling consumers in England acquired equipment for brewing and drinking tea. Ann Smart Martin, "'Fashionable Sugar Dishes, Latest Fashion Ware': The Creamware Revolution in the Eighteenth-Century Chesapeake," *Historical Archaeology of the Chesapeake,* edited by Paul A. Shackel and Barbara J. Little (Washington, D. C.: Smithsonian Institution Press, 1994), p. 181. Carson, "The Consumer Revolution in Britain and America: Why Demand?," p. 505.

46. Martin, "Fashionable Sugar Dishes," pp. 169–187. McKendrick et al., *The Birth of a Consumer Society,* p. 2.

47. Many families took their tea on Pembroke or breakfast tables by 1790. Martin, "Fashionable Sugar Dishes," p. 174. (The percentages for "Cream/pearlware" that appear in the "1750–59" column should appear in the "1770–79" column.)

48. This version of "A Ladies' Adieu to her Tea Table" appeared in the *Pennsylvania Gazette,* February 2, 1774, item 54810. Roth, "Tea Drinking in 18th-Century America," p. 444.

Figure 1   The Morris suite of painted furniture
shown in the oval room from Willow Brook—
one of the houses depicted on the furniture—
now installed in the Baltimore Museum of Art.
(Courtesy, Baltimore Museum of Art; gift of the
city of Baltimore, installation and renovation
made possible by contributors to the Willow
Brook Fund.) The card table in the center of the
room is from the Buchanan suite.

Lance Humphries

Provenance,
Patronage,
and Perception:
The Morris Suite
of Baltimore
Painted Furniture

▼ I N B A L T I M O R E , Maryland, the history of patronage, use, and collecting of painted furniture spans over two centuries. One of the most fascinating and complex suites (fig. 1) is associated with John B. Morris, a nineteenth-century Baltimore lawyer, businessman, and banker. Renowned for its imagery, which includes views of country estates in and around the city, this suite has received a great deal of attention in scholarly publications. Much about this furniture has been discovered, yet the motivation for its creation has remained a mystery. The Morris suite continues to offer a particularly rich opportunity to explore how objects were shaped not only by their makers, but also by those who commissioned them, and how their existence was determined by cultural factors that fostered and encouraged a need for their production.

The Morris suite is remarkable for several reasons, not the least being its size. Comprised of ten armchairs, two settees, and a pier table, the suite may have included at least two additional chairs. Although not supported by contemporary documentation, the suite was apparently made by the renowned Baltimore furniture makers John and Hugh Finlay and decorated with seventeen medallions depicting country houses and other buildings in and around the city by landscape painter Francis Guy (see app. 1–16 and pier table). The latter's oil on canvas paintings often feature local country seats depicted in a similar manner. Advertisements by the Finlays suggest that the suite dates circa 1803–1805. The brothers illustrated a side chair of the same form as the armchairs in the Morris suite in 1803 (fig. 2) and offered to produce furniture "with or without views adjacent to the city" through 1804.[1]

Although there is no evidence they owned the Morris suite, members of the Gilmor family of Baltimore owned two of the houses depicted on the

John and Hugh Finley

HAVE opened a fhop at No. 190½, Market-ftreet, oppofite Mr Peter Wyant's inn, where they have for fale, and make to any pattern, all kinds of FANCY and JAPANNED FURNITURE, viz.

Japanned and gilt card, pier, tea, dreffing, writing and fhaving TABLES, with or without views adjacent to the city.

Ditto cane feats, rufh and windfor CHAIRS, with or without views.

Ditto cane feats, rufh and windfor SETTEES, with or without views.

Ditto Window and Recefs Seats.

Ditto Wafh and Candle Stands.

Ditto Fire and Candle Screens.

Ditto   Ditto.   with views.

Ditto Bedfteads, and Bed and Window Cornices, &c.

Which they warrant equal to any imported.

They as ufual execute Coach, Sign and Ornamental Painting.

Military ftandards, drums, mafonic aprons, all kinds of filk transparencies, &c. in the neateft manner, and on the fhorteft notice.

☞ Old chairs repainted.

N. B. Apply as above or at their manufactory No. 3, South Frederick-ftreet.

October 24.   d

Figure 2 Advertisement by John and Hugh Finlay in the October 24, 1803, issue of the *Federal Gazette & Baltimore Daily Advertiser.* (Courtesy, Maryland Historical Society.) This advertisement for the Finlay firm depicts a side chair of the same form as the armchairs in the Morris suite, with the splat in the form of two gothic-arched panels flanking a central tablet.

Figure 3 Pier table, Baltimore, Maryland, 1815–1830. Yellow pine and maple; rosewood graining, gilt plaster, hollow cast lead (mono-pedia), ormolu, and glass. H. 37¼", W. 45", D. 23⅛". (Courtesy, Baltimore Museum of Art; bequest of Elizabeth Curzon Hoffman Wing, in memory of Hanson Rawlings Duval, Jr.) The description of Robert Gilmor, Jr.'s pier table suggests that this form may date earlier than traditionally believed.

Figure 4 Sofa illustrated in *Catalogue of the Celebrated Dr. William H. Crim Collection of Genuine Antiques, To be Sold . . . In the Fourth Regiment Armory, Beginning Wednesday, April 22ᵈ 1903* (Baltimore, Md.: A. O. Kirkland, 1903), lot 1127.

furniture: Beech Hill, the country residence of Robert Gilmor, Sr., and The Vineyard, the country estate of his son William Gilmor (app. 5, 16). Surprisingly, none of the houses can be associated with Robert's eldest son, Robert Jr., one of the country's most prominent art collectors and, apparently, the most aesthetically inclined member of the family. However, documentary evidence regarding Robert Jr.'s possessions and their dispersal demonstrates that throughout the nineteenth and early twentieth centuries wealthy and socially prominent Baltimoreans often bought furniture at auction from the sales of various family members as well as those of their social peers. Extant auction catalogues document only a fraction of the sales that occurred and an even smaller percentage of the furniture that changed hands in the city. In many instances, these consumption patterns make traditions of original family ownership problematic. As is the case with the Morris suite, many pieces of Baltimore furniture cannot be documented before the late nineteenth century.[2]

Several examples of painted furniture that reportedly belonged to Robert Gilmor, Jr., illustrate this problem. A card table (Maryland Historical Society) has been linked to him through oral tradition, and a lounge (Hampton National Historic Site) has been associated with him through its descent in the family of his brother William. Although it is possible that Gilmor was the original owner of both objects, there is no documentary evidence to support that conclusion. He clearly owned many pieces of furniture that have not been identified. In 1815, Harriott Horry of Charleston, South Carolina, noted that his drawing room contained furniture upholstered in crimson damask: "the outsides of the arms of the Sofas are a sort of griffin in Bronze with brass or gilt heads, a marble slab supported in the same manner in the middle pier has a looking glass fixed under it and the chairs have loose cushions with tassels." The pier table illustrated in figure 3 may have also have belonged to Gilmor. Oral tradition maintained that the table came from the Hoffman family house at Cathedral and Franklin Streets, but it may have been acquired at the 1910 sale of J. Latimer Hoffman—a cousin and collateral descendant of Gilmor who lived further east on Franklin. Similarly, Gilmor may have owned the sofa (fig. 4) that subsequently entered the antique collection of Baltimore physician William H. Crim. This elaborate seating form had metal supports like those mentioned in Horry's diary.[3]

Although Crim's sale had an illustrated catalogue issued by A. O. Kirkland in 1903, published records for auctions held during the early to mid-nineteenth century are scarce. A notable exception is the estate sale of John Eager Howard, whose house Belvidere is depicted on the Morris suite (app. 1). Copies of the auction catalogue and a manuscript list of purchasers survive, indicating that Howard had three sets of painted furniture: a blue suite comprised of chairs, settees, and brackets; a set of white armchairs; and a yellow suite comprised of settees, armchairs, and window benches. Howard's sons, Benjamin and Charles, bought the white and blue sets, and Charles Carnan Ridgely of Hampton acquired the yellow (see figs. 5–6).[4]

Figure 5 Armchair, Baltimore, Maryland, 1800–1806. Maple and walnut . H. 32¾", W. 21", D. 16". (Collection of Hampton National Historic Site, National Park Service; photo, Gavin Ashworth.)

Figure 6 Detail of the decoration on the crest rail of the armchair illustrated in fig. 5. (Photo, Gavin Ashworth.) Unlike the houses on the Morris suite, decorations like that on the crest rail of this chair could have been painted by a craftsman from images in pattern books.

Figure 7 Side chair, Baltimore, Maryland, 1810–1820. Maple and cherry. H. 34", W. 20½", D. 24¼". (Collection of Mrs. George M. Kaufman; photo, Gavin Ashworth.) Recent pigment analysis indicates that this suite of chairs is painted with chrome yellow. In 1814 Robert Gilmor wrote that chromate of iron was found in the Bare Hills area seven miles north of Baltimore on the Falls turnpike: "Perhaps in no part of the world has so much been discovered at one place: it furnishes the means of preparing the beautiful paint called the chromic yellow, with which carriages and furniture are now painted in Baltimore." Gilmor's observation that the pigment was used on carriages and furniture suggests that the Finlays—who worked in both trades—may have been using chrome yellow as early as 1813. Considering the abundant local supply, the use of this pigment may have reflected local pride. See Robert Gilmor, Jr., "A Descriptive catalogue of Minerals occurring in the vicinity of Baltimore," *American Mineralogical Journal* 1, no. 4 (1814): 231–32. In 1818 Gilmor presented examples of granular and octahedral chromate of iron from the Bare Hills to the British Museum. He noted that the octahedral examples were the first "that had ever been seen in Europe" (Henry Ellis, British Museum, to Robert Gilmor, Jr., January 10, 1818, private collection).

Unlike Howard's sets, many important pieces of Baltimore painted furniture remain poorly documented. Furniture scholars have long maintained that the set of chairs represented by the example illustrated in figure 7 was associated with the Abell family or their relatives throughout the nineteenth century. However, the branch of the Abell family that owned them at the turn of the twentieth century bought furniture in the classical style at local auctions. Mrs. Edwin Franklin Abell, for example, purchased the sofa at the Crim sale (fig. 4). Therefore, the Abells could have acquired the side chairs now associated with them through avenues other than family descent. The same can be said of John B. Morris and the painted suite traditionally associated with him.[5]

Although the forms of the Morris suite are elegant and refined, it is their decoration that sets them apart from most other painted furniture (see figs. 8, 9). The extraordinary nature of this work is amply demonstrated by comparing it to that found on a suite of painted furniture made for the Buchanan family of Baltimore and traditionally attributed to John and Hugh Finlay. The Buchanan suite included at least sixteen pieces: ten side chairs, two window seats, two card tables, a settee, and a pier table

Figure 8 Armchair attributed to the shop of John and Hugh Finlay with crest rail medallion attributed to Francis Guy, Baltimore, Maryland, 1803–1805. Maple and ash. H. 33¾", W. 21⅝", D. 20¹⁵⁄₁₆". (Courtesy, Baltimore Museum of Art, gift of Lydia Howard de Roth and Nancy H. DeFord Venable in memory of their mother Lydia Howard DeFord and Purchase Fund; photo, Gavin Ashworth.)

Figure 9 Detail of the decoration on the crest rail of the armchair illustrated in fig. 8. (Photo, Gavin Ashworth.)

(figs. 10–15, 31, 32). Attrition may account for the fact that both suites have ten chairs, since sets typically came in multiples of six. The patron who commissioned the Morris suite chose the more costly armchair form—apparently for a room where cards were not intended to be played—and

Figure 10 Side chair attributed to the shop of John and Hugh Finlay, Baltimore, Maryland, 1803–1806. Maple, ash, and mahogany. H. 33¼", W. 19", D. 19¼". (Courtesy, Baltimore Museum of Art, George C. Genkins Fund by exchange; photo, Gavin Ashworth.) This chair is from the Buchanan suite.

Figure 11 Detail of the decoration on the crest rail of the side chair illustrated in fig. 10. (Photo, Gavin Ashworth.)

specified that the crest rails and skirts of all the furniture be decorated with paintings of buildings. Only the pier table and card tables from the Buchanan suite are decorated in that manner (figs. 12–15, 32, 33). The crest rails on all of the chairs and window seats are embellished with various armorial, musical, and floral trophies (see figs. 10, 11).[6]

The extravagant display of effort in the decoration of the Morris suite is its most notable feature. Decorators in the Finlays' shop may have relied on designs in drawing books to paint trophies like those on the Buchanan suite as well as imaginary landscapes; however, the depiction of actual buildings required the artist to visit the site. Assuming that Francis Guy was responsible for the views on the Morris suite, he undoubtedly made preliminary sketches in the field before executing the paintings in his

Figure 12 Card table attributed to the shop of John and Hugh Finlay with skirt medallion attributed to Francis Guy, Baltimore, Maryland, 1803–1806. Maple and mahogany veneer with yellow pine and oak. H. 30⅜", W. 38¾", D. 17³⁄₁₆" (closed). (Courtesy, Baltimore Museum of Art, Friends of the American Wing Fund; photo, Gavin Ashworth.) The mate to this table from the Buchanan suite is illustrated in figs. 32 and 33.

Figure 13 Detail of the decoration on the skirt of the card table illustrated in fig. 12 showing the panel depicting a country house of the Buchanan family of Baltimore. (Photo, Gavin Ashworth.)

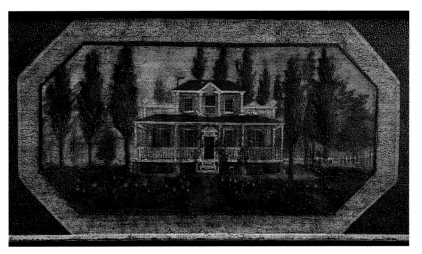

Figure 14 Pier table attributed to the shop of John and Hugh Finlay with skirt medallion attributed to Francis Guy, Baltimore, Maryland, 1803–1806. Yellow pine, tulip poplar, and maple. H. 35⅞", W. 45⅛", D. 20". (Courtesy, Baltimore Museum of Art, George C. Jenkins Fund by exchange; photo, Gavin Ashworth.) This pier table is from the Buchanan suite.

Figure 15 Detail of the decoration on the skirt of the pier table illustrated in fig. 14. (Photo, Gavin Ashworth.) This panel depicts houses on Gay Street traditionally thought to have been built by William Buchanan for his daughters.

studio or the Finlays' shop. Although Guy painted oil on canvas landscapes depicting three of the houses on the suite and could have reused some of his own studies, the chronology of these images is not known. The suite could be earlier than the landscapes. In an era before photography and easily obtained transportation, the expense and effort that went into obtaining the seventeen views of buildings on the Morris suite would have been obvious to anyone using the furniture—and that was undoubtedly the whole point of the commission.[7]

One of the earliest published descriptions of the Morris furniture is in Letitia Stockett's *Baltimore: A Not Too Serious History* (1928). While touring the Mount Vernon area, she stopped at 401 North Charles Street, the former residence of Francis Key Howard (1826–1872) and his wife Lydia E. Hollingsworth Morris (d. 1921). Lydia's parents John B. (1785–1874) and Anne Marie (Hollingsworth) Morris (d. 1847) have traditionally been the earliest owners associated with the painted suite. Stockett observed that the Howards' house had been furnished with "beautiful and lovely things," including a set of furniture (figs. 16, 17) made "by Lindley [*sic*] and decorated with miniatures of famous country estates in and near Baltimore." After noting that several of the houses were no longer standing, Stockett expressed her concern about where these "chairs and tables so intimately

Figure 16 Circa 1927 photograph of the interior of 401 North Charles Street, Baltimore, Maryland. (Courtesy, Maryland Historical Society.) This view shows the "yellow drawing room" in the residence of the Frank Key Howard family. The settee with Montebello depicted in the center of its crest rail and two chairs from the Morris suite are visible. One of the chairs has Grace Hill depicted on its crest rail.

Figure 17 Circa 1927 photograph of the interior of 401 North Charles Street, Baltimore, Maryland. (Courtesy, Maryland Historical Society.) This view shows the "pink room" in the residence of the Frank Key Howard family. The settee with the Banks of the City depicted in the center of its crest rail and the pier table from the Morris suite are visible in the far right and left.

associated with our history will find a home." Her anxiety probably arose from the recent sale of the house, the dismantling of its contents, and the marriage of two daughters who would live elsewhere.[8]

By the 1930s, the Morris suite was achieving local and national distinction, not only as superb examples of Maryland decorative arts, but, as Stockett had suggested, as a record of early Baltimore houses that had largely disappeared. In 1930 one of the chairs appeared in an article on Maryland furniture in *Antiques,* and in 1936 the Peale Museum included photographs of the buildings depicted on the suite in an exhibition on early Baltimore country houses. Later in that same year, the *Index of American Design* recorded the chair with Willow Brook depicted on its crest rail (fig. 18).

Figure 18 Lillian Causey, rendering of an armchair from the Morris suite, ca. 1936. Watercolor, gold ink, and graphite on paper. 14" x 10½". (Courtesy, National Gallery of Art.) Charles Morris Howard owned this chair when Causey painted it.

The rendering was subsequently included in an exhibition at the National Museum in Washington, D.C., devoted to the fruits of this WPA project. By 1937, when furniture historian Edgar G. Miller illustrated several pieces from the suite in his two-volume book, *American Antique Furniture,* the suite had become well established in the canon of American furniture. Over the next several years the Baltimore Museum of Art received most of the furniture in the Morris suite on loan (with the exception of two chairs), and in 1966 the institution acquired the entire suite.[9]

When the photographs of the suite were exhibited at the Peale Museum in 1936, the *Baltimore Sun* reported that the furniture had been "used at Claremont (or Clearmont), the country home of the late John B. Morris." Since Morris' daughter Lydia and her husband Frank Key Howard were deceased at that time, the *Sun*'s information apparently came from their surviving children, Lydia Howard DeFord or Charles Morris Howard. However, after the suite came to the Baltimore Museum of Art, tradition asserted that the furniture had been "made for" John B. Morris in about 1805, and "had never been out of the family of its original owner." This interpretation persisted until 1981, when decorative arts scholar Stiles Colwill posited that John B. Morris was not yet living in Baltimore and was too young to have commissioned the suite. Colwill suggested that Morris might have acquired the furniture second hand sometime after his marriage in 1817. Although Colwill's theory is probably correct, there is no documentation placing the suite in Morris' possession.[10]

Stockett failed to publish any information about the history of the furniture, but she apparently knew of the list associated with it. Written on stationary from 401 North Charles Street, this list and a nearly identical one penned by the same hand (private collection) are the oldest manuscripts pertaining to the suite. Early accounts stated that an "old family memorandum" accompanied the furniture, but the lists are relatively modern. Both pieces of stationary have 1904 watermarks, which indicate that the lists were made between that date and before 1928, when Stockett misread "Lindley for Findlay."[11]

The manuscript list illustrated in figures 19 and 20 is titled "Names of Country Seats/ on the Clermont Furniture" on the outside and "List of

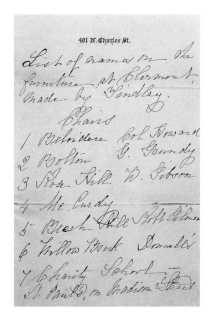
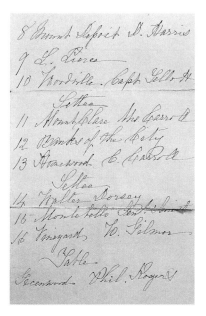

names on the/ furniture, at Clermont,/ made by Findlay" on the inside. These inscriptions establish that the furniture was at this country house northwest of Baltimore by the twentieth century and that it possibly remained there until it was moved to 401 North Charles Street, photographed in situ, and apparently removed by circa 1928. Although the precise date that John B. Morris acquired Clermont is not known, he either rented or owned it by 1835. In July of that year, his sister-in-law Lydia E. Hollingsworth wrote that the family would be spending the summer there to avoid the heat. Morris subsequently gave or sold Clermont to his daughter Lydia and her husband, who were recorded as the owners in 1873.[12]

By the turn of the twentieth century when the list was made, whatever Lydia Morris Howard knew about the history of the suite consisted of very old memories, because her father had been deceased for nearly thirty years and her mother for even longer. Considering that the furniture is at least a century older than the list, some caution should be taken regarding the manuscript's accuracy. In the absence of a contemporary bill of sale, it raises important questions about knowledge of the Finlays' work at the beginning of the twentieth century. Why this list was made is not known, but two scenarios regarding its creation seem likely—the Howards either copied or adapted an earlier list, or they made a list for the first time. With the exception of the pier table, which is not numbered on the manuscript, the numerals on the list correspond with those painted on the rear seat rails of the chairs and settees (see fig. 21). These numbers were probably

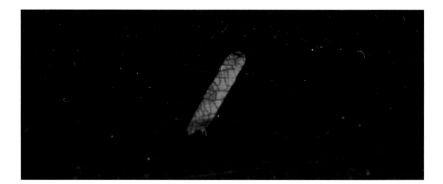

Figure 21 Detail showing the *"1"* mark on the rear seat rail of the armchair with Belvidere depicted on its crest rail (app. 1). (Photo, Gavin Ashworth.) The slant of the numbers on the Morris suite is similar to that of the numbers on the manuscript lists illustrated in figs. 19 and 20. These numbers may be by the same hand.

added to the suite when the list was made since the numerals on the seating furniture and the document appear to be by the same hand. Although Lydia Morris Howard may have been involved in making the list, her daughter Lydia Howard DeFord probably wrote it. It cannot be a coincidence that Belvidere, the ancestral country seat of Lydia DeFord's great-grandfather, John Eager Howard, is number one on the list. The primacy of this home would only have been this important to John Eager Howard or his descendants, particularly since no Morris family house is depicted on the furniture.[13]

Although the suite has been associated with John B. Morris since the 1930s, the furniture has an alternate provenance. The earliest reference to the suite—the catalogue of a 1914 Baltimore exhibition celebrating the centennial of the writing of the Star Spangled Banner—noted that the furniture belonged to Lydia Morris Howard, was loaned by her daughter Miss Nancy H. Howard, and came from Belvidere. In this exhibition the Morris pieces, which were apparently one of the most significant attractions, were complemented by furniture from the Ridgely family that was originally from Belvidere (see fig. 5). Catalogued one after the other, the similar provenance was undoubtedly thought to be important. By this time the Ridgelys were also descendants of John Eager Howard, so it is highly likely that these cousins knew each other and their furniture. The Belvidere provenance for the Morris furniture was repeated fourteen years later when Lydia Howard DeFord loaned one of the settees and three chairs for an exhibition at Homewood House on the campus of Johns Hopkins University. The catalogue noted that the furniture was originally from Belvidere, "the home of John Eager Howard." This Howard-Belvidere provenance, which would have been tremendously interesting and important to Baltimore audiences, was never published after 1928. Nancy H. Howard died unmarried in 1926, and perhaps with her the origin of the Belvidere provenance. However, her estate records indicate that before her death the suite was divided between Lydia Morris Howard's children, although the furniture would later be reunited as members of Nancy's generation died. Lydia's planned division of the furniture may explain the creation of multiple copies of the manuscript list describing the suite. Although Nancy's sister Lydia Howard DeFord may have told the organizers of the Homewood exhibition that her furniture came from Belvidere, the same pieces were published with the Morris family provenance by the late 1930s as were two chairs from the suite owned by her brother Charles Morris Howard. The Morris provenance was apparently first put forward when photographs of the images were exhibited at the Peale Museum in 1936.[14]

The Belvidere provenance for the Morris suite is unlikely. Frank Key Howard's father Charles did purchase a suite of blue painted furniture at his father's sale that was similar in composition to the Morris suite, but it is doubtful that the auctioneer would have mistaken blue for black. Moreover, John Eager Howard's blue suite did not have a pier table and included side chairs rather than armchairs. Perhaps the 1936 exhibition at the Peale Museum brought the Belvidere auction catalogue to the attention of Lydia Morris Howard's children, encouraging them to revise their thoughts on the origin of their suite. The Howards—or those who assembled the 1914 and 1928 catalogues—may simply have believed the furniture was from Belvidere because that house is depicted on the Morris suite and was at the time owned by descendants of John Eager Howard. Why, however, would Howard have commissioned a suite of furniture and placed his house on a chair, while using the larger reserve on the pier table for an image of a Rogers family house (see figs. 24, 25)?[15]

The creation of the manuscript list identifying the buildings on the suite would seem to be a Colonial Revival exercise in recapturing history. A 1914 newspaper article by Amy D'Arcy Wetmore extolled the virtues of these country seats and lamented the fact that they were vanishing as the city expanded. Since the Howards' methods of identifying the houses are not known, it is difficult to judge the accuracy of their lists. If they were working from an earlier manuscript, it may have contained only last names and not identified the respective houses. Three of the names on the list ("McCurdy," "L. Pierce," and "Walter Dorsey") do not have property designated (figs. 19, 20), which suggests that the Howards were not able to figure these out. Even after the suite came to the Baltimore Museum of Art, difficulty arose in attempting to learn more about the various buildings, and some of the identifications remain uncertain.[16]

Many of these buildings were torn down without ever being photographed, and conclusive identification of several of the structures depicted on the suite may not be possible. For nearly a century, the images on the suite have been treated as irrefutable evidence of how the buildings actually appeared, thus the suite has perpetuated the identifications found on the manuscript list. Confident attributions are possible for approximately two thirds of the seventeen buildings, because photographs, paintings, or prints offer some visual evidence to corroborate the identifications on the Howards' list. There are obvious mistakes, including numbers 3 "Rose Hill W. Gibson," and 4 "McCurdy" (app. 3 and 4). The depictions of Rose Hill on Warner & Hanna's 1801 map of Baltimore (figs. 22, 23) and in the background of Francis Guy's views of Bolton indicate that William Gibson's house was a five-bay Georgian building with a central pediment, whereas the house painted on the chair numbered 3 is only three bays wide. This

Figure 22 WARNER & HANNA's PLAN *of the City and Environs of Baltimore Respectfully dedicated to the Mayor City Council and Citizens thereof by the Proprietors, 1801.* (Courtesy, Maryland Historical Society.)

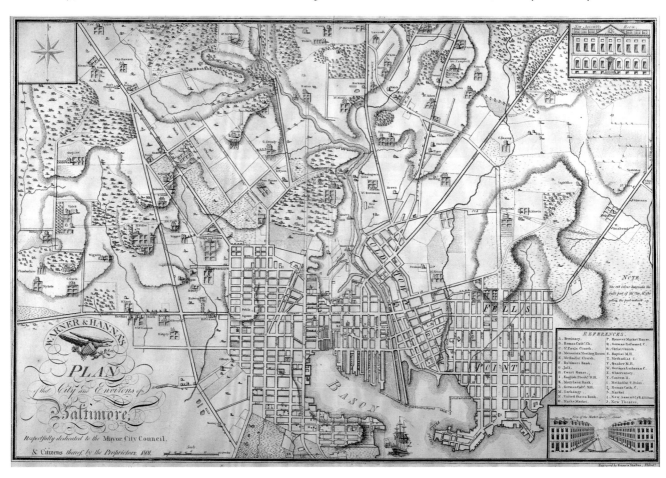

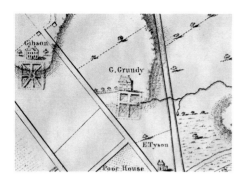

Figure 23   Detail of the map illustrated in fig. 22 showing William Gibson's house Rose Hill northwest of George Grundy's house Bolton. Both houses are similarly depicted on chairs in the Morris suite.

has led scholars to believe that numbers 3 and 4 are simply reversed, and that the house depicted on chair number 3 was Hugh McCurdy's residence Grace Hill. However, an 1803 insurance policy issued by the Baltimore Equitable Society suggests that his country seat was five bays wide and had a raised basement and a balcony or porch extending across its long side, making it highly unlikely that this building was the one depicted on the chair numbered 3.[17]

The uncertainty in these identifications is important. Unlike previous interpretations of the Morris suite, which considered the decoration as merely representative views of important country houses in the Baltimore area, this article posits that the houses and buildings depicted on the furniture are bound together in a nexus of social connections specific to only one individual or patron. While the owners of these buildings do not easily coalesce into a readily identifiable matrix, they were among the elite of Baltimore society. Some of the property owners were from old Maryland families, such as John Eager Howard of Belvidere, and Charles Carroll, Jr., of Homewood. Others were from families that became prominent after the Revolutionary War, and some, like the Gilmors, had arrived in Baltimore during the last quarter of the eighteenth century. Most of the owners were Episcopalians or Presbyterians, and one, Charles Carroll, Jr., was Catholic. Some of those whose houses are on the suite were Federalists, whereas others were Republicans. John Eager Howard and Samuel Smith (Montebello), for example, were staunch political rivals. These two men may have been the most politically powerful individuals represented on the suite, although the placement of their country houses, on a chair and settee, respectively, does not accord them much prominence or equality.[18]

If the representation of important houses was the sole reason for the depiction of these buildings on the suite, it is difficult to explain why certain ones were omitted. Charles Carnan Ridgely's country house Hampton is not represented, yet it was one of the most sophisticated and imposing domestic buildings in the state. Some of the houses depicted on the suite were brand new, whereas others were not, and there is considerable variation in their apparent cost, style, and architectural significance (see app.). William Gilmor's The Vineyard is a modest dwelling with an end gable roof, and William Gibson's Rose Hill and Jeremiah Yellott's Woodville are rather simple five-bay Georgian structures with central pediments. Warner & Hanna's map (fig. 22) shows many examples of similar houses, but it does not include all of the buildings depicted on the suite. Some of the houses represented on the furniture were built after the map's publication, and some may have been omitted for practical reasons. The location of Willow Brook is covered by the dedicatory legend, and Homewood and The Vineyard were much further north than the area represented. Considering the geographic range covered by the buildings depicted on the suite, it is clear that dozens if not hundreds of other houses could have been chosen but were not. All of these factors point to a very specific reason for choosing the depicted structures.[19]

Figure 24 Pier table attributed to the shop of John and Hugh Finlay with skirt medallion attributed to Francis Guy, Baltimore, Maryland, 1803–1805. Maple; marble. H. 36⅜", W. 48⅜", D. 24⅛". (Courtesy, Baltimore Museum of Art, gift of Lydia Howard de Roth and Nancy H. DeFord Venable in memory of their mother Lydia Howard DeFord and Purchase Fund; photo, Gavin Ashworth.)

Figure 25 Detail of the decoration on the skirt of the pier table illustrated in fig. 24. (Photo, Gavin Ashworth.)

Until all of the houses can be firmly identified, theories regarding the link that connects them remain in the realm of speculation. However, several possibilities warrant exploration, including the centrality of the pier table to the suite and the preeminence of the image on that piece (figs. 24, 25). The image of the house represented on the skirt is nearly twice as large as the houses on the crest rails of the chairs and settees and would have been the only image visible when the furniture was in use; all of the remaining images would have been covered by the sitters. If the pier table was the only one in the suite—which appears to have been the case with several surviving sets—the image chosen for it must have been even more important. The fact that the table does not have a numeral on its rear rail and is not numbered on the Howard list also suggests that it may not have had a mate.[20]

The Howard list identifies the house on the pier table as Greenwood, the country residence of Philip Rogers, a brother of the more famous Nicholas Rogers. The image is somewhat damaged, but a chair from another partial suite of furniture has the same view on its crest rail (figs. 40, 41). No documentation accompanied the chair, but the house depicted on it has been

Figure 26 Francis Guy, *View of the Seat of Colonel Rodgers, Near Baltimore*, ca. 1811. Oil on canvas. 18⅞" x 31¾". (Courtesy, Maryland Historical Society; bequest of Mrs. Geneva D. Richardson.) Guy eliminated some details. By 1811 Druid Hill was stuccoed and painted yellow.

Figure 27 Circa 1860 photograph of Druid Hill. (Courtesy, Maryland Historical Society.) This image shows the house with the front portico largely removed at the time the dwelling was being converted into a pavilion for Druid Hill Park.

published as Greenwood based on the pier table image. The dwelling is highly unusual among those represented on the suite and among country houses in the Baltimore vicinity. It is a one-story building above a raised basement with a crowning balustrade and a central parapet with a carved swag. In form, this house appears to be nearly identical to Druid Hill, the country residence built by Philip Rogers' brother Nicholas, who was an amateur architect (figs. 26, 27). Several authors have stated that Nicholas Rogers designed a very similar house for Philip—based solely on the image on the Morris suite—but such an occurrence seems unlikely.[21]

Little of Nicholas Rogers' architecture survives, but his known work suggests that he experimented with different styles, forms, and motifs. There is no reason to believe that he would abandon this proclivity and design a house identical to Druid Hill for his brother. As a gentleman architect, Rogers realized that houses could be extensions of an owner's

Figure 28 Charles-Balthazar-Julien Févret de St. Mémin, *Harriet Rogers,* Baltimore, Maryland, ca. 1806. (Courtesy, Maryland Historical Society; gift of Helen Hubbard, Mrs. Walter Oakman, and the estate of Mrs. J. H. Ten Eyck Burr.) While in Baltimore, Saint-Mémin depicted several sitters with landscape backgrounds. Of the firmly identified images, that depicting Harriet Rogers, the daughter of Nicholas and Eleanor Rogers, is the only one in which a residence of the sitter is shown, suggesting that the Rogers family strongly identified themselves with Druid Hill.

personal identity as well as emblems for subsequent generations. This was certainly true of his family. Druid Hill figures prominently in the background of Charles-Balthazar-Julien Févret de St. Mémin's profile portrait of Rogers' only daughter Harriet (fig. 28).[22]

If Philip's house was identical to Druid Hill, how would contemporary observers know which Rogers house was being referenced in the suite of painted furniture? Topography and garden plantings may have provided clues, as is the case with similar five-bay Georgian structures like Rose Hill (fig. 23, app. 4) and Woodville (app. 10); however, the house on the pier table appears elevated, resembling the hillside setting of Druid Hill (see fig. 26).

Other evidence may have led architectural historian Michael Trostel to speculate that the house on the pier table represents Druid Hill rather than Greenwood. The image long assumed to be Greenwood looks nothing like the structure identified as Philip Rogers' residence on Warner & Hanna's map (fig. 29). It appears that the latter house was destroyed and replaced

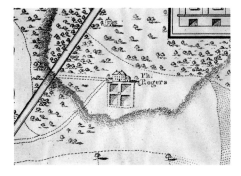

Figure 29 Detail of the map illustrated in fig. 22 showing Philip Rogers' house Greenwood. The house apparently burned shortly after this map was made and was replaced by another structure of a different form.

with a new one by 1801. An insurance policy issued by the Baltimore Equitable Society in that year noted that Greenwood was made of brick, measured sixty-two by forty-four feet and had "one story above the water table"—a description that does not correspond with the traditional Georgian house shown on the map. An 1815 policy valued the house at $3,000 and mentioned that it had a "kitchen etc. underneath, plain finished." In comparison, an insurance policy for Druid Hill described it as a brick building measuring sixty-five by forty-seven feet "with Basement story, in which is a large Kitchen with other necessary rooms. It is one & half stories and rough cast, having a flat roof & center part covered with cement. Well finished with good materials." In 1824, Druid Hill was valued at $8,000.[23]

Although similar in size, Greenwood and Druid Hill were different. The former was a one-story brick dwelling, whereas the latter was a story and a half and had brick walls finished with stucco—"cement" and "rough cast." Furthermore, Greenwood was "plain finished," while Druid Hill was "[w]ell finished with good materials." All of this mattered to an insurance company that would have to pay for the building to be rebuilt if destroyed. If Greenwood had replicated Druid Hill it would have been appraised at a similar value. Given these descriptions, the image depicted on the pier table is most likely Druid Hill.

By the beginning of the twentieth century, the Howards may not have realized that the Druid Hill known to them was Nicholas Rogers' house. If they compiled their list of houses depicted on the suite from an earlier list or from memory, this building may have been known simply as the "Rogers house." The city of Baltimore purchased Nicholas' house from his son Lloyd in 1860 and subsequently altered it by removing the parapet and original porch (see fig. 27) and adding a cupola and a large, encircling Italianate-style porch. With these changes, the house became the centerpiece of the park that the city created out of the property. A newspaper article written at about the same time that the Howards created their list indicates that many Baltimoreans did not understand the unusual design of the original house. Ferdinand C. Latrobe reported that "the Mansion as it stands today is the original home of the Rogers family, but what was the first floor has been made a sort of basement and the second floor has become the first floor." He did not realize that the house was designed as a piano nobile resting over a raised basement story. This misconception would have influenced contemporary views regarding the original elevation. Aside from this residence and the supposed McCurdy house, the identities of other structures depicted on the suite are not being called into question, in most cases for lack of comparative documentation.[24]

Another image central to understanding the suite depicts Mount Clare, the house built by Charles Carroll, barrister (app. 11). Aside from Mount Clare, only one other house represented on the suite survives (see app. 13). By the time the furniture was made, the barrister had long been dead and his wife Margaret (Tilghman), who had spent the previous two decades making significant alterations to the residence and gardens, occupied the house. Remarkably, the Howards' list notes that Mount Clare was the property of "Mrs. Carroll" (fig. 20). No other property was identified as being owned by a woman. Considering the personal stamp that Margaret placed on this house and the fact that she was the resident and taxpayer during the period when the furniture was commissioned, the image on the suite probably pertained to her rather than her deceased husband. Similarly,

Woodville (app. 10) became associated with Mary Hollingsworth Yellott after her husband Jeremiah died in 1805. On October 1, 1810, the *American & Commercial Daily Advertiser* reported that Mary's father had died at "Woodville, the seat of Mrs. Yellott." Thus, where no man was involved, a country house could be understood as representing the woman of the household.[25]

Two other images that shed light on the suite are public buildings. The central medallion on one of the settees (figs. 30, 31) depicts a structure known as the Banks of the City, and the crest rail of a chair has a representation of St. Paul's Charity School (figs. 8, 9). Completed about 1801, the Banks of the City building housed the Bank of Baltimore, the Bank of Maryland, and the Office of Discount and Deposit, which was part of the Bank of the United States. In 1797 members of the Bank of Maryland approached their counterparts in other financial institutions to establish "regulations for the convenience and protection of the several banks of the city." The participating organizations created a committee comprised of three members of each institution's board to consult with the other banks on matters of mutual interest. In 1800 the Office of Discount and Deposit encouraged the other two banks to establish offices in the country to avoid the "malignant fever" that currently afflicted the city. The directors of the participating banks understood the importance of a safe location. Many

Figure 30 Settee attributed to the shop of John and Hugh Finlay with crest rail medallions attributed to Francis Guy, Baltimore, Maryland, 1803–1805. Maple and ash. H. 33⅞", W. 51³⁄₁₆", D. 22⅛". (Courtesy, Baltimore Museum of Art, gift of Lydia Howard de Roth and Nancy H. DeFord Venable in memory of their mother Lydia Howard DeFord and Purchase Fund; photo, Gavin Ashworth.)

Figure 31 Detail of the central panel on the crest rail of the settee illustrated in fig. 30 showing the building housing the Banks of the City. (Photo, Gavin Ashworth.)

were prominent merchants who were undoubtedly concerned that their businesses would suffer if communication, trade, and banking were imperiled by the fear of illness or death. At a following meeting the parties authorized the purchase of land upon which to erect a "suitable building" for the "accommodation of the three banks in the vicinity of the city." They subsequently acquired property at North Avenue and Bolton Street, which was then in the country. As these meetings were held near the close of 1800, the building was probably erected shortly thereafter.[26]

The houses of three individuals involved in the formative stages of the Banks of the City are represented on the suite: George Grundy, Robert Gilmor, Sr., and David Harris, the cashier of the Office of Discount and Deposit (see app. 2, 5, 8). Although the residences of some directors of the participating banks are also depicted, those of many are not. None of the directors of the Bank of Maryland in 1803 and 1804—likely years for the furniture's production—are represented. This suggests that the commission for the suite did not originate from the Banks of the City, but from other circles and interests.[27]

The Howards' list identifies the other public building on the suite as the "Charity School–St. Paul's, on Madison Street." This school was built in 1801 under the direction of the Benevolent Society of the City and County of Baltimore, a charitable organization founded in 1799. Although an offshoot of St. Paul's Protestant Episcopal Church, this school for orphan and indigent girls was supported by individuals from various religious denominations. Since the school was one of several charitable organizations active in the city during the period when the suite was made, its depiction must have been purposeful.[28]

The Benevolent Society was the vision of Eleanor Buchanan Rogers, the wife of Nicholas of Druid Hill. Considering the position of their house in the hierarchy of images on the suite, it is not surprising that the Charity School is among them. In 1799 she persuaded other women in the city to help sell subscriptions to raise money for the school, which they accomplished without the assistance of men. Once they met their goals and insured the success of the project, the women assembled a board of male trustees, as required by law, to run the financial and legal aspects of the school, and obtained a charter from the State of Maryland. Throughout its early history the school was run by a group of female managers and governed by men, including Nicholas Rogers who was one of the first trustees. Despite the legal necessity of having male trustees, the women of the society took every effort and precaution to keep the management and leadership of the organization within their control. According to their constitution, male subscribers had to contribute fifty dollars to vote for the trustees, whereas female subscribers only had to contribute five dollars to have this privilege. These trustees were empowered to select the managers from the Episcopalian women who were annual subscribers or from the "wives, sisters, or daughters" of male annual subscribers, who apparently need not have been Episcopalian. Thus a significantly higher number of women were able to participate in shaping the governance of the school, as was true in other charity schools in Baltimore.[29]

In 1811 the society published an *Address to the Members of the Protestant Episcopal Church* with a list of donations to date and two lists of annual subscribers, including lapsed and current subscriptions. The individuals specified as current subscribers were undoubtedly those most concerned with the promotion of the school. They included Harriet Carroll, Margaret Carroll, William Gibson, Mrs. Robert Gilmor, William Gilmor, George Grundy, Margaret Howard, and Nicholas Rogers, all of whom owned houses depicted on the suite (see app. 1, 2, 4, 5, 11, 13, 16, and pier table). In addition, Mrs. David Harris is listed as a twenty-dollar donor, and Jeremiah Yellott, who died six years earlier, is listed as a fifty-dollar donor (see app. 8, 10). According to this publication, Yellott left the Charity School $500 in his will. Margaret Carroll and Nicholas Rogers also left bequests to the Benevolent Society, as may have other supporters of the school. Thus eleven of the structures depicted on the suite are all linked with the Charity School, not just tangentially, but by individuals heavily invested in this benevolent cause. Importantly for the reidentification of the image on the pier table as Druid Hill, neither Philip Rogers nor his wife Mary Woodward Rogers had anything to do with the school, and thus it seems unlikely that their house would be centrally referenced here.[30]

Although many of the benefactors whose names appear in the *Address* were women, the actual number of female donors may have been higher. Men's names may have been attached to some donations for reasons of propriety or simply because they controlled the money. Considering the strong female presence in the formation and management of the Charity School, it is possible that the images on the suite are tied to the women who lived in the houses, perhaps more than to the men. This may explain why Robert Gilmor, Jr.'s house does not appear on any of the furniture, since his first wife died in 1803, and he did not remarry until 1807. If the suite was associated with Eleanor Rogers and the Charity School, it would also explain why Hampton is not depicted. Charles Carnan Ridgely was a trustee of the Orphaline Charity School, founded in 1801. Like the St. Paul's Charity School, this organization had female managers, but they tended to be the wives of tradesmen. Although relatives of Ridgely were contributors to the Benevolent Society, there is no evidence that he was involved. His and Philip Rogers' absence from this circle may have arisen from their religious affiliation; both were among a small group of wealthy Marylanders who were instrumental in the establishment of Methodism in Baltimore. The absence of the Orphaline School and other charitable organizations among the buildings depicted on the suite indicates that the image of the St. Paul's Charity School was especially meaningful to the patron who commissioned the furniture. Although the Morris suite is strongly connected to the Benevolent Society and several of its benefactors, it is doubtful that the furniture was commissioned for use in the Charity School. Its cost would probably have been prohibitive, and its fragility and elegance would have been inappropriate for that environment.[31]

Furniture historian Wendy Cooper has recently suggested that painted furniture may have been intended for use in country houses, more specifically in rooms adjacent to gardens. By the late nineteenth century, many pieces of Baltimore painted furniture were in country house settings, but their presence there does not preclude their earlier use elsewhere. This furniture may have been considered old fashioned and not appropriate for newer drawing rooms in town. Photographs of the interior of the Howard house at 401 North Charles Street demonstrate how discordant the Morris suite looked in rooms furnished largely with late nineteenth-century furniture and decorations (figs. 16, 17).[32]

Although Cooper's hypothesis may apply to some painted furniture, it is unlikely that the Morris suite was commissioned for a country house. Ever critical of Baltimore society, Betsy Patterson Bonaparte reported from Paris in 1816: "The waste of life which takes places with us shut up in our melancholy country houses where we vegetate for months alone is happily not endured here." Although wealthy Marylanders often entertained guests at their country houses, the power, prestige, and social connections reflected in the furniture's imagery would have been more potent in an urban setting. Moreover, why would one need images of one's country house when in the country? In an urban context these images would have reminded the viewer that most of the individuals represented by the views had the financial resources to maintain a house in town and in the country.[33]

The symbiotic relationship between town and country is aptly displayed on Warner & Hanna's map (fig. 22), where the dense city blocks are shown with a legend listing key public buildings in town, including the courthouse, banks, and churches. Surrounding the town are numerous country seats, which were, in general, neither working farms nor year-round residences. Most of these estates had limited acreage and were pleasure retreats, largely for summer use. In 1808 the city contemplated annexing additional parts of the countryside because the lands owned by these "rich proprietors" derived "all their high value from the proximity to the commercial parts, to the markets, to the navigation &c.," which justified taxation to assist in the city's maintenance. Considering that the Morris suite was probably made in the first decade of the nineteenth century, the images on the furniture may have held special meaning as sanctuaries for the elite during the various yellow fever epidemics that plagued the city in the late

1790s. At the dawn of the nineteenth century these estates represented wealth, comfort, and social power unattainable for much of Baltimore's population.[34]

Considering the diverse images depicted on the suite, it is unlikely that it was made for a private patron. In this regard, the furniture made for the Buchanan family offers a valuable comparison. Although this suite is comprised of sixteen pieces, including several table and seating forms, only the pier table and the two card tables have buildings depicted on them (figs. 12–15, 32, 33). Family tradition maintained that the suite was used in one of two townhouses owned by the three daughters of merchant William Buchanan. The paired buildings depicted on the pier table represent these houses which were located on Gay Street (figs. 14, 15). This placement of

Figure 32 Card table attributed to the shop of John and Hugh Finlay with skirt medallion attributed to Francis Guy, Baltimore, Maryland, 1803–1806. Tulip poplar and pine with oak. H. 28¾", W. 38⅝", D. 17½". (Courtesy, Winterthur Museum; bequest of Henry Francis du Pont.) This card table is from the Buchanan suite.

Figure 33 Detail of the decoration on the skirt of the card table illustrated in fig. 32. This panel depicts the pair of townhouses built by James Buchanan and John Hollins on Monument Square in 1799.

the most important image on the pier table suggests a similar use in the Morris suite. The building on the card table shown in figure 12 probably represents the Buchanan family's country house (fig. 13), whereas the corresponding image on its mate depicts the pair of townhouses built by William Buchanan's son James and John Hollins on Monument Square in 1799 (figs. 32, 33). All other pieces in the Buchanan suite are decorated with agricultural, musical, or armorial trophies (see figs. 10, 11). A similar decorative scheme occurs on a set of chairs that descended in the Ridgely family. Although only three examples are currently known, one has a view of Hampton while the others have landscape views. Thus for furniture intended for a private residence, only buildings relating to that family appear to have been appropriate. This suggests that Nicholas and Eleanor Rogers did not commission the Morris suite for Druid Hill.[35]

During this period there is only one location where the wealth, social connections, and charitable benevolence manifest in the imagery on the Morris suite would have been appropriate—the Baltimore Dancing Assembly Rooms. As the eighteenth century closed, the city had several hotels and inns used for assemblies, which were fashionable in both Britain and the United States. These assemblies were intended to encourage a public and genteel mixing of the sexes through conversation, dancing, card playing, and light refreshments (fig. 34). As the wealth of Baltimoreans increased, the Dancing Assembly endeavored to create a more exclusive and beautiful

Figure 34 Rules of the Baltimore Assembly, printed by W. Goddard and J. Angell, Baltimore, Maryland, ca. 1789. (Courtesy, Maryland Historical Society.)

Figure 35 Detail of the map illustrated in fig. 22 showing the building housing the Dancing Assembly Rooms.

Figure 36 City Assembly Room and Library illustrated in John H. B. Latrobe, *Pictures of Baltimore,* ca. 1832. (Courtesy, Maryland Historical Society.)

environment for their activities. In 1796 a group of subscribers raised $36,000 to erect a building for the organization, which had been in existence since the 1780s. Construction appears to have begun in 1797, and the new building, located at the northeast corner of Holliday and Fayette Streets (the current site of War Memorial Plaza), opened for assemblies in January 1799. Significantly, Nicholas Rogers designed the structure (fig. 35).[36]

Although descriptions of the Dancing Assembly Rooms are scarce, an 1800 city directory noted that the edifice had "perhaps the most elegant exterior of any building in the city." The section of the structure that could be entered from the side door on Holliday Street housed the Library Company of Baltimore (fig. 36). On the right hand side of the ground floor was the card room and "the requisite number of dressing rooms, housekeepers'

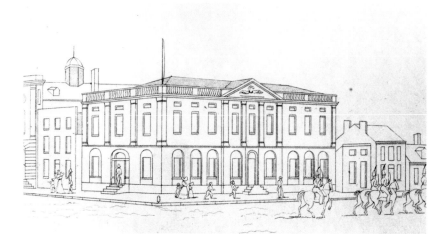

room, &c." The second floor had a large ballroom on the left, an adjoining supper room to the right, and smaller reception rooms and the staircase behind the supper room. This trio of rooms—ball, supper, and card—seems to have been standard for the planned functions of assemblies. The furniture forms in the Morris suite would have been most appropriate for the supper, ball, or reception rooms, since there are no card tables. Later in the history of the Dancing Assembly, an Englishman claimed that "the suite of dancing and refreshment rooms, in which the regular winter balls are held, are not surpassed in beauty by any in Europe. There are many much larger; but for richness, taste, and effective decoration, nothing can be more chastely beautiful than these."[37]

This elegant building was the first monumental one in the city that was not governmental or ecclesiastical in nature. According to architectural historian Robert Alexander, "it commemorated the powerful position of the group that underwrote and used it, an oligarchy that conducted public and private business by association." Importantly, this private building was built half a decade in advance of the new Baltimore City courthouse, which in size and overall architectural composition mimics the earlier structure. After the Dancing Assembly Rooms were completed, they outranked any of the previous assembly rooms that had been carved out of the various hotels in town. The erection of a purpose-built structure was not the norm in the United States at this time, demonstrating its importance in the social life of the city.[38]

The Dancing Assembly Rooms were where wealthy Baltimoreans went to see and be seen—they were the stage of their social pageantry. Membership was strictly by invitation, only men could be subscribers, and males living in the environs of Baltimore could not attend functions unless they were members. While the very nature of such assemblies was to be exclusive, the membership would have included a number of overlapping circles of relations, acquaintances, and business associates. Naturally, the invitation-only policy and the exclusive nature of the organization created friction between some members. In 1798 Robert Smith (brother of Samuel Smith) questioned Robert Oliver's ability to choose individuals of high character, an insult which almost escalated to a duel. Their conflict suggests how important it was to be represented in this select group. For apparently multiple reasons, the Baltimore Dancing Assembly was also plagued by financial difficulties. In 1817 the Dancing Assembly Rooms were sold, but the assembly put together a new set of subscribers, some of whom were members of the original group, to buy back the building. This new management continued until June 1835 when the Dancing Assembly Rooms were sold at auction and purchased by Benjamin Cohen, who refitted them and reopened them again for the same purpose. Apparently to make the rooms more profitable, Cohen added a third story to the structure shortly after his purchase. A few records survive for this period, suggesting a degree of continuity in the subscribers. Cohen's venture also failed, and in 1844 the city bought the building and converted it to the Central High School (fig. 37). The building continued to be used as a school until it burned in 1873.[39]

No complete list of the members of the Dancing Assembly survives, but many of the owners of the houses represented on the Morris suite were subscribers (see app. 1, 2, 5, 6, 8, 10, 13, 14, 16, and pier table). Although admired for their "richness, taste, and effective decoration," specific details regarding the furnishings of these rooms are not mentioned in any documents currently known. The furniture was, however, important to both the managers and members. As the rooms were nearing completion, the subscribers were required to pay an additional seventy-five dollars to "complete the building and purchase the necessary furniture, &c." Considering the exigencies of any construction campaign, one wonders whether this additional levy was sufficient to finish the building and purchase furniture, or if the latter was put off to a later date. If used at the Dancing Assembly Rooms, the Morris suite could have been commissioned to augment furniture already there, perhaps more utilitarian pieces that had been acquired when the building first opened. The number of seating pieces in the suite seems small, but images of the Pump Room at Bath from the mid-eighteenth century to the mid-nineteenth century indicate that it was sparsely furnished. Such rooms were for parading of society, and attendees were apparently expected to spend most of their time standing or dancing. As the assemblies were only held once or twice a month during the winter season, infrequent use may account for the furniture's survival. The 1836 Dancing

Figure 37 1860s photograph of Central High School, Baltimore, Marlyand. (Courtesy, Maryland Historical Society.) This image shows the Dancing Assembly building after the third story was added in the 1830s. The ballroom, with large palladian window, was on the second floor, apparently extending five bays across the front of the building. The entrance to the rooms occupied by the Library Company of Baltimore is visible at the center.

Assembly rules and regulations stated the directors of the assembly had the "privilege of using the Rooms (including also the furniture) without charge." By this period, whatever furniture had been used in the rooms at the time the Morris suite was made may no longer have been there, but nineteenth-century accounts suggest that the furnishings were an essential complement to the interior architecture.[40]

Although traditionally thought of exclusively as furniture makers, the Finlays marketed themselves as orchestrators of Baltimore's social pageantry, and on several occasions they clearly performed that function. In 1803 and 1804 they advertised that they were capable of making Masonic and military banners, and painting coaches (fig. 2)—all items used by the city's elite to signal their position in society and inform others that they possessed good taste. The Finlays were also involved in important and symbolic events, including both interior and exterior celebrations. For the 1814 dinner celebrating Commodore Oliver Hazard Perry's victory at Lake Erie, one of the Finlays decorated the banquet room of the Fountain Inn with American flags and an American eagle suspended from the ceiling and recreated the quarter-deck of a ship to serve as a stage for seating Perry, President James Madison, and other distinguished guests. Other emblematic decorations filled the room and adorned the tables, while the stage was backed by a transparency representing Perry's capture of the British fleet. In the following year the Finlays were involved with the ceremonies dedicating the Washington Monument and Battle Monument. When the cornerstone of the Washington Monument was laid in 1815, Rembrandt Peale recalled that "Mr. [Hugh] Finlay, an upholsterer of taste got up a decorative display depicting the column and a portrait by Peale of George Washington, and surrounded the whole with festoons of drapery and flags of the union." Later in that same year, John Finlay and Rembrandt Peale collaborated to create the "funeral car" that led the procession to the future site of architect Maximilian Godefroy's Battle Monument. The "plan" that surmounted the car may have been a model of the monument.[41]

Considering the importance of the Dancing Assembly Rooms in Baltimore social life, there is every reason to believe that the Finlays would have been involved in decorating and furnishing them with objects that demonstrated the wealth, taste, and benevolence of certain subscribers. Their firm also decorated and refurbished coaches for various subscribers. In 1806 and 1807 Robert Oliver paid the Finlays for providing thirty-eight chairs and two settees for his new house and "repairing" (probably repainting) his carriage. The former's patronage suggests the Finlays were the premier firm for such services. From the opening of the Dancing Assembly Rooms until well into the 1830s, the assembly association published guidelines to direct how coaches would arrive and depart from the building. John H. B. Latrobe recalled that it "was necessary to have the reputation for wealth in those days to justify keeping a carriage."[42]

Evidence suggests that painted furniture was considered more appropriate for spaces that accommodated public receptions than mahogany furniture during the early nineteenth century. In 1809 the White House purchased painted furniture designed by Benjamin Henry Latrobe and decorated by the Finlays for the Blue Room (Oval Room). This suite was replaced by gilded furniture after the White House burned. The Finlays' involvement may have arisen from a recommendation by Baltimore congressman Samuel Smith, whose house is depicted on the Morris suite. In a March 10, 1809, letter to Dolly Madison, Smith referred to "Finlay" as "our Man of Taste." This endorsement suggests that Smith had firsthand knowledge of the Finlays' ability to decorate and furnish important public interiors such as the Dancing Assembly Rooms—Baltimore's premier reception space in this period. Moreover, Smith's language implies a communal acceptance of the Finlays' local role far beyond that which would have been achieved by the furnishing of any one particular house.[43]

One clue suggesting the use of painted furniture in the service of social pagentry is a chair from a set reputedly made for a banquet in honor of Marquis de Lafayette's visit to Baltimore in 1824 (figs. 38, 39). Although oral tradition maintained that the chair was made for a dinner Lafayette attended with a committee of citizens of the corporation of Baltimore, it is more likely that the set was made for the ball and "renowned 'Silver Supper'" held for him in the Dancing Assembly Rooms. According to historian Thomas Scharf, the "splendor of this fete was long remembered by the

Figure 38 Side chair, Baltimore, Maryland, ca. 1824. Unidentified woods. H. 30½", W. 17¾", D. 15⅜". (Courtesy, Baltimore Museum of Art, gift of Randolph Mordecai; photo, Gavin Ashworth.) Although this set of chairs has yet to be linked to the Finlays, their firm specialized in providing furniture and decorations for symbolic events such as the "silver supper."

Figure 39 Detail of the decoration on the crest rail of the side chair illustrated in fig. 38. (Photo, Gavin Ashworth.)

fashionable society of the city." Lafayette was paraded through the rooms in a carefully orchestrated sequence of events, including a receiving line, the ball itself, and two seatings of dinner at which he and the managers of the evening sat at a head table. This event also suggests that the Dancing Assembly Rooms were where prominent Baltimoreans celebrated their history and their collective achievements. The year of the "Silver Supper" Thomas Waters Griffith gave seven lectures there on the history of Maryland.[44]

Although the life of Baltimore's bon ton rotated around the activities in these rooms, some cultural leaders questioned the gaiety and extravagance that such entertainments entailed. Sir Richard Hill's *An Address to Persons of Fashion, Relating to Balls,* reprinted in Baltimore in 1807, suggested that individuals involved in such "vain amusements" might better spend their time in religious pursuits. He argued that the "fashionable diversion of Balls" was "entirely inconsistent with the spirit of Christianity" and "it is not possible to be present at them without incurring great guilt." Hill further questioned the merits of squandering "away in diversions, what would contribute to the support of so many of our poor distressed fellow-creatures." The fact that prominent Baltimoreans including Prudence Gough Carnan purchased copies of Hill's work immediately upon its release indicates that such concerns existed at the very moment of the Morris suite's production. Thus, individuals like Eleanor Rogers who were heavily involved in religious and charitable activities had every reason to want to display their benevolence in the Dancing Assembly Rooms—the place in which these "vain amusements" occurred—to counter any criticism that could be leveled at them.[45]

Considering the Finlays' knowledge of Masonic imagery and their advertised ability to depict various kinds of trophies on their furniture, it is likely that the decoration of the Morris suite functioned symbolically or emblematically. The two public buildings depicted were undoubtedly chosen for specific and timely reasons. The depiction of the Banks of the City offered a convenient and succinct way to represent the mechanisms of commerce by which the subscribers who built the Dancing Assembly Rooms had amassed their wealth. The ability of this image to symbolically represent all banking in the city ended with the establishment of the Union Bank of Maryland in 1805 and its occupancy of an imposing new building in 1807. The Charity School of the Benevolent Society represented wealth put to good use—a pressing societal concern. For members of the Dancing Assembly, the image of this building would have represented the intimate connection between commerce and charity. Furthermore, these two buildings represent masculine and feminine spheres of influence, an important distinction given the purpose of the Dancing Assembly Rooms.[46]

The goal of bringing men and women together for the public good may be further explored in the decoration of the suite, notably in the bow, arrows, and quiver that decorate the centers of the splats and front seat rails (see figs. 8, 30). These devices almost certainly constitute the trophy of love that the Finlays specifically offered as a decorative motif. Flanked on the seat rail by oak leaves and surrounded on the splat by grapevines, the trophies may allude, respectively, to masculine and feminine love coming together in conjugal happiness. Since at least the seventeenth century, the fruitful vine and the oak tree had been used symbolically to suggest the relationship of the sexes. Such conjugal happiness in the home was integral to civic virtue—morals that were largely guided in the United States, as Alexis de Tocqueville suggested, by women. This connection between male and female love may also allude to one of the main functions of assemblies—introducing young men and women to appropriate matches. If Baltimoreans followed British precedent, a successful meeting might be followed by an invitation to spend time at one party's country house.[47]

The images of country houses depicted on the suite represented, in and of themselves, the kind of refinement and gentility that was the raison d'être of the assemblies. This may explain why a view of the Dancing Assembly Rooms was chosen as an inset on Warner & Hanna's map (figs. 22, 35). After visiting Belvidere in 1796, Englishman Thomas Twining reported that such country villas were "evidence of the refinement towards which society in America was advancing." Like many of his peers, Twining equated improvements in the country with prosperity. For the owners of the houses depicted on the suite as well as in Francis Guy's larger landscapes, these properties symbolized leisure, improvement, and refinement as well as communal achievement. The imagery on the suite would have been especially powerful if the furniture was made for the Dancing Assembly Rooms where the elite celebrated themselves through genteel amusements.[48]

If the suite was made for these rooms, the commission could have been instigated by the wives, sisters, or daughters of the male members. In this period religion, charity, and the domestic arena were among the few avenues of social expression open to women. Jane Austin's novels offer a glimpse into the contemporary feminine sphere and occasionally mention assemblies. In Persuasion (1818), Elizabeth Elliot told her father in the "first ardour of female alarm [she], set seriously to think what could be done [about their financial problems]" and "finally proposed these two branches of economy, to cut off some unnecessary charities, and to refrain from new furnishing the drawing-room." The decoration on the Morris suite can be interpreted as intersecting all of these areas of social expression.[49]

It is possible that funds for commissioning the suite were brought together by subscription—a contribution ensuring the depiction of a house selected by each benefactor. The women in Eleanor Rogers' charity circle clearly had experience and success in similar fund raising endeavors. A larger than average donation may have ensured a place on one of the settees, as these two pieces would have been more expensive than the chairs. Perhaps Eleanor Rogers paid for not only the pier table (figs. 24, 25), but also the chair depicting the Charity School (figs. 8, 9). Druid Hill was built on land inherited by Eleanor, suggesting that both of these properties may have been heavily identified with her. Furthermore, there is the depiction of Margaret Carroll's house Mount Clare and the residences of two pairs of sisters: Willow Brook (Ann Smith Donnell), The Vineyard (Mary Ann Smith Gilmor), Belvidere (Margaret Chew Howard), and Homewood (Harriet Chew Carroll). With the exception of Ann Smith Donnell, all of these women were important members of the Charity School. These connections support the hypothesis that the concept and funding of the suite emanated from a group of women.

Considering that women were the guardians of cultural morality during this period—a guardianship achieved by involvement in such a charity—it is only logical that an organization as influential as the Benevolent Society would be represented on a suite commissioned by female members of the Dancing Assembly. By contrast, the inclusion of this image might never have occurred to their male counterparts. Sir Richard Hill's moralistic criticisms were aimed almost entirely at women. He implored "mothers and aunts" to keep their "daughters and nieces" from the vanities and concerns over ball gowns that attending assemblies entailed. Hill had, in fact, written his tract after hearing a "young lady affirm, that she saw no harm in going to a Ball." If female members of the Dancing Assembly commissioned the suite, they may have specified the image of the Charity School to remind observers that commerce and the luxuries of elegant assemblies did not preclude them from benevolent causes.[50]

A close connection with the female managers of the Charity School and this suite of furniture is no coincidence. Francis Guy, who is believed to have painted the various views of the buildings, was both an artist and a religious man. In 1803 the *Federal Gazette & Baltimore Daily Advertiser* reported that he would deliver a lecture to "prove the Divinity of the Scripture by the goodness of its fruits" and explain why Deism was bad for the individual and society in general. The artist offered to donate the whole admission price of twelve and one-half cents "to such orphan's school or schools in this city, as the company then present may think most worthy their benevolence." Although there were several orphan asylums in Baltimore at this time, Guy was playing a tune that Eleanor Rogers and her benevolent compatriots wanted to hear. They could learn more about the social benefits of religion—as they were ably demonstrating at their school—and if they arrived en masse they had the possibility of raising a contribution for their charity. Through such connections, Eleanor and her circle would have known Guy when it came time to commission their suite of furniture, and they understood him to be in agreement with their mission.[51]

The Charity School circle, however, cannot at present explain all of the buildings depicted on the suite. Samuel and Margaret (Spear) Smith, the owners of Montebello (app. 15) do not appear to have been involved with the Charity School, nor were several other families whose houses are represented. It is possible that the images of certain houses emanated from sources other than the residents, perhaps children or relatives who considered this particular dwelling their family seat or friends who wished to acknowledge others. The identification of the Smiths' house is quite secure, as photographs and other images record the unique appearance of Montebello. This is not the case with some other houses, such as that said to have been Hugh McCurdy's. Although there is no documentary evidence pertaining to this dwelling other than the Howards' list, it is tempting to speculate that it may have been the residence of William MacCreery, who was a significant donor to the Charity School and an early member of the Dancing Assembly. It is possible that the Howards misread the name on an earlier list and substituted "McCurdy" for MacCreery. The absence of a first name suggests they did not know much about the owner.[52]

Some of the references outside the Charity School circle may be linked to Eleanor and Nicholas Rogers' communal acquaintances. While serving on the Baltimore City Council until his retirement in 1801, Nicholas would have become familiar with political leaders such as Walter Dorsey. In 1799 Dorsey became chief justice of the criminal court of Baltimore City and County, a position important in a suite of furniture that deals with town and country. Equally important, the Dorseys in Walter's line were members of St. Paul's Protestant Episcopal Church, and therefore either Eleanor or Nicholas Rogers could have interacted with him or his wife Hopewell (Hebb) socially.[53]

Other than the Charity School circle, only one other organization had a similar membership—the Library Company of Baltimore. Surviving records indicate that nearly every individual represented on the Morris suite was a member of the Library Company. Since this organization was a private subscription library sharing some of the same board members as the Dancing Assembly, it is safe to assume that most of the individuals who were members downstairs were also members upstairs.[54]

When the Library Company moved into the building housing the Dancing Assembly Rooms in May of 1798 (fig. 36), the managers ordered seven Windsor chairs from Jacob Daley and a desk, tables, and bookcases from an unnamed joiner. This selection suggests that the Library Company's furniture was largely utilitarian. Their minutes for the first decade of the nineteenth century do not mention the purchase of any furniture similar to the Morris suite or donations of furnishings by interested members. If the minutes thoroughly and accurately document the Library Company's activities, this would preclude that the suite was made for them. However, their membership indicates that the building the Library Company shared with the Dancing Assembly was the place in town where the people represented by the images on the Morris suite came together.

Figure 40 Side chair attributed to the shop of John and Hugh Finlay with crest rail medallion attributed to Francis Guy, Baltimore, Maryland, 1803–1806. Woods not recorded. H. 34¼", W. 17½", D. 15¾". (Courtesy, Baltimore Museum of Art, Middendorf Foundation Fund; photo, Gavin Ashworth.)

Figure 41 Detail of the decoration on the crest rail of the side chair illustrated in fig. 40 showing the panel depicting Druid Hill. (Photo, Gavin Ashworth.)

Figure 42 Side chair attributed to the shop of John and Hugh Finlay with crest rail medallion attributed to Francis Guy, Baltimore, Maryland, 1803–1806. Woods not recorded. H. 34¼", W. 17½", D. 15¾". (Courtesy, Baltimore Museum of Art, Middendorf Foundation Fund; photo, Gavin Ashworth.)

Figure 43 Detail of the decoration on the crest rail of the side chair illustrated in fig. 42 depicting an unidentified country house. (Photo, Gavin Ashworth.)

Although it is likely that the Morris suite was made for the Dancing Assembly Rooms, it may not have been the only furniture used there. Three side chairs, a card table, and a pier table (see figs. 40–47) with buildings depicted in a manner similar to those on the Morris furniture may have been made for the card room. In *Baltimore Painted Furniture,* William Voss Elder noted that the tables descended in the Maynadier and Key families, and that both pieces had been used at Belvoir in Anne Arundel County, Maryland. Two of the side chairs reputedly descended in the family of Christopher VanDeventer and his wife Sally Birckhead, but it is unlikely that he was the original owner. Christopher was born in 1788 and would have been in his teens when the chairs and accompanying tables were made. As is the case with many surviving examples of Baltimore painted furniture, these pieces probably became associated with their respective families later in the nineteenth century. The identical decorative schemes of these tables and chairs suggest that they were made as a suite, one that clearly included additional side chairs and probably a second card table.[56]

Like many of its counterparts, the Baltimore Dancing Assembly Rooms had a space dedicated to card playing. This pastime was so commonplace among "people of fashion" that Sir Richard Hill questioned whether "every lady who frequents Card-tables" was "clothing herself with the whole armour of God, and working out her own salvation with fear and trembling?" Because of concerns regarding propriety, card playing and charity went hand in hand in some social arenas. When Miss Mary Boardman Crowninshield visited Secretary of State James Monroe in Washington in 1816, she reported "We played loo and I won—I am afraid to say how much, but [I] shall give it to the orphan asylum." Thus the strictures that found attending balls and card playing frivolous may have obliquely shaped the way the Dancing Assembly Rooms were furnished.[57]

Too little of this second suite is known to determine much about it. Of the five houses depicted on the furniture, two have not yet been securely identified. The tablet of one of the side chairs depicts Druid Hill (formerly Greenwood) (figs. 40, 41), the card table bears an image of Mount Clare (figs. 44, 45) and the pier table is decorated with a house that may be Green Mount (figs. 46, 47)—the country house of Robert Oliver, an early

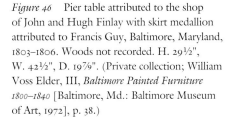

Figure 46 Pier table attributed to the shop of John and Hugh Finlay with skirt medallion attributed to Francis Guy, Baltimore, Maryland, 1803–1806. Woods not recorded. H. 29½", W. 42½", D. 19⅞". (Private collection; William Voss Elder, III, *Baltimore Painted Furniture 1800–1840* [Baltimore, Md.: Baltimore Museum of Art, 1972], p. 38.)

Figure 47 Detail of the decoration on the skirt of the pier table illustrated in fig. 46. The panel depicts a country house, possibly Robert Oliver's Green Mount.

member of the Dancing Assembly. If these objects were made for the Dancing Assembly Rooms, the suite may have originated in a social circle slightly different from that responsible for the Morris suite: Robert and Elizabeth (Craig) Oliver, Margaret Carroll, the Rogers, and the Howards (the Howards' house Belvidere appears on a recently discovered third chair). Notably, Mount Clare, Druid Hill, and Belvidere are the only

Figure 48 Armchair attributed to the shop of John and Hugh Finlay with crest rail medallion attributed to Francis Guy, Baltimore, Maryland, 1803–1806. Maple with unidentified ring-porous hardwood. H. 34½", W. 21³⁄₁₆", D. 18¼". (Collection of Stiles Tuttle Colwill; photo, Gavin Ashworth.)

Figure 49 Detail of the decoration on the crest rail of the armchair illustrated in fig. 48. (Photo, Gavin Ashworth.) The structure depicted on the panel has not been identified, but it may represent a public building.

houses that appear twice on any painted furniture known today. Three of the women of these households were major players in the St. Paul's Charity School.[58]

Outside of the objects discussed here, few pieces of Baltimore painted furniture have houses or buildings depicted on them. Recently three dark blue armchairs with structural and decorative details similar to those in the Morris suite have surfaced. Unfortunately, none of the buildings depicted on their crests has been identified, although one is clearly a large brick structure in town (figs. 48, 49) whereas the others are houses in landscape settings. Although the Finlays offered furniture "with or without views adjacent to the city," it appears from surviving examples that few clients specified depictions of buildings. This may have arisen from the Finlays' business arrangement with Francis Guy, which may have been brief or otherwise limited. The extravagant use of building views may also have been considered more appropriate to public spaces than domestic ones. If so, that too would have curtailed production. Assuming that the Morris suite was made for the Dancing Assembly Rooms, John B. Morris could have purchased the furniture at any number of occasions when the rooms were sold or after they finally closed in the 1840s. Advertisements for the sale of the rooms in 1817 and 1835 do not mention furniture, although the contents were surely sold, possibly more than once. The most likely date for Morris to have acquired the suite is 1835. In August of that year, all of the contents of Morris' townhouse on South Street were destroyed by mobs enraged by a banking scandal. Although Benjamin Cohen purchased the rooms in May, some of the furniture may have been sold at a later date. Acquiring the suite would have been a symbolic gesture for Morris, linking himself with the early titans of business who had pushed Baltimore into its golden age of commerce, including the Gilmors and others who had survived earlier banking ventures unscathed. The fact that Samuel Smith's home Montebello was depicted on the suite would have furthered Morris' connections to this earlier period, as Smith was instrumental in calming the disorders of the riots and was elected mayor later in the year. If Morris purchased the furniture after his townhouse was destroyed, he could have used it either at his new residence on Mulberry Street or in the country. In the absence of a contemporary bill of sale, many questions still remain unanswered about this suite, leaving only intriguing theories about the commission and use of this unique set of furniture.[59]

ACKNOWLEDGMENTS   The author thanks James Archer Abbott, Curator of Decorative Art, Baltimore Museum of Art, for his enthusiastic support of the research for this article and dedicates this work to the memory of his mother, Brenda.

1. The standard literature on the Morris suite is found in William Voss Elder, III, *Baltimore Painted Furniture 1800–1840* (Baltimore, Md.: Baltimore Museum of Art, 1972), pp. 20–27; and William Voss Elder, III, and Jayne E. Stokes, *American Furniture 1680–1880, From the Collection of the Baltimore Museum of Art* (Baltimore, Md.: Baltimore Museum of Art, 1987), pp. 45–47 (chairs), 59–60 (settees), 161–62 (pier table). A settee from the suite was included

in the seminal publication *Baltimore Furniture: The Work of Baltimore and Annapolis Cabinetmakers from 1760 to 1810* (Baltimore, Md.: Baltimore Museum of Art, 1947), pp. 156–57. The Baltimore Museum of Art will hereafter be cited as BMA. Stiles Tuttle Colwill was the first to suggest that Francis Guy painted the decorative panels in his *Francis Guy 1760–1820* (Baltimore, Md.: Maryland Historical Society, 1981), pp. 23–25. The visual similarities between Guy's oil on canvas works and the views on the furniture are compelling. Colwill also observed that Guy did not advertise between 1804 and 1806, the period when the Finlays boasted of their ability to supply furniture with landscape views. This suggests that the artist may have been in their employ during those years. Since the Finlays advertised their ability to supply furniture with painted views as early as 1803 (pp. 24–25), it is likely that Guy could have been working for them at this time as well. In addition to the newspaper advertisement reproduced here, an advertisement in the August 11, 1804, issue of the *American & Commercial Daily Advertiser* states that the Finlays "hold the exclusive right" to supply "views on their chairs & furniture" (pp. 24–25). The 1803–1805 date range here assigned to the Morris suite is based on three main factors: the Finlays' advertisement from 1803; the fact that Homewood, one of the houses depicted, was not completed until 1803; and the fact that at least one of the individuals whose house is depicted, Jeremiah Yellott, died in 1805. Other issues pertaining to the date will be discussed below.

2. See Lance Humphries, *Robert Gilmor, Jr. (1774–1848): Baltimore Art Collector and American Art Patron*, 2 vols. (Ann Arbor, Mich.: University Microfilms International, 1998), passim. The numerous auction catalogues and manuscript documents regarding sales used for this study were instrumental in forming the author's opinions regarding the problems with local furniture provenance. At many of these sales, members of the Gilmor and the related Howard and Hoffman families were purchasing their own family furniture, while at the same time pieces were slipping out of their families. Throughout much of the nineteenth century, the Register of Wills for Baltimore City maintained Accounts of Sales. If an auction was part of the settlement of an estate, a complete record of the items sold, as well as the purchaser and price paid, was recorded. These Accounts of Sales document hundreds if not thousands of sales for which no auction catalogues survive.

3. For more on the card table, see Gregory R. Weidman, *Furniture in Maryland 1740–1940: The Collection of the Maryland Historical Society* (Baltimore, Md.: Maryland Historical Society, 1984), p. 180. Although Gilmor could have owned this table, the author has found no evidence documenting its sale out of his family into the Riggs family, whose descendants believed their ancestor had acquired it from Gilmor's estate sale. The lounge, also attributed to the Finlays, but from a later period, is mentioned in Wendy A. Cooper, *Classical Taste in American 1800– 1840* (New York: Abbeville Press, 1993), p. 274, nt. 31, as belonging to Robert Gilmor, Jr. This object was apparently acquired from a descendant of his brother William in 1905, but there is no evidence that it belonged to Robert Gilmor, Jr. (Lance Humphries to Lynne Hastings, Hampton House National Historic Site, June 17, 1997). Harriott Horry Diary, June 9, 1815, Harriott Horry Ravenal Papers, ms. 11-332B-5, South Carolina Historical Society, Charleston. The author thanks Maurie McInnis for this reference. For a partial provenance of the pier table, see Elder, *American Furniture 1680–1880*, pp. 165–66. J. Latimer Hoffman was a collateral descendant of Robert Gilmor, Jr., and owned many firmly documented art objects from his collection. In the auction catalogue a pier table nearly identical to that illustrated in fig. 3 is shown in the parlor of Hoffman's house (*Catalogue of Fine Old and Original Antique Furniture and Rare and Original Oil Paintings, Engravings and Old Original Colored Prints, Many Colored in the Plate. Collection of Old English Cut Glass, Sheffield Plate, Sterling Silver, Sevres, Dresden and Other Ornaments at the Residence of J. Latimer Hoffman, Jr., Esq. No. 112 East Franklin Street, Baltimore, Maryland. Commencing Tuesday May 31st, 1910 and Continuing Each Day Thereafter at Same Hour Until The Entire Collection is Disposed of.* [Baltimore, Md.: Pattison & Gahan, 1910], lot 147.) Copies of this catalogue are at the BMA and the Enoch Pratt Free Library. Neither is annotated, thus the author has not been able to learn who purchased the table at the auction. With its metal, monopodial supports, this pier table form is highly unusual among extant Baltimore painted furniture. Baltimore antiques dealer Faris C. Pitt owned a very similar pier table but with a different skirt. See the illustration of his shop window in *Orphan's Court Sale Extraordinary of the Entire Collection and Stock of Rare and Valuable Oil Paintings, Ceramics, Bronzes, Oriental Rugs, Antique Furniture and Objects of Art, Belonging to the Estate of the Late Faris C. Pitt, Beginning Monday, May 15th, 1922* (Baltimore, Md.: N. B. Lobe & Co., 1922). The window display shown in the catalogue appears to have been an historic photograph, and not an illustration of items sold in this particular sale.

Pitt acquired a number of works directly from J. Latimer Hoffman, many of which were reputedly in Gilmor's collection. Thus, the pier table illustrated in Pitt's shop window could have been Gilmor's as well. See, for instance, lot 220, a Pembroke table that Pitt purchased from Hoffman, "who said it came from the Robert Gilmor Estate."

4. *Catalogue of the Furniture, Plate, &c. of the Late Col. Howard, To be Sold in Obedience to his Last Will and Testament, at Belvidere-House, On Monday, the 5th Nov. 1827* (Baltimore, Md.: J. Robinson, 1827). Two copies of the catalogue are in the collection of the Maryland Historical Society (hereafter cited MdHS). See the manuscript list, "Sales at Auction of the Personal Estate of Col. John E. Howard at Belvidere House on the 5th + 6th Novr. 1827," ms. 2450, MdHS. These items were lots 247, 89, and 47, respectively. On the suite at Hampton, see Lynne Dakin Hastings, *A Guidebook to Hampton National Historic Site* (Towson, Md.: Historic Hampton, Inc., 1986), pp. 48–49.

5. Elder, *Baltimore Painted Furniture*, p. 61, states that the Abell family of Baltimore owned the furniture and used it in their country house Woodbourne, but no dates of ownership are provided. In *American Furniture 1680–1880*, pp. 50–51, Elder suggests a provenance going back to Arunah S. Abell. More recently Gregory R. Weidman has observed that this suite "descended through the Abell family of Baltimore and were at one time used at Woodbourne. Since A. S. Abell did not come to Baltimore until 1837, the set of chairs may have originally come from Charles and Mary Ann Carroll of Litterluna in Baltimore County, whose granddaughter Elizabeth Laurenson (Mrs. Edwin Franklin Abell) lived at both that Greek Revival house and at Woodbourne" (Gregory R. Weidman, "The Furniture of Classical Maryland, 1815–1845," in Weidman and Jennifer F. Goldsborough, et al., *Classical Maryland 1815–1945: Fine and Decorative Arts from the Golden Age* [Baltimore, Md.: Maryland Historical Society, 1993], p. 96). *Catalogue of the Celebrated Dr. William H. Crim Collection of Genuine Antiques, To be Sold . . . In the Fourth Regiment Armory, Beginning Wednesday, April 22^d 1903* (Baltimore, Md.: A. O. Kirkland, 1903), lot 1127. A number of partially annotated copies of this catalogue survive, but none is fully annotated. One copy in the Library of the Gallery of the MdHS is partially annotated and has newspapers tipped into it noting who purchased some of the pieces at each day's sale. This sofa was sold to one J. C. Rodgers, who according to the Gallery copy bought it for "Mrs. Abell." Other works purchased by Rodgers were similarly noted as being for Mrs. Abell, who is listed as "Mrs. E. F. Abell," apparently Elizabeth Laurenson (Mrs. Edwin Franklin Abell). According to her obituary, Elizabeth Laurenson Abell lived at Woodbourne until her husband's death in 1904. As she was his second wife, and they had no children, her survivors and heirs were her husband's children by his first marriage. Obituary of Elizabeth Laurenson Abell, August 14, 1934, Dielman-Hayward file, MdHS.

6. This suite is no longer intact, but most of it is split between the Baltimore Museum of Art and the Winterthur Museum. See entries in Elder, *Baltimore Painted Furniture*, pp. 28–33; Elder, *American Furniture 1680–1880*, pp. 47–48 (three chairs), 60–61 (window seat), 135–36 (card table), 162–63 (pier table); and Charles F. Montgomery, *American Furniture, The Federal Period in the Henry Francis du Pont Winterthur Museum* (New York: Viking Press, 1966), pp. 451–53 (card table, three chairs, settee, window seat). Two chairs, formerly in the collection of the BMA, were exchanged with the Metropolitan Museum of Art. A ninth chair is still in the possession of Buchanan descendants, and a tenth chair was reputedly destroyed in a house fire many years ago.

7. Finlay advertisement for "Fancy Landscape[s]" in the *Federal Gazette & Baltimore Daily Advertiser,* February 4, 1806. A side chair with an imaginary romantic landscape on its crest rail is illustrated in Weschler's, *American Furniture and Decorations,* Washington, D. C., April 27, 1996, cover and lot 171 (one of three chairs in this lot). This chair is remarkably similar in form and decoration to furniture from a partial suite (window seats, card and pier tables) included in Elder, *Baltimore Painted Furniture,* pp. 33–35. A pair of armchairs of the same form as those in the Morris suite, but with romantic landscapes on the crest rail, is illustrated in *Baltimore Furniture: The Work of Baltimore and Annapolis Cabinetmakers from 1760 to 1810,* p. 159. These chairs have been repainted white and redecorated, with the exception of the romantic landscape and flanking panels on the crest rails. Reputed to have come from Brooklandwood and passed from Mrs. George Brown to her daughter (the owner at the time of publication), these two chairs are probably among those visible in earlier photographs of that house (Newton W. Elwell, *The Architecture, Furniture and Interiors of Maryland and Virginia During the Eighteenth Century* [Boston, Mass.: George W. Polley & Co. Publishers, 1897], pls. 3, 4, 8). The photographs show them in dark, probably black, paint. Their overall ornamentation was originally very similar to the chair that sold at Weschler's (see above). On the use of a draw-

ing book of decorative patterns for ornamenting painted furniture, see Nancy Goyne Evans, "The Christian M. Nestell Drawing Book: A Focus on the Ornamental Painter and His Craft in Early Nineteenth-Century America," in *American Furniture,* edited by Luke Beckerdite (Hanover, N. H.: University Press of New England for the Chipstone Foundation, 1998), pp. 99–163. Guy painted landscapes depicting Mount Deposit, Bolton, and Druid Hill. His depiction of Druid Hill was apparently the one exhibited in 1811, suggesting that it is later than the suite. For images of these works, see Colwill, *Francis Guy,* pp. 59, 63–65, 67. In several landscapes Guy also tucked in images of houses depicted on the suite, including a tiny depiction of Willow Brook, which appears in the lower right distance of his *View of the Bay From Near Mr. Gilmor's* (ibid., p. 52), and two depictions of Rose Hill, shown just to the left of Bolton (ibid., pp. 63, 65). William Russell Birch's *The Country Seats of the United States of North America, with some Scenes connected with them* (Springland near Bristol, Pennsylvania: Designed and Published by W. Birch, 1808[–09]) included views of several Maryland country houses, notably Montebello, which appears on the suite, and Hampton. Although these published images could have been used as inspiration for ornamental painters—allowing an artist or artisan to include them on furniture of this kind without traveling to the site—Birch's book was published after the date assigned to the Morris suite. Birch's engravings of Montebello and Hampton are reproduced in Laura Rice, *Maryland History in Prints 1743–1900* (Baltimore, Md.: Maryland Historical Society, 2002), pp. 36–37.

8. Letitia Stockett, *Baltimore: A Not Too Serious History* (1928; reprint with a new foreword by Harold A. Williams, Baltimore, Md.: Johns Hopkins University Press, 1997), p. 218. Based on the Baltimore city directories, the Howards had lived at this address since at least shortly after the Civil War. From the late 1860s until the mid 1880s, the address is given as 101 North Charles. Beginning with the city directory for 1887, the address is listed as 401 North Charles because the streets were renumbered the previous year. See *R. L Polk & Co.'s Baltimore City Directory for 1887* (Baltimore, Md.: R. L. Polk & Co.), pp. 45, 634. The author has not located a detailed genealogy of John B. Morris and his family, but some of it can be gleaned from a genealogy of his wife's family (*Descendants of Valentine Hollingsworth, Sr.* [Louisville, Ky.: John P. Morton & Company, 1925], pp. 46–47.) The author has relied heavily on the Dielman-Hayward file (a clipping file of obituary and marriage notices from the local newspapers) at the MdHS for genealogical information regarding these and other families discussed below. Stockett, *Baltimore: A Not Too Serious History,* p. 218. Stockett's observation that the house was sold previous to the publication of her book is confused by a newspaper article titled "Old Howard Residence on Charles Streets Sold," which has a typed date of June 1929 (Lydia Howard de Roth Papers, ms. 1906, MdHS). Other articles in this collection make it clear that Lydia Howard DeFord (Mrs. Herbert C.) de Roth and her sister Nancy Howard DeFord (Mrs. Edward) Venable were for a time living abroad with their husbands. These sisters were the only children of Lydia Howard (Mrs. William Howard) DeFord. As their names are confusing, they will be referred to respectively as Lydia DeFord de Roth, Nancy DeFord Venable, and Lydia Howard DeFord, even though this is not uniformly how they were called during their lifetimes.

9. See Henry J. Merkley, "Early Maryland Furniture," *Antiques* 18, no. 3 (September 1930): 210. Although the caption of the illustrated chair (then in the collection of Lydia Howard DeFord) stated that it was the one depicting the "McCurdy mansion," it was actually the chair depicting George Grundy's house Bolton. The caption was also incorrect in stating that the chair was "[one] of a set of twelve with settee." Acknowledging that the suite was attributed to "John Findlay, fancy furniture maker," the caption also states that "the decorator is said to have been an English artist." It is intriguing to think that the "decorator" was Francis Guy, but the reference is vague, and Merkley may have been referring to Finlay. On the Peale Museum's show, see Katherine Scarborough's review of the exhibition, "Unique Record of Baltimore Mansions: Medallions of Old Homes Adorn Baltimoreans' Furniture," *The Sun* (Baltimore), March 1, 1936. At the time of this exhibition, Lydia Howard DeFord owned eleven of the pieces, and her brother Charles Morris Howard owned two chairs. See Index of American Design Data Report Sheet MD-FU-25a, (b) (1943.8.4390), on file with the Department of Modern Prints and Drawings, National Gallery of Art, Washington, D.C. The author thanks Charles Ritchie of that department for his assistance in locating this material. The recorded chair, which has an image of Willow Brook on its crest rail, was one of the two owned by Charles Morris Howard. The project recorded "original owner" information, here stated to be "John B. Morris of Charmont." On the exhibition see "Old Baltimore Design Depicted in WPA Art," *Evening Sun* (Baltimore), July 7, 1936. See Edgar G. Miller, Jr., *Amer-*

ican Antique Furniture, 2 vols. (1937; facsimile reprint, New York: Dover Publications, 1966), 1: 208–9, no. 290 for the chair depicting Bolton; 1, 290–91, no. 515 for the settee that has Montebello depicted in the center of the crest. Both pieces were then in the collection of Lydia Howard DeFord, "members of a family for whose ancestor they were made" (1: 208). The pier table is not illustrated. Lydia Howard DeFord initially loaned eight chairs, the two settees, and the pier table to the Baltimore Museum of Art. Her two daughters, Lydia DeFord de Roth and Nancy DeFord Venable, inherited these pieces as well as the two other chairs owned by their uncle Charles Morris Howard. The entire suite was on loan to the BMA until the museum acquired it by gift and purchase in 1966. The suite had been offered to Henry Francis du Pont in 1961 (Nancy Howard Venable to Mr. du Pont, March 11, 1961, Winterthur Museum Archives). The author thanks Wendy Cooper for bringing this document to his attention. Du Pont did not acquire the suite because he felt the asking price of $110,000 was too high (Henry Francis du Pont to Mrs. Edward Venable, April 8, 1963, Private collection).

10. Scarborough, "Unique Record of Baltimore Mansions." See, for instance, J. G. D. Paul, "Art, History and A Baltimore Cabinet-Maker," *Baltimore Museum of Art News* (June 1944): 4–5; "Furniture Exhibit Recalls Banks' Venture of 1801," *Evening Sun* (Baltimore), June 16, 1944; "Craftsman's Triumph," *The Sun* (Baltimore), May 4, 1952. This information apparently emanated from promotional material prepared at the Baltimore Museum of Art, which entered such published sources as Miller's *American Antique Furniture* (see 1: 208). It was repeated on page 21 in Elder's *Baltimore Painted Furniture.* Colwill, *Francis Guy,* pp. 76–77. Colwill suggests that Morris could have purchased the suite at the auction sale of the property and furnishings of the Fountain Inn (formerly James Bryden's Coffee House), which was advertised in the October 30, 1817, issue of the *Federal Gazette & Baltimore Daily Advertiser.* This building had a room decorated with murals by Guy and was the location of several of his sales (Colwill, *Francis Guy,* pp. 20–22). At least part of Bryden's Coffee House also acted as assembly rooms, but it is unlikely that this suite was commissioned to be used in a space available to the general public. In John B. Morris' will, he divided various monies and properties between his children and grandchildren, including his house on Mulberry Street, which he left to his son Thomas H. Morris. The latter also inherited all his father's books, maps, prints, and engravings hanging in this house. Specific bequests of furniture are not noted. No inventory was taken of John B. Morris' personal property, only of his stocks. See Will of John B. Morris, Wills, Liber J. H. B. (41), fols. 114–121; and Inventory of John B. Morris, Inventories, Liber J. H. B. (101), fols. 341–342, Register of Wills, Baltimore City. No sales of personal property were held from the estate.

11. One copy of the list accompanied the suite when it was given to the BMA. The other, found in the house of Nancy DeFord Venable, is in a private collection. The information on the lists is identical with only minor word variations. The list in the private collection retains its original envelope labeled, in the same hand: "Painted Furniture." J. G. D. Paul, "Art, History and A Baltimore Cabinet-Maker."

12. Although the author has not yet investigated the land records regarding the estate, Morris owned or rented Claremont as early as 1835. In a letter written by Lydia E. Hollingsworth—the sister of Ann (Hollingsworth) Morris who lived with the John B. Morris family—she noted that the family expected "to leave South Street next week to go to Clermont and remain during the warm weather" (Lydia E. Hollingsworth to her cousin Rachel Tobin, June 12, 1835, typescript of an apparently lost original, Hollingsworth Family Letters, 1802–1837, MdHS). See *F. Klemm's Map of Baltimore and Suburbs* (Baltimore, Md.: F. Klemm, 1873), where "F. K. Howard" is shown owning Claremont to the south of the Liberty Road. Since Frank Key Howard died in 1872, the property may have been owned by his wife Lydia, who was Morris' daughter. "Mrs. Davis," possibly Morris' daughter, Nancy, who had married Henry Winter Davis, owned an adjacent property. This suggests that Morris may have sold or given his properties to his children before his death.

13. Debbie Parr, an independent conservator who has recently worked on the suite, noted that the numbers are old and probably oil based. Paint analysis of the white pigment might refine this interpretation, as some white pigments were not available in the early nineteenth century. Lydia Morris Howard's increasing age may have motivated her children to record what she knew about the suite and the buildings depicted. In *American Furniture 1680–1880,* Elder suggests that the list may have been written by Lydia Howard DeFord (p. 45), and this author is inclined to agree. The handwriting is very similar to other examples of her hand. The list does not seem to be in her mother's hand, and it is clearly not in the hand of her brother Charles Morris Howard. Lydia DeFord's other brother Frank Key Howard appears to have

become unstable, and examples of their sister Nancy H. Howard's hand have not yet been located. The lack of a Morris family house on the suite did not trouble earlier writers, including those who noted that the furniture was made for the Morris family (see "Furniture Exhibit Recalls Banks' Venture of 1801," *Evening Sun* [Baltimore], June 16, 1944). It is illogical that a patron would commission a suite of furniture depicting houses, and not include his own.

14. See the catalogue of *Historical Exhibits Collection: National Star Spangled Banner Centennial, Peabody Art Galleries, September 7th to 20th, 1914* (Baltimore: 1914), cat. 313, "Settee and Chair from Belvedere, home of John Eager Howard," loaned by John Ridgely of Hampton; and cat. 314 "Two decorated settees and chairs from 1800, from Belvedere, home of John Eager Howard. Showing medallions, Mount Clare, Montibello, Belevedere and other country seats." This listing of buildings confirms that the two settees were included along with the chair depicting Belvidere. Mrs. John Ridgely was on the committee involved with classification and creation of the catalogue, but her role in providing specific details is not known. Lydia Morris Howard's son Frank Key Howard was also involved in planning this exhibition, but what he knew about the suite is also not known. He was thanked by the mayor for his efforts (James H. Preston to Frank Key Howard, November 4, 1914, Lydia Howard de Roth Papers, ms. 1906, MdHS). That the suite was thought to be a vital part of the exhibition is documented by its presence on an early list of the objects slated to be exhibited (Historic Exhibits Committee to Louis H. Dielman, Peabody Institute, July 4, 1914, Archives of the Peabody Institute, Executive Secretary, Correspondence, Gallery of Art 1911–1928, Series IV. A.1). The other exhibition was held at Homewood House on the campus of Johns Hopkins University, June 9–24, 1928 (Friends of Art, *Homewood Exhibition* [Baltimore, Md.: Friends of Art, 1928], items on display in the Music Room). The author thanks Catherine Rogers Arthur at Homewood for bringing this exhibition to his attention and for her assistance with other questions regarding the Carroll and Rogers families and their furniture. The records of the Friends of Art shed no further light on this provenance, as the Friends seem not to have preserved research notes used to compile the catalogue. See the folders for this exhibition in Municipal Art Society of Baltimore, Records, 1905–1949, Ms. 2840, box 2, MdHS. When Lydia Morris Howard died in 1921 she divided her estate between her children, Lydia, Nancy, and Charles Morris, and placed an equal share in trust for her son Frank Key (Lydia E. H. Howard Will, Wills, H.W.J. [137], fols. 115–117, Register of Wills, Baltimore City). All of these children apparently lived with her at 401 North Charles Street. Lydia Morris Howard's inventory lists stocks, and only one page of personal items including several pieces of furniture. This was clearly not enough to furnish this house (Lydia E. H. Howard Inventory, Inventories, H.W.J. [231], fols. 368–372, Register of Wills, Baltimore City). It appears that by this time her children had informally inherited or divided the contents of the house, including the suite. Nancy H. Howard was the first of Lydia Morris Howard's children to die. She left her furniture equally to her three siblings. In the inventory of her possessions at 401 North Charles Street, Nancy's part of the suite is specifically itemized under a heading "Painted furniture from Clearmont made by Findlay." According to the inventory, she owned the chairs depicting Belvidere and the St. Paul's Charity School, and the settee depicting Montebello at the center of the crest (Will and Inventory of Nancy H. Howard, estate #2651, Register of Wills, Baltimore City). When Lydia Howard DeFord died in 1945, her inventory included "8 Small chairs, 2 seats, 1 console Table," valued at $1,200, which were listed as being at the Museum of Art (Inventory of Lydia Howard DeFord, estate #42404, Register of Wills, Baltimore City). Charles Morris Howard left all of his furniture to Lydia Howard DeFord's two daughters, so the two chairs he owned were re-united with the rest of the suite (Will of Charles Morris Howard, estate #46237, Register of Wills, Baltimore City). Frank Key Howard died in 1929. Presumably, the pieces he had inherited passed to his sister Lydia Howard DeFord, who had earlier acquired the furniture owned by Nancy. Throughout the 1930s, Charles Morris only owned two chairs, including the one that depicted Willow Brook. Either Lydia DeFord de Roth or her sister Nancy DeFord Venable owned a copy of Scarborough's "Unique Record of Baltimore Mansions." Neither made corrections to Scarborough's observation that the suite had been used by John B. Morris at Claremont, suggesting that they did not find her account in error. See Lydia Howard de Roth Papers, ms. 1906, MdHS. Some other articles and obituaries in this collection are corrected or annotated.

15. The fate of the blue suite of furniture purchased by Charles Howard is not known. When he died in 1869 he left all of his property to his wife Elizabeth Phoebe (Key) (Will of Charles Howard, Wills, J.H.B. [35], fols. 376–377, Register of Wills, Baltimore City). His

estate was not inventoried, nor was there any further administration. Elizabeth died intestate in 1897. If the blue suite was among her possessions, it was not inventoried as a readily identifiable group (Inventory of Elizabeth P. K. Howard, Inventories, T.W.M. [164], fols. 568–572). Both Charles and Elizabeth's obituaries state that they died at their country home Oakland in Allegheny County. Although they had lived at the northeast corner of Mount Vernon Square for many years, that property was sold and Elizabeth died at their home at 919 Cathedral Street. As they had a number of children, the suite could have been given or bequeathed to any one of them. The white and yellow suites in the auction catalogue were both described as including armchairs, as were other suites of chairs in the house. As the description of the blue suite simply stated "chairs," these seating forms were most likely side chairs (*Catalogue of the Furniture, Plate, &c. of the Late Col. Howard,* lots 47, 89, 247). Two copies of the auction catalogue are in the collection of the MdHS. One copy was owned by Charles Howard, but descended in the family of Charles McHenry Howard, a cousin of the Howards under discussion. The other copy was owned by Benjamin Chew Howard, whose descendants, even more distant cousins of the Howards under discussion, gave it to the MdHS. For the 1914 exhibition the committee provided forms to each potential lender, with spaces to describe each object. A blank form is in a large group of documents regarding this exhibition in Mayor James H. Preston's Papers at the Baltimore City Archives.

16. Amy D'Arcy Wetmore, "Old Country Seats Scenes of Gaiety. Baltimoreans of 1800 to 1850 Enjoyed Suburban Life in Country. Many Old Homes are Now Passing. City was Formerly Encircled by Places where the Owners Entertained Friends," *Baltimore News,* July 25, 1914. In this article, Wetmore discusses many of the houses depicted on the Morris suite but does not mention the furniture. Since she also mentions the Morris country house, Claremont, Wetmore may have known of the furniture. Although her article preceded the *National Star Spangled Banner Centennial* exhibition by several months, she could have heard of the suite during the planning stages of this exhibition or known the Howards socially. Another manuscript document, also apparently in the hand of Lydia Howard DeFord, accompanied the suite when acquired by the BMA. On it, she listed three of the houses, Willow Brook, Bolton, and Montebello, and living descendants of the original owners. She may have contacted these individuals for information about the houses. However, as the manuscript also has a brief list of "Collectors," including Mrs. Miles White and Mrs. William H. Whitridge, the individuals listed may have been people who might have had an interest in purchasing the suite. As the list also notes that Mrs. H. Irvine Keyser gave a building to the Maryland Historical Society (the Enoch Pratt House), it was created sometime after 1916. It is possible that some of the properties depicted on the suite did not have names. A typed list headed "Key List to Houses represented on furniture" is in the file for the suite at the BMA. Although no author for this list is noted, local historian Dr. J. Hall Pleasants created it. J. G. D Paul's "Art, History and A Baltimore Cabinet-Maker," noted that the BMA was indebted to Pleasants' research, and he is credited for information concerning the set in *Baltimore Furniture: The Work of Baltimore and Annapolis Cabinetmakers from 1760 to 1810,* p. 156. For some reason, numbers 3 and 5 were omitted from this list. Pleasants noted the uncertainty of the identifications and locations of several houses, in particular those that are not named on the list. Some of his research notes on the suite are in his file on John and Hugh Finlay (J. Hall Pleasants Studies in Maryland Painting, MdHS).

17. The suite's images are treated as securely identified "documents" regarding the appearance of the buildings in the 1936 exhibition at the Peale Museum and in Robert L. Raley, "The Baltimore Country-House 1785–1815" (master's thesis, University of Delaware, 1959). Although unpublished, this thesis is often cited. Warner & Hanna's map shows the location of Gibson's house, indicating that this structure is the house to the left of Bolton in several landscapes by Francis Guy. See Colwill, *Francis Guy,* pp. 63, 65. The correction of numbers 3 and 4 is noted in Elder, *American Furniture 1680–1880,* p. 47, nt. 7. See Baltimore Equitable Society, policy 1355, November 1, 1803. McCurdy's seat, described as being near that of Jeremiah Yellott, was brick, measured 50' x 22' 3", and had a "well finished Balcony along the whole front of twelve feet wide." The house had two stories, with "about two thirds of the Cellar part above the surface of the Earth." This description does not relate to the image said to be McCurdy's house. The Equitable Society records are one of the few resources available to document the size and general appearance of buildings from the early nineteenth century. Unfortunately, in this period few of the owners of the houses illustrated on the suite insured their country residences with this company.

18. Whitman H. Ridgway, *Community Leadership in Maryland 1790–1840: A Comparative*

Analysis of Power in Society (Chapel Hill, N.C.: University of North Carolina Press, 1979), chapter 4 and appendices.

19. Willow Brook or its precursor is visible on the 1799 edition of the Warner & Hanna map. The map indicates that the house was owned by (Thorowgood) "Smith," who built the dwelling and subsequently sold it to John Donnell. A change in the shape of the dedicatory legend hid this building in the 1801 version of the map.

20. The author thanks J. Laurie Ossman for suggesting that the images would have been hidden when the seating furniture was in use.

21. The image on the chair was identified as Greenwood in Elder, *Baltimore Painted Furniture*, p. 41. Correspondence from the previous owner of these chairs, in the accession file for the work at the museum, makes no mention of the identification of the buildings on the pieces. For more on Druid Hill see Edith Rossiter Bevan, "Druid Hill, Country Seat of the Rogers and Buchanan Families," *Maryland Historical Magazine* 44, no. 3 (September 1949): 190–99. The house and its builder are also discussed in Robert L. Alexander, "Nicholas Rogers, Gentleman-Architect of Baltimore," *Maryland Historical Magazine* (hereafter cited *MHM*) 78, no. 2 (summer 1983): 84–105. No earlier authors questioned the identifications of the buildings painted on the suite, and in the past the images have been used as historical documents without questioning the accuracy of the depictions or their identification. Greenwood's similarity to Druid Hill is noted by Bevan, "Druid Hill, Country Seat of the Rogers and Buchanan Families," p. 197, nt. 16; and Alexander, "Nicholas Rogers, Gentleman-Architect of Baltimore," pp. 87–88. Both authors used only the pier table image as evidence of the appearance of Greenwood. Bevan found the image on the pier table "rather reminiscent" of Druid Hill, while Alexander found it a "virtual replica." Noting that the pier table image is damaged, Alexander observed slight differences in the windows in the parapet and in the stairway and columns. It appears that neither author knew of the more intact image on the chair (fig. 41).

22. In his Baltimore period, Saint-Mémin produced a number of images with suggestive landscape settings. The Rogers piece is unique among the known images for its inclusion of an actual house. Two other Saint-Mémin portraits depict buildings, but the sitters and structures have not been identified. See Ellen G. Miles, *Saint-Memin and the Neoclassical Profile Portrait in America* (Washington, D.C.: National Portrait Gallery and the Smithsonian Institution Press, 1994), pp. 122, 268, 382, 418. The author thanks Ellen Miles for her thoughts on this portrait.

23. Architect Michael F. Trostel restored Druid Hill a number of years ago. In his copy of Elder's *Baltimore Painted Furniture,* he annotated the image of Greenwood "now known to be Druid Hill." Precisely how Trostel came to this conclusion is not known. The author thanks Peter Pearre, Trostel's partner in the firm of Trostel & Pearre, for his assistance with this article. For Greenwood, see Baltimore Equitable Society, policy 4135, February 1, 1815. An earlier policy 896 and 897, February 1, 1801, does not mention the kitchen underneath. On February 1, 1808, it was renewed as policy 2107 with the same description as 1801, both valued at $2,666.67. When renewed in 1815, the phrase about the kitchen was added, and the valuation increased to $3,000.00. For Druid Hill, see Baltimore Equitable Society, policy 7883, January 26, 1824. As of this time the house was owned by Nicholas Rogers' son Lloyd Nicholas Rogers. The author thanks Peter Pearre for these insurance references.

24. The author has also speculated that an earlier manuscript could have listed the house as that belonging to "Col. Rogers" which could have been mistaken for "Phil. Rogers" if written in a particularly flowery hand. A newspaper article discussing one of Lloyd Nicholas Rogers' daughters gave a history of the Rogers family and an account of the sale of Druid Hill to the city ("She Lived in Druid Hill, Mrs. Goldsborough last Occupant of Mansion at Sale," *The Sun* [Baltimore], March 6, 1905).

25. The listing of "Mrs. Carroll" on the Howard manuscript has only been acknowledged in the catalogue for the 1928 Friends of Art *Homewood Exhibition.* Michael F. Trostel, *Mount Clare: Being an Account of the Seat built by Charles Carroll, Barrister, upon his Lands at Patapsco* (Baltimore, Md.: National Society of Colonial Dames of American in the State of Maryland, 1981). After the barrister died, his wife Margaret had only a life interest in the property. At her death it was to become the property of the Barrister's nephew James (Maccubbin) Carroll, who did not take possession of the house until 1817 (see ch. 5 and p. 91). Margaret is listed as the tax-paying owner of the property for the 1798 federal tax and is listed on the 1804 tax list for precincts surrounding Baltimore Town (George J. Horvath, Jr., *The Particular Assessment Lists for Baltimore and Carroll Counties 1798* [Westminster, Md.: Family Line Publications,

1986], pp. 59, 138). It is unlikely that this house references James Carroll. He had never resided there before the suite was made. Jesse Hollingsworth obituary, *American & Commercial Daily Advertiser,* October 1, 1810, Dielman-Hayward file, MdHS. The fact that the Howard list does not refer to "Mrs. Yellott" or "Mrs. McCurdy" as it does to "Mrs. Carroll," suggests that the suite may have been made before the deaths of Jeremiah Yellott and Hugh McCurdy in 1805, although "McCurdy," as mentioned, may simply be in error.

26. J. Thomas Scharf, *History of Baltimore City and County,* 2 vols. (1881; facsimile reprint, Baltimore, Md.: Regional Publishing Company: 1971), 1: 454. Scharf also discussed the subsequent use of this building by the Mount Hope College, which apparently purchased it in 1828. He described it as being seventy feet long, and states that it was probably built "about 1800" (ibid., 2: 853). Scharf's account of the Banks of the City appears to be one of the few extant, and is often quoted and paraphrased.

27. Scharf, *History of Baltimore,* 1: 452–56. Gilmor was a committee representative from the Bank of Maryland around 1797, when the Banks of the City was in its formative stages. Grundy and Harris represented the Office of Discount and Deposit in different meetings in 1800. During later years, Gilmor, Samuel Smith, and Jeremiah Yellott represented the Bank of Maryland, and Grundy and Harris represented the Office of Discount and Deposit. The boards in this period seem to have only undergone minor changes each year. In 1795 Nicholas Rogers and Hugh McCurdy supervised the sale of subscriptions for the Bank of Baltimore, but they were not among the list of directors in 1796, 1803, or 1804.

28. Information on the early years of this school is found in the Benevolent Society's publication *An Address to the Members of the Protestant Episcopal Church, in the City and County of Baltimore* (Baltimore, Md.: Joseph Robinson, 1811). Scharf's *History of Baltimore* only mentions the St. Paul Charity School in a footnote (2: 521, nt. 1]) where he states that a performance was for the benefit of the "Female Charity School, under the direction of the Benevolent Society." Other early charities include the Charitable Marine Society (1796); the Baltimore Orphan Asylum (prior to 1801), first known as the Female Humane Association Charity School, and then as the Orphaline Charity School and St. Peter's School and Orphan Asylum (1806) (ibid., 2: 592, 594). It is unclear whether each institution had a building. St. Peter's School could have been founded after the suite was made. On the subsequent history of the St. Paul's Charity School, see Mary H. Bready, *Through All Our Days: A History of St. Paul's School for Girls* (Hunt Valley, Md.: Braun-Brumfield Inc., Sheridan Group, 1999). The author thanks Bready for her assistance with his research.

29. *The Laws of Maryland, Volume II,* edited by William Kilty (Annapolis, Md.: Frederick Green, 1800), ch. 44, "An Act to incorporate a society for the maintenance and education of poor female children, by the name of The Benevolent Society of the City and County of Baltimore." *An Address to the Members of the Protestant Episcopal Church,* pp. 9, 11. When The Orphaline Charity School was rechartered in 1807, similar voting structures were put in place, and it was affirmed that women had the right to vote for the trustees, indicating that this issue was important to the managers. *The Laws of Maryland, Volume III,* edited by William Kilty, et al. (Annapolis, Md.: J. Green, 1820), ch. 145, "An Act for incorporating a Society to educate and maintain Poor Orphan and other destitute Female Children, by the name of The Orphaline Charity School, and to repeal an Act of Assembly therein mentioned." The school was first chartered in 1801 as the Female Humane Association Charity School.

30. *An Address to the Members of the Protestant Episcopal Church,* pp. 6, 13–19. For Margaret Carroll's bequest, see Trostel, *Mount Clare,* p. 88. Will of Nicholas Rogers, Wills, W.B. (11), fols. 354–356, Register of Wills, Baltimore City.

31. On Ridgely as a trustee, see Kilty, *The Laws of Maryland, Volume III,* ch. 145, where it is also mentioned that by this time the charity had a "school-house." Scharf, *History of Baltimore,* 2: 592, states this school was organized several years previous to its charter in 1801. On this school's complicated history, see Ron Pilling and Pat Pilling, *Pickersgill Retirement Community: Two Centuries of Service to Baltimore* (Towson, Md.: Pickersgill Retirement Community, 2002). The Pillings state that as of 1802 several of the female managers were married to tanners and riggers (p. 12). These women and their families were from a different social class than those associated with the Morris suite. Several Ridgelys made donations to the Benevolent Society, but not Charles Carnan Ridgely or his wife Priscilla Dorsey Ridgely. See *An Address to the Members of the Protestant Episcopal Church,* p. 16, for Charles Sterrett, Nicholas G. and Rebecca, who were donors; and p. 18 for Rachel and Rebecca as discontinued subscribers. Rebecca was probably Charles Carnan Ridgely's aunt. On the instrumental roles of Philip Rogers and

Charles Carnan Ridgely in establishing Methodism in Baltimore, see *Those Incredible Methodists: A History of the Baltimore Conference of the United Methodist Church,* edited by Gordon Pratt Baker (Baltimore, Md.: Commission on Archives and History, Baltimore Conference, 1972), p. 15, 27ff.

32. See Wendy A. Cooper, "American Painted Furniture: A New Perspective on Its Decoration and Use," *Antiques* 161, no. 1 (January 2002): 212–17. The Morris suite was used in a country house by about 1904. Painted armchairs and side chairs similar to those in the Morris suite were in George Brown's country house Brooklandwood by 1897 (Elwell, *The Architecture, Furniture and Interiors of Maryland and Virginia,* pls. 3, 4, 8). Although several objects illustrated in Elder's *Baltimore Painted Furniture* were used in country settings, few can be documented there before the early twentieth century.

33. Betsy Patterson Bonaparte to John Spear Smith, August 22, 1816, Bonaparte Collection, ms. 142, box 3, MdHS. The author thanks Helen Jean Burn for this reference. John Spear Smith was the son of General Samuel Smith, owner of Montebello. Written a century after Patterson's account, Wetmore's "Old Country Seat Scenes of Gaiety" suggests a more active life in the country. The patronage and display of landscapes like those painted by Francis Guy are not well documented. Harry Dorsey Gough's views of his estate Perry Hall were part of the furnishings of his house in Baltimore (Colwill, *Francis Guy,* p. 111). A valuable comparison is found in two of Flemish artist Hendrik De Cort's (1742–1810) views of Castle Howard and its grounds, commissioned by the Fifth Earl of Carlisle specifically for his town house in London (*Castle Howard* [Yorkshire, England: Castle Howard Estate Ltd., 1997], pp. 60–61). These works were apparently painted after De Cort came to England in 1790. As the earl had in the 1770s commissioned four views of the estate by William Marlow (1740–1813) that were used in the castle (see ibid., pp. 53, 60), this second commission suggests an increased interest in the use of country views in the city.

34. *Records of the City of Baltimore,* vol. 4 (1818), as quoted in Sherry H. Olson, *Baltimore: The Building of an American City* (1980; revised and expanded ed., Baltimore, Md.: Johns Hopkins University Press, 1997), p. 54.

35. Elder, *Baltimore Painted Furniture,* pp. 28–33; Elder, *American Furniture, 1680–1880,* pp. 47–48, 60–61, 135–36, 162–63; and Montgomery, *American Furniture,* pp. 451–53. Although this suite of furniture is not the focus of the article, the houses and furniture are discussed in "Buchanan Family Reminiscences," *MHM* 35, no. 3 (September 1940): 262–69. This article gives one the earliest known accounts of the furniture, and a drawing closely replicating the image on the pier table is included on page 265. By 1940 some of this furniture had been sold to individuals outside the family. In "Buchanan Family Reminiscences," the building on the card table is described as "the town-house," but it is not specifically associated with James A. Buchanan. Elder identified the building in *American Furniture 1680–1880,* p. 136, nt. 2. Documentation for the date of the building is found in Thomas Waters Griffith, *Annals of Baltimore* (Baltimore, Md.: W. Wooddy, 1824), p. 169. The chair with the view of Hampton and its accompanying seating forms are thought to be English and only decorated in Baltimore. A chair from this set is illustrated in Miller, *American Antique Furniture,* 1: 205, no. 278. At that time, Miss Harriet R. Chew, a Ridgely descendant, was the owner. Two chairs remain at Hampton, one with the house depicted on the crest rail, the other with a garden ruin. The crest rail image of Hampton is illustrated in Hastings, *A Guidebook to Hampton National Historic Site,* p. 74. The author thanks Lynne Hastings for information on these pieces. There is no evidence that Eleanor and Nicholas Rogers owned the Morris suite. Eleanor died before her husband and, as was typical, no estate was entered into probate. Nicholas died with a will, but no inventory was taken of his personal possessions (Will of Nicholas Rogers, Wills, W.B. [11], fols. 354–356, Register of Wills, Baltimore City). As mentioned, his son Lloyd Nicholas Rogers subsequently owned Druid Hill, selling it immediately before he died. The recording of his estate took place shortly after he had moved out of the mansion. In the detailed inventory of his house on Mulberry Street in Baltimore, nothing corresponds to the Morris suite (Lloyd N. Rogers Inventory, Inventories, I.P.C. [79], fols. 91–100, Register of Wills, Baltimore City). However, several pieces of caned furniture were listed including "5 Cane Seat Chair[s]" and "2 Cane Seat Hall Chair[s]" in the hall and "5 Cane Seat Chairs" in the garrets. These seating forms may well have constituted the suite of twelve white painted chairs of New York or Massachusetts origin possibly used at Druid Hill. For the armchairs, see Weidman, *Furniture in Maryland 1740–1940,* pp. 110–11. John B. Morris was in law partnership with Lloyd Nicholas Rogers and probated his will. Morris could have acquired the suite from Rogers any number of times, including when the latter

sold Druid Hill. Coincidentally, Rogers' townhouse was very close to the residences of Morris and Morris' daughter Lydia Morris Howard.

36. Most accounts of the rooms are drawn from Scharf, *History of Baltimore,* 2: 679–80, who noted that they opened in January 1798. Robert Alexander stated that the rooms opened in January of the following year (Alexander, "Nicholas Rogers," p. 88). On assembly rooms as part of a larger culture of social refinement in the United States, see Richard L. Bushman, *The Refinement of America: Persons, Houses, Cities* (New York: Knopf, 1992), pp. 50–51, 160–61, 186–88.

37. *The New Baltimore Directory, and Annual Register; for 1800 and 1801* (Baltimore, Md.: Warner & Hanna, [1800–1801]), p. 22. The author thanks Helen Jean Burn for leading him to this reference. The city directory published in 1799 did not mention the rooms, perhaps because they were not yet open. [John H. B. Latrobe], *Picture of Baltimore, Containing a Description of All Objects of Interest in the City; and Embellished with Views of the Principal Public Buildings* (Baltimore, Md.: F. Lucas, Jr., 1832), p. 192. The building is illustrated opposite p. 191. This publication notes that the function of the rooms had recently been changed. The best description of the rooms and their sizes is found in the sale announcement for 1817 ("Trustee's Sale . . . Dancing Assembly," *Federal Gazette & Baltimore Daily Advertiser,* March 31–May 7, 1817, announcing the sale which took place on May 8). See also James S. Buckingham quoted (without noting that it is him) in Alexander, "Nicholas Rogers," p. 90.

38. Alexander, "Nicholas Rogers," p. 90. For a brief discussion and illustration of this building, see Mills Lane, *Architecture of the Old South: Maryland* (New York: Abbeville Press, 1991), pp. 88–90. In *Refinement of America,* Bushman observes that "these special structures for cultured events were less common in America than taverns with special rooms for assemblies" (p. 161). Bushman does not specifically discuss the Baltimore Dancing Assembly Rooms. The author thanks Charles Brownell for his thoughts on assembly rooms in this period.

39. This denial of admission to males in the area is noted on "Baltimore Assembly" (Baltimore, Md.: W. Goddard and J. Angell, n.d.). Two copies of this broadside detailing the "rules" of the assembly are in the Broadside Collection, MdHS. Although not dated, one is inscribed on the reverse: "Assembly Tech [? sp]1789/ Mr. Harris." This copy was apparently inscribed to David Harris, a very early subscriber to the assembly. The other is inscribed to "W. H. Dorsey (of [?])." This copy may have been sent to William Hammond Dorsey, the brother of Walter Dorsey. Similar guidelines are found in much later rules. See "Extracts from Proceedings of Directors and Managers, Relative to Baltimore Assemblies," December 23, 1836, Broadside Collection, MdHS. "Though the membership encompassed a larger group than any one individual's circle of friends, the assemblies were self-consciously and resolutely exclusive" (Bushman, *Refinement of America,* pp. 50–51). After attending a concert in Baltimore in 1827, Robert Gilmor, Jr., wrote: "There was a large company of our acquaintance invited, but many of those present were not of our circle, though very respectable people, who came to see their daughters perform" ("The Diary of Robert Gilmor," *MHM* 17, no. 3 [December 1922]: 249, entry for January 18, 1827). Gilmor's many diary entries document the close family circle that dominated his social activities, as well as the larger circle of friends and acquaintances with whom he interacted. While numerous, the friends in no way represent all of wealthy Baltimore society. Both Gilmor and his father were members of the Dancing Assembly. The contentious exchange between Smith and Oliver, which ended without bloodshed, is noted in John Bosley Yellott, Jr., "Jeremiah Yellott—Revolutionary War Privateersman and Baltimore Philanthropist," *MHM* 86, no. 2 (summer 1991): 183–84. John Yellott states that Robert Oliver blackballed Robert Smith from membership, but this author read the original source and interpreted it differently. Smith, who was a member, criticized Oliver's respectability, as he believed Oliver had cashed a check that was not his. Oliver stated that it was his right as a Dancing Assembly stockholder to follow his judgement in voting on nominations. See *Federal Gazette & Baltimore Daily Advertiser,* December 21, 23, 26, 31, 1798. The subscribers are documented in "New Dancing Assembly Association," April 16, 1817, vertical file, Manuscripts Department, MdHS. This document gave Isaac McKim, James Sterrett, and John Spear Smith the authority to purchase the rooms for the association's use by dividing the cost into shares that would be purchased by those signing the document. The manuscript also notes that as soon as the building was purchased, the subscribers would convene to adopt regulations necessary for the management of the property. This sale required an act of the Maryland Legislature, which appears to have been proposed in 1816 and passed on January 30, 1817. See *The Laws of Maryland Volume V,* edited by William Kilty, et al. (Annapolis, Md.: J. Green, 1820), ch. 191, "An Act for the Sale of the Baltimore Dancing

Assembly Rooms." The notice of the sale appeared in *Federal Gazette & Baltimore Daily Advertiser* as "Trustee's Sale . . . Dancing Assembly." The second sale was first advertised in "Baltimore Dancing Assembly Rooms for Sale," *American & Commercial Daily Advertiser,* April 10, 1835, and the advertisement ran through June 1, 1835, the day of the sale. The lot is described as 48' x 95', apparently the size of the building. On June 2, 1835, the *American & Commercial Daily Advertiser* reported that B. I. Cohen had bought the rooms for $10,000, and that "it is intended to retain the building for the purpose for which it was originally designed, and that it will undergo material repairs and improvements in order the better to adapt it to this object." *Matchett's Baltimore Director. Corrected up to May, 1837. For 1837–8* (Baltimore, Md.: Baltimore Director Office, 1837), p. 19, noted that the building had "lately been altered in height from two to three stories, and otherwise improved." See "Baltimore Assembly Record Books," 1837–1839, ms. 53, Manuscripts Department, MdHS. This volume lists the subscribers to balls in this period. A note by Mendes Cohen, who donated the volume to the MdHS in 1915, states that he purchased it from a dealer "some year ago." According to this note, the volume also included invitations addressed to "the Misses Cox," but the invitations are no longer in the volume. They are, however, probably the invitations seen by Scharf and noted in his *History of Baltimore,* 2: 678. The sale of the building is noted in *Historical Sketch of the Central High School of Baltimore: Its Wants and Claims, by a Friend of Education* (Baltimore, Md.: Samuel S. Mills, 1856), pp. 14–15. "Messrs. Cohen" owned the building when it was purchased by the city. The sale was first suggested in 1842 and completed in 1844. At the time of the purchase, the property was described as the "Old Assembly Rooms and tavern." This tavern, apparently a building between the Dancing Assembly Rooms and the Holliday Street Theater, was torn down to make way for a playground. The building with its third story is illustrated in the school's 1860 annual report. See also Rice, *Maryland History in Prints 1743–1900,* p. 195. The fire spread to the former Dancing Assembly Rooms from the Holliday Street Theater (*The Sun* [Baltimore], September 10, 11, 1873). It appears that the second and third stories were largely destroyed, or at least heavily damaged. Whether the building was torn down shortly thereafter is not mentioned.

40. "Baltimore Dancing Assembly," *Federal Gazette & Baltimore Daily Advertiser,* September 5, 1798. Although built in the 1770s, the Maryland State House was apparently not uniformly furnished until 1797 (William Vose Elder, III, and Lu Bartlett, *John Shaw: Cabinetmaker of Annapolis* [Baltimore, Md.: Baltimore Museum of Art, 1983], pp. 127–28). Elder and Bartlett note that "A new State House did not necessarily entail all new furniture; some furnishings accumulated in the sixty-five year history of the second State House would have survived." Although the Dancing Assembly Rooms were new in 1799, a similar situation could have arisen with that organization's furnishings. This author believes it likely that the rooms were not immediately equipped with all new furniture. See J. C. Nates' 1804 engraving of the Pump Room in Barry Cunliffe, *The Roman Baths at Bath: Authorised Guide Book* (Bath, Eng.: Bath Archaeological Trust, 1993), p. 40. This illustration as well as one from the mid-nineteenth century are in Diana Winsor, *Historic Bath* (Norwich, Eng.: Jarrold Publishing, 1987), n.p. The 1804 view shows no furniture, while that from mid-century shows a few chairs and settees lining the walls. These pieces do not appear to be upholstered. "Extracts from Proceedings of Directors and Managers, Relative to Baltimore Assemblies."

41. See the reproductions of their advertisements in the *Federal Gazette & Baltimore Daily Advertiser,* October 24, 1803, and the *American & Commercial Daily Advertiser,* August 11, 1804, reproduced in Colwill, *Francis Guy,* 24. A detailed account of this celebration is in "Commodore Perry," *American & Commercial Daily Advertiser,* February 2, 1814: "The whole of the arrangements, paintings, and decorations, under the management of that ingenious artist, Mr. Findley, who displayed a taste, and a spirit, such as have not been witnessed in our city on any former occasion." See also Rembrandt Peale, "Reminiscences. Desultory," *The Crayon* 3, no. 1 (January 1856): 6. Peale recounted this story to explain how he had been, in his opinion, responsible for the change in Robert Mills' design for the column. Peale does not mention the first name of the Finlay involved. A contemporary account of the festivities observed that Peale's portrait and a painting by Henry Warren of Mills' design "were richly decorated by Mr. Hugh Findley, forming, together, an appropriate trophy for the occasion" (*An Authentic Account of all the Proceedings on the Fourth of July, 1815, With Regard to Laying the Corner Stone of the Washington Monument Now Erecting in the City of Baltimore* [Baltimore, Md.: John Horace Pratt, 1815], p. 4). Scharf, *History of Baltimore,* 1: 267.

42. Robert Oliver Papers, ms. 626.1, MdHS; Journal 1805–1808, fol. 159, August 7, 1806, and fol. 270, January 31, 1807. "The Baltimore Dancing Assembly," *Federal Gazette & Balti-*

more Daily Advertiser, January 12, 1799; and the 1836 "Extracts from Proceedings of Directors and Managers, Relative to Baltimore Assemblies." Both publications indicate that the heads of the horses pulling the carriages should face Gay Street on arrival and departure. John E. Semmes, *John H. B. Latrobe and His Times 1803–1891* (Baltimore, Md.: Norman, Remington Co., 1917), p. 190. Latrobe believed that by 1824 there may have been fewer than a dozen private carriages "because the style of living was plainer, and that strife had not arisen in which victory constituted outdoing your neighbor in dress and equipage." Latrobe was too young to have personally remembered the period in which the Dancing Assembly Rooms were built, and by 1824 the financial pressures of the late 1810s may have altered the extravagant displays of earlier times. Interestingly, Latrobe's discussion of carriages immediately precedes his discussion of balls, indicating they were linked in his mind.

43. For more on the White House furniture, see Betty C. Monkman, *The White House: Its Historic Furnishings and First Families* (New York: Abbeville Press, 2000), pp. 38–40. When President Monroe redecorated this room after the fire, his agent Joseph Russell informed him that "mahogany is not generally admitted in the furniture of a Saloon, even at private gentlemen's houses." Russell subsequently supplied him with a gilded suite (p. 61). Samuel Smith to Dolly Payne Madison, March 10, 1809, receivers copy, White House. The author thanks Catherine Thomas of the BMA for bringing this highly important document to his attention. It has been published in Monkman, *The White House,* p. 40. On Finlay's behalf, Smith asked for Dolly Madison's "friendly interference" with Latrobe "that he may participate in the furnishing of the Presidential House."

44. The chair depicting Lafayette was given to the Baltimore Museum of Art by a descendant of William Patterson. Family tradition apparently held that it was made for Patterson to use at a dinner given in Lafayette's honor during his visit to Baltimore. Since as early as 1936, this visit has been associated with a reference in J. Thomas Scharf's *The Chronicles of Baltimore, Being a Complete History of "Baltimore Town" and Baltimore City From the Earliest Period to the Present Time* (Baltimore, Md.: Turnbull Brothers, 1874). On page 415, Scharf mentions two dinners attended by Lafayette with members of the corporation of Baltimore. This is the source cited by Elder, *Baltimore Painted Furniture,* p. 69. Its 1936 association with the chair is documented on the Index of American Design Data Report Sheet MD-FU-56 (1943.8.4397), on file with the Department of Modern Prints and Drawings, National Gallery of Art, Washington, D.C., which also cites this source. When a photograph of this chair was included in the Index of American Design exhibition at the National Museum in Washington, a local newspaper account incorrectly stated that this chair had been used for a dinner given for Lafayette at Fort McHenry ("A Catalogue of U.S. Artisans," *The Sun* [Baltimore], August 2, 1936). As Scharf's *Chronicles of Baltimore* does not discuss the dinner and ball at the Dancing Assembly Rooms, the possibility of the chair having been made for this occasion has not to date been suggested. In addition to the two dinners he documents, Scharf only notes that there was a "splendid ball given in [the] Holliday Street Theater, which had been fitted up for the occasion." He amended this in his *History of Baltimore,* 2: 679, where he notes that the impressive dinner that followed the ball was held at the Dancing Assembly Rooms. *Plan of Arrangements for The Ball, In Honour of General La Fayette* (Baltimore, Md., 1824). A copy of this program is in the collection of the MdHS. Contrary to Scharf's account, the program indicates that the ball and dinner were held in the Dancing Assembly Rooms, while the Holliday Street Theater was used as holding rooms for the guests. At the head table at the dinner, Lafayette was seated with "several gentleman entitled to seats . . . attended by the five elder Managers, and the Chairman of the Committee of Arrangement" (p. 5). The gentleman and "elder Managers" were not named, but William Patterson was included in most of the short lists of those in Lafayette's company while in Baltimore (Scharf, *Chronicles of Baltimore,* pp. 409–15). Thomas Waters Griffith, *Annals of Baltimore* (Baltimore, Md.: W. Wooddy, 1824); and Thomas Waters Griffith, Notebook, 1824, ms. 412, MdHS. This notebook bears a handwritten title page "Seven Lectures on Chapters on Maryland History read by the late Thomas W. Griffith in the Baltimore Assembly Rooms in 1824." Depending on the dates of his lectures, Griffith may have been asked to speak after the publication of his volume.

45. On the general cultural criticism in this period, see Bushman, *Refinement of America,* pp. 186–93. [Sir Richard Hill], *An Address to Persons of Fashion, Relating to Balls: With a Few Occasional Hints Concerning Play-houses, Card-tables &c. In Which is Introduced the Character of Lucinda, With an Appendix, Containing Some Extracts From the Writings of Eminent Pious Men, Against the Entertainments of the Stage, and Other Vain Amusements. By a Member of the Church of England* (Baltimore, Md.: Printed by J. Robinson, for Cole and I. Bonsal, Warner &

Hanna, and George Hill, 1807). Sir Richard Hill (1733–1808) was a British author. This work was first published in 1761. The author thanks Mary Herbert, Curator of Manuscripts at the MdHS, for bringing this reference to his attention and for sharing her work on the Morris suite. Ibid., pp. v–vi, 25–26. One copy of this volume (MdHS) is annotated on the front fly leaf "P Gough 1807"; on the title page "P Gough"; and on page 7 "Prudence G. Ridgely." The volume was probably owned by Prudence Carnan Gough (1755–1822), the sister of Charles Carnan Ridgely of Hampton, and perhaps later by her granddaughter Prudence Gough Carroll (1795–1822), who married John Ridgely (1790–1867) of Hampton in 1812. The author thanks Lynne Hastings at Hampton for assistance in sorting out the ownership of this volume.

46. The Finlays advertised "Trophies of Music, War, Husbandry, Love, etc., etc.," indicating that they were thinking of their decorations in symbolic ways (*Federal Gazette & Baltimore Daily Advertiser,* February 4, 1806). The Union Bank is the next bank chartered after the three that were housed in the Banks of the City (Scharf, *History of Baltimore,* 1: 456). On the building designed by Robert Cary Long, Sr., see Lane, *Architecture of the Old South: Maryland,* pp. 106–7. The sculpture on the bank's pediment depicted Neptune and Ceres, representing maritime commerce and agriculture. The Commercial and Farmers Bank, built later, had an arched entry with spandrels depicting Mercury and Ceres, representing commerce and agriculture (pp. 122–23). Therefore, in this period Baltimoreans were used to thinking of commerce in abstract representational ways, suggesting that they may have viewed the buildings depicted on the suite in this manner. The author thanks Martin Perschler for this observation regarding masculine and feminine spheres.

47. See for instance H. Rodney Nevitt, Jr., *Art and the Culture of Love in Seventeenth-Century Holland* (Cambridge, Eng.: Cambridge University Press, 2003), p. 6. See also Cesare Ripa, *Baroque and Rococo Pictorial Imagery; The 1758–60 Hertel Edition of Ripa's 'Iconologia' with 200 Engraved Illustrations,* introduction by Edward A. Maser (New York: Dover Publications, Inc., 1971), pls. 9, 53: where "Earth" and "Assistance" use a grapevine twined around a staff to symbolize fruitfulness and "conjugal assistance." This metaphor would blossom throughout the nineteenth century into the commonplace "clinging vine" and "sturdy oak." Alexis de Tocqueville, *Democracy in America,* 2 vols., translated by Henry Reeve (1837), 1: chapter 17. De Tocqueville noted that while religion was often powerless to keep men from the temptations of life, its "influence over the mind of women is supreme, and women are the protectors of morals. There is certainly no country in the world where the tie of marriage is more respected than in America or where conjugal happiness is more highly or worthily appreciated." Robert Gilmor, Jr., had a commemorative medal made for the fiftieth wedding anniversary of his parents Robert Sr. and Louisa (Airey). The back of the medal depicted Cupid with the motto: "To Conjugal Happiness." This medal was presented at a ceremony at the Gilmors' country residence Beech Hill (Humphries, *Robert Gilmor, Jr.,* 1: 111). Prescriptive discussions of conjugal happiness, religion, and love were so commonplace at this time that they appeared in almanacs published locally. See, for example, Abraham Weatherwise, *The Rural Almanac for the Year of Our Lord 1806* (Baltimore, Md.: Printed by John West Butler, 1806), for a discussion on "Love": "There is something in the rich endowment of a woman's love, which exceeds all human bliss. . . . It not only inspires our morals, but even our religion is cold philosophy without it." See Mark Girouard, *Life in the English Country House: A Social and Architectural History* (1978; reprint, Harmondsworth, Eng.: Penguin Books, 1980), p. 232. "Ambitious parents had to engineer marriages rather than arrange them [as they had in the eighteenth century], by seeing that their daughters met the right sort of young man in the right circumstances. London balls, or balls in the local Assembly Room, were a good venue for striking up a first acquaintance; but the relaxed atmosphere of a house-party was ideal for the last stages before the proposal." This source is helpful on the role of assemblies in this period.

48. Thomas Twining, *Travels in America 100 Years Ago* (New York: Harper and Brothers Publishers, 1893), p. 116. Twining believed this, as much of the country he traveled through on his journeys between cities was still forested. Like many of his peers, he equated progress with inhabiting and taming wild land.

49. Kathleen D. McCarthy, *Women's Culture: American Philanthropy and Art, 1830–1930* (Chicago: University of Chicago Press, 1991), pp. 4–5. Jane Austen, *Persuasion* (1818), ch. 1.

50. On this cultural guardianship, Bushman, *Refinement of America,* pp. 189–90, observes: "Men and women shared equally in the softening of American character, but women played a particular role, because of an assumed greater susceptibility to genteel vanities. . . . On the positive side, women were more naturally delicate and sensitive and so more open to refining

influences; on the negative, they suffered from an inclination to vanity and delight in pleasure." Bushman notes in the late eighteenth century "criticism grew in volume and force" at the very moment that country houses, elegant town houses, and "the construction of assembly rooms" was increasing (p. 191). Hill, *An Address to Persons of Fashion, Relating to Balls,* pp. iii, 31. In a note on page 25, Hill gives a mock accounting of expenditures on "diversions" versus money spent "for the relief of the sick and needy." The first item among the diversions, the price of an annual subscription to an assembly, includes the cost of ball dresses, indicating that Hill's tract was largely aimed at women.

51. See the transcription of Guy's notice in the *Federal Gazette & Baltimore Daily Advertiser,* March 12, 1803, in Colwill, *Francis Guy,* p. 130. At subsequent lectures Guy donated the "surplus" of the admission price to either "the benefit of Orphans" or "the poor" (transcriptions of *American & Commercial Daily Advertiser* advertisements for June 29, 1809, July 8, 1809, and March 2, 1813, ibid., pp. 132–33).

52. MacCreery was an annual subscriber to the school, and one of the original donors (*An Address to the Members of the Protestant Episcopal Church,* p. 19). On his involvement with the assembly, see Scharf, *History of Baltimore,* 2: 679.

53. On Rogers' public service, see Alexander, "Nicholas Rogers," p. 88. Dorsey served on the new Court of Oyer and Terminer and resigned his post in 1808 (Scharf, *Chronicles of Baltimore,* p. 286). Scharf, *History of Baltimore,* 2: 728, erroneously states that Dorsey died in 1808. He also notes that Nicholas Rogers was one of five judges appointed in 1788 when this criminal court was first assembled.

54. Other than these two organizations, no other business or social organization is known which connects so many of the individuals represented on the suite. Considering Samuel Smith and John Eager Howard's political rivalry, and their different religions, their presence together is perhaps the most extraordinary. On a rare occasion when they did come together, in the corporation of the Baltimore and Frederick Turnpike company, other key figures are not involved with the suite, such as the company's president, Jonathan Elliott. John Donnell was the only other manager whose house is depicted on the suite. See the list of managers in a notice in the *Federal Gazette & Baltimore Daily Advertiser,* May 14, 1805. For more on the Library Company, see "The Library Company of Baltimore," *MHM* 12, no. 4 (December 1917): 297– 311; and Stuart C. Sherman, "The Library Company of Baltimore, 1795–1854," *MHM* 39, no. 1 (March 1944): 6–24. Also see their papers, Library Company of Baltimore Papers, ms. 80, MdHS.

55. See Treasurer's Account Book, January 1796–April 1806, entries for July 27, 1798, and September 14, 1798, box 4, Library Company of Baltimore Papers, ms. 80, MdHS. The payment to the joiner was made through Robert Cary Long, the builder of the Dancing Assembly Rooms. This reference to Daley, a local chair maker, precedes his first appearances in the city directory in 1804. For the directory reference, see Weidman, *Furniture in Maryland,* p. 276. The library board of directors met monthly and reported the business addressed at each meeting. Gifts to the library were acknowledged in the minutes. If the suite was purchased by the library or given by a group of subscribers it would probably have been mentioned in the minutes. There does not appear to be any mention of such furniture in the first volume of the board minutes (Record Book, January 20, 1798–April 5, 1809, box 2, Library Company of Baltimore Papers, ms. 80, MdHS). In the minutes, mention is made of a "director's room," but the location of this space is not known. This exclusive location might have been more appropriate for furniture such as the Morris suite. During this period several of the male individuals associated with the Morris suite were on the library board, but at no time are the individuals exactly the same.

56. For additional information on these pieces, see Elder, *Baltimore Painted Furniture,* pp. 37–38, 41. At the time of the publication the pier table was in the collection of Mr. and Mrs. William M. Maynadier. The Maynadiers had recently sold the card table to the house museum Mount Clare. No previous owners or dates of ownership are indicated. The chairs reputedly descended in the Birckhead and VanDeventer families, and were acquired from a family member who in 1972 reported that they were used in a house in Washington, D.C. (Robert VanDeventer to Baltimore Museum of Art, August 19, 1969; and Robert VanDeventer to William V. Elder, March 1, 1972). The third chair, owned privately, was sold at auction in 1996 (Weschler's, *American Furniture and Decorations,* Washington, D.C., April 27, 1996, lot 171). This lot included three painted chairs, but the one similar to those in the BMA collection was not illustrated.

57. Hill, *An Address to Persons of Fashion, Relating to Balls,* p. 12. *Letters of Mary Boardman*

Crowninshield, edited by Francis Boardman Crowninshield (New York: Riverside Press, 1905), p. 59, as quoted in Montgomery, *American Furniture,* p. 319. Hill, *An Address to Persons of Fashion, Relating to Balls,* p. 25. In his mock account of funds spent on diversions, Hill specifically included money lost at loo.

58. The building on the side table is remarkably similar to Oliver's country house, which apparently went through at least two building campaigns. Depicted on the 1801 Warner & Hanna map as a three-bay house, this dwelling was subsequently extended to five bays. Much later, it gained an enormous Doric portico on its side. Although the building depicted on the side table is missing a middle window on the second floor (probably more an artistic error than an actuality), it does have a center chimney—a distinctive feature shared by Oliver's house. If built as a five-bay house originally, it is more likely that chimneys would have only been used on the outside walls. The house as remodeled with the addition of the portico is illustrated in Lane, *Architecture of the Old South: Maryland,* p. 107.

59. The author thanks Stiles Colwill for information on these pieces, acquired from a San Francisco collection with connections to Baltimore in the early twentieth century. The furniture was believed to have come from Rosewood, a house in the Caves Valley near Baltimore. Morris' sister-in-law who lived with the family reported "the utter destruction of every article within our long cherished paternal home," including parts of the house such as doors, shutters, and mantles that were either destroyed or stolen. This destruction necessitated the family moving to the "fine large house" on Mulberry Street, which they rented in September from the widow of Eaton R. Partridge. Here there was no "feeling of home. [N]o furniture the eye had rested on all our lives" (Lydia E. Hollingsworth to Rachel Tobin, December 10, 1835, Hollingsworth Family Letters, 1802–1837, MdHS).

Appendix

This appendix suggests the kinds of materials that are currently available to document the appearance of the buildings depicted on the Morris suite. Since the construction and destruction dates of many of these structures have not been determined, that information is not provided here. Some dates, however, given in the references are cited. In each entry, the name of the building is followed by the number and identification provided on the Howard list, the owners' names, and their life dates when known.

Known affiliations with either the Baltimore Dancing Assembly or the Library Company of Baltimore are provided. Members of the Baltimore Dancing Assembly are documented through sources cited in the text, and their earliest known date of membership is given. Some members cannot be documented before 1817, but were undoubtedly members much earlier. Because the legal managers were men and so few sources pertaining to the organization survive, the presence of any particular women cannot currently be established. Stockholders of the Library Company are documented in the Accounts Ledgers 1799–1834, Library Company of Baltimore Papers, ms. 80, box 14, MdHS, where yearly accounts were kept beginning in 1799. All stockholders as of this date continued to be stockholders through the first decade of the nineteenth century, with the exception of Jeremiah Yellott, who died in 1805 but whose wife, Mary, continued his subscription. Nearly all of the stockholders in the Library Company were men.

Members involved with the Charity School of the Benevolent Society are documented in the list of subscribers in *An Address to the Members of the Protestant Episcopal Church, in the City and County of Baltimore* (Baltimore, Md.: Joseph Robinson, 1811). This publication included lists of donors and annual subscribers with the numbers of years they had subscribed, suggesting the year of first membership listed below. Religious affiliations are provided when known, and may not reflect the religions of both husband and wife.

Where possible, selected references to substantive histories or published images of the buildings are included. All of the photographs in the appendix are by Gavin Ashworth.

Chairs

BELVIDERE
1 Belvidere Col. Howard
John Eager Howard (1752–1827)
Margaret Chew Howard (1760–1824)
Baltimore Dancing Assembly, 1817;
Library Company stockholder, 1799;
Benevolent Society (John Eager Howard,
donor, Margaret Howard, annual sub-
scriber, ca. 1800); Episcopalian

Several drawings and photographs document the appearance of Belvidere before
it was torn down. These, in addition to
the image on the 1801 Warner & Hanna
map, are similar to the house depicted on
the Morris suite.

References: Mills Lane, *Architecture of
the Old South: Maryland* (New York:
Abbeville Press, 1991), p. 94 (photograph).

BOLTON

2 Bolton G. Grundy
George Grundy (1755–1825)
Mary Carr Grundy (1763–1797)
Baltimore Dancing Assembly, 1817;
Library Company stockholder, 1799;
Benevolent Society (George Grundy,
donor, and annual subscriber, ca. 1799,
and trustee as of 1811; daughter Mary
Grundy [1788–1818], manager as of
1811); Episcopalian

Three paintings by Francis Guy and the
1801 Warner & Hanna map document
the appearance of this house. Late
nineteenth-century photographs
(MdHS) show the house modified by
the addition of an attic story.

References: Stiles Tuttle Colwill,
Francis Guy 1760–1820 (Baltimore, Md.:
Maryland Historical Society, 1981),
pp. 63–65 (illustration of three Francis
Guy landscapes depicting Bolton).

GRACE HILL
(corrected traditional, although apparently incorrect, identification)
3 Rose Hill W. Gibson
Hugh McCurdy (ca. 1765–1805)
Grace Allison McCurdy (1775–1822)
Library Company (not a stockholder, but given permission to use someone else's share circa 1803); Presbyterian

As discussed in the text, number 3 on the Howard list identifies William Gibson as the owner of Rose Hill, a house that did not look like that represented on the chair bearing the number 3. The traditional assumption has been that numbers 3 and 4 are reversed. While this may be so, the house represented on the chair bearing the number 3 does not match an insurance description of McCurdy's country house (see text). No images are known to document the appearance of this house.

ROSE HILL
(corrected traditional identification)
4 McCurdy
William Gibson (1753–1832)
Sarah Morris Gibson
Library Company stockholder, 1799;
Benevolent Society (William Gibson,
donor and annual subscriber, ca. 1799);
Episcopalian

As discussed in the entry for Grace
Hill, the identities of these two buildings were probably reversed on the
Howard list. In addition to the image
of Gibson's property on the 1801
Warner & Hanna map, Rose Hill is
depicted in the background of two
paintings of Bolton by Francis Guy.

References: Stiles Tuttle Colwill,
Francis Guy 1760–1820 (Baltimore, Md.:
Maryland Historical Society, 1981),
pp. 63, 65 (illustrations of two Francis
Guy landscapes of Bolton).

BEECH HILL

5 Beech Hill Robt. Gilmor
Robert Gilmor (1748–1822)
Louisa Airey Gilmor (1745–1827)
Baltimore Dancing Assembly, 1798;
Library Company stockholder, 1799;
Benevolent Society (Robert Gilmor,
donor, Mrs. Robert Gilmor, annual
subscriber, ca. 1799); Presbyterian

The depiction of the Gilmor property
on the 1801 Warner & Hanna map is
not like that found on the Morris suite.
The map image shows only a single
block with no wings. However, later
images of Beech Hill, including a drawing, engraving, and a photograph
(MdHS) indicate that it evolved into
a five-part house. By the 1830s, classi-
cally inspired details had replaced the
Chinese lattice on the porches, visible
in the image on the Morris suite.

References: Laura Rice, *Maryland
History in Prints 1743–1900* (Baltimore,
Md.: Maryland Historical Society,
2002), p. 103 (engraving of Beech
Hill).

WILLOW BROOK
6 Willow Brook Donnell's
John Donnell (1754–1827)
Ann Teackle Smith Donnell (1781–1858)
Baltimore Dancing Assembly, 1817;
Library Company stockholder, 1799;
Episcopalian

No photographs depicting the facade
of this building are known, although
there are mid twentieth-century photographs of the rear (MdHS). The only
known early image of Willow Brook
appears in the background of a landscape by Francis Guy. A nineteenth-
century engraving of Union Square
shows the facade with the wings raised
to two stories.

References: Edith Rossiter Bevan,
"Willow Brook, Country Seat of John
Donnell," *Maryland Historical Maga-
zine* 44, no. 1 (March 1949): 33–41.
William Voss Elder, III, *The Oval
Room from Willow Brook* (Baltimore,
Md.: Baltimore Museum of Art, 1966).
Stiles Tuttle Colwill, *Francis Guy
1760–1820* (Baltimore, Md.: Maryland
Historical Society, 1981), p. 52 (*View
of the Bay From Near Mr. Gilmor's*).

CHARITY SCHOOL

7 Charity School—St. Paul's, on Madison Street.

The only known image of this building appears on an 1869 bird's eye view map of Baltimore. The overall form of the structure appears to be similar to that of the building depicted on the Morris suite.

References: Mary H. Bready, *Through All Our Days: A History of St. Paul's School for Girls* (Hunt Valley, Md.: Braun-Brumfield Inc., Sheridan Group, 1999), endpapers reproduce a detail of E. Sachse & Co.'s *Bird's Eye View of the City of Baltimore*.

MOUNT DEPOSIT

8 Mount Deposit D. Harris

David Harris (ca. 1752–1809)

1) Sarah Crockett Harris (d. 1785)

2) Frances Holton Chase Harris
(1745–1815)

Baltimore Dancing Assembly, 1798;
Library Company stockholder, 1799;
Benevolent Society (Mrs. David Harris,
donor); Presbyterian

Francis Guy painted a view of this
house.

References: Stiles Tuttle Colwill,
Francis Guy 1760–1820 (Baltimore, Md.:
Maryland Historical Society, 1981),
p. 59 (illustration of Francis Guy landscape depicting Mount Deposit).

OAKLEY (traditional identification)
9 L. Pierce
Levi Pierce (ca. 1769–1821)
Mary Elizabeth Williamson Pierce
Library Company stockholder, 1814;
Presbyterian

No known images document the
appearance of this house. The Howard
list does not identify the house owned
by "L. Pierce," who may have been
Levi Pierce. When Levi died he owned
a property called Oakley. Whether he
lived in this dwelling at the time the
Morris suite was made is not known.

WOODVILLE
10 Woodville Capt. Yellott
Jeremiah Yellott (ca. 1750–1805)
Mary Hollingsworth Yellott
(1760–1811)
Baltimore Dancing Assembly, 1798;
Library Company stockholder, 1799;
Benevolent Society (Jeremiah Yellott,
donor, and left bequest in his will);
Episcopalian

This house is depicted on the 1801
Warner & Hanna map, at the time
owned by its builder Charles Ghequire.
In form it is similar to the building
identified as Woodville on the Morris
suite.

References: Edith Rossiter Bevan,
"Woodville-Baltimore," typescript,
vertical file, MdHS.

Settees

MOUNT CLARE

11 Mount Clare Mrs. Carroll
Charles Carroll, Barrister (1723–1783)
Margaret Tilghman Carroll (1742–1817)
Benevolent Society (Margaret Carroll,
donor and annual subscriber, ca. 1801);
Episcopalian

Mount Clare survives and is a house
museum. The wings and dependencies
shown on the Morris suite were replaced by dependencies of a different
form.

References: Michael F. Trostel, *Mount
Clare: Being an Account of the Seat built by
Charles Carroll, Barrister, upon his Lands at
Patapsco* (Baltimore, Md.: National Society
of Colonial Dames of America in the State
of Maryland, 1981).

BANKS OF THE CITY
12 Banks of the City

No known images document the
appearance of this building, although
the footprint of the structure on Pop-
pleton's 1823 map of the city indicates
that the structure was H-shaped in
plan, which is consistent with the
Morris suite image.

HOMEWOOD

13 Homewood C. Carroll
Charles Carroll, Jr. (1775–1825)
Harriet Chew Carroll (1775–1861)
Baltimore Dancing Assembly, 1801;
Library Company stockholder, 1801;
Benevolent Society (Harriet Carroll,
annual subscriber, ca. 1800); Catholic
and Episcopalian, respectively

Homewood survives and is a house
museum.

References: *Building Homewood: Vision
for a Villa 1802–2002* (Baltimore, Md.:
Homewood House Museum, Johns
Hopkins University, 2002).

WALTER DORSEY HOUSE
(traditional identification)
14 Walter Dorsey
Walter Dorsey (1771–1823)
Hopewell Hebb Dorsey (ca. 1773–1853)
Baltimore Dancing Assembly, 1798;
Library Company stockholder, 1799;
Episcopalian

No known images document the
appearance of this house.

M O N T E B E L L O
15 Montebello Genl. Smith
General Samuel Smith (1752–1839)
Margaret Spear Smith (1759–1842)
Library Company stockholder, 1799;
Presbyterian

The appearance of this house is well
documented by a contemporary
engraving and photographs taken
before it was torn down (MdHS).

References: J. Gilman D. Paul,
"Montebello, Home of General Samuel
Smith," *Maryland Historical Magazine*
42, no. 4 (December 1947): 253–60.

THE VINEYARD

(traditional identification)

16 Vineyard W. Gilmor

William Gilmor (1775–1829)

Marianne (Smith) Drysdale Gilmor
(1778–1852)

Baltimore Dancing Assembly, 1817;
Library Company stockholder, 1799;
Benevolent Society (William Gilmor,
annual subscriber, ca. 1801); Presbyterian (?)

Photographs (MdHS) said to represent
The Vineyard depict a house much
larger than that represented by the
image on the Morris suite. However,
the back of one photograph has a plan
that suggests that the house in the
photograph may encapsulate a much
smaller dwelling, one that in shape and
size was probably similar to that on the
Morris suite.

Pier Table

DRUID HILL
(new identification)
Greenwood Phil. Rogers
Colonel Nicholas Rogers (1753–1822)
Eleanor Buchanan Rogers (1757–1812)
Baltimore Assembly, 1798; Library
Company stockholder, 1799; Bene-
volent Society (Eleanor Rogers,
founder and manager as of 1811,
Nicholas Rogers, donor and annual
subscriber, ca. 1799, and trustee as of
1811); Episcopalian

For the re-identification of this building see the text. The appearance of
Druid Hill is documented by several
images, including photographs and a
painting by Francis Guy (both MdHS).
Other than the image of Greenwood
on the 1801 Warner & Hanna map,
which apparently depicts an earlier
house on the site, no known view documents the appearance of the dwelling.

References: Edith Rossiter Bevan,
"Druid Hill, Country Seat of the
Rogers and Buchanan Families,"
Maryland Historical Magazine 46,
no. 3 (September 1949): 190–99. Stiles
Tuttle Colwill, *Francis Guy 1760–1820*
(Baltimore, Md.: Maryland Historical
Society, 1981), p. 67 (illustration of
Francis Guy landscape depicting Druid
Hill). [Edith Rossiter Bevan?], "Green-
wood," typescript, vertical files, MdHS.

Edward S. Cooke, Jr.

The Long Shadow
of William Morris:
Paradigmatic Problems
of Twentieth-Century
American Furniture

▼THE STUDY OF American furniture from the last half of the twentieth century has been hindered by a pervasive scholarly balkanization. The terms decorative arts, design, art, and material culture have come to be distinct in terms of subject matter, approach, scholarship, and representation. For example, the works of Wendell Castle, Charles Eames, Robert Venturi, and Donald Judd tend to appear in different exhibition and publication venues, elicit different interpretive questions, and figure in different histories of American domestic goods. Such a state contrasts noticeably with British design history, which has taken a more ecumenical and theoretically-based view of material culture, one that looks at material expression whether a craftsperson, designer, architect, or artist has had a hand in its production, while American scholars of twentieth-century material culture remain mired in the celebration of either individual craftspeople or designers and emphasize historical narrative at the expense of critical analysis or interpretation. This essay focuses specifically on the decorative arts ideology deployed in the study of studio furniture, exploring its beginnings and demonstrating how this fissure might be repaired.[1]

In its most public guises—museums and journals—the past century's material culture rarely exists as a coherent package. Many museums have departments of American decorative arts that focus on work made before 1920 (up through the arts and crafts movement, celebrated as the last gasp of the individual craftsman) and assign responsibility for the twentieth century to different departments of design or contemporary art. In some other museums, departments of American decorative arts focus on one-off craft objects and luxury goods of the twentieth century, identifying them as the logical extensions of the historical collections, and thereby include only a small part of the period's material culture. Such institutions reject the industrial or commercial products of the past century, seeing them as commonplace kitsch. Few institutions collect and display a wide variety of objects from the twentieth century. The split is also seen in the mutually exclusive contents of design magazines such as *Metropolis* and *Design Issues,* on the one hand, and decorative arts periodicals such as *Antiques* and *American Craft,* on the other. The origin of manufacture, the role of machinery, the numbers produced, and the market all play an important role in distinguishing an object's taxonomical category, exhibition relations, publication venue, and scholarly attention. Separate, distinct discourses characterize the American field.[2]

Compartmentalization can also be seen in much of the scholarship on American studio furniture produced in the past quarter of a century. A

Figure 1　Sam Maloof working in his shop, 1978. (Photo, Jonathan Pollock.)

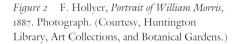

Figure 2　F. Hollyer, *Portrait of William Morris,* 1887. Photograph. (Courtesy, Huntington Library, Art Collections, and Botanical Gardens.)

recent example, *The Furniture of Sam Maloof,* is the latest and largest consideration of that individual furniture maker (fig. 1). Much of the work on Maloof celebrates his singular genius, draws on a general context to provide background for hagiography, makes uncritical use of the maker's own words and philosophy to bestow meaning on the work, and relies on a descriptive consideration of the objects that focuses upon technique. Such an approach links current work on studio craft to the conservative decorative arts canon, discussed by Jonathan and Katherine Prown in the 2002 volume of *American Furniture,* rather than examining this work within the context of various modes of furniture production or under the lens of material and visual culture theory. Why has this canon colored the focus of twentieth-century decorative arts, favoring the studio crafts and precluding design and theory? The investigation of this question leads back to William Morris (1834–1896), the English designer-craftsman, social critic, writer, and socialist (fig. 2).[3]

Morris was one of the first writers, and certainly the most prolific and influential, to use the term "decorative arts" in the manner in which we commonly understand it today, as "that great body of art, by means of which men have at all times more or less striven to beautify the familiar matters of everyday life." By focusing on "ornamental workmanship," Morris sought to elevate quotidian objects so that society ascribed value to them even though they might not equal the "higher" "arts of the intellect" (architecture, painting, and sculpture). In his call for serious consideration of this class of artistic production, Morris popularized the term decorative art, rejecting the other period terms such as "industrial arts" and "applied arts" because of their manufacturing and commercial connotations. Morris' extensive writings inspired many American cultural capitalists and early museum professionals, who then began to collect and institutionalize decorative arts at the turn of the century, thereby ensuring that Morris' terms and criteria became the foundation for the field. Therefore it is important to recognize Morris' particular construction of the decorative arts. Two themes stand out in his writings on the subject—his sense of history and his great esteem for the maker.[4]

Responding against the misery, alienation, and inequities of the contemporary British economy, Morris looked back to the fourteenth and fifteenth centuries as an idealized organic past. He wrote how craftsmen at that time had their own fields or lived adjacent to sites of agricultural production, were complete masters of their tools, enjoyed a rhythm of work that combined artisanal freedom and harmonious cooperation, and produced worthy objects. A certain communalism, born of the agrarian life and fostered by church fellowship, circumscribed the craftsman:

> The theory of industry among these communes was something like this. There is a certain demand for the goods which we can make, and a certain population to make them: if the goods are not thoroughly satisfactory we shall lose our market for them and be ruined: we must therefore keep up their quality to the utmost. Furthermore the work to be done must be shared amongst the whole of those who can do it, who must be sure of work always as long as they are well behaved and industrious.

For Morris, we should learn from history and use it as a template for reform and restructuring. History was the supreme teacher that would guide and inspire those living in the present. Morris also believed that object making was ultimately a local activity, rooted in a specific context for an immediate audience.[5]

The other tenet central to Morris' writings was his supreme regard for the individual craftsman as the heart of a successful society. Morris celebrated the craftsman for his ability to create a "new art of conscious intelligence" that was distinct from "mechanical toil," the useless work that provided the baubles of contemporary fashion. Deriving great pleasure in his activity, the true craftsman used dexterity and thoughtfulness within the comforts of the guild and the local community to improve the built environment. To Morris, there was direct linear linkage from harmonious thoughts and processes to beautiful built environments and harmonious societies. In celebrating the medieval craftsman who designed his own products, Morris wrote:

The medieval man sets to work at his own time, in his own house; probably makes his own tool, instrument, or simple machine himself, even before he gets on to his web, or his lump of clay, or what not. What ornament there shall be on his finished work he himself determines, and his mind and hand designs it and carries it out; tradition, that is to say the minds and thoughts of all workmen gone before, this, in its concrete form of the custom of his craft, does indeed guide and help him.

The imaginative work of a fully skilled craftsman ensured pleasure in making and use.[6]

Morris' idealized vision of production relations led ultimately to a critique of commercial capitalism, the products of which were "trivial, mechanical, unintelligent, incapable of resisting the changes pressed upon them by fashion or dishonesty." With the rise of the division of labor at the expense of the master designer-maker and a concern for profit rather than livelihood, the maker became "condemned for the whole of his life to make the insignificant portion of an insignificant article of the market." As the all-around craftsman gave way to the narrow specialist, items for use gave way to items for sale. Morris thus made selective use of Karl Marx to focus on the process of manufacture as a determinant in the ultimate value of the object and paid little attention to the reception or social meaning of such objects. It is easy to see how Morris' ideology influenced decorative arts scholarship that celebrated the individual craftsman, identified the colonial and early national periods as the Golden Age of American craftsmanship, and linked the colonial craftsman to the myth of the self-sufficient American farmer.[7]

Such a privileging of the individual craftsman working directly with low technology to produce objects of exchange precludes both the notion of a professional industrial designer who works with a team to develop prototypes and then plans or orchestrates manufacture, as well as the concept of a craft object existing as a commercial commodity with recursive meanings. Morris has thus cast a long shadow over the scholarship of the decorative arts, limiting the focus of study to the idealized shop floor, the time period of study to a preindustrial period, and the meaning of the product to decontextualized original use. Reliance on Morris' terms fails to engage with the twentieth-century discourse on new forms of production, the rise of batch and mass production, and the possibility of multiple simultaneous meanings. Decorative arts scholars remain tied to the issues raised by Morris without considering the work of Walter Benjamin or Jean Baudrillard on production or Karl Marx, Pierre Bourdieu, or Frederic Jameson on commodity. While the disciplines of art history and cultural studies constantly engage in theoretical exercises, the field of decorative arts remains an anachronistic fiction. The decorative arts scholars deploy a technologically obsessed formal study of one-off objects and leave the vast universe of recent material culture to design historians, who, in America, remain focused upon the heroic individual designer and the exceptionalism of American design as a way to legitimize the practice of industrial design as something different from and elevated above mere product design for mass production. Thus Morris' terms seem to have cast a shadow even on American industrial design.[8]

To overcome the limits of the Morris paradigm, we should draw inspiration from English design historians and look at decorative arts and design as a whole, to examine production, reception, and theorization of a whole range of domestic material culture. To demonstrate the possibilities of this approach, the work of Sam Maloof and other pioneering studio furniture makers will be examined in a more theoretical manner.[9]

Sam Maloof (b. 1916) has been making furniture in his own shop for the past fifty-five years. In an early article on the woodworker, art journalist Sherley Ashton described him in a manner that strikingly recalls Morris' idealized craftsman:

> Working with disciplined hands and a free spirit, Maloof is rewarded with great warmth in his designs; but achieving warmth in his designs is a fetish with him. In his opinion the weakness in much contemporary American furniture is its coldness, a result of the fact that, in the United States, designer and maker are usually two people instead of one. . . . His one enthusiastic concern is that every piece he turns out shall demonstrate usefulness, beauty, and craftsmanship. . . . Maloof thrives on the freedom and demands of his one-man operation. In the course of the day he may be salesman, designer, craftsman, supply buyer, truck driver, but he is sublimely free to design and build, without interference from such commercial factors as cost accountants, advertising executives, sales managers, or shop superintendents whose foibles tend to destroy the subtleties of craftsmanship for the sake of profits.

His happy lot was further linked to the pleasant lemon grove surrounding his shop (fig. 3). All subsequent writings on Maloof have repeated the importance of his pastoral utopia in the San Bernardino Valley of California and unwavering commitment to the designer-craftsman as distinct from and superior to industry.[10]

Figure 3 Exterior view of the Sam Maloof home and studio, Alta Loma, California. (Photo, Jonathan Pollock.)

The privileging of the independent, rural maker can be seen in the biographies of Maloof's peers as well. Wharton Esherick (1887–1970), whom Maloof referred to as the "dean of American craftsmen," lived and worked on a heavily wooded hilltop in Paoli, Pennsylvania. In his organic house

Figure 4 Exterior view of the Wharton Esherick home and studio, Paoli, Pennsylvania. (Courtesy, Wharton Esherick Museum.)

and studio (fig. 4), which he built over a period of forty-five years, Esherick enjoyed the freedom of making furniture and interiors for friends. Working only with one or two assistants, he eschewed large or complicated jobs "that get out of my hands" because he worked for his own pleasure, did not want to worry about employees, and believed it important to know about everything happening in his studio. The process of making sculptural furniture thus became an act of friendship and respect in which the finished object served to link maker and client as friends (fig. 5). His

Figure 5 Living room interior of the home owned by Lawrence and Alice Seiver, Villanova, Pennsylvania. (Courtesy, Wharton Esherick Museum.) Esherick provided much of the paneling, built-in furniture, lighting, and movable furniture in the 1950s and 1960s.

rugged integrity, expressive work, and isolation (he lived and worked at the top of the hill while his wife and children lived in a farmhouse below the studio) led one writer to refer to him as the "Thoreau of post-War

America." Among his friends was Ford Maddox Ford, who wrote of the woodworker and his environment in Morrisian terms:

> A dim studio in which blocks of rare woods, carver's tools, medieval look-ing carving gadgets, looms, printing presses, rise up like ghosts in the twi-light while the slow fire dies in the brands. . . . Such a studio built by the craftsman's own hands out of chunks of rock and great balks of timber, sinking back into the quiet woods on a quiet crag with, below its long windows, quiet fields parceled out by the string-course of hedges . . . And let Esherick be moving noiselessly about in the shadows, with a plane and a piece of boxwood . . .Or pouring a hundred times, heavy oil and emery powder on one of the tables he has designed, and rubbing it off with cloths to get the polish exactly true, and bending down again and again to see the sheen of the light along the polished wood. . . . Those are the conditions you need for thought. . . . There have always been craftsmen and the craftsmen have always been the best men of their time because a handicraft goes at a pace commensurate with the thoughts in a man's head.

For the craft writers of the 1950s and 1960s, as for Morris in the late nine-teenth century, the noble, free craftsman worked in an independent shop, located in a rural or town setting, and had his hand in all parts of the endeavor, from design conception through choice of materials and con-struction to marketing and sales. Such a freeholder had a stake in society and contributed to a democratic society distinct from the totalitarianism of Cold War Russia.[11]

The romantic lure of creative small shops exerted considerable influence on an American middle and upper class, who were increasingly white-collar, service professionals removed from the "art, trade, and mystery" of the crafts. Through public performances and writings, many of the studio fur-niture makers working from the 1950s into the 1970s actively played to this eager audience. In interviews, public lectures, or instructional workshops, Maloof talks modestly about how his work ethic enables him to survive without his wife ever taking a job outside the house, how he brings his skills to bear on every object that leaves his shop, how he has maintained close friendships with his clients, and how he has taken such pleasure in a life-time of craft. Certainly the imprint of William Morris is clear, a connection implicitly noted by Maloof's followers. The ultimate result of his presenta-tions is an awed audience that reverently approaches him and seeks more assurances about the values of the craftsman lifestyle. Viewers of his furniture also approach the objects with a similar sense of respectful deference.

A crafts mystique also lies at the heart of public adulation of James Krenov (b. 1920), an American woodworker who trained and worked in Sweden before returning to the United States in the early 1970s. Over the course of the decade, he became the philosophical conscience of the "woodraft" segment of the field, one that was decidedly non-commercial. Beginning with a 1967 article in *Crafts Horizons* and developed further in four books published between 1976 and 1981, Krenov poetically argued that respect for the material and delicate, sensitive work, reliant on sharp edge tools (hand planes, chisels, spokeshaves, and scrapers), would lead to a personal approach in woodworking (figs. 6, 7). He became the stri-dent defender of the "quiet craftsman" and "impractical cabinetmaker,"

Figure 6 James Krenov, cabinet. Fort Bragg, California, 1982. Maple, red oak, and partridge. H. 67", W. 27", D. 11". (Courtesy, Pritam & Eames.)

Figure 7 View of the cabinet illustrated in fig. 6 with the door open.

predominantly amateurs or semi-professionals, whose love of wood and focus on hand tools led to works of uncompromising quality and intense sensitivity. He admitted that a really good craftsman would not reach a broad public because "this craftsman is the one who does the work himself, and gives people something very personal; not very much of it, but very personal and therefore not accessible to everyone." In his seminal 1976 book, *A Cabinetmaker's Notebook,* Krenov criticized contemporary American studio furniture for being fashion-oriented, superficial, and market-driven. Rather than offering how-to technical information, he provided a craft philosophy that allowed the reader to tap into their own creative soul.

With total sales exceeding half a million, his books echoed the spirit of Morris and inspired many to take up furniture making or to build similarly refined, subtle work. His workshops, as well as his teaching at the College of the Redwoods, a community college in rural Fort Bragg, California, engendered a loyal band of disciples who seek to follow the attitudes, principles, and even forms of the master.[12]

But what lies below this placid surface of reverence and adulation? Essential to a more rigorous analysis of studio furniture practice is the recognition that pastoralism and an emphasis on the aura of craftsmanship often mask commercialism. While Maloof's gross production would not qualify him as an industry (except in the eyes of Krenov), he certainly demonstrates a very conscious interest in maintaining his public image. Although he claims to have worked "not for recognition or for monetary reward," the evidence in the literature on him suggests otherwise. His prominent leadership roles within local and national organizations such as the Southern California Designer-Craftsmen and the American Craft Council from the 1950s through the 1980s not only reveals his responsibility to give something to the field but also suggests his willingness to help write craft history with himself as a major protagonist. When friends and publishers began to suggest in the 1970s that he write a book, he dismissed any solicitation of a mere how-to book but held to his conviction that he was worthy of a well-illustrated monograph that celebrated his contributions to woodworking and studio crafts. His talks have consistently dwelt on first-person stories, providing narratives that feature him, celebrate his work, and relegate other makers to secondary roles.[13]

While priding himself as a full-time maker rather than as a teacher who made just a few pieces of furniture, Maloof has made it a priority to take time away from the shop to attend important conferences and keep his name in circulation. He began in the 1970s to devote increasing amounts of time to travel in order to lecture, teach workshops, and talk about his work in conjunction with the growing number of craft or furniture exhibitions. However, Maloof's use of public lectures, demonstrations, and workshops—the staples of American craft marketing—to promote his work is hardly unique. The public seems to crave firsthand exposure to iconic figures like Maloof and Krenov, and the makers simply respond to that demand. Yet each maker has his own particular spin: Maloof prides himself as the most successful full-time working craftsman, Krenov presents himself as the guardian of meaningful refined workmanship, and Wendell Castle (b. 1932) identifies himself as the leading art furniture maker. Each has taken up a facet of the Morris idealized craftsman.

Pricing is another area in which Maloof's activity can be interpreted in different ways. Throughout his autobiography he constantly recalls how people told him his work was underpriced or confesses his unfamiliarity with pricing. In 1971 he told one such story: "Most people tell me I don't charge enough. But my problem is setting a price myself. I'm hesitant. One friend said he wouldn't buy any more furniture from me unless I raised my prices. He'd contracted for a piece. I sent him the bill. And he sent me $200 more than I asked for." Such posturing could be interpreted as either naiveté or a strategic form of self-deprecation intended to stir up additional commercial interest, but the frequency with which price is discussed in print or in conversation leads one to believe the latter.[14]

Strategic pricing of a more explicit sort has guided Wendell Castle. During much of the 1950s and 1960s, three- and low four-figure prices characterized the field, but he aggressively challenged that market structure in 1983 when New York gallerist Alexander Milliken showed Castle's fine furniture, a body of work inspired by the products of French *ébéniste* Emile-Jacques Ruhlmann. Castle stunned the studio furniture world by putting a price of $75,000 on a desk and two chairs (fig. 8). Milliken then convinced Castle to develop a body of work not exclusively defined by function as furniture, resulting in a 1985 exhibition of thirteen clocks (fig. 9). For this

Figure 8   Wendell Castle, lady's desk with two chairs, Scottsville, New York, 1981. Curly English sycamore, purpleheart, ebony, delrin, and Baltic birch plywood. Desk: H. 40¾", W. 41½", D. 22¼"; chair: H. 34¾", W. 21", D. 26". (Courtesy, Wendell Castle.)

ensemble, Castle continued to push the pricing of his work. The prices for these clocks ranged from $75,000 to $250,000, a reflection of their large size, luxurious materials, and labor intensive work by Castle's skilled employees as well as of a new marketing strategy. Milliken sought to raise the maker's prices in order to take advantage of the buoyant New York art market of that period and to allow Castle to focus on his own work rather than rely on commissions.[15]

Astute business practices can also be seen in Maloof's record keeping and awareness of milestones. He kept track of when he first produced a particular form, proudly recalled the number of firsts for which he was responsible (maker of the first piece of contemporary furniture accessioned by the Museum of Fine Arts, Boston; maker of the first piece of contemporary furniture in the White House collection; first woodworker elected Fellow of the American Craft Council; first craftsman to receive a

Figure 9   Wendell Castle, *Ziggeraut,* Scottsville, New York, 1985. Gabbon ebony, curly koa veneer, leather, and gold-plated brass; weight-driven movement. H. 71", W. 39", D. 15". (Courtesy, Wendell Castle.)

Figure 10   Brand used by Sam Maloof from the late 1950s to 1971. (© Smithsonian Institution; photo, Jonathan Pollock, 2001.)

MacArthur Grant, etc.), and adapted his practice of signing furniture. Initially he used a brand that linked him to more commercial practices (fig. 10). Beginning with the *Woodenworks* exhibition of 1972, he began to sign his work with an electric burning pen. Upon his election as an ACC Fellow in 1975, he burned in his signature, the number of that example in that year's work, and the initials "fACC" (Fellow of the American Crafts Council) (fig. 11). After he received an honorary degree from the Rhode

Figure 11   Burned signature used by Sam Maloof from 1975 to 1992. (Courtesy, Museum of Fine Arts, Boston.)

Figure 12 Burned signature used by Sam Maloof after 1992. (© Smithsonian Institution; photo, Jonathan Pollock, 2001.)

Island School of Design in 1992, he substituted "d.f.a. r.i.s.d." (doctorate of fine arts, Rhode Island School of Design) for "fACC" (fig. 12). While such signatures surely embody his pride of accomplishment, they also provide a sense of commercial identity and authorship that are useful in the marketplace for custom furniture. Initially he found the stamp sufficient to link him to the design community of Southern California, but his subsequent switch to his actual signature signals an interest in emphasizing the involvement of the human hand and the authenticity of the author-maker. His subsequent inclusion of a serial number and his honorific legitimization suggest his pursuit of a larger and different market—the national studio crafts market.[16]

Wendell Castle also has employed a number of different signing strategies. For his stack-laminated work of the 1960s, he would carve a simple "WC" and the last two digits of the year in unobtrusive locations such as underneath a seat or along the base (fig. 13). The initials and date follow the conventions used by Wharton Esherick, whose sculptural furniture had been an inspiration to Castle. The main intent of these marks seems to be documentation for a knowing, familiar clientele. By 1978, as Castle began to show at New York art galleries, he altered his marking. He began to carve "W. Castle" and the last two digits of the year in more visible areas, such as along the front of the work (fig. 14). A promotional pamphlet of this period states that "Each piece of furniture is signed as it leaves the studio, the guarantor of our commitment to artistic integrity and uncompromising craftsmanship." With more success in the early 1980s, he expanded

Figure 13 Carved inscription used by Wendell Castle before 1978. (Courtesy, Museum of Fine Arts, Boston.)

Figure 14 Carved inscription used by Wendell Castle from 1978 to 1984. (Courtesy, Museum of Fine Arts, Boston.)

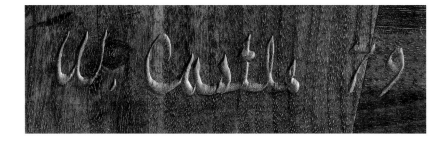

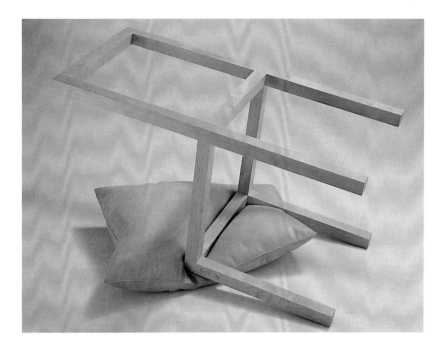

the signature to include "Wendell Castle" and the full four-digit year and signed these features rather than carving them (fig. 15). Such an evolution reveals Castle's expanding market and his attempt to offer "signed" works of art to an unfamiliar audience. The blurred distinction between individual signature and stamp of authenticity thus highlights the commercialization and commodification of craft.[17]

Closer scrutiny of Maloof's shop activities also provides some distance from the Morris ideal. Much of his ability to focus upon his shop was enabled by his wife and helpmate Freda, who selflessly served as business manager and salesperson, while also running the household, for fifty years. He recognized her many contributions to his success, but it is important to see her not only as an enabler or inspiration, but rather as a full-time unpaid partner who oversaw the books, managed Maloof's time, entertained clients, and ran the showroom, which also happened to be their home. Employee relationships rather than pleasurable work characterize other aspects of Maloof's shop. For consistent production, he has hired a number of workers whose main tasks remain the tedious acts of sanding, finishing, and clean-up, freeing Maloof to focus on and control the riskier "signature" elements such as cutting out parts, assembling, and rough shaping. Maloof believes that good pay and benefits rather than providing opportunities for satisfying craftsmanship or training apprentices are the most important part of his relationship with these workers. Gendered and wage-based relationships seem more modern than those guild relationships favored by Morris and call into question the myth of the happy small shop. The intensification of a domestic type of production in order to accommodate aspects of market capitalism also links the Maloof enterprise to the rural New England craft shops of the early national period of American history, when decreased agricultural returns and increased markets for consumer goods spurred widespread familial exploitation and outwork.[18]

Figure 16 Sam Maloof workshop, 1981. (Photo, Jonathan Pollock.)

Freda's role in the Maloof shop should not be underestimated. As a teacher at Santo Domingo Pueblo and then director of arts and crafts at the Indian School in Santa Fe, she had extensive experience in the commercialization of authentic crafts and how to pitch the handcrafted object to the modern world. Maloof's self-effacing posturing, use of signatures, parlaying of demonstrations as marketing spectacles as well as technical instruction, and domestic showcasing of products all had parallels in the world of Pueblo ceramics. Freda's business orientation can also be seen in her interest in the third day of the Asilomar conference of 1957, where a session on "professional practices" focused on business ethics, production problems, and distribution methods.[19]

Maloof's role as a craftsman is also complicated by the milieu in which he worked. As a designer-maker in the 1950s, he belonged to a spectrum of furniture producers working in a loosely soft modern or Scandinavian modern vein. Like his contemporary Walker Weed (b. 1918), Maloof's product was not inevitably or obviously the work of an individual, but in fact resonated with the work of Danish designer-craftsmen like Finn Juhl and Hans Wegner, whose furniture was shown at Frank Brothers in Long Beach, and

Figure 17 Sam Maloof, armchair, Alta Loma, California, 1975. Walnut and black vinyl. H. 38", W. 30", D. 22½". (Courtesy, Museum of Fine Arts, Boston; purchased through funds provided by the National Endowment for the Arts and the Gillette Corporation.)

American designers such as Paul McCobb and Edward Wormley, who produced designs for large firms such as Winchendon and Dunbar. Maloof's practical organization and link to larger operations is also born out by his stockpiling of parts; reliance on labor-saving devices such as templates; embrace of simple joinery and screwed construction; and willingness to use such powered equipment as electric drills and routers (fig. 16). Maloof does not really make one-off pieces of furniture but rather relies on free workmanship executed on powered equipment such as the bandsaw and slight variations of modeling achieved with the Surform, rasps, and spokeshaves to develop a line of furniture that shared basic features with slight differences in final finish. For example, Maloof offers ten basic chair forms with a variety of different permutations for details (types of seats, backs, crest rails) that enables him to make fifty different chairs (figs. 17–19). The main difference between the work of Maloof and that of McCobb or Wormley was the market: the former was for local clients who knew the maker while the latter were marketed throughout the country by retailers.[20]

In the 1960s Maloof became linked not to the design world of the 1950s but rather to the emerging counter-culture craft world of California. The

Figure 18 Sam Maloof, armchair, Alta Loma, California, 1975. Walnut and black vinyl. H. 38½", W. 30", D. 25¾". (Courtesy, Museum of Fine Arts, Boston; purchased through funds provided by the National Endowment for the Arts and the Gillette Corporation.)

Figure 19 Sam Maloof, armchair, Alta Loma, California, 1975. Walnut. H. 39¾", W. 22", D. 23". Courtesy, Museum of Fine Arts, Boston; purchased through funds provided by the National Endowment for the Arts and the Gillette Corporation.)

emphasis on pastoral lifestyles, designing and making, and self-reliance provided a new context in which his work prospered. Self-taught and committed to woodworking, Maloof fostered an aesthetic that played into these values: celebration of "inferior" second-grade walnut, replete with contrasting sapwood and heartwood; expedient but decorative joinery; and emphasis on shaping and finishing. While fitting in with the gentle revolutionaries, he was no recluse but maintained his businesslike approach. Unswayed by changing fashion or artistic impulses and working within a restricted universe of formal composition, he took greater advantage of the marketing system developed within first the local and then the national craft field. This practicality proved invaluable as the craft world professionalized in the 1980s and offered new national markets through exhibitions

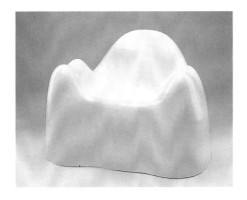

Figure 20 Wendell Castle, *Molar* chair, manufactured by Northern Plastics Corporation for Beylerian Limited, 1969–1970. Glass-reinforced polyester. H. 26", W. 36", D. 30". (Courtesy, Detroit Institute of Arts.)

Figure 21 Wendell Castle, protoype for the *Atlantis* desk, designed for the Gunlocke Company, 1982. Ebonized and lacquered cherry, flakeboard, beeswing narra veneer, plastic inlay, and gold-plated brass. H. 29", W. 72", D. 36". (Courtesy, Wendell Castle.)

Figure 22 Wendell Castle, *Huevos* table, 1999. Mahogany. Dimensions not recorded. (Courtesy, Wendell Castle.)

in museums and galleries. It was through these venues as well as magazines and summer craft programs that a national audience came to know and lionize Maloof and his work. [21]

Whereas Maloof restricted his basic forms and techniques to achieve slight variations within a batch production strategy, Wendell Castle followed a different design philosophy by undertaking work for contract furniture firms in order to make his work available to a broader audience. In response to the pop furniture of the 1960s featured in the Italian design magazine *Domus,* Castle developed plastic versions of his stack-laminated wooden furniture. For his "Molar Chair" series (fig. 20), he built a series of stack-laminated and putty-filled prototypes, from which he then fabricated molds. The furniture firms Stendig and Beylerian then molded and distributed the plastic furniture. Although this venture did not lead to success, Castle did not abandon the idea of broader markets. In the 1970s he used templates for "limited signed editions" in which the basic forms were similar, but different woods and slight variations in shaping led to the uniqueness of each object. Castle attempted to enter the design world

again in 1982, when he developed prototype designs for the Gunlocke Company, an office furniture company in Wayland, New York. He drew up designs for four different lines of office suites; the *Atlantis* desk (fig. 21) was available in lacewood, fiddleback maple, or Tchitola veneer, and the donut-shaped feet were lacquered in turquoise, peach, or magenta. Once again, Castle found it difficult to use a small shop to compete in the contract design world.[22]

More recently, he has developed a hybrid operation that complements his own studio. In establishing Icon Design, he set up a separate manufacturing shop overseen by one of his former students, developed a series of clean-lined forms that he calls the Wendell Castle Collection (fig. 22), and invested in templates and jigs to ensure consistent production. However, this is not mass-produced furniture, as he points out: "Even though we call this a production company, we're not production in the [conventional] way where there's an assembly line and conveyor belt. In this price range, furniture's not made that way. Furniture's pretty much made one at a

Figure 23   Stamp used by Wendell Castle on his designs for Icon Furniture. (Courtesy, Wendell Castle.)

time." The furniture in the line retails from $2,000 to $20,000, the starting price for Castle's own one-off work, and features a "WC" stamp rather than his full signature (fig. 23). Castle's distinction between the different parts of his production points to the way in which he adheres to the Morris paradigm while also taking advantage of the possibilities of the design world; the two worlds are not mutually exclusive: "I see the Wendell Castle Collection as a way to grow. The art furniture depends on me. I have to be involved with every aspect or it isn't the way I want it. For the Wendell Castle Collection, I can develop certain designs and work them out and then repeat them. With a one-of-a-kind piece, you only get one shot."[23]

Although the preceding discussion of the production of Maloof and his contemporaries offers important adjustments to the received history, it is in the reception of that furniture where more recent scholarship can shed dramatic new light. In the 1950s and 1960s most studio furniture embodied use value and consistently remained true to the function of furniture. Much of this early work continues to be used and enjoyed by the families who originally bought it from the maker. There remains a personal connection that exists outside the marketplace and a sense that those works were simply locally made versions of modern furniture. More complex to unwrap are those pieces bought from the 1970s on, when the changing context of the crafts world shifted the meaning of studio furniture. Maloof's furniture itself remained remarkably consistent in terms of form and process, with only slight refinements such as scooped wooden seats, hard-lined edges, and stronger router joints where the legs met the seat. However, what changed dramatically were the motives and expectations of the audience. Some clients might have bought his work at the shop, but more began to order it based on seeing images of the furniture in print or seeing it on view in gallery shows or museum exhibitions. Some of these new buyers even made the pilgrimage to Maloof's shop in Alta Loma.

It was in the 1970s and early 1980s that Maloof and other pioneer studio furniture makers achieved name and product recognition beyond the small craft community and familiar regional clients. The 1972 *Woodenworks* exhibition at the Renwick Gallery of the Smithsonian Institution showcased the work of Wharton Esherick, Sam Maloof, George Nakashima, Art Carpenter, and Wendell Castle and provided a national stage. In 1975 the Museum of Fine Arts, Boston initiated a "Please Be Seated" program to provide public seating in the galleries and tapped Maloof, Castle, and Nakashima to make the first pieces of furniture. Another exhibition, *New Handmade Furniture,* opened at the American Craft Museum in 1979 and featured the pioneers as well as emerging younger makers. The debut of a journal dedicated to fine furniture making, *Fine Woodworking,* further helped canonize Esherick, Maloof, Castle, and Krenov as pioneers in that field.[24]

However, different people invested different meaning in this work. Makers, both small shop woodworkers as well as serious hobbyists, flattered the pioneers by copying them. Some honored Maloof's furniture by copying Maloof's chairs, shaping, and joinery; others made stack-laminated forms similar to Castle's, and still others made cabinets on stands in homage to

Figure 24 Sam Maloof, settee, Alta Loma, California, 1987. Curly maple. H. 30", W. 42", D. 25". (Photograph 2003 © Metropolitan Museum of Art; gift of the artist and purchase, anonymous gift.)

Krenov. The knock-offs or imitations do not detract from the originals, but in fact the simulacra have created additional aura and raised the value of the authentic original.[25]

In the late 1970s and 1980s, the changing marketplace, especially the emergence of a body of clients who could be considered collectors, elevated the work of the early studio furniture makers, especially Maloof. Purchasing fine furniture because it might make them feel happier or more fulfilled, allow them to express their discerning individuality, or demonstrate their social power, these new clients often followed trends and asked for a well-publicized Maloof form. Maloof also began to offer his work in curly maple (fig. 24), a showier wood that appealed to the new clients, in addition to his familiar black walnut. The fetishizing of the craft object thus triggered the emergence of a well-understood Maloof style, making a recognized fashion line out of what had once been a decidedly anti-fashion, styleless pursuit.[26]

One particular Maloof form underscores this transformation—the rocker. Maloof made his first spindle-back rocker in about 1960, then began to think about its market potential when President John Kennedy's doctor endorsed the rocking chair as a relaxing therapeutic seat for those with lower back pain. However, Maloof's rocker remained a slow seller for

much of that decade. He sold only one in 1963 or 1964 and was able to sell only five in 1969 (fig. 25). He then included a walnut rocker in *Woodenworks* and another one for the "Please Be Seated" program at the Museum of Fine Arts, Boston, in 1975 (fig. 26). Even though the latter example was on display for only a short time and was never used for public gallery seating, it had an enormous impact on the demand for Maloof's work. By 1980 Maloof had built about one hundred rockers, then priced at $2,500, and had orders for another sixty. Joan Mondale, the wife of Vice President Walter Mondale, bought a rocker for the vice president's house in 1979, and in 1981 a rocker purchased at the auction celebrating the twenty-fifth anniversary of the American Craft Museum was donated to President Ronald Reagan (fig. 27). The rocker became a celebrity item, purchased by entertainment figures such as Anthony Quinn, Gene Kelly, and Jim Henson; serious craft collectors such as George and Dorothy Saxe of San Francisco, Sydney and Frances Lewis of Richmond, and Peter and Daphne Farago of Providence; and three presidents (Reagan, Carter, and Clinton).[27]

In the 1980s Maloof averaged between twenty-five and thirty rockers a year, with prices in 1989 that ranged from $8,000 for walnut to $12,000

Figure 26   Sam Maloof, rocking chair, Alta Loma, California, 1975. Walnut. H. 44½", W. 27¾", D. 46". (Courtesy, Museum of Fine Arts, Boston; purchased through funds provided by the National Endowment for the Arts and the Gillette Corporation.)

Figure 27   President Ronald Reagan accepting the gift of a Maloof rocking chair, November 11, 1981. (Courtesy, Sam Maloof.) Sam and Freda Maloof and Clement Conger look on.

Figure 28   Sam Maloof sitting in one of his rocking chairs. (Photo, Rick Mastelli.)

for maple to $15,000 for rosewood. In two important 1980s exhibitions—*California Woodworking* (1980) and *Craft Today: Poetry of the Physical* (1986)—Maloof placed a rocker. But the real popularizer was a 1986 article on him in *People* magazine, titled "King of the Rockers," that followed his receipt of the MacArthur Grant in 1985. In the 1990s rockers comprised more than half of his yearly production.[28]

Thus, over the past quarter century, the rocker has come to represent or stand in for Sam Maloof (fig. 28). Maloof's furniture began to symbolize the maker; purchase of a Maloof rocker translated to acceptance of the myth of the American craftsman and control over the creative producer, or Morris' master of "ornamental workmanship." Distinguished from elements of mass culture by the attention to workmanship and detail implied in the concept of craftsmanship, the rocker embodied the optimism, warmth, and masculine individuality of its maker. Yet there is a certain contradiction at play. The rocker, more limited in function in comparison to Maloof's other seating, and more space intensive in terms of its action, became the signature object for the woodworker who presented himself as a designer-craftsman committed to functional straightforward furniture.

Returning to Marx's notion of commodity, it is important to note that one can thus look at a Maloof rocker as a commodity, a tool or implement that commercial capitalism uses to lull its audience into passivity and acceptance, and an aesthetic object purchased more for financial or social investment than for functional need or as a local purchase. As the rustic furniture maker Dan Mack commented: "Nobody needs a Sam Maloof chair. A Maloof chair has become an attractive cultural icon of the 1950s, of an elder craftsman, of a noble savage, of conspicuous consumption, of museum-endorsed taste." The reference to the happy craftsman toiling in his own shop thus reinforces the desired belief that handcraft remains an economically viable option even as many inequitable and exploitative forms of production persist to provide desired consumable goods. In this light, Maloof's conscious marketing strategies can also be read as symptoms of the larger socio-economic structure of commercial capitalism.[29]

The foregoing reexamination of the furniture made by Sam Maloof and other early studio furniture makers reveals the complicated nature of production and reception. These artisans have produced beautiful objects for more than a half century, but one needs to situate this work outside of aesthetic appreciation and a Morrisian paradigm. More recent theoretical scholarship can shed light on a variety of meanings embodied in this furniture and ascribed to it. This is our task, to recognize the need to go beyond William Morris in the analysis and interpretation of late twentieth-century American furniture.

ACKNOWLEDGMENTS   The author thanks Glenn Adamson, Tim Barringer, Bebe Johnson, Warren Johnson, John Kelsey, Rick Mastelli, and Jonathan Prown for their comments on an earlier version of this essay.

1. Good examples of the British approach include the *Journal of Design History* or Tanya Harrod's *The Crafts in Britain in the 20th Century* (New Haven, Conn.: Yale University Press, 1999). For a helpful discussion about the differences between British design history and American design studies, see *Design Issues* 11, no. 1 (Spring 1995).

2. Museums with separate decorative arts and design departments include the Metropolitan Museum of Art and the Detroit Institute of Art. Museums that link the studio crafts with the decorative arts include the Museum of Fine Arts, Boston, and the Philadelphia Museum of Art. The Mint Museum of Craft and Design is a recent noticeable exception to this division, but there the focus is exclusively on the twentieth century.

3. The most recent publication is Jeremy Adamson, *The Furniture of Sam Maloof* (New York: W. W. Norton, 2001). Other helpful publications on Maloof include Sherley Ashton, "Maloof . . . designer, craftsman of furniture," *Craft Horizons* 14, no. 3 (May–June 1954): 15–19; Glenn Loney, "Sam Maloof," *Craft Horizons* 31, no. 4 (August 1971): 16–19, 70; Sam Maloof, *Sam Maloof, Woodworker* (New York: Kodansha, 1983); Michael Stone, *Contemporary American Woodworkers* (Salt Lake City: Gibbs Smith, 1985), pp. 64–81; Rick Mastelli, "Sam Maloof," *Fine Woodworking* 25 (November/December 1980): 48–55; and *Sam Maloof. Woodworking Profile* (Newtown, Conn.: Taunton Press, 1989), videotape. A critical review of the 2001 Maloof exhibition at the Smithsonian's Renwick Gallery in Washington points out the shortcomings of this conservative approach, remarking that the craftsman's all-consuming emphasis on technique and wood has made him an anachronism: "as his archaic skills took over, he faded out of the contemporary conversation; he managed to pull his career back in time, to somewhere around the turn of the century." See Blake Gopnik, "Going Through the Motions: Renwick's Maloof Show Honors a Master Craftsman, but No Artist," *Washington*

Post, October 7, 2001, p. G12; Jonathan Prown and Katherine Hemple Prown, "The Quiet Canon: Tradition and Exclusion in American Furniture Scholarship," in *American Furniture,* edited by Luke Beckerdite (Hanover, N.H.: University Press of New England for the Chipstone Foundation, 2002), pp. 207–27; Jonathan Bizen, "Assessing an Icon: Sam Maloof," *Home Furniture* 13 (November 1997), pp. 66–71.

4. William Morris, *The Decorative Arts: Their Relation to Modern Life and Progress* (London: Ellis and White, 1878), pp. 4, 25. In *Art and Its Producers* (1888; reprint, London: Longmans & Co., 1901), p. 3, Morris used the term "architectural arts" to describe "the addition to all necessary articles of use of a certain portion of beauty and interest, which the user desires to have and the maker to make."

5. William Morris, "Art and Industry in the Fourteenth Century" (1890) in *The Collected Works of William Morris,* edited by May Morris, 24 vols. (1910–1915; reprint, New York: Russell and Russell, 1966), 22: 386. See also William Morris, "Architecture and History" (1884) in ibid., 22: 296–317; and *William Morris on History,* edited by Nicholas Salmon (Sheffield, Eng.: Sheffield Academic Press, 1996).

6. William Morris, "The Prospects of Architecture" (1881) in May Morris, ed., *The Collected Works of William Morris,* 22: 119–51. William Morris, "Architecture and History" (1884) in ibid., 22: 312. See also "Textile Fabrics" (1884) and "Art and Its Producers" (1888) in ibid., 22: 270–95, 342–55.

7. Morris, *The Decorative Arts,* p. 4. Morris, "Architecture and History," in May Morris, ed., *The Collected Works of William Morris,* 22: 308. For an insightful exploration of this myth, see Laural Thatcher Ulrich, *The Age of Homespun* (New York: Alfred A. Knopf, 2001). See also Mary Douglas, "American Craft and the Frontier Myth," *New Art Examiner* 21 (September 1993): 22–26.

8. Walter Benjamin, "The Work of Art in the Age of Mechanical Production," in *Illuminations: Walter Benjamin,* edited by Hannah Arendt (1968; reprint, New York: Schocken Books, 1988), pp. 217–51; Jean Baudrillard, *The Mirror of Production* (St. Louis, Mo.: Telos, 1975); Karl Marx, *Capital* (1867), translated by Samuel Moore and Edward Aveling (Moscow: Progress, 1954); Pierre Bourdieu, *Distinction* (London: Routledge, 1984); and Frederic Jameson, *Postmodernism, or the Cultural Logic of Late Capitalism* (Durham, N.C.: Duke University Press, 1991).

9. On the definition of studio furniture maker, see Edward S. Cooke, Jr., and Gerald W. R. Ward, *The Maker's Hand: American Studio Furniture, 1940–1990* (Boston: Museum of Fine Arts, Boston, 2003), pp. 10–15.

10. Ashton, "Maloof . . . designer, craftsman of furniture," pp. 15, 18.

11. The best period description of Esherick and his studio, from which the quotations are taken, is Gertrude Benson, "Wharton Esherick," *Craft Horizons* 19, no. 1 (January/February 1959), pp. 32–37. Other helpful sources include *Woodenworks: Furniture Objects by Five Contemporary Craftsmen* (Washington, D.C., and Minneapolis, Minn.: Renwick Gallery and Minnesota Museum of Art, 1972), pp. 22–29; Stone, *Contemporary American Woodworkers,* pp. 2–17; and Robert Aibel and Robert Edwards, *Wharton Esherick, 1887–1970: American Woodworker* (Philadelphia: Moderne Gallery, 1996). Garry Knox Bennett, who began to make furniture in the late 1960s in his Oakland studio, is the exception that proves the rule about the pastoralism of studio furniture; he celebrates that his work is "made in Oakland": Ursula Ilse-Neuman et al., *Made in Oakland: The Furniture of Garry Knox Bennett* (New York: American Craft Museum, 2001). Ford Maddox Ford, *Great Trade Route* (New York: Oxford University Press, 1937), p. 202.

12. James Krenov, "Wood: . . . the friendly mystery . . . ," *Craft Horizons* 27, no. 2 (March/April 1967): 28–29 and 54; James Krenov, *A Cabinetmaker's Notebook* (New York: Van Nostrand, 1976); James Krenov, *The Fine Art of Cabinetmaking* (New York: Van Nostrand, 1977); James Krenov, *The Impractical Cabinetmaker* (New York: Van Nostrand, 1979); and James Krenov, *Worker in Wood* (New York: Van Nostrand, 1981). Useful insights into Krenov's philosophy and influence include Michael Stone, "The Quiet Object in Unquiet Times," *American Craft* 44, no. 1 (February/March 1984): 39–43; and Glenn Gordon, "James Krenov: Reflections on the Risks of Pure Craft," *Fine Woodworking* 55 (November/December 1985): 42–49. Krenov, *A Cabinetmaker's Notebook,* p. 16. See James Krenov, *With Wakened Hands: Furniture by James Krenov and Students* (Bethel, Conn.: Cambium Press, 2000); and Ross Day, "A Krenov Student's Notebook," *Fine Woodworking* 146 (winter 2000/2001): 98–103.

13. Maloof, *Sam Maloof, Woodworker,* p. 23. Jonathan Fairbanks' introduction to this autobiography also takes a narrow view of commercialism and projects the Morris paradigm onto

Maloof: "In other words, the entire Maloof production is that of an artist's studio, with each work tailored to the needs of maker and buyer. There is no speculative production other than the periodic introduction of three or four new forms each year, made specifically for clients and then included in Sam's repertoire. . . . No commercial firm can produce or market the Maloof product" (p. 16). Yet, as Caroline Jones points out, the artist's studio was becoming increasingly more commercial in orientation at this time: *The Machine in the Studio* (Chicago: University of Chicago Press, 1996). On his aspirations for a proper book, see Adamson, *The Furniture of Sam Maloof,* p. 192.

14. Quotation from Loney, "Sam Maloof," p. 17. On pricing, see Maloof, *Sam Maloof, Woodworker,* esp. pp. 31, 39, 41, and 45.

15. On Castle's prices, see Carolyn Meyer, *People Who Make Things: How American Craftsmen Live and Work* (New York: Atheneum, 1975), pp. 165–72; Urbane Chapman, "Wendell Castle Tries Elegance," *Fine Woodworking* 42 (September/October 1983): 68–73; and Roger Holmes, "Wendell Castle's Clocks," *Fine Woodworking* 59 (July/August 1986): 80–83.

16. The role of signature and authorship in design is well theorized in Frederic Schwartz, *The Werkbund: Design Theory & Mass Culture before the First World War* (New Haven, Conn.: Yale University Press, 1996).

17. Quotation from a ca. 1980 brochure titled "The Signed Edition Series" (in the Wendell Castle file in the Arts of the Americas Department, Museum of Fine Arts, Boston). On Castle's interest in broadening his market from local craft consumers to the New York art market, see Davira Taragin et al., *Furniture by Wendell Castle* (New York: Hudson Hills, 1989), esp. pp. 54–89.

18. Maloof's perspectives on employees are presented in Maloof, *Sam Maloof, Woodworker,* pp. 49–52. On the intensification of domestic craft production in the early national period, see Christopher Clark, *The Roots of Rural Capitalism: Western Massachusetts, 1780–1860* (Ithaca, N.Y.: Cornell University Press, 1990); and Edward S. Cooke, Jr., *Making Furniture in Preindustrial America: The Social Economy of Newtown and Woodbury, Connecticut* (Baltimore, Md.: Johns Hopkins University Press, 1996).

19. On the savvy marketing of Pueblo pottery, see Ruth Bunzel, *Pueblo Potter: A Study of Creative Imagination in Primitive Art* (New York: Columbia University Press, 1929); and Barbara Babcock, "First Families: Gender, Reproduction and the Mythic Southwest," in *The Great Southwest of the Fred Harvey Company and the Sante Fe Railway,* edited by Barbara Babcock and Marta Weigle (Phoenix, Ariz.: Heard Museum, 1996), pp. 207–18. On Freda Maloof's interest in business, see Adamson, *The Furniture of Sam Maloof,* esp. pp. 70–71; and Jonathan Binzen, "Alfreda Maloof: An Appreciation," *Fine Woodworking* 134 (February 1999): 36.

20. Photographs of Maloof's shop interior reveal stacks of certain parts such as spindles and legs that suggest outsourcing. In the 1950s Don Wallance commented on how "creative craftsmanship" in the highly industrialized America incorporated a spectrum of locations from the small shops of designer-craftsmen to the design laboratories of certain industrial designers to small-scale industry: *Shaping America's Products* (New York: Reinhold, 1956). On workmanship and variation within free workmanship, see David Pye, *The Nature and Art of Workmanship* (New York: Cambridge University Press, 1968).

21. On the local California craft world of the 1950s and 1960s, see Olivia Emery, *Craftsman Lifestyles: The Gentle Revolution* (Pasadena, Calif.: California Design Publications, 1976); and on the national scene, see Edward S. Cooke, Jr., "Wood in the 1980s: Expansion or Commodification?" in Davira Taragin et al., *Contemporary Crafts and the Saxe Collection* (New York: Hudson Hills, 1993), pp. 148–61.

22. On Castle's early efforts in production and limited edition work, see Taragin et al., *Furniture by Wendell Castle,* pp. 42–45 and 71–73.

23. On the Wendell Castle Collection, see Steven Fennessey, "Carving a New Niche," *Rochester Democrat and Chronicle,* July 19, 1999, pp. 1C and 6C; and *Americanstyle* (fall 1999): 18.

24. Adamson, *The Furniture of Sam Maloof,* pp. 149–91.

25. Mastelli, "Sam Maloof"; and *California Woodworking* (Oakland, Calif.: Oakland Museum of Art, 1981). On the effect of Maloof and his contemporaries on other makers, see Dona Meilach's *Creating Modern Furniture: Trends, Techniques, Appreciation* (New York: Crown, 1975); Dona Meilach, *Woodworking: The New Wave* (New York: Crown, 1981); and the several *Fine Woodworking Design Books* published since 1977 (Newtown, Conn.: Taunton Press, 1979). *Woodshop News* published a spirited group of editorials and letters to the editor from December 2001 through April 2002 that focused upon the widespread copying of Maloof's chair designs.

26. Cooke, "Wood in the 80s"; and Adamson, *The Furniture of Sam Maloof,* p. 224.

27. Mastelli, "Sam Maloof," p. 52; and Adamson, *The Furniture of Sam Maloof,* pp. 114, 120–23, 175, 185–89, 203, and 216–17.

28. *California Woodworking,* p. 14; and Paul Smith and Edward Lucie-Smith, *Craft Today: Poetry of the Physical* (New York: American Craft Museum, 1986), pp. 142–43. Barbara Manning, "Master Craftsman Sam Maloof is King of the Rockers Because He Rocks by the Seat of His Pants," *People Magazine,* January 6, 1986.

29. Dan Mack, "Thoughts on Chairs and Change and Creativity's Eternal Vitality," *Woodshop News* 12, no. 11 (October 1998): 12. On the commodification of the craftsperson, see Peter Dormer, "The Ideal World of Vermeer's Little Lacemaker," in John Thackara, *Design After Modernism* (New York: Thames and Hudson, 1988), pp. 135–44; and Gloria Hickey, "Craft Within a Consuming Society," in *The Culture of Craft,* edited by Peter Dormer (Manchester, Eng.: Manchester University Press, 1997), pp. 83–100.

Figure 1   Martin Johnson Heade, *Sunset Harbor at Rio*, 1864. Oil on canvas, 20⅛" x 35". (Courtesy, Pennsylvania Academy of the Fine Arts, Henry C. Gibson Fund.)

Peter M. Kenny

From New Bedford to New York to Rio and Back: The Life and Times of Elisha Blossom, Jr., Artisan of the New Republic

▼ DURING THE EARLY national period over a thousand cabinetmakers labored in the small pre-industrial workshops and manufactories of New York City. Together they invented and sustained one of the premier schools of American cabinetmaking that today universally is associated with the name of Duncan Phyfe. Among the unsung journeymen who contributed to the growth and development of this school was Elisha Blossom, Jr. Taken by his family at a young age from New Bedford, Massachusetts, to the larger and more cosmopolitan city of New York, Blossom worked at several occupations during his lifetime, including shipwright, cabinetmaker, shop clerk, and accountant. But probably the most exciting episode of his life was a sojourn he made as a young man to the exotic port of Rio de Janeiro (fig. 1), where he worked as an agent for a New York cabinetmaking firm involved in the venture cargo trade. This phase of Blossom's career is chronicled in his daybook for the years 1811 to 1818. The daybook reveals that he made a variety of furniture forms for four different masters and gives the amounts he received on a piecework basis for his labor. Blossom's descriptions and charges provide an excellent point of comparison with contemporary New York cabinetmakers' price books, which published descriptions of various furniture forms and charges for journeymen's labor in three separate editions and two supplements and revisions before 1818.[1]

This article will analyze and interpret Blossom's daybook by comparing his entries with information gleaned from price books and other period documents concerning the manufacture and sale of furniture. It will also examine Blossom's business relationships with his employers and define his place in the robust New York cabinetmaking industry of the 1810s, especially that segment of the industry involved in marketing ready-made furniture locally through auction and in ports in the American south, the Caribbean, and South America. Similarly, notations in Blossom's daybook and information on his personal life reveal concerns about mobility that must have been common among multi-talented artisans. Like many of his peers, he relished the autonomy of the independent mechanic's life but eventually succumbed to the steady income of an office job—work he admittedly found a bit "too confining."

Elisha Blossom, Jr., was born on September 8, 1789, in New Bedford, Massachusetts, a sixth-generation descendant of one of the original settlers of Plymouth Colony. His father Elisha Sr. (1767–1812), was a shipwright who married Elizabeth (Betsy) Loring (1770–1822) in 1788. Approximately

Figure 2 William J. Bennett, *Bowling Green, north on the west side of Broadway,* New York City. Aquatint, 13½" x 9⅜". (© Collection of the New-York Historical Society.) Bennett's view depicts Bowling Green about 1826. No. 1 Broadway is the first house on the left in the foreground and has a pedimented, projecting center bay. According to *Iconography of Manhattan Island,* 6 vols. (New York: Robert H. Dodd, 1915–1928), 3: 589–90, No. 1 Broadway was the site of a boarding school for young ladies before Innocent Loring established her fashionable boardinghouse. It became the private residence of Robert Kennedy in 1798 and Nathaniel Prime in 1810.

four years later the couple took their eldest child, Elisha Jr., and his younger brother, Eliphalet (1790–1793), to New York City. The precise reasons why the family left New Bedford for New York remain uncertain, but perceived economic opportunities and kinship ties may have precipitated their move. Betsy Blossom's mother, Innocent Loring (1749–1816), had already moved from New Bedford to New York. From 1792 to 1796, Innocent ran a boardinghouse at her residence at No. 1 Broadway in lower Manhattan. This area was one of the city's most fashionable neighborhoods (fig. 2). Elisha and Betsy arrived in 1793 and may have lived with her mother. According to tradition Innocent's husband, Joshua Loring (1741–ca. 1801), a house carpenter by trade, also removed to New York; however, his name does not appear in the city directories. Given the peripatetic nature of house carpenters, it is possible that he split his time between New Bedford and New York.[2]

In 1796 Innocent Loring moved her boardinghouse uptown to 147 Harman Street in the city's Seventh Ward. This change of address must have dramatically altered the demographics of her clientele from the merchants and other elites who stayed with her on lower Broadway to the mechanics and tradesmen who populated the outer or mechanics' wards. Her new establishment may have been "a craft boardinghouse where for as little as three dollars per week [journeymen]. . . could get meals, a place to bed down, and word of mouth about available jobs in the city." Because her boardinghouse was near the shipyards along the East River many of her boarders were probably shipwrights. One of them was her son-in-law, Elisha, who is documented in the city directory at this address from 1796 to 1800. Between 1800 to 1812, he, and presumably his wife and children as well, moved from Oliver Street, to Cherry Street, to Clinton Street, to Henry Street, and finally back to Harman Street, all addresses in the outer wards near his places of employment at the East River shipyards. Although frequent relocation was relatively common among New York journeymen and their families, all these moves must have been difficult for Elisha and Betsy Blossom, who by 1802 had brought eight children into the world. By 1804 four of the eight had died, including Eliphalet (1790–1793), the toddler who had accompanied the family from New Bedford to New York, and Ansel (1793–1794), the first child born to Elisha and Betsy in New York. Given the fact that one of the boys died in the late summer and the other early in the fall, it is possible that they perished from yellow fever. That disease swept through the port of New York with frightening regularity during the summer months and was especially devastating on the lower tip of Manhattan, where Innocent Loring kept her first boarding-house. Although this scenario is purely conjectural, the deaths of the two little boys from yellow fever could have hastened Innocent's move to an outer ward where the risk of contracting the disease was somewhat reduced. More misfortune visited the Blossoms and Lorings in 1801 when Innocent's husband died. Elisha Jr. probably began serving his apprenticeship in that year or the following one after he turned thirteen.[3]

Elisha Jr.'s résumé is spelled out clearly in the pages of his daybook: shipwright, cabinetmaker, bookkeeper, and accountant. When and with whom he acquired the skills to perform these jobs, however, is far less certain. His training as a shipwright was a direct consequence of his father's involvement in that trade and probably came first. Becoming a journeyman shipwright was a demanding pursuit that required the longest period of apprenticeship of any of the mechanics' trades in Federal New York. The city's master shipbuilders maintained strict control of their trade, enforcing full-term apprenticeships that lasted seven years well into the nineteenth century. Given these strict requirements, it is uncertain whether Elisha's father, apparently a journeyman all his life, would have been qualified to train his son, although the possibility exists that he did. Regardless of who trained him, Elisha Jr. met the challenge of this rigorous apprenticeship and became a member of the New York Society of Journeymen Shipwrights and Caulkers.[4]

Elisha Blossom, Jr., may have acquired his bookkeeping skills as part of the apprenticeship agreement struck between his parents and his master. (Masters were often charged with educating apprentices as well as training them in a particular craft.) Elisha Jr. must have become quite proficient with numbers. In 1815 he received an annual salary of $600 from Henry Eckford, the legendary New York shipbuilder. Eckford was an immigrant Scot, a skilled artisan, and dynamic businessman who became extremely successful, especially after the War of 1812. In 1817 he won the commission

Figure 3   Launch of the Battleship Ohio at the New York Navy Yard, Brooklyn, Tuesday Morning, May 30, 1820, attributed to William J. Bennett, New York City. Watercolor, 14¼" x 23". (© Collection of the New-York Historical Society.) The ship's figurehead depicting Hercules, carved by Jeremiah Dodge (1781–1860) and Cornelius Sharp (active ca. 1810–d. 1828), is in the collection of the Peabody Essex Museum, Salem, Massachusetts.

to produce the federal government's ship-of-the-line, *Ohio,* one of the largest vessels built in the East River shipyards in the early national period (fig. 3). Later Eckford received lucrative contracts to build several large warships for Latin-American states and for the Greeks during their war for freedom from the Turks (1825–1826). He died in Constantinople in 1832 while organizing a navy yard for the Sultan and was returned to New York preserved in a cask of wine. One can only imagine the colorful personalities and important deals that Elisha was privy to during his employment with Eckford.[5]

Elisha's career as an accountant was relatively short, lasting at the most from 1815 to 1818. After that date, and until his death in December 1823, he appears to have made his living solely as a shipwright. During these five years he may have worked at Eckford's East River yards, or possibly for the shipbuilding partnership of Stephen Smith and John Dimon. In 1819–1820 he may have participated in a partnership referred to as "Blossom, Smith & Demon, shipyards, Stanton M. I." in city directories. According to historian Robert Greenhalgh Albion, Smith was one of Eckford's apprentices and was the principal builder of the firm, whereas his partner Dimon attended to repairs. The profitability of this arrangement is evidenced by a remark credited to Dimon: "Smith builds the ships and I make the money."[6]

If Elisha Jr.'s apprenticeship began in 1802, he would have completed his term by 1809. Afterward, he may have spent his first few years as a journeyman working aboard ships at sea or in port for a variety of master shipbuilders. His early years as a journeyman may have been lean ones, however, due to the declining state of the American economy. The Embargo Act of 1807, which forbade American vessels from foreign trade, was particularly devastating for shipwrights, sail makers, and chandlers and brought port activity along the eastern seaboard to a virtual standstill. The act was repealed after a year, but the modest recovery that followed was interrupted by the War of 1812. With his prospects as a shipwright somewhat in doubt, Elisha Jr. may have hedged his bets by seeking additional training as a cabinetmaker.

Elisha Jr. may have learned the cabinetmaking trade from his maternal uncle, David Loring (1784–1849), who served his apprenticeship back in New Bedford with Elisha's first cousin, Samuel Blossom. In the October 23, 1802, issue of the *Columbian Courier, and Weekly Miscellany,* Blossom advertised: "Runaway from the subscriber, on the 9th inst. an indented Apprentice to the Cabinet-Making business, named David Loring; aged about 17 years. . . . reward of FIFTY CENTS." Whether Loring returned or fled directly to New York is unknown. In October 1803 Blossom died, and Loring, by then almost nineteen years old, would have been on his own.[7]

The earliest reference to David Loring in New York City is March 7, 1807, when the *People's Friend & Daily Advertiser* reported that the "Partnership of Loring & Ryer, Cabinetmakers, was this day dissolved by mutual consent." After the break up, Loring worked on his own at 40 Beekman Street until 1810 when he took Abraham S. Egerton of the New Brunswick, New Jersey, family of cabinetmakers as his second partner. Their association lasted about a year; by 1811 Loring was working independently at 25 Beekman Street, the same address he shared with Egerton. His dreams of success as a cabinetmaker in New York were cut short by a devastating fire in 1814 that completely destroyed his shop and wareroom. After the fire Loring left New York for Cincinnati, Ohio, where he first established a window blind manufactory and later ran a grocery. Eventually he became a very successful merchant and one of Cincinnati's leading citizens.[8]

Elisha Blossom, Jr.'s Daybook, Rio de Janeiro, June 10–October 26, 1811
Elisha Blossom, Jr., arrived in Rio de Janeiro by June 10, 1811, the date recorded on the front page of his daybook (fig. 4). None of his impressions

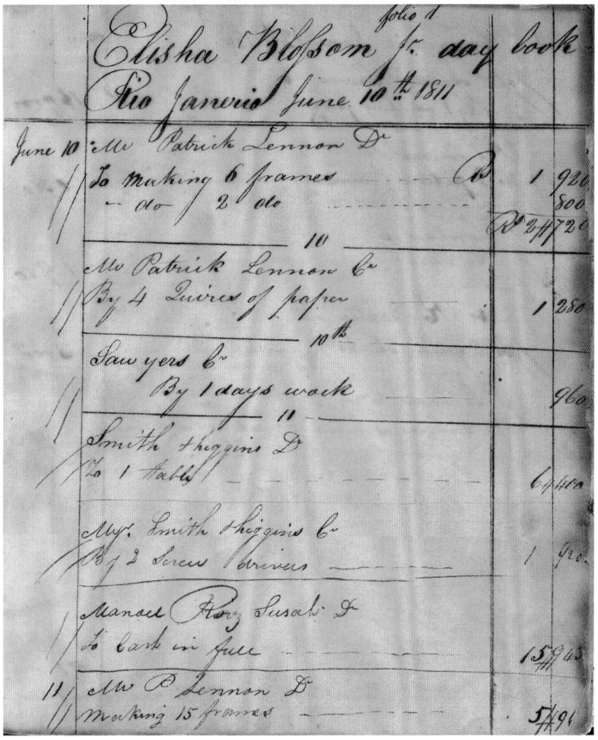

Figure 4 Page 1 in Elisha Blossom, Jr., Daybook, Rio de Janeiro and New York, 1811–1818. (© Collection of the New-York Historical Society.) This daybook was half of a two-part bookkeeping system that also included an alphabetized ledger where daily credits and debits were totaled up under the names of the individual with whom Blossom made transactions. The ledger is missing.

regarding his sojourn survive, but there can be little doubt that Elisha was just as awed by the majesty of this exotic, tropical port as other nineteenth-century travelers, one of whom claimed, "The day one first enters this magnificent harbor may well be regarded as an epoch in his life, for it is without question the finest in the world" (see fig. 1). Blossom probably moved to Rio to serve as an agent for mercantile interests back in New York. This supposition is borne out by account activity recorded in his daybook on July 16, 1811: a debit of 300 mill reas (one Portugese mill rea [1,000 reas] equaled approximately $1.25) to the cabinetmaking partnership of Loring & Egerton on a "Bill of exchange on Balch & Ridgway," a second debit of 30 mill reas/563 reas charged David Loring "To [a] Bill on Loring & Egerton," and a credit of 54 mill reas/657 reas to Loring & Egerton "By [a] Bill given on you in favor of D. Loring." A block of entries, crossed out but still legible and dated August 22, 1811, appears to be a summary of activities that confirm Blossom's agency relationship with his uncle and his partner. Some of these notations reference dates before the start of Blossom's daybook, which may indicate that he sold off some of Loring & Egerton's venture cargo at ports of call along the way or that Elisha was in Rio earlier than the dateline of his daybook indicates. The earliest entries in this block were for a "Commission charg'd Loring & Egerton Jany 19th 1811" of 17 mill reas/375 reas; a "Commission charg'd on sales febry 23" of 23 mill reas/100 reas; and "do on purchases" totaling 6 mill reas/322 reas. Blossom also recorded but did not date a "loss on coffee" of 42 mill reas and an "allowance on wood" of 19 mill reas. The former may indicate that Blossom reinvested some of his commissions in the produce of the region, the latter that he used some mahogany or other wood belonging to Loring or Egerton for projects in Rio. Other entries in this block include a credit of 21 mill reas/937 reas to David Loring "By[a] commission charg'd him July 10," as well as a "Commission on goods advanced [illegible] Oct. 11 as p Bill 2-½ p cent" and a "Commission on goods advanced per ship Triton." Both commissions were minor totaling 873 reas. All told, Blossom earned commissions totaling 69 mill reas/607 reas from David Loring and Loring & Egerton. In an era when a fully employed journeyman carpenter or cabinetmaker earned about $400.00 a year, these commissions clearly were a significant part of Blossom's annual income.[9]

Among all the goods Blossom sold on commission, the percentage represented by furniture cannot be determined due to the lack of descriptive information. However, numerous other transactions listed throughout the daybook describe individual furniture forms—mostly tables—sold by Blossom in Rio. Thirty-six pieces of furniture are recorded between June and October 1811, including twenty-six tables of unspecified types ranging in value from 4 mill reas to 10 mill reas; four wash stands valued at 7 mill reas/500 reas; one desk of indeterminate value; one music table of indeterminate value; one stool valued at 1 mill rea/400 reas; and one clothes horse valued at 1 mill rea/600 reas. The most expensive piece of furniture Blossom sold—and the most suprising entry in the entire daybook—was a "cradle for his Royal Highness the Infanta of Spain." This cradle, which sold for

Figure 5 Cradle, New York City, 1815–1825. Mahogany and mahogany and rosewood veneers with white pine; brass inlay. L. 45". (Courtesy, Metropolitan Museum of Art, Sylmaris Collection; gift of George Coe Graves, by exchange.) The crotch mahogany veneer on the dome, separated by brass line inlay, radiates from a brass star inlaid at the center in a rosewood field; the dome is lined with the original cream-colored silk. Matching silk or mull draperies, suspended from the dome, very likely completed the cradle's sumptuous original decorative scheme.

45 mill reas to Maestro Gerde Rinaldo on September 21, 1811, must have been exceptional for its cost was that of a mid-grade sideboard. A New York cradle (fig. 5) with a brass-inlaid circular crown, rich crotch-mahogany veneers, and its original silk lining may represent a comparable form, although it is impossible to determine whether the Infanta's cradle was brought from New York or made by Blossom in Rio. One sale recorded in the cabinetmaker's daybook suggests the latter. On September 3, 1811, Blossom debited Patrick Lennon 27 mill reas for six tables, a stool, and a clothes horse and credited Leonard Sawyer 6 mill reas/800 reas "for turning." Sawyer's piecework may have been the legs for the tables and stool and components for the clothes horse.[10]

Although most venture cargo shipments assembled by cabinetmakers and merchants were diverse to meet the demands of consumers in different ports of call, the furniture that Blossom sold in Rio lacked variety. A remarkable handwritten notebook kept by an anonymous American trader in Rio indicates that large cargoes of furniture in a wide range of forms were being sold for a good profit. The "proportion" and "assortment" of wares he mentioned may have resembled the mix of furniture that Loring & Egerton sent to the port less than two years later. This document also helps explain why men like Blossom accompanied furniture cargoes abroad:

Cabinet Wares or Furniture

This article will answer well in any reasonable quantities, and will generally sell at an advance of 75 to 80 per % from the first cost. Several considerable parcels have arrived from the United States of late, & they appear to have been much demanded, as the Inhabitants have really been hurrying for a choice, and they have all sold in a few days, and for a very handsome profit.

The kinds most suitable for this market at this moment, are Dining, Pembroke, Card, Dressing and Night Tables, Bureaus, Bidets, Wardrobes, Secretaries, writing desks with book cases, Sideboards, Sofas with and without Cushions & with Chairs to match, wash stands, Bedsteads &c. &c. – Of writing Desks the market appears to be well supplied – and if more are shipped immediately, they will become quite a drug, but whenever they are shipped, they ought to be furnished with Inkstands, Sand boxes &c. &c. & generally furnished with shaving apparatus.

Common or Windsor chairs & Sofas, are also abundant in the market, but when a sale is made, it is generally at a very handsome price.

A few well made and well contrived Counting room Desks would sell to advantage, and perhaps a few counting room Cases for Papers, Books &c. –

The following may be considered as to proportion, as a good assortment, viz –

6 Side Boards	12 Dining Tables, singles & in setts	20 Pembroke Tables
30 Night Tables	12 Dressing Tables	50 Bidets
20 Bedsteads	6 Wardrobes	12 Secretaries & field & high posts Bookcases
8 pair Card Tables	3 Counting room Desks	3 do Cases for Books
12 Bureaus	6 doz, Chairs	12 washstands, Sofas &c. &c. –

This furniture should be of the best workmanship & mahogany, or eather it should be so in appearance, but it ought not be of the highest priced and most expensive kinds. They ought also to be well packed and secured from injury, and if a Cabinet Maker was in the Ship to put them in good order when opened and repair any damage they may have sustained on the passage, his services would be useful. Your bedsteads or some of them at least ought to have a sacking bottom & other wooden bottoms, but all prepared for sacking bottoms. Care should also be taken to have all the locks in this furniture of the very first kind, and as you can get no mahogany here to repair with, you had better have a little, as if you lose a leg to your tables, or anything of that kind you will find it useful to repair with.[11]

The aforementioned Patrick Lennon played a major role in Blossom's economic life and subsistence in Rio. Between June 10 and June 14, 1801, Elisha made this merchant and dry goods grocer thirty-seven frames (presumably for prints) and sold him "40 brass rings" to hang them. Lennon later purchased twenty-seven pieces of furniture and several additional frames and commissioned Blossom to repair and alter objects the merchant already possessed. In exchange, Lennon supplied Blossom with trousers, shirts, stockings, butter, potatoes, tea, farina, porter, rum, quires of paper, and a pitcher and tumblers. The merchant seldom paid in cash, both men apparently preferring to work within the typical system of debits and credits found in a barter economy. On October 21, 1811, Blossom and Lennon settled their accounts as the former prepared to board ship for his eventual return to New York. Adjacent entries in the cabinetmaker's daybook— "Mr. P. Lennon's Bill, 341-350 (341 mill reas/350 reas)" followed by "Mine 305-310 (305 mill reas/310 reas)"—indicate that Lennon owed Blossom 36 mill reas/40 reas. The merchant settled his debt with cash and twenty-one bottles of porter, perhaps to be enjoyed by Elisha on his long voyage home.

Blossom's single greatest expenditure with Lennon occurred on June 30, 1811, when he recorded a credit to him of 108 mill reas/800 reas "By 1 Boy," obviously a slave. Blossom may have had problems with this slave since he exchanged him for another two weeks later. On July 15, 1811, Elisha credited Lennon 19 mill reas/20 reas for the "difference between the Black boys." The second slave evidently suited Blossom's needs. On July 12, 1811, the cabinetmaker charged a Mr. Maden for seven days of carpentry work as well as one day's "Negro hire," the latter of which came to 960 reas. Between August 20 and 22, 1811, Blossom repaired furniture for a Mr. Halkman and a Mr. Morgan, charging the former half a day's "Negro Hire," presumably for general shop work, and the latter a full day's "Negro hire [for] carrying tables & wardrobe." Although it is unlikely that the slave received remuneration, Blossom purchased him a pair of shoes on October 9, 1811. No further reference to the slave occurs in the daybook, which suggests that Blossom leased him from Lennon on a short-term basis, principally as a porter but also perhaps as a general shop hand and carpenter's helper.

Halkman and Morgan, who may have been furniture importers, provided Blossom with plenty of repair work in Rio. Sometimes these tasks earned him significant sums. Elisha charged John Morgan 14 mill reas/500 reas for repairing a French press on August 17, 1811, and an additional 12 mill reas/800 reas for repairing eighteen tables on August 21. Another entry on August 21 debited Lewis F. Halkan 16 mill reas for Blossom's repair of another French press. The surcharge of 480 reas added to Halkan's account may have been a half-day's "Negro hire," probably for a porter to pick up and return the press. Except in parts of Canada and the Mississippi River Valley, the French press was a new furniture form in early nineteenth-century America. Its case design was based on the traditional French *armoire,* but it typically had neoclassical turnings and moldings (see fig. 6). New York

Figure 6 French press, New York City, ca. 1810. Mahogany with yellow poplar and white pine. H. 83½", W. 54½", D. 20¾". (Courtesy, Boscobel Restorations, Inc.)

furniture makers coined the term "French press" during the first decade of the nineteenth century, and by 1810 the designation had become popular enough to be included in the New York cabinetmakers' book of prices. Although neither Morgan nor Halkman are known to have worked there, they may have served as agents for New York firms like Loring & Egerton. The final entry for Halkman and Morgan in Blossom's daybook is dated October 25, 1811. He credited the former 60 mill reas "by [a] bill of Exchange" and 28 mill reas "in Rice," and the latter 284 mill reas/60 reas "By Sundries." No cash payments were recorded for these significant sums.

Blossom supplemented his income in Rio with various types of house and ship carpentry. On June 16, 1811, he charged a Mr. Conolly for "Shelves in Kitchen," "Pieces for a hencoop," "11-¼ yds. of canvass for Blinds," and "4 frames, Rollers, Brackets for blinds." Other tasks performed by Blossom included putting on a roof, making doors and door cases, and unspecified work on the *Piscataquay* and the *Osprey,* the ship he took to New York later that fall. He charged 1 mill rea/600 reas for his day labor on the ships, which was forty percent more than what he received in New York the following year. This differential stemmed from the high demand for shipwrights and other woodworkers in the South American port, an enviable situation for a skilled, multitalented man like Blossom.

The purchases recorded in Blossom's daybook indicate that he had a comfortable life in Rio and that his credit was good with the local merchants. Patrick Lennon seems to have supplied most of his staples and some of his apparel. In fact, Elisha bought clothing and shoes with considerable frequency, perhaps because he chose to travel light on his journey from New York. He purchased a pair of shoes from Cyrus Bridge and nine shirts from Lennon on June 13, bought four more shirts from Antonio Joze Mendes on July 19, and acquired two pairs of "trowsers" from Lennon on July 22. On June 28 he made a rare cash payment of 20 reas to Portuguese tailor Antonio Mellendes for six pairs of pantaloons—tight-fitting dress pants—a vest, and alterations to his coat. These were the clothes of a merchant craftsman, a role Elisha seems to have assumed in Rio.

Another entry in Blossom's daybook documents a second New York journeyman cabinetmaker in Rio in 1811. On June 25 Elisha debited Andrew Hill for a pair of shoes purchased from Cyrus Bridge. This may have been the same Andrew Hill who was a member of the New York Society of Cabinet Makers in 1810. The Andrew Hill in Rio repaid his debt by "Making [a] table for Mr. Bridge" on July 26. Two other men whose names appear in the daybook may also have been cabinetmakers in Rio, although neither of them appears in New York City directories. Andrew Laurie's debit entries on September 26 and October 11 totaled 38 mil reas/400 reas for a work bench, a dozen boards, a compass, bead and tooth planes, files, sandpaper, a glue pot, varnish, castors, bed caps, and other items. Similarly, Patrick Robinson owed Elisha 70 mill reas for tools, a chest, a plane, and patterns purchased on October 12. Blossom, who departed Rio two weeks later, seems to have been disbanding his workshop.[12]

Little details gleaned from the daybook add texture to Blossom's life. Along with his stylish coat, vest, and pantaloons, Blossom had a pocket watch, which Messrs. Barrow and Westwood repaired on July 14. The cabinetmaker's leisure hours may have been spent hunting tropical birds in the mountain forests around Rio with a fowling piece he purchased from Andrew Laurie for 16 mill reas. Elisha may also have had an appreciation for the arts. Soon after returning to New York, he charged Mathias O'Connor twelve dollars for "4 pictures of Paul & Virginia," the innocents in Jacques-Henri Bernardin de Saint Pierre's sentimental prose idyll, *Paul et Virginie* (1788). A notation in the margin of Blossom's daybook indicates O'Connor returned the pictures on October 24, 1812, twelve days after their purchase. It is possible that Blossom had acquired the prints in Rio from Patrick Lennon, the merchant for whom he made so many picture frames.

According to historian Sean Wilentz, approximately twenty-five percent of New York journeymen were "single men in their twenties with flat purses and high hopes, the proverbial craft novices in search of . . . a quick savings." This characterization certainly fits Blossom, who was remarkably industrious during his time in Rio. Elisha recouped his monthly rent and made a small profit by subletting space to Barrow & Whitehead, the watch repairers; Mr. Bridge, the shoemaker; and Mr. Fidae, whose occupation is unknown. Blossom appears to have been leasing a commercial building/warehouse, where he and possibly others lived and worked. On September 9, 1811, Elisha recorded payment for six months rent at 38 mill reas/400 reas per month. In comparison, rental on a typical journeyman's house in an outer ward of New York City was approximately $55.00 a year in 1809. The high rate that Blossom paid suggests that he leased a large building in a good location and that the mercantile interests he represented in New York assumed all or some of the cost. The advance payment of the rent was also a harbinger that Blossom's days in Rio were numbered and that David Loring and/or other New York artisans and merchants were trying to maintain a foothold in Rio for future shipments and trade.[13]

On October 26, 1811, he recorded a debit of 80 mill reas, "Cash in full for passage to New York on Ship Osprey." No further entries appear in his daybook between that date and late February 1812, a four-month period that roughly represents the duration of his voyage.

New York City, February 23, 1812–December 28, 1818
Blossom's daybook entries in New York document his activities as a journeyman working for several master cabinetmakers as well as his abandonment of the trade for a steady salaried job before returning to ship carpentry, his first-learned skill. Still single when he returned from Rio, Elisha "Began Board with Loring & Blossom" on February 23, 1812, for a weekly charge of $3.00, or $3.31 when it included washing. Precisely which Loring and which Blossom is referred to in the daybook is uncertain, however. It could be his grandmother, Innocent Loring, who ran boardinghouses in the city for years, and Elisha's mother, Betsy Loring Blossom. On the other hand it could be Blossom himself and his uncle David Loring who might

have shared the annual rent on 25 Beekman Street, Loring's business address from the time of his partnership with Egerton in 1810–1811 until 1814, when the property was destroyed by fire. An entry in the daybook on March 7, 1812, crediting Innocent Loring $6.00 for two weeks board supports the latter scenario. Even after Elisha Jr.'s marriage to Maria Ann Anderson on October 31, 1812, the couple boarded with Loring & Blossom. On January 30, 1813, they began paying a new weekly rate of $4.50. Elisha and Maria did not continue in this living situation for long; their final payment for board with Loring & Blossom occurred on May 13, 1813, about the time Elisha departed—albeit temporarily—from his uncle's shop.

Neither the city directory nor the daybook provide clues as to where the couple lived in the year after Elisha parted with David Loring, but it's possible they moved in with Blossom's mother, Betsy, at 431 Pearl Street, where she ran a millenary shop. Tragically, Betsy Blossom was widowed on September 6, 1813, when her husband died from wounds he received in a naval engagement between the U. S. Brig *Enterprise* and *H. M. S. Boxer* during the War of 1812. A particularly poignant entry in Blossom's daybook occurred on Independence Day 1812, when he debited the account of "Mr. E. Blossom Senr." seven dollars for "Passage Paid Capt. Tripp to New Bedford." With America declaring war on Britain on June 14, 1812, Elisha and his father may have unwittingly bid their final farewells to each other on that fateful day in July.

From 1814–1815 until his death in 1823, Blossom appeared in the New York City directory every year except 1818. During this period, he is listed as plying three separate occupations: cabinetmaker (1814–1815), accountant (1815–1818), and finally shipwright (1818–1823). The master cabinetmakers he worked for are discussed below.

David Loring

Elisha Blossom probably trained as a cabinetmaker with David Loring, worked for him in Rio, and served as a journeyman in the latter's shop at 25 Beekman Street immediately after he returned to New York. Elisha made only ten pieces of furniture while working for Loring in 1812. The first two pieces recorded in Blossom's daybook on May 9, and 16, 1812, were Pembroke tables—classic New York forms with double-elliptic leaves. His labor charge for the more elaborate table, which had reeded legs, inlaid banding, and a sham drawer with a bead in the end rail, was $5.52. In comparison, he charged $4.80 for the other table, which had plain tapered legs and no end drawer. The following month, Blossom made a relatively expensive sideboard for which he charged $30.00—the second highest amount recorded in his daybook. Based on Elisha's description, this object may have been what New York cabinetmakers termed a "French sideboard" (see fig. 7). On August 1, 1812, Loring instructed Blossom to complete an English-style, two-part wardrobe—as opposed to the French-style armoire or press described earlier—for which the latter charged $25.94.

Although constructing the wardrobe took a considerable amount of time, over five months passed before Blossom made another piece of furniture.

Figure 7   French sideboard, New York City,
1810–1820. Mahogany and mahogany veneer with
yellow poplar. H. 57½", W. 73⅜", D. 25½".
(Courtesy, New York State Museum; partial gift
of the Wunsch Foundation.)

On January 22, 1813, he recorded labor charges for a pair of Pembroke tables
with reeded legs. During the preceding September and October, he tided
himself over by working for George James, a shipwright who paid him a
day rate of $1.44, presumably for building or repairing ships. Between Jan-
uary 22 and April 3, 1813, Blossom received only four furniture-making
projects from Loring. These included a Pembroke table with reeded legs, a
counting house desk, another English-style wardrobe, and a pillar-and-
claw Pembroke table with fashionable, Grecian-style saber legs and four
columns on a block-like plinth. Blossom's labor charge for the latter object
was $9.44, almost twice what he charged for Pembroke tables with turned
and reeded legs. Moreover, this charge was exclusive of any expenses Loring incurred for having the table ornamented in typical New York fashion
with distinctive water-leaf carving on the legs (claws) and columns (pillars)
(see figs. 8, 9). Carving was generally restricted to specialists, who either
worked for larger shops or as independent contractors. Loring may also
have purchased the plinth columns from a turner if he did not have such a
tradesman in his employ. Turners typically furnished cabinetmakers with
legs, stretchers, and other components on a piecework basis. Journeymen
cabinetmakers like Blossom performed other tasks such as sawing, joinery,
running molding, veneering, and finishing. The parameters of their work
are clearly delineated in New York cabinetmakers' price books, and cor-
roborated by entries in Blossom's daybook.[14]

A section of David Loring's daybook photocopied by furniture historian
Jane Sikes Hageman records the sale of furniture during a two-month
period from mid-March to mid-May, 1813, a time frame that partially over-
laps Blossom's tenure in his uncle's shop. During this period, Loring sold
only seven pieces of furniture, a testament, perhaps, to the depressed state
of the trade. Two of the sales were to cabinetmakers: On April 26, 1813,

Figure 8   Pembroke table, New York City, 1810–1820. Mahogany and mahogany veneer with white pine and cherry. H. 28¾", W. 35¾", D. 48¾" (open). (Courtesy, Metropolitan Museum of Art.)

Figure 9   Detail of the side apron of the table illustrated in fig. 8, showing the two hinged "flys" that support the leaf. In the 1810 New York price book only one "fly" on each side was standard for both turned leg and pillar-and-claw pembroke tables. A charge of 1s.4p. was assessed for each additional fly.

Loring charged John Linacre $67.00 for "One sideboard payable the 20ᵗʰ of July next" (possibly the same sideboard Blossom made for Loring in January 1813), and on May 26, Loring debited William Turner $82.00 for "One Sopha." A consistent, albeit little-known presence, in the New York furniture trade from 1806 to 1818, Turner kept his shop a few blocks from Loring at 50 Beekman Street. Such close proximity obviously was helpful in the cooperative environment that characterized the furniture trade in Federal New York. On May 8, 1812, the *New-York Gazette & General Advertiser* reported that Turner maintained a "Cabinet Ware-Room" at 163 William

Street and had an extensive selection of furniture, including "Side-Boards, Sophas, Secretaries, Bureaus, Card and Tea Tables, sets of Dining Tables, wash hand Stands, Bedsteads, &c." This was followed by another advertisement on May 25 for the "Sale of Elegant Cabinet Furniture/ By [auctioneer] M'Mennomy Tuesday, at 10 o'clock at the Warehouse of Wm Turner." The objects mentioned in this notice were the same ones that Turner had advertised earlier, with the addendum that "all [were] manufactured of the best materials and very highly finished in the most modern fashionable style." That style, of course, was the French-inspired *gout antique*, or rich antique style. M'Mennomy did not state that all of the furniture being auctioned was made by Turner. Indeed, Turner's purchase of a sofa from Loring in 1813 suggests that the former sold mixed lots. Some New York cabinetmakers took exception to this practice, believing that selling furniture only of their own manufacture provided potential buyers with the best guarantee of quality. That is not to say that Turner or Loring sold shoddy goods; rather that they responded to the demand for well-made furniture at a reasonable price as did most of their contemporaries. Such tradesmen produced furniture for stock-in-trade, auction, and export. A French sideboard labeled by William Turner and dated May 1813 (fig. 10) is typical of this class of furniture,

Figure 10 French sideboard, possibly by William Turner, New York City, 1813. Mahogany and mahogany veneer with unrecorded secondary woods. H. 35½" (to top), W. 77¼", D. 22¾". (Courtesy, Christie's.) The sideboard has a partial label that states: "AK[ER]/No. 50 Beekman Street/ New York/ All orders Thankfully Received and Favor[ably] attended to/ May, 1813." William Turner was listed at this address in the 1813 New York City directory.

Figure 11 Charles-Honoré Lannuier (1779–1819), French sideboard, New York City, 1812–1819. Mahogany and mahogany veneer with yellow poplar, mahogany, white pine, ash; *vert antique.* H. 57", W. 76⅜", D. 27¾". (Courtesy, Metropolitan Museum of Art; gift of Fenton L. B. Brown.)

but it does not approach the level of work achieved by Charles-Honoré Lannuier (see fig. 11) or his peers in the upper echelon of New York's cabinetmaking trade.[15]

Even within the short period covered by Sikes' photocopies of Loring's daybook, it is apparent that he did business with other New York cabinetmakers, including two tradesmen who worked nearby. He sold eighty feet of cherrywood to John Dolan on March 23, eight feet of mahogany "joist" to John L. Everitt on April 22, and sixty-eight feet of white pine to Dolan on April 26. Dolan evidently closed his shop at 30 Beekman Street the following month. On May 12, 1813, he advertised his benches, tools, wood, the lease on his house and shop and his stock, which included "a large assortment of Sideboards, sets of dining Tables and Ends, Tea and Breakfast Tables, high post and canopy Bedsteads, Bureaus, &c. manufactured out of seasoned wood . . . in the first stile of fashion and elegance." Peremptory sales like this were relatively common in nineteenth-century New York. They underscore the risks associated with running a furniture manufactory and wareroom and illustrate the problems associated with balancing inventories with fluctuating demand, especially in the uncertain economic times brought on by the War of 1812. Everitt, on the other hand, endured the hardships and later sought markets for his furniture in the American South. In 1816 he auctioned off a large quantity of furniture in Richmond, Virginia, and two years later began marketing his wares through an agent in Charleston, South Carolina. Besides being involved in the export trade, Everitt's career had another point of intersection with Loring's; he also employed Elisha Blossom, Jr., in 1813.[16]

John L. Everitt
Between April 14 and May 15, 1813, Everitt made a series of cash payments to Blossom for making a set of pillar-and-claw dining tables. For his labor, Blossom received twenty-eight dollars, part in advance, part while working

on the tables, and a final payment upon completion. Advances as well as payments exceeding the amounts stipulated for piecework in the journeyman cabinetmaker's price books were two strategies employed by master cabinetmakers to attract labor. Thus, it may have been the promise of fast cash that lured Blossom to Everitt's shop, where he worked for roughly two months from May until July 1813.

During the time he was employed by Everitt, Blossom made ten pieces of furniture including the aforementioned set of dining tables, four Pembroke tables with double elliptic leaves, two "square dining tables," a crib, and a bedstead. The "square dining tables" were eight feet long and nine feet long respectively, and each had two "fast" (fixed) legs and falling leaves supported by moveable "flys" or flaps (see appendix). The most elaborate and stylish piece Blossom made for Everitt was a French bureau, a form that resembled and functioned as a small sideboard more than the French-inspired commode or bureau that its name suggests. During the 1810s, French bureaus gained popularity owing to their compact size, which was well suited to the typical narrow townhouses in the city. Their strong architectural character also conveyed the style and monumental character of French Empire furniture.

The description of the French bureau in Blossom's daybook indicates that it shared features with the example illustrated in figure 12, including gilt-brass lion's paw castors, a long top drawer divided in two at the center with a banded rail below, and a backboard, albeit of a plainer type without the finials or the broken pitch-pediment. Blossom's labor charges totaled $22.48 with the work accounted for as follows:

Figure 12   French sideboard, New York City, 1810–1820. Mahogany and mahogany veneer with white pine. H. 59¾", W. 61⅜", D. 22¼". (Courtesy, Museum of Art, Rhode Island School of Design; bequest of Martha B. Lisle, by exchange; photo, Erik Gould.) The addition of two tall, narrow bottle drawers between the cupboard doors is frequently found on small-form French sideboards from New York.

May 22, 1813

Making french Bureau
Start   3.8.6

6 inches in length & height	7.6
plinth on front and ends	6.3
glueing on block for pilasters and breaking plinth round ditto	4.6
sinking groove in plinth	2.8
sunk panel in plinth	6.9
mitering reeds	.9
therm feet each side ½	9.4
fitting on claw castors	1.1
2 pannell Doors	8.3
veneering panels	2.4
Banding doors 4.8 (crossed out)	3.8
mitering Band	1.4
hanging doors with centre hinges	2.
filet between doors	1.
Banding of rail under draw	.7
dividing draw	5.
laping each draw 2/6	5.
draw sides mahogany	1.
cutting legs to lengthen draw	1.

account continued on next page
amt. Brot over   £6.2.10

Back board	4.
Veneering do	1.1
Pilasters on do	2.8
Beading do	1.7
Brass railing	5.
Pilasters	11.
Scroll & caps	8.
Veneering pilaster	.10
escutcheon	.2
polishing ends	1.8
glueing block on back legs	.8
1 false bottom	.1
Joint in top & bottom rail	1.
frieze rail	2.8
mitering ends of top rail	1.6
Joint in top	1.

               £9.2.10   £8.17.2 (crossed out)
Deduct molding on Doors   3/£8.19.10 $22.48

The brass side rails, backboard, top drawers, and lower cupboard section leave little doubt that the principal function of Blossom's French bureau was for the display and storage of silver, cut glass, porcelain, and other serving and ornamental objects used in the dining room. For all intents and purposes the form was a sideboard. Elisha's extra charge for two paneled doors eliminated the lower two drawers of the three specified in the list of revisions to the 1810 New York price book issued before 1814. Conversely, his introduction of one "fast," or fixed, shelf instead of drawers or sliding trays behind the doors reduced his labor cost. The disconnect between the term "French bureau" and the form's use arises from the object's hybrid nature. As the 1810 price book indicates, "French sideboards" were fashionable somewhat earlier than French bureaus. Master cabinetmakers seeking to meet, or generate, demand for a compact sideboard simply melded these two French-derived forms to create a new one. This apparently caused some consternation among journeymen when it came to pricing their labor. The 1817 New York price book attempted to remedy the situation stating: "When a French bureau exceeds five feet in length, [the labor charges are] to be taken from [the] French sideboard." The official "start" charge for the French bureau was £4.3, whereas the charge for the French sideboard was £8.17 shillings, with a discount of 1s.3s. for every inch the piece was reduced in length or width. This clause, which was intended to avoid future conflicts between journeymen and masters, reveals that journeymen were extremely aware of the need for reevaluation and revision of the price books.[17]

Blossom's daybook entry for the French bureau is the earliest reference to the form based on the revised list of additional prices issued as an addendum to the 1810 New York price book. Elisha almost certainly owned a copy of the price book, and he probably owned or had access to the addendum. The descriptions of his labor and the amounts he charged were clearly informed by them. If he owned the addendum, he may have attached it to his copy of the price book as did Daniel Turnier, another New York journeyman cabinetmaker. Blossom's daybook records the sale of a price book in January 1814, just before he quit the trade for the first time.[18]

Charles Christian

The most important individual Elisha Blossom, Jr., worked for was master cabinetmaker and auctioneer Charles Christian, who in 1814 made furniture for the Governor's Room and Mayor's office in the recently completed New York City Hall. Christian arrived in New York in 1798 and established his business at 61 New Street. Two years later, he moved to 73 Broad Street, where he advertised: "Charles Christian, Cabinet Maker, Late Foreman to the Furniture Ware Room, of the Society of Cabinet Makers, Philadelphia. . . has removed to Broad street. . . in consequence of several years practice in the first shops of Europe and America, he may venture to solicit a portion of the public patronage. . . N. B. A few good workmen wanted . . . An apprentice wanted." Although a competent businessman, Christian was an ill tempered man notorious for mistreating his apprentices. In 1803 the court found him guilty on several counts of beating four apprentices, refusing to supply them with sufficient clothing, and, worst of all, failing to teach them the fundamentals of the trade. Christian may have treated his journeymen somewhat better. Blossom's daybook indicates that he received payment in a timely fashion.[19]

Christian was appointed an auctioneer for the City and County of New York in April 1803. For the next five years, he and his partner, Samuel Paxton, conducted auctions at their store "for the reception and sale of Furniture at auction or on commission" at 7 Burling-slip. One of Christian's first sales included "his valuable stock of Furniture, all of which is his own manufacture." Regrettably, only two advertisements document the auctions run by the partners. One described a sale consisting of mixed lots of household furniture, linens, kitchen utensils, and plated wares, whereas the other featured sumptuous imported goods: "Two sets of most splendid India Paper Hanging, a rich Marble Chimney-piece, made in Rome, by an eminent artist, a Sofa and Chair, of Satin damask, made at Lyons, in France." In addition to conducting sales, Christian repaired "Second Hand Furniture for auction. . . at the cheapest rate." His advertisements touted "the advantage of employing an Auctioneer who is a perfect judge of the value and quality of Cabinet and other Furniture."[20]

No record of Christian conducting sales after 1805 is known; however, it is possible that his sales occurred on such a regular basis that advertisements were not necessary. By mid June 1813, he had "recommenced the Cabinet Making Business at No. 35 Wall-street." This coincided with his hiring Blossom, who recorded labor advances from Christian for two writing tables and bookcases, the first on July 10 and the second on August 1. Blossom's tenure in Christian's shop was relatively short, lasting only until mid October when the former received final cash payments for work on a pine bookcase and a portable desk. Altogether, Blossom made seven pieces of furniture for Christian including the four mentioned above, and five Pembroke tables with reeded legs and double-elliptic leaves. A labeled Pembroke table from Christian's shop (figs. 13, 14) probably resembles those made by Blossom.[21]

Blossom described his labor for making the first two Pembroke tables on September 25, 1813 (fig. 15). It is significant that Christian ordered two examples of the same form, a possible indication that he was amassing an

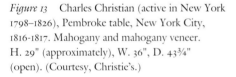

Figure 13   Charles Christian (active in New York 1798–1826), Pembroke table, New York City, 1816-1817. Mahogany and mahogany veneer. H. 29" (approximately), W. 36", D. 43¾" (open). (Courtesy, Christie's.)

Figure 14   Detail showing the label on the Pembroke table illustrated in fig. 13. Partition and Fair Streets were joined to form Fulton Street in 1816. When this occurred, Christian's Fair Street address changed to 90 Fulton Street, and he adjusted his label in ink accordingly. In May 1817 he moved his shop to No. 58 Fulton.

inventory for his new wareroom. The leg stiles of each table had square paterae with canted corners, probably of figured mahogany veneer. This detail may have been new for Blossom, since none of the pieces he made Loring or Everitt had paterae. Christian placed a second order for two Pembroke tables on September 27, 1813, and a third order for a single one on the same date. This effectively meant that Blossom produced five handsome mahogany tables in succession, an efficient procedure that may have kept him in the good graces of his temperamental employer. It may also explain why Christian paid Elisha in advance and on time. According to the descriptions in Blossom's daybook, the last three Pembroke tables lacked paterae, but the other features of all five were similar. The double-order tables were three feet eleven inches wide when open and three feet long on the bed, or frame; whereas the single table was three feet ten inches wide when open and two feet ten inches long on the bed. The standard starting size for a Pembroke table in the 1810 New York price book was three feet four inches wide when open and two feet six inches long on the bed. As one might expect, the size and ornament of the tables determined Blossom's labor charges. The two tables with the paterae were $6.93¾ each, the other pair was $6.20¾, and the single was $6.16½. Christian may have wanted several Pembroke tables with different prices and decorative options to appeal to the tastes and pocketbooks of his diverse clientele. Alternatively, the most elaborate examples could represent a custom order.

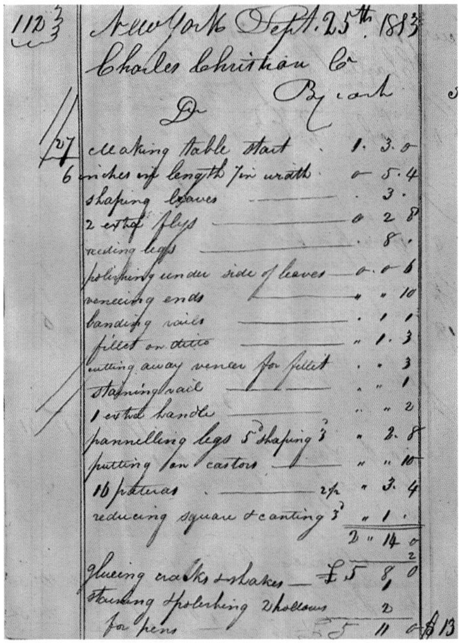

The writing tables and bookcases, which also represent a double order by Christian, were new to Blossom's repertoire. At the top of the entry for these two pieces are the dates "August/1/21," the only time such a dating system appears in the daybook. In all other instances only one start date is given. This dating system could mean one of two things—that Blossom began work on the first writing table and bookcase on August 1 and completed it on or before August 21 or that he began working on both pieces simultaneously and completed them in three weeks time. The first scenario seems the most likely as Blossom's labor charge for one of these pieces came to approximately twenty dollars, or just over a dollar a day. According to furniture historian Charles Montgomery, American journeymen worked six days per week and approximately eleven hours per day, which means that Blossom put in eighteen to nineteen days labor for Christian during this three-week period. Montgomery also stated that journeymen averaged one dollar per day through much of the Federal period. Given the fact that Blossom had received as much as $1.44 a day for shipwright's work, it is difficult to understand why he continued in the cabinetmaking trade.[22]

Blossom's daybook entries (fig. 15) reveal that the design of his writing tables and bookcases was distinctive when compared to most surviving examples of this rather neglected form. The writing table and bookcase illustrated in figure 17 shares some features with those made by Elisha, in particular the veneered, temple-form pediment board with flanking pedestals and urns and the book-matched "joint in [the] veneer of [the] Draw front." Blossom's pediment board, which was "hollow" on top, may have resembled the backboard on the small, French sideboard shown in figure 12.

Figure 15 Folio 112 in Elisha Blossom, Jr., Daybook. This page records Blossom's work on a Pembroke table for Charles Christian under the date September 27. Blossom credited Christian $5.00 for a cash payment three days earlier.

CHARLES CHRISTIAN DR	
Writing table & Book case £	3.12.0
6 inches in length	0.6.0
1 Do framing	0.0.8
1 Do ends	0.0.8
Joint in veneer of Draw front	0.0.2
pannells in legs	0.0.8
reeding rails	0.0.6
Do legs	0.7.0
Putting on castors	0.0.10
partitions in draws	0.2.3
2 Joints in top	0.0.8
clamping top	0.2.0
veneering top	0.1.6
veneering panels in fall	0.1.10
Banding fall	0.3.6
Mitres in fall	0.1.0
Banding center of fall Long	
banding	0.1.0.
Loose cornice {equal to solid top}	
5 feet crotch band 6-1/2	0.2.8
cock beading 10 feet 3d	0.2.6
4 mitres 1-1/2	0.0.6
Pediment board	0.4.6
veneering do	0.0.8
hollow on top 2 ft. 8 in. 3d	
mitres	0.0.10
Pedestals on front corners	0.2.0
3 small draws	0.7.6
1 partition across Case	0.1.8
16 letter holes 7d	0.9.4
8 upright partitions	0.8.0
scolloping Do 4d	0.2.8
3 Joints in top & Bottom	0.1.0
sinking veneer in front edge	
of bottom	0.1.3
Joints in Pannells of falls	0.0.7
polishing ends	0.2.4
pannells in back	0.3.0
Joint in draw Bottom	0.0.4
partition for sand and ink	0.1.3
hollow for pens to tilt	0.1.3
beveld piece for wafers	0.0.3
2 urns	0.0.8
Bringing pannells in fall	
forward	0.1.0
8 grooves for uprights	0.1.4
putting piece mahogany	0.1.6
moulding on edge of ends	0.0.6
	8.4.2
Deduct for mouldings on fall	0.2.9
Quarter round on pediment	0.0.8
	0.3.5
£	8.0.9

A WRITING TABLE AND BOOK CASE

The table two feet six inches long, two feet wide, the framing six inches deep, and one drawer in ditto veneered and cock-beaded ; four plain legs, a bead or band on the lower edge of the frame ; one joint in the top and edge of ditto banded. The book case two feet three inches high, the ends one foot wide, the front framed with two flat panels, or flush and veneered, the inside flush and lip'd for cloth, solid top, square edge, — 3 12 0

Each inch more in length, extra		0	1	0
Ditto in height, width of book case ends, or depth of table frame,	-	0	0	8
Ditto in width of table,	-	0	0	6
Each extra long drawer,	-	0	5	3
Dividing ditto into two,	-	0	4	0

Framing the ends two feet two inches deep, with inner ends to form a knee hole; two flat panelled doors in front, or square clamp'd, veneered on both sides, and cock-beaded, one shelf in each cupboard, — 2 0 0

Each inch more in depth of framing, 0 1 0

When made with drawers, deduct for doors and shelves — — 0 19 0

Each short drawer, veneered and cock-beaded 0 4 3

A plain arch, veneered, 0 4 0

A bead or band on the sweep edge of ditto, 0 3 0

A flap ten inches wide, hung to the edge of the table top, (to turn over as a card table) two lopers to support ditto, cock-beaded; three pieces mitred on the back part of the top, under the book case, — 0 14 0

A slider in front, under the top of the table, Square clamp'd and lip'd for cloth, 0 6 0

When the book case is made with two flat panelled doors, to be the same price as with fall in preamble.

For work inside of Book Case, see Counting House ditto.

Figure 16 Transcriptions from the Elisha Blossom, Jr., Daybook and the 1810 New York cabinetmakers' book of prices showing side-by-side comparison of the "Writing table and Book case" Blossom made for Charles Christian and the price book entry for the same form, which Blossom used as the basis for his charges.

Both of his upper cabinet sections had fall fronts "lip'd for cloth" and interior compartments for letters, bills, receipts, and business ledgers. The compartments consisted of sixteen pigeon-holes arranged around a core of eight tall partitions with scalloped front edges which formed slots for the ledgers and three shallow drawers below the "1 partition across [the] Case." Two writing tables and bookcases in institutional collections (Yale University Art Gallery and New York State Museum) have similarly fitted interiors, indicating that these pieces served as the business center in many nineteenth-century households. Functional, unadorned counting house desks with fitted interiors, on the other hand, were used in most offices and shops. The two furniture forms' shared features and functions are recalled in the 1810 New York price book entry for a "Writing Table and Book Case" (fig. 16): "For work inside of Book Case, see Counting House ditto." Options listed for the writing table and bookcase included a hinged writing fall "to turn over like card table" (with sliding supports), a recess, or "kneehole," at the center, and glazed bookcase doors with mullions arranged in handsome geometric patterns. The most important surviving example of this stylish type is a labeled and dated writing table and bookcase made in the shop of Duncan Phyfe in August 1820.[23]

While Blossom was working on the writing tables and bookcases, his wife, Maria, became ill. Given the fact that they had been married exactly nine months, it is possible that her problems were associated with pregnancy. On September 18, 1813, Elisha noted that he had paid $5.50 to Doctor Samuel Torbert for "medicine & attendance" and $10.50 to Mrs. Mooney for "3 weeks Nursing wife." Nine days later Blossom credited David Loring $8.25 for a cradle which he may have purchased in preparation for a new baby's arrival. A Blossom family genealogy states that Elisha and Maria Ann Anderson had only one child, Elisha William, born August 12, 1816, but it is possible that the couple had another earlier baby who never reached full term.

John Linacre

After leaving Christian's shop, Blossom found employment with John Linacre, who worked as a journeyman for cabinetmaker John Hewitt in 1811. Linacre established his own business at 382 Pearl Street in 1812 but left the cabinetmaking trade three years later. He was listed in the city directory as a merchant in 1815 and as a grocer in subsequent years. Linacre's experience was not unique among New York journeymen in the 1810s. Many small cabinet shops emerged in New York City, especially after the War of 1812, causing owners of larger, more established shops to complain that their business suffered from too much competition. This set the stage for the consolidation that occurred in the cabinetmaking trade in the late 1820s and 1830s.[24]

Blossom first referred to Linacre on October 23, 1813, when he credited his new master with the first of five cash payments ending on November 20, 1813 and totaling $42.00. During this same period he posted debits totaling $54.20. These charges included nine dollars for "1 clarinet bought by Mr. Rosetti," $1.50 for "finishing Dining Tables," and $43.70 for "Making [a] Sideboard." Based on Blossom's description, the latter object was a French sideboard. It had an overhanging frieze with drawers at the top and four doors and columns in the lower section. The "start" charge of nine pounds was the same as that given for the basic model of this form in the 1810 New York price book.[25]

By 1813 French sideboards were all the rage in New York. The example made by Blossom had many optional refinements: a "hollow" molding under the top, a frieze rail with cross-banded crotch mahogany, three top drawers—the center one with book-matched veneers and all three with solid mahogany sides—veneered paneled doors with cross-banding on the stiles and rails, and four columns with crotch veneers. Although not specified, the columns probably had carved capitals. All of these features can be observed on the French sideboard made by Lannuier (fig. 11). According to Charles Montgomery, the retail price of a piece of furniture was usually three and one half times the cost of the labor. Therefore, Linacre may have priced Blossom's sideboard as high as $150.00. By comparison, John Hewitt paid journeyman Thomas Constantine forty dollars each for

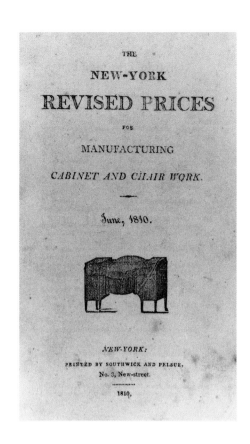

Figure 18 Title page from *The New-York Revised Prices for Manufacturing Cabinet and Chair Work, June, 1810*. (Courtesy, Winterthur Library: Printed Book and Periodical Collection.) This page from Duncan Phyfe's personal copy depicts a pedestal-end sideboard that was more Anglo-inspired than the "French sideboard" also listed (for the first time) in the 1810 price book. During the early 1810s, elite New Yorkers probably considered the latter form more avant-garde.

three French sideboards in April, May, and June 1812, $46.34 for another example in March 1813, and thirty dollars for a "French sideboard plain" the following May. In turn, Hewitt sold at least two French sideboards in 1812, one for $110 and another for $115.00. The sideboard that Blossom made for David Loring in June 1812 may have been comparable to the "plain" example made by Constantine. The labor charges for both journeymen were the same, and the daybook entry for Elisha's sideboard describes a relatively simple form. On April 28, 1814, Linacre advertised a variety of furniture, including pillar-and-claw card tables, tea tables, and dining tables along with "an elegant Sideboard on a new construction of a superior quality." Although it is impossible to determine if the sideboard in the advertisement was the one Blossom made five months earlier, it is obvious that Linacre had enough confidence in his journeyman to assign him the job of making one of these valuable and impressive forms.[26]

Blossom's other work for Linacre included two worktables, one completed on December 11, 1813, and the other on December 31; a cradle completed on December 15; and two Pembroke tables with turned, reeded legs completed on January 22, 1814. The worktables were the first examples of that form recorded in Blossom's daybook.

Blossom left Linacre's shop by January 22, 1814, when the former sold the latter "1 Book of prices Bound" for $1.50. This may have been the 1810 New York book of prices (fig. 18), possibly with the supplement issued somewhat later. Nine days later Elisha wrote that he had "Engaged and Commenced as a clerk With Richard Scott Book Seller for $375 per year Paid." An adjacent notation in the cabinetmaker's daybook indicates that Blossom "could not agree as [the clerk's job] . . . was too confining & Quit 10th Feby." Although his candid admission suggests that he preferred the relatively independent life of a journeyman, economic imperatives caused him to return again to the security of a salaried job in 1815.

Return to David Loring's Shop and Subsequent Abandonment of the Trade
The same day Blossom left Scott, he "Returned by mutual Consent" to his uncle's cabinetmaking shop, debiting Loring $160 for "1 chest of tools & work bench as per agreement." Business must have been relatively slow, for Elisha received only half a dozen furniture making projects between March 5 and July 6, 1814. These included the end section of a dining table with "octagon" (canted) corners on a single hanging leaf, a bookcase, two corner basin stands, and three pillar-and-claw Pembroke tables. Blossom's relationship with Loring ended when he completed the last Pembroke table on July 6. The latter's shop burned later that year, and Loring and his family moved west, traveling by stage over the Allegheny Mountains to Pittsburgh before completing their journey by keel-boat down the Ohio River to Cincinnati.[27]

Entries in Blossom's daybook summarizing "Wages Earnd . . . from May 1st 1814" to September 9, 1814, suggest that he was concerned about his finances and wanted to gauge his income over a fixed period of time. Some of the furniture making projects and odd jobs listed during that period do not appear in the main body of the daybook, but the wages he earned making furniture for his uncle during this time frame are recorded. Loring always paid the exact charges Blossom recorded in his daybook for specific furniture forms. These charges matched those prescribed in the 1810 New York price book (fig. 18) and later addendum, indicating that Loring accepted the wage scale set by the masters and journeymen of the city and that he considered Blossom's work to be of good quality. Obviously, masters were not obligated to pay journeymen the amounts specified in the price book for substandard work.[28]

Between May 1 and September 9, 1814, Blossom received additional income from making cheap "press boards" (probably ironing boards), a fireboard, a coffin, and a mill of some sort for $5.00. He also produced six pieces of furniture—three breakfast tables, a pair of circular washstands, and a bookcase—that do not appear in the main part of his daybook. Odd jobs performed by Blossom included taking a sideboard out through a window, minor house repairs, "writing" for a church (probably bookkeeping), and "3 Months service at Society"—presumably the New York Society of Journeyman Shipwrights and Caulkers, of which Blossom was a member in 1818, or the New York Society of Cabinet Makers. Elisha's wages for this four month period totaled $100.46¾. This translates into an annual wage of $304.41, or $70.59 less than the salary he was promised by the bookseller Richard Scott and approximately $100 less than the average annual wage of a journeyman house carpenter.[29]

Blossom performed fifteen days of unspecified labor for John Linacre in December 1814 but appears to have received little other work after leaving Loring's shop. Elisha made only three entries in his daybook during the following seven months and none pertained to cabinetmaking. Several possibilities might explain this radical drop in activity. Blossom could have left the city in search of work or lost his tools in the fire that destroyed Loring's shop. Alternatively, he simply may have become dispirited by that disastrous turn of events and dropped out of the work force for a while. One yearns to know more about this difficult time in Blossom's life, how he reacted to adversity, and what brought him to the decision finally to abandon cabinetmaking for good.

On July 1, 1815, Blossom "Began to write For Henry Eckford . . . @ $600 per year house rent free of expense." The salary alone was far more than Elisha could have earned as a journeyman cabinetmaker, not to mention rent-free housing. Blossom's landlord excused him from his current lease, which was due to expire November 30, 1815, for "ten dollars in consideration of his taking the house off my hands for the remainder of the year." Evidently, Blossom's new salary allowed him to engage in other income producing activities. In 1815–1816 he recorded sales of lumber, pitch, nails, brads, and other hardware, most to Henry Eagle of Oswego, New York. On February 19, 1816, Elisha paid state and city taxes on a "House in Mott Street" that he leased for £31, or $77.50, annually.[30]

Blossom probably kept Eckford's books for about three years beginning on July 1, 1815. New York City directories listed Elisha as an accountant through June 30, 1818. Although not recorded in the 1818–1819 directory, he was listed as shipwright the following year and worked in that trade until his premature death at the age of thirty-four on December 22, 1823.[31]

The entries in Blossom's daybook end around the time he left Eckford. Dated December 28, 1818, the last entry is a debit to Robert Bogardus "To cash for a Judgement of Bodie and McKean against Andrew Anderson assigned to me in full for $40.00." Blossom made note of a few rental agreements for the years 1820 to 1822 but declined to record any of his activities as a shipwright. It is likely that he maintained another ledger for that purpose. Nearly half of his calf-bound folio daybook (probably assembled from the four quires of paper Elisha acquired immediately upon his arrival in Rio) remains empty.

With the exception of his ten-day hiatus with bookseller Robert Scott, Blossom worked as a journeyman cabinetmaker in New York for just over three years. Between May 16, 1812, and July 1, 1815, he recorded the production of forty-eight pieces of furniture for which he charged $962.36. If Blossom had received the standard journeyman's wage from all his masters, as he did after resuming work in David Loring's shop in 1814, his average annual wage from cabinetmaking (assuming he was fully employed) would have been about $320. However, Blossom received only $183.60 between May 16, 1812, when he got his first furniture-making project in New York from his uncle, and May 22, 1813. In contrast, New York journeyman cabinetmaker Thomas Constantine made $453.20 during the same period. Blossom may not have been as skilled or as proficient as Constantine, or he may not have received the same amount of work. Either or both of these factors could have contributed to Elisha's decision to abandon the cabinetmaking trade.[32]

Elisha Blossom was never an important figure in the New York cabinetmaking trade. Were it not for the survival of his daybook, his life and career would be as transparent as those of many other New York journeymen and apprentices who failed to attain the status of Thomas Constantine, much less Duncan Phyfe. As a group, however, these unrecognized artisans helped create one of the most recognizable and renowned schools of cabinetmaking in early nineteenth-century America.

ACKNOWLEDGMENTS   For assistance with this article the author thanks David Barquist, Elaine Bradson, Luke Beckerdite, Andrew Brunk, Jane Sikes Hageman, Charles T. Lyle, Thomas Michie, John Scherer, Leslie Symington, and Karen Zimmerman.

1. The author respectfully borrows the phrase "Artisan of the New Republic" from Howard B. Rock's *Artisans of the New Republic, The Tradesmen of New York City in the Age of Jefferson* (New York: New York University Press, 1979). This excellent book brought Blossom's daybook to the author's attention. Only three other New York City cabinetmakers' account books from the early nineteenth century are known: John Hewitt, 1800–1803 and 1810–1813 (New Jersey Historical Society); Fenwick Lyell, 1800–1811 (Monmouth County Historical Society), and David Loring (whereabouts unknown).

2. William Duncan, *New-York City Directory* (1793). The 1795 edition was the first to give Innocent Loring's occupation. See *Iconography of Manhattan Island, 1498–1909,* edited by I. N. Stokes, 6 vols. (New York: Robert H. Dodd, 1915–1928), 3: 589–90 for a discussion of the successive

occupants of No. 1 Broadway. Stokes states that from 1792 to 1797 Loring kept a fashionable boardinghouse on the premises. Sean Wilentz, *Chants Democratic, New York City & the Rise of the American Working Class, 1788–1850* (New York: Oxford University Press, 1984), p. 52.

3. David Longworth, *Longworth's American Almanack, New-York Register, and City Directory, 1797–1812* (1819). Wilentz, *Chants Democratic*, p. 52. Elizabeth Blackmar, *New York for Rent, 1785–1850* (Ithaca, N.Y.: Cornell Unversity Press, 1989), pp. 213–14. Genealogical information on the Blossom family is available at <http://members@aol.com/dashmom/ blossom/html>. Innocent Loring is listed as a widow in the 1802 New York City Directory for the first time. Evidently her husband died the year before.

4. Wilentz, *Chants Democratic*, p. 135.

5. Elisha Blossom, Jr.'s Daybook, 1811–1822 (hereafter cited Blossom Daybook), August 1815, New-York Historical Society. Blossom's daybook will only be cited when no specific dates are given in the text. For Eckford, see Robert Greenhalgh Albion, *The Rise of the New York Port, 1815–60* (New York: Charles Scribner's Sons, 1939), pp. 288–89.

6. Longworth, *Longworth's American Almanack*. Albion, *Rise of the New York Port*, pp. 292, 299.

7. Elton W. Hall, "New Bedford Furniture," *Antiques* 113, no. 5 (May 1978): 1118. Samuel Blossom's death date is given in *Vital Records of New Bedford, Massachusetts to the Year 1850*, edited by Florence Conant Howes, 3 vols. (Boston, Massachusetts: New England Historic Genealogical Society, 1941), 3: 26. Samuel Blossom was the son of Benjamin Blossom (1753–1837), brother of Elisha Blossom, Sr., and Rebekah (Blossom) Tobey (1757–1832) of Fairhaven, Massachusetts. Samuel appears to be the first Blossom trained as a cabinetmaker, and he may have apprenticed with Lemuel Tobey (1749–1829) of Dartmouth, Massachusetts. Margaret K. Hofer, "Furniture Makers and Allied Craftsmen in Plymoth and Bristol Counties, Massachusetts, 1760–1810," *Antiques* 159, no. 5 (May 2001): 812. Lemuel Tobey's account is in the collection of Old Sturbridge Village, Sturbridge, Massachusetts and is discussed in Philip Zea, "Rural Craftsmen and Design" in Brock Jobe and Myrna Kaye, *New England Furniture: The Colonial Era: Selections from the Society for the Preservation of New England Antiquities* (Boston: Houghton Mifflin, 1984), pp. 64–65. The author thanks Leslie Symington for compiling genealogical information on the Blossoms and Lorings for this article.

8. *People's Friend & Daily Advertiser,* March 7, 1807; *New-York Evening Post,* May 19, 1810. For more on Abraham Egerton, son of Matthew Egerton, see Marilyn A. Johnson, "John Hewitt, Cabinetmaker," *Winterthur Portfolio* 4 (1968): 200, n. 34. For more on the destruction of Loring's business and move to Cincinnati, see Jane E. Sikes, *The Furniture Makers of Cincinnati, 1790 to 1849* (Cincinnati, Ohio: Cincinnati Historical Society, 1976) pp. 147–49. One of Loring's account books which survived the 1814 fire was among the possessions brought with him to Cincinnati. Historian Jane Sikes Hageman examined this document for the aforementioned study and illustrated a page from it dated March 16, 1813. Although the account book's current whereabouts is unknown, Hageman photocopied a few pages dated between March 16, and May 20, 1813, and was kind enough to share these with the author.

9. William S. Auchincloss, *Ninety Days in the Tropics, or Letters from Brazil* (1874), pp. 27–28, in Katherine Emma Manthorne, *Tropical Renaissance, North American Artists Exploring Latin America, 1839–1879* (Washington, D.C.: Smithsonian Institution Press, 1989), p. 144. The value of the U. S. dollar in relation to the Portuguese rea is based on the 1809 rate given on page 93 in "Notebook of an Unidentified American Trader," Rhode Island Historical Society, microfilm, Downs Manuscript Collection, Winterthur Library, Winterthur Delaware, M6.: $1.00 U.S. equals 750 Portuguese reas. For carpenters' and cabinetmakers' wages, see Rock, *Artisans of the New Republic,* pp. 251–53.

10. Honoré Lannuier charged a Mr. Brinckerhoff of New York $42.00 for "A Mahogany Crebe." The bill for the cradle is illustrated in Peter M. Kenny, Frances F. Bretter, and Ulrich Leben, *Honoré Lannuier Cabinetmaker from Paris: The Life and Work of a French Ébéniste in Federal New York* (New York: Metropolitan Museum of Art, 1998), p. 231.

11. "Notebook of an American Trader," p. 131. Salem cabinetmaker Nehemiah Adams sent a cargo of furniture valued at $869.90 (Mabel Munson Swan, "Coastwise Cargoes of Venture Furniture," *Antiques* 55, no. 4 [April 1949]: 280.)

12. A printed list of the ninety-two members of the New York Society of Cabinet Makers is bound into a copy of *The New-York Revised Prices for Manufacturing Cabinet and Chair Work* (1810) in the library at the Museum of Fine Arts in Houston. This copy is inscribed by New York journeyman cabinetmaker Daniel Turnier, one of Blossom's contemporaries. Hereafter the various editions of the price books will be referred to as *New York Price Book* followed by the date of publication.

13. Wilentz, *Chants Democratic,* p. 49. Blossom Daybook, July 24 and August 5, 1812. Barrows & Whitehead paid 1 mill rea/820 reas rent up to July 21 (July 24). Mr. Bridge paid 12 mill reas/800 reas for one month's rent "due 5th September," and Mr. Fidae 21 mill reas/300 reas rent "due this day" (both August 5). A journeyman carpenter's estimated annual budget made in 1809, including an average house rental of $55.00 (Rock, *Artisans of the New Republic,* p. 253).

14. Blossom's "start" charge for the sideboard was £9, or about $22.50, the same start charge given for a French sideboard in the 1810 New York price book. It had the form's usual four cupboard doors below three frieze drawers, a backboard, and reeded legs and castors, but lacked many of the extras that made some examples very expensive. For more on the French sideboard and its sources in France, see Kenny et al., *Honoré Lannuier,* pp. 83–84.

15. The author thanks Jane Sikes Hageman for providing photocopies of pages from David Loring's daybook. Despite repeated attempts to locate Loring's daybook through family descendants in Cincinnati, it still remains to be found. *New-York Gazette & General Advertiser,* May 8, 1812; and *New-York Gazette & General Advertiser,* May 25, 1812. Christies, *Important American Furniture, Silver, Prints and Folk Art,* New York, May 29, 2002, lot 185.

16. *New-York Gazette & General Advertiser,* May 12, 1813. Dolan is listed as a cabinetmaker in New York City directories from 1802 to 1814. From 1815 to 1825 he ran a hardware store. A card table with reeded legs and a treble-elliptic top labeled by Dolan when he was at the 30 Beekman Street address (1809–1813) is shown in *Antiques* 80, no. 4 (October 1961): 298. A nearly identical card table is in the collection of the Museum of the City of New York, and was included in the catalogue *Furniture by New York Cabinetmakers* (New York: Museum of the City of New York, 1957), p. 60, no. 96. Forsyth M. Alexander, "Warehousing in the Southern Atlantic, 1783-1820," *Journal of Early Southern Decorative Arts* 15, no. 2 (November 1989): 16.

17. See *New-York Evening Post,* May 13, 1817, for an advertisement by Charles Christian mentioning "large and small Side Boards." The list of *Additional Revised Prices* (n.d.) is bound into the previously cited *New York Price Book* (1810). "A French Sideboard," is listed on p. 42 of the aforementioned price book. In the 1817 edition of the *New York Price Book,* "A French Sideboard" is listed on p. 71.

18. The aforementioned *New York Price Book* (1810) has the following inscription above table 4, p. 62: "This Book is all most [sic] out of use for the next comes first April 6th 1817 T. C. for D T n [probably Daniel Turnier]." Blossom Daybook, January 22, 1814: "Mr. John Linacre [debit] To 1 Book of prices Bound $1.50."

19. For Christian's commission at City Hall, see Kenny et al., *Honoré Lannuier,* pp. 142–43. *Daily Advertiser,* May 8, 1800. For more on the Philadelphia furniture wareroom and the Society of Cabinet Makers, Philadelphia, of which Christian was president in 1796, see Charles F. Montgomery, *American Furniture, The Federal Period in the Henry Francis du Pont Winterthur Museum* (New York: Viking Press, 1966), pp. 22–23. For Christian's mistreatment of apprentices, see Kenny et al., *Honoré Lannuier,* pp. 63; 100, n. 75.

20. *New York Directory, 1808. American Citizen,* April 16, 1803; March 11, 1805; and May 3, 1804; and February 6, 1805; and *New-York Commercial Advertiser,* May 20, 1805. *New-York Evening Post,* November 2, 1803.

21. *Statesman,* June 15, 1813; *Columbian for the Country,* June 16, 1813; *New-York Evening Post,* June, 18, 1813; and *National Advocate,* June 22, 1813.

22. Montgomery, *American Furniture,* p. 23.

23. Never very popular with collectors because their upper cabinet sections were paneled rather than glazed and, therefore, unusable for the display of ceramics, glass or other collectibles, examples of this form are in three public collections: Yale University Art Gallery in New Haven, Connecticut; House of History in Kinderhook, New York; and the New York State Museum in Albany. Gerald W. R. Ward, *American Case Furniture in the Mabel Brady Garvan and Other Collections* (New Haven, Conn.: Yale University Art Gallery, 1988), pp. 357–59 shows Yale's writing table and bookcase with the fall front closed and open. Nancy McClelland, *Duncan Phyfe and the English Regency, 1795–1830* (New York: William R. Scott, 1939), pl. 167 illustrates the writing table and bookcase in the House of History. *New York Price Book* (1810), pp. 32, 33, 35, 37. See McClelland, *Duncan Phyfe,* pl. 251 for the labeled 1820 writing table and bookcase by Phyfe.

24. John Hewitt Account Book, New Jersey Historical Society, Newark, New Jersey, unpaginated as cited in Johnson, "John Hewitt, Cabinetmaker," p. 187, n. 6. A photocopy of the account book is in the scholarship files of the American Wing, Metropolitan Museum of Art.

Linacre is included at the back of the account book among a group of journeymen who worked for Hewitt, along with their aggregate charges for furniture making in 1812–1813. For competition among cabinetmakers in New York, see Kenny et al., *Honoré Lannuier,* p. 45.

25. *New York Price Book* (1810), pp. 42-43.

26. John Hewitt Account Book, "Work Done by Thos. Constantine," as cited in Johnson, "John Hewitt, Cabinetmaker," p. 196. *New-York Evening Post,* April 28, 1814.

27. Sikes, *Furniture Makers of Cincinnati,* p. 148.

28. Some master cabinetmakers failed to follow the established wage scale for journeymen. This problem was addressed on p. 1 in the preface to the 1817 revised *New York Price Book:* "[the committee of journeymen who worked on the price book] have endeavoured to equalize the prices in such manner, that two men working at different pieces of work, will not be paid, one more than the other, which has been hitherto, in many instances, the cause of much jealousy of men, working for the same employer." With regard to the issue of quality of workmanship, the committee stated that the prices listed "are considered for work of good quality, and when not such, to be valued and paid for accordingly" (p. 6).

29. For a carpenter's annual wage in New York City, see Rock, *Artisans of the New Republic,* p. 252.

30. *New York City Directory, 1815.* New York City directories covered the period of July 1 in any given year until June 30 of the next, and information for them began to be compiled after May 1, which was traditionally moving day. Blossom lived at 25 Roosevelt Street and gave his occupation as cabinetmaker in May, but by July 1 he had abandoned that trade. Blossom Daybook, November 4, 1815. On June 18, 1816, Blossom charged the "Estate of I Loring" $11.75 for "cash paid for her burial."

31. *New York City Directories, 1816–1823.* As previously stated, Blossom appears to have been a partner in the firm listed in New York City directories as "Blossom, Smith & Demon." The firm's shipyards were located at "Stanton, M. I.," the same address given for Blossom when he worked for Eckford.

32. John Hewitt Account Book, "Work Done by Thos. Constantine," as cited in Johnson, "John Hewitt, Cabinetmaker," p. 196. For all his furniture-making activities between February 14, 1812, and April 29, 1814, Constantine's wages totaled $1,060.26. That averages out to about $489.00 per year, or just under one-and-one-half times more than Blossom's annual earnings from cabinetmaking. Constantine was an unusually motivated artisan. Although he ran away from his master John Hewitt in 1811, Constantine displayed considerable energy in establishing a Cabinet Furniture Store at 157 Fulton Street in 1817. There he sold English pianos, patent bedsteads, and the latest "Elastic Spring Sofas," which were reportedly "not the description of spring seat sofas made some time since in Europe, . . . but . . . an improvement in the mode of making and applying them, by which the elasticity is never lost." In 1819 he won a contract to make desks and chairs for the House of Representatives in Washington. See the *Commercial Advertiser,* June 18, 1811, and *Mercantile Advertiser,* October 2, 1822, and *New-York Daily Advertiser,* November 2, 1819.

Appendix

Furniture Made by Elisha Blossom, Jr., for New York Master Cabinetmakers, 1812–1814:

Daybook Entry	Employer	Form	Charge
May 16, 1812	D. Loring	"Pembroke table"	$5.52
" "	" "	" "	$4.80
June 20, 1812	" "	"Sideboard"	$30.00
August 1, 1812	" "	"wardrobe"	$25.97
January 22, 1813	" "	"pair Breakfast tables"	$12.41
February 20, 1813	" "	"Single counting house Desk"	$11.98
February 27, 1813	" "	"Breakfast table"	$6.21½
March 27, 1813	" "	"Wardrobe"	$26.00
April 3, 1813	" "	"Pillar & Claw table"	$9.44¾
May 1, 1813	J. Everit	"Pillar & Claw Dining Tables"	$28.83
May 22, 1813	" "	"French Bureau"	$22.48
June 19, 1813	" "	"Breakfast table" x2	$11.83
" " "	" "	"Breakfast table"	$4.22
" " "	" "	"table"	$5.54
June 26, 1813	" "	"crib"	$4.00
" " "	" "	"Bedstead"	$3.25
July 10, 1813	" "	"Dining table"	$3.65½
" " "	" "	"Dining table"	$3.49
August 1/21, 1813	C. Christian	"Writing table & Book case"	£16.2.3 (only)
September 5, 1813	C. Christian	"table" x2	$13.87½
" 27 "	" "	" "	$12.41½
" " "	" "	"table"	$6.16½
October 2, 1813	" "	"pine Book case"	$10.00
November 17, 1813	J. Linacre	"finishing Dining Tables"	$1.50
" " "	" "	"Sideboard"	$43.70
December 11, 1813	" "	"work table"	$10.25
December 15, 1813	" "	"cradle"	$4.00
December 31, 1813	" "	"work table"	$10.21
January 22, 1814	" "	"2 breakfast tables"	$12.12½
March 5, 1814	D. Loring	"end dining table"	$10.85
March 26, 1814	" "	"book case"	$9.86
April 23, 1814	" "	"Pembroke table" [pair?]	$21.60
May 7, 1814	" "	"breakfast table"	$5.94
" " "	unknown	"Breakfast Table"	$6.50
May 28, 1814	D. Loring	"2 corner bason Stands"	$9.68½
June 10, 1814	unknown	"pair Breakfast tables"	$12.25
July 6, 1814	D. Loring	"pair pillar & claw Pembroke tables"	$22.20
August 1, 1814	unknown	"pair circular work stands"	$9.12½
August 3, 1814	unknown	"Book case"	$4.00

Book Reviews

Adam Bowett. *English Furniture, 1660–1714: From Charles II to Queen Anne.* Woodbridge, England: Antique Collectors' Club, 2002. 368 pp.; numerous illus. $89.50.

"I have attempted to write this book from first principles," Adam Bowett writes in the preface to this new history of early English furniture, "and, in the main, from primary evidence—bills, inventories, and of course, the furniture itself" (p. 10). He holds fast to this self-imposed limitation throughout, picking carefully along the upper reaches of courtly furniture in search of secure footing. Bowett's aim is not a cultural narrative but a chronology of documented and hence datable pieces, against which other objects may be judged. The narrow, laser-like focus of this exercise may prove disconcerting to material culture scholars who have been schooled in interdisciplinary theoretical models, and even those in the relatively conservative field of furniture connoisseurship may find Bowett's subject matter to be bafflingly circumscribed. He provides no information about vernacular traditions or regionalist comparison, and very little about broad social context—only the lineage of the most advanced furniture of the day.

It would be easy to dismiss Bowett's book as out-of-date. With its old-fashioned title (are we really still marking time by monarchs in the twenty-first century?) and Antique Collectors' Club imprint, it seems like it could have been written thirty years ago. The fact remains, however, that it was not; and it badly needed to be written. Certainly, it would have been possible for Bowett to write a more broad-minded book—by including even a cursory account of the recent scholarship published under the auspices of the Regional Furniture Society, for example. But even so, this book fills a huge gap in the literature, and it does so admirably. Until now there has been no reliable account of the furniture style that most furniture historians still call "William and Mary." Many readers of this journal, I suspect, would be hard pressed even to define the term "scriptor," though that furniture form was nearly universal in the aristocratic interiors of late seventeenth-century England. Here, though, is a full accounting of the scriptor, its construction and evolution, and an explanation of how it gradually transformed into the desk-and-bookcase we all know so well.

In his reconstruction of such developments, Bowett draws largely on bills submitted to wealthy patrons by top tradesmen such as Richard Price, Gerrit Jensen, and Thomas Roberts (a chair maker who provided Queen Anne's coronation throne). He supplements this rich trove of information with other documents, ranging from national export figures to Joiners' and Upholsterers' Company Minute books. Throughout, his treatment of these texts is unstintingly exhaustive. He even extracts new insights from such chestnuts as John Stalker and George Parker's *Treatise of Japanning and Varnishing* (1688) and William Salmon's *Polygraphice* (1672), which he affectionately prizes for its "endearing, kitchen sink quality" (p. 62). Bowett's explication of period finish recipes is wonderfully detailed—unless you are a professional conservator, you'll never need to look further on the topic—and he includes a helpful index of woods used in furniture of the period (similar to, but more comprehensive than, a list he compiled for Amin Jaffee's recent book *Furniture From British India and Ceylon* [2001]).

For its tabulation of useful information alone, then, Bowett's book deserves to find a place on every decorative art historian's shelf. But the volume is also unexpectedly absorbing (if not entirely satisfying) on the level of method. When testing extant furniture against textual evidence, Bowett applies a combination of hard-won expertise and good old common sense. For American readers his no-nonsense prose style will be eerily reminiscent of the writings of the late Benno M. Forman, who, like Bowett, possessed a seemingly instinctive ability to get inside the head of the period craftsman. Bowett's book is filled with offhand observations that, in the aggregate, do a great deal to explore the mindset of the English cabinetmaker. Typical of his elegant argumentation is a passage on unusual three-part desk-and-bookcases, in which the desk and the lower drawers are set within separate carcasses. Bowett reasons that this was done so that different specialist workers in the shop could execute these portions of the piece simultaneously. The molding between each piece allowed for a margin of error when it came time for the various makers to fit their components together into a unit (p. 223). In a similar vein, Bowett notes that the famous black, slim clock cases that house the works of Ahasuerus Fromanteel could not have been made by a specialist clockmaker, as has often been assumed. His logic is disarmingly simple: the tall-case clock form itself was new, and the skills necessary to make it complex. Fromanteel's cabinetmaker must have been well versed in other forms, and surely would not have stopped making those forms once he had learned to make clocks (p. 46).

This is as inductive as Bowett gets. Unlike Forman, he never resorts to ingenious guesswork; because of the ever-present backdrop of documentary evidence, he doesn't need to. His factual conclusions therefore have a degree of authority that would be impossible to match in the American context. Readers will be amazed and gratified to see how Bowett is able, for example, to pin down the introduction of "floral" marquetry to the years between 1664 and 1670, based on subtle differences between two editions of John Evelyn's book *Silva* (p. 55). He is also able to date the introduction of turned cane chair stiles to 1690, the appearance of tassel feet and fully-raked back legs on such chairs to 1709, and the concept of a "desk and bookcase" to 1698 (see pp. 255 and 220). Bowett is equally helpful when parsing period terminology. He notes that chairs that are today called banister backs, because their backs are composed of baluster-shaped half turnings, were actually called "rib-back" chairs in England. This is significant because period references to banister backs could well be caned chairs; indeed, Bowett cites two bills for "Cane chairs" which also had "bannister backs"—meaning simply that they had turned banister-shaped stiles (p. 234).

Nowhere is Bowett's attention to documentary detail more rewarding than in his discussion of the impact of continental manufacture. In general, he is much less inclined than previous writers have been to stress the contributions of the Huguenots who emigrated from France and Holland to England. He begins by noting that the word "foreigner," which appears often in Joiners' Company documents, does not mean an immigrant craftsman, but simply someone who was not a member of the guild: "This is why the majority of foreigners listed in the Company's Minute books had English surnames" (p. 31). Furthermore, Bowett writes, there were only nineteen cabinetmakers listed in the parish records of London's Huguenot churches between 1660 and 1713, and of these, only one achieved any known prominence. This evidence calls into question the contention of scholars such as Gervaise Jackson-Stops, who have portrayed the Huguenot population in London as a key ingredient in England's post-Carolean cosmopolitan makeover. Bowett is most contentious on this point when he cuts through the mythology surrounding the figure of Daniel Marot, a Huguenot who has been credited as being tremendously influential on the basis of his published engravings of furniture designs. Bowett's examination of the bills furnished to the court of William III reveals no furniture by Marot, however, and even Marot's *Livres* of designs were unlikely to have been very important in London, given that "No English edition was produced and . . . only one complete edition is known to survive in an English collection" (p. 188). Other Frenchmen such as Francis Lapiere and Jean Poitevin were probably much more significant than Marot in the English context. The fact that they were probably not Huguenots may make their story less romantic to the modern mind, but as Bowett says, "the important point is not that particular craftsmen were Huguenots or Catholics, but that they were French" (p. 34).

Bowett's text bristles with such welcome skepticism, and he always focuses tightly on the particulars of a given question. On the whole the book is perhaps too particular for casual perusal; though Bowett claims it was "written for the non-specialist reader" (p. 11), it is difficult to imagine that anyone but the truly committed will pore through it cover to cover. Here and there he even adopts the format of a reference work, as when he resorts to itemized lists when describing the typical construction of cabinets during a given period. All this density makes the book feel a bit wonkish, an effect that is exacerbated by the uneven photography, which ranges from superlative to truly awful (many chairs are pictured with either their crest rails or their front stretchers badly out of focus).

Such idiosyncrasies can be excused given Bowett's intentions—this is, after all, a book of analysis, not synthesis. More disappointing from the American perspective is the lack of a comprehensive context for the documented pieces that Bowett takes as his subject. There is very little furniture in the book that could be considered a direct counterpart or precedent to furniture made in the New World. Apart from a few pages on middle-class cane chairs, Bowett gravitates exclusively toward elite artifacts—and he is neither apologetic nor defensive on this point. He argues that for purposes of establishing chronology, it is useless to pretend that stylistic periods were homogenous and unified across social classes. Rather, he writes, periods are best defined in terms of "marker goods" such as "looking glasses, pendulum clocks, upholstered and caned chairs, oval tables and walnut or olivewood furniture" (p. 25). This is a good theory, as far as it goes, but it is useful only for describing and identifying the inception of a style, not for discussing its impact on the broader culture.

Bowett occasionally falls prey to glibness on this score, as when he writes of the furnishings made for William III: "There were relatively few men who could afford to build on this princely scale, but just as the minor apartments at Hampton Court were equipped with walnut and japanned furniture rather than lacquer and gilt, so more modest houses could be furnished less lavishly but no less fashionably" (p. 184). If this comparison— between separate rooms of a king's palace on the one hand, and entire social classes on the other—seems too pat, it is because Bowett has little to say about the world outside the English country house. Some of the forms introduced at Hampton Court may have appeared shortly thereafter in the homes of courtiers, but what happened next? If we care anything about Bowett's chronological sequencing, then surely we also care about the answer to that question. But to infer even the dating (much less the interpretation) of the vast majority of surviving furniture on the basis of the information presented here would be a difficult task indeed. Bowett actually implies that it would be impossible to do so reliably, because new furniture forms percolate downwards chaotically, in what he calls a "halting interaction between fashionable and vernacular culture" (p. 25). Bowett does make a few attempts to suggest the overall complexity of this interaction, as when he observes that "the same pressures that induced a townsman to buy a set of caned chairs for his parlour might have the reverse effect on a countryman" (p. 25) or when he isolates japanning as a stylistic innovation that "narrowed the gulf between the super-rich and the merely well-off, for how many people could reliably tell the difference between true lacquer and good japanning?" (p. 22).

For the most part, however, Bowett never strays far from the royal bills. He leaves the messy process of extrapolating from his carefully assembled chronology to others. Had he chosen to do this himself, it would have required him to venture quite a bit further into the realm of the speculative, but his book would have been far stronger for it. The dust jacket of *English Furniture, 1660–1714* modestly notes of Bowett: "This is his first book and he is still learning." My own vote would be that in his next effort (which, as he teasingly reveals in a footnote on page 289, will cover the next "phase" of English cabinet work), he might apply his formidable skills to a broader range of material evidence. In the meantime, we Americans should be glad to have this important book, and draw conclusions from it as best we can.

Glenn Adamson
The Chipstone Foundation

Thomas Moser, with Brad Lemley. *Thos. Moser: Artistry in Wood*. San Francisco: Chronicle Books, 2002. 192 pp.; numerous color and bw illus. $60.00.

Thomas Moser may arguably be the best-known contemporary American furniture maker working outside the production or contract field. Through advertisements in magazines like *The New Yorker*, retail stores in major urban centers (New York, Chicago, San Francisco, Charleston, and Washington, in addition to Freeport, Maine), and institutional work (especially for university libraries), Moser and his traditionally based contemporary hardwood furniture have maintained high visibility for the past fifteen years. He produced the book under review with the intention of conveying "the thinking behind the aesthetic and structural design choices I have made" (p. 60). He charts his development as a maker, then follows with chapters on his preference for cherry wood, his design aesthetic, and his notion of craftsmanship. Lavishly illustrated with images of his furniture—environments as well as single works and details—the format also includes sidebars on particular topics such as his failures in toy manufacturing, the development of a special form like the deacon's bench, and an homage to George Nakashima. The overwhelming use of color images, in which the saturated auburn hues of cherry dominate, and the celebratory journey from humble beginnings to worldwide appreciation link this volume to a genre of seductively illustrated autobiographies of contemporary woodworkers such as Sam Maloof and George Nakashima, a link Moser seems to desire.[1]

Moser views himself as the lineal descendant of the nineteenth-century vernacular cabinetmaker, one who employed a skilled economy to make simple, well-proportioned, utilitarian forms of local woods. When he first left his academic job and opened a shop in 1972, he parlayed knowledge of historical furniture and antique restoration to build pine case pieces and tables in federal-period and Shaker styles, often using paint as a finish. In 1976 Moser grew concerned about imitation, realizing that by copying the work of old New England craftsmen, he was merely "enhancing their stature, not our own" (p. 48). Yearning to build a market niche on more than his "workmanship, sharp tools, and quick hands," Moser made a conscious decision to create his own aesthetic, celebrating black cherry, with an oil finish, as the primary wood and ash as a secondary wood for spindles, turned legs, and drawer linings. Like the studio furniture makers of the 1950s, he responded favorably to the warmth, depth, and translucence of cherry and began to use it to make comfortable, durable, and traditionally constructed (dovetailed carcasses and drawers, mortise-and-tenoned panels, etc.) furniture loosely inspired by federal and Shaker examples. In 1980, in response to the increased appreciation of furniture made during the arts and crafts movement earlier in the century, Moser began to incorporate visible joinery as part of his design aesthetic. Such an interest in explicit workmanship may have also developed from the studio furniture field's devotion to technical virtuosity in the 1970s. In the 1990s, Moser's firm expanded beyond its rectilinear vocabulary and began to explore more curvilinear work.

Although an autobiography can often cross the line into boosterism and promotional claims, Moser's volume contains some elements of interest to furniture historians. His chronicle of the early years of his shop provides insights into the motivations and decisions of many who pursued craftwork in the 1970s as an alternative career. The frustrations and limitations of white-collar work, even university teaching, and the allure and satisfaction of making things and integrating thought and action are key to his story. The most obvious and consistent theme in the book is his sense of the role of craftsmanship. Neither an impractical romantic hung up on the moral value of handwork nor a self-indulgent maker who spends thousands of hours creating "a frivolity for the elite few" (p. 146), Moser expresses very specific opinions on the need for keeping a production mentality while making what William Morris referred to as "good citizen's furniture." This sort of work is unpretentious, timeless, functional, and geared toward the human body. Establishing his first shop in New Gloucester, Maine, right near the Shaker community of Sabbathday Lake, Moser lauds the Shakers as the historical standard for this approach and seeks to update that same philosophy. It is no surprise that just as the Shakers relied on the circular saw and extensive outwork systems to make their work efficient and economical, Moser has embraced labor saving equipment like a computer-guided core cutter to shape his plank seats, justifying the use of such mechanized tools in conjunction with finishing handwork as the proper balance of efficiency and inefficiency. He acknowledges that some critics see this as a compromise of principles, but he lays out a shop floor mentality in which the fast production of parts with an eye to quality and safety should be wed to careful skilled handwork in the assembly and finishing stages. Drawing inspiration from Danish cabinetmaking firms that he visited, Moser even set up his shop with these two elements separate.

Another striking aspect of Moser's story is his commitment to hiring and teaching a wide variety of help. Over the years he has employed people with advanced degrees as well as working-class Mainers, and he has consistently hired women. Many people found their true calling as craftspeople, with twenty-three going on to start their own furniture business. In Maine you can construct a family tree of Moser employees who have taken some aspect of the Moser philosophy and developed their niche in a small shop situation, whether producing Shaker inspired work (Chris Becksvoort), arts and crafts (Kevin Rodel), or even batch production (Doug Green). Others have developed personal styles in small shops in Maine (Bill Huston and Lynette Bretton) or moved to Vermont (Jim Becker) or even Seattle (Stewart Wurtz) to set up small shops offering similar lines. In this manner, the Moser shop has served as an important training ground for northern New England small-shop furniture makers and as a catalyst for the field's growth. However, Moser does not acknowledge that his influence as a teacher was greatest in the first fifteen years of his business, when his shop relied heavily on skilled workmanship to achieve efficiency.

In his emphasis on the personal qualities of workmanship and teaching, Moser offers a selective history of his firm that links his work to that of prominent contemporary woodworkers like George Nakashima or more historical figures such as the Shakers or Gustav Stickley. The book's format, plethora of color images of details, and language of craftsmanship reveal Moser's intention to be considered as an equal to studio furniture makers and to earn a reputation as a consummate designer-craftsman. However, the emphasis on process and workmanship obscures other aspects of the Moser operation, particularly its evolution from small shop to production shop similar in scale to Danish firms like Johannes Hansen, who manufactured much of Hans Wegner's work. Employing more than a hundred workers and enjoying sales that exceeded fifty-eight million dollars in 1998, Moser oversees a large sophisticated plant (approximately sixty-five thousand square-feet) with some skilled furniture makers but a greater number of specialized workers. He first expanded his manufacturing and retail operations in the mid-1980s, but initially found it difficult to sustain such a widespread endeavor. In about 1990, he developed a more profitable arm of his business—corporate and library commissions. The images in the volume and the role of his son Aaron as manager of "corporate and institutional selling efforts" (p. 56) suggest that these large commissions play an increasingly important role in the firm's economic health, but there is little discussion of them in the text. Even a partial list of clients suggests the success of this venture: the J. Paul Getty Trust Center, the law school libraries at Yale and UCLA, the arts library at Harvard, the libraries at the University of Pennsylvania and Seton Hall University, the Thoreau Institute Library, and the offices of *The New Yorker*.[2]

Moser's misreading of the English design historian David Pye is instructive in placing Moser somewhere between the studio furniture maker and the contract furniture industry. Whereas Pye extolled the virtues of the "workmanship of risk," Moser misquotes him and celebrates the "manufacture of risk" (p. 160), revealing his approach to the field. Like his contemporary Charles Webb in Cambridge, Massachusetts, Moser emerged from a studio furniture background and benefited from employing a number of individuals interested in craft as an alternative career, but in the mid-1980s he changed directions. He consciously sought to parlay the look and values of the individual shop in the manufacturing realm. Moser's work itself does not compare favorably to that of studio furniture makers like Walker Weed, Sam Maloof, or George Nakashima who preceded him; it seems stiff, derivative, and overly self-conscious. While the individual work suffers when compared to that of some designer-craftsmen, the designs and workmanship of the library and institutional work rise above the standard millwork usually found in those locations. It is in the realm of manufactured craftsmanship that Moser has really made his mark and will be remembered. It is unfortunate that his book does not lay out that particular story in greater detail, distinguishing between the earlier and later phases of his firm. The book is less a history of the firm than Moser's treatise on craftsmanship that telescopes or blurs that history.[3]

Edward S. Cooke, Jr.

Yale University

1. George Nakashima, *The Soul of a Tree: A Woodworker's Reflections* (Tokyo, New York, and San Francisco: Kodansha International Ltd., 1981); and Sam Maloof, *Sam Maloof, Woodworker* (New York: Kodansha, 1983).

2. Studio furniture makers are independent producers, either self-taught or academically trained, who work in small shops or studios. While these makers use machinery, and may employ assistants or specialists, they produce a limited number of works. Their work is often custom-made for commissions, or sold through galleries, specialized shows, and personal connections with buyers. For additional insight into the term and its historical development, see Edward S. Cooke, Jr., Gerald W. R. Ward, and Kelly H. L'Ecuyer, with the assistance of Pat Warner, *The Maker's Hand: American Studio Furniture, 1940–1990* (Boston: MFA Publications, 2003). See Zachary Gaulkin, "The Many Sides of Thomas Moser," *Fine Woodworking*, no. 128 (January/February 1998): 70–73. A 1984 small, largely black-and-white catalogue available at the Cumberland Avenue store in Portland, Maine, asserted that all Moser furniture was made with historical joinery and that "there is no mass production in our workshop. Each item of furniture is built entirely by one or by small groups working together and orders are filled, each in their turn."

3. See David Pye, *The Nature and Art of Workmanship* (1968; reprint, New York: Van Nostrand Reinhold, 1971).

Bradford L. Rauschenberg and John Bivins, Jr., *The Furniture of Charleston, 1680–1820*. Frank L. Horton Series. 3 vols. Winston-Salem, N.C.: Old Salem, Inc., and the Museum of Early Southern Decorative Arts, 2003. Vol. 1, *Colonial Furniture*. Vol. 2, *Neoclassical Furniture*. Vol. 3, *The Cabinet-makers*. xxxv + 1388 pp., numerous color and bw illus., maps, appendices, bibliography, concordance, index. $325.00.

The much-anticipated work of Bradford L. Rauschenberg and John Bivins, Jr., *The Furniture of Charleston, 1680–1820*, lends proof to the adage, good things come to those who wait. After more than twenty years of fieldwork and research, the authors have produced a monumental tome. Composed of three volumes with more than one thousand pages, it features hundreds of color and black and white photographs of more than four hundred pieces of furniture plus maps, appendices, bibliography, concordance, and index. Weighing nearly sixteen pounds, the book is a goldmine of information for furniture scholars, collectors, and dealers interested in the Carolina Lowcountry's unique material culture. As the preface by Gary J. Albert notes, it combines "Rauschenberg's tenacious research skills and mastery of microscopic wood analysis" with "Bivins' encyclopedic knowledge of all American furniture forms and unique insight into an artisan's approach to construction" (p. ix).

Recognizing that an opus of this size cannot be produced in isolation, the authors acknowledge generously the many individuals and institutions whose support, both financial and otherwise, made the book possible. The research was partially funded by the Research Tools and Reference Works program of the National Endowment for the Humanities, and the Chipstone Foundation provided valuable support for the expense of extensive color photography. The book has been published as part of the Frank L. Horton series, an endowed fund created by the Museum of Early Southern Decorative Arts (MESDA) especially for the publication of monographs on southern crafts and craftsmen. Previous titles in the series include John Bivins, Jr.'s *The Furniture of Coastal North Carolina* (1988), Benjamin H. Caldwell, Jr.'s *Tennessee Silversmiths* (1988), and Harold Eugene Comstock's *The Pottery of the Shenandoah Valley Region* (1994). As the fourth and most recent installment in this distinguished series, *The Furniture of Charleston* symbolizes MESDA's ongoing commitment to the serious study of southern material culture.

In the first few pages, Brad Rauschenberg provides furniture scholars with a noteworthy anecdote for the historiography of their field. For decades, the renaissance of interest in southern furniture has been attributed to the reaction sparked by a comment made at the 1949 Williamsburg Antiques Forum by Joseph Downs, curator of the American Wing at the Metropolitan Museum of Art, that "nothing of artistic merit was made south of Baltimore." Rauschenberg demonstrates that Milby Burton (1898–1977), then director of the Charleston Museum, had addressed this issue fully eight years earlier in a 1941 interview with a Richmond, Virginia, newspaper. In his published remarks, Burton decried the established biases of both "the Plymouth crowd and the Jamestown crowd" and made the pithy remark that he was "so damned tired of hearing the Boston crowd infer there was no silver or furniture making in the South" (p. xxvi).

Published in 1955, Milby Burton's book *Charleston Furniture, 1700–1825* launched the first serious examination of Charleston's early furniture production. For decades, the subject then lay dormant until 1986, when John Bivins penned a significant article, "Charleston Rococo Interiors: The 'Sommers' Carver," in the fall issue of the *Journal of Early Southern Decorative Arts*. Since then, interest in Charleston furniture has skyrocketed, both in scholarly venues and in the marketplace. Important monographs in recent issues of this journal have included Luke Beckerdite's analysis of the French Huguenot influence on South Carolina's seventeenth-century furniture, Thomas Savage's research on Martin Pfeninger and Charleston's pre-Revolutionary German cabinetmakers, and John Bivins' discussion of Scottish, German, and Northern influences on Charleston's post-Revolutionary cabinetwork (each in *American Furniture* 1997), as well as an examination by Maurie D. McInnis and the author of this review of the New York City cabinetmakers Deming and Bulkley and their impact on Charleston's nineteenth-century furniture (*American Furniture* 1996). Similarly, in *Southern Furniture, 1680–1830: The Colonial Williamsburg Collection* (1997), Ronald L. Hurst and Jonathan Prown shed new light on a number of pivotal Charleston objects, and, in recent years, a distinguished coterie of southern scholar-dealers—Sumpter Priddy, Deanne Levison, Milly McGehee, Harriett and Jim Pratt, and George Williams—have made groundbreaking discoveries in the realm of Charleston furniture studies. Today, *The Furniture of Charleston* stands on top of this mountain of research, which collectively presents a powerful tribute to the life's work of Frank L. Horton and the research resources he has created at MESDA.

As the introduction states, this book is not simply "a catalog" of the Charleston furniture in MESDA's collection; rather, it is a highly detailed analysis of the cabinetmaking industry in a sophisticated urban center, Charleston, and a compilation of the known furniture it produced. Arranged chronologically, the first two volumes move from the colonial period in volume one to the neoclassical period in volume two, and each volume carefully analyzes the construction and stylistic features that allow shop groups to be identified. In the section on neoclassical bedsteads, for example, a chart examines the characteristics of forty surviving bedsteads and suggests the presence of seven distinct shop groups that either employed or contracted with at least six turners and three carvers between the years 1785 and 1815 (p. 805). Throughout the book, the authors succeed in building important relationships between the individual objects and the region's supporting documentation. So, while Charleston's most famous cabinetmaker, Thomas Elfe (ca. 1719–1775), remains elusive without the discovery of a single signed, labeled, or documented example of his production, the authors' expert analysis showcases his surviving day books for the years 1768 to 1775 and how they illuminate the intricacy of Charleston's early cabinet trade.

Through furniture, the authors illustrate how Charleston evolved from an early outpost of the British colonial empire into a thriving capital and cultural center. Founded in the late seventeenth century by an assortment of British, French, Dutch, German, Swiss, and Sephardic Jewish settlers, Charleston became a place where by 1740 Eliza Lucas Pinckney could say, "the people live very Gentile and very much in the English taste." Deeply imbued with British style, Charleston's colonial furniture reflects the city's rising level of sophistication. Charleston's eighteenth-century cabinet wares typically feature paneled backs, full or three-quarter length dustboards, center drawer muntins, and other construction characteristics that typify urban British craftsmanship. By 1770 Charleston possessed one of the most professional and diverse cabinetmaking communities in British North America. Composed of English, Scottish, French, German, Swedish, and African American professionals, Charleston's cabinetmakers fashioned some of the finest furniture produced in early America. The Edwards library bookcase, for example, with its complex construction, triple serpentine form, polychrome marquetry and ivory inlay, made in Charleston between 1770 and 1775, is, as the authors describe, "unparalleled in American furniture" (p. 168). In his 1997 article on this piece and its relationship to the German-born cabinetmaker Martin Pfeninger (d. 1782), Savage explains how it presents "a synthesis of British and Continental structural and decorative features within the context of Charleston taste and patronage."[1]

After the Revolution, Charleston's urbane consumers continued to support talented emigré craftsmen. In the city's post-Revolutionary economic and cultural environment, Scottish furniture makers such as Robert Walker

Figure 1 Wardrobe, Charleston, South Carolina, 1785–1790. Mahogany and mahogany veneer with white pine and cedar. H. 91", W. 53¼", D. 25¾". (Collection of Mrs. George M. Kaufman; photo, Dirk Bakker.)

Figure 2 Double-top sideboard, Charleston, South Carolina, 1790–1800. Mahogany and mahogany veneer with ash, tulip poplar, and white pine. H. 45½", W. 66½", D. 31". (Courtesy, Rivers Collection; photo, Gavin Ashworth.)

(1772–1833), who arrived in 1793 with copies in hand of Thomas Sheraton's *The Cabinet-Maker and Upholsterer's Drawing Book* and *The Cabinet-Makers' London Book of Prices,* competed with German- and English-born craftsmen like Jacob Sass (1750–1836) and John Ralph (ca. 1743–1801), whose businesses had been established in Charleston some twenty years earlier. As Germanic features first seen in the Edwards library bookcase continued well into the 1790s (see fig. 1), and Scottish furniture forms such as the double-top sideboard became relatively commonplace in Charleston (see fig. 2), the city's neoclassical furniture expressed the happy coexistence of these disparate styles. By the early nineteenth century, Charlestonians could boast a cosmopolitan culture that combined their native-grown society with imported influences from abroad as well as those from the northern states, most especially New York and Massachusetts. The authors fully describe the impact of imported northern-made furniture on early nineteenth-century Charleston's cabinet trade, how it influenced local styles and led to the industry's eventual decline.

While the organization of these first two volumes seems innovative, it is perhaps not likely to be repeated. Each piece of furniture is assigned a unique number based on the period (early, colonial, neoclassical), the form (case furniture, tables, chairs, beds), and finally the sequence in which it appears in the book. So, for example, the first colonial-period table is CT-1 and so forth. Each piece is then catalogued with a complete discussion of its primary and secondary woods, dimensions, construction details, markings or inscriptions, and provenance. Honed by MESDA's many years of field research, the descriptions of construction seem particularly excellent, and the concordance allows readers to find every page on which a particular piece might be mentioned. However, due to the page design and layout, this reader found the overall organization frequently difficult to follow, and to track a particular detail, it was sometimes necessary to use all three vol-

Figure 3 Double chest, Charleston, South Carolina, 1750–1760. Mahogany and mahogany veneer with cypress and white pine. Descended in the Holmes family. H. 72", W. 44⅝", D. 24". (Courtesy, Charleston Museum; photo, Gavin Ashworth.)

umes simultaneously, flipping pages from volume one to volume two to the references to a specific cabinetmaker contained only within volume three.

The third volume features a comprehensive biographical dictionary of all the furniture-related craftsmen discovered by MESDA's documentary research on the Carolina Lowcountry. With more than six hundred artisans listed, it cites all the known references to each one found in the region's court records, newspaper advertisements, directories, and manuscripts, both published and unpublished. Also included are photographs of all the known signed, labeled, or documented examples of an artisan's work. The volume contains three appendices: an alphabetical listing of tradesmen, a chronological listing, and tradesmen clustered by street address intended, as Rauschenberg notes, to provide "a rare glimpse into the relationships and evolution of artisans and partnerships, as well as the rise and fall of business" (p. 871). Unfortunately, this volume does not include a fourth appendix that divides the furniture-related artisans into their specific subcategories: joiners, turners, cabinetmakers, chair makers, carvers, painters/gilders, upholsterers/paperhangers, picture-frame makers, even Venetian blind makers. An appendix of this kind would have underscored one of book's main points, the complex and increasingly specialized nature of Charleston's cabinetmaking community.

However, the darkest lining in the silver cloud of this book was undoubtedly the death of the co-author, John Bivins, in August 2001. A swashbuckling figure in the American decorative arts, John was a consummate craftsman and scholar. During his career at MESDA, he served as the director of restoration and as the curator of crafts, and, later, as the director of publications, editing two journals, *The Luminary* and *The Journal of Early Southern Decorative Arts,* during a golden age of that museum's insti-

Figure 4 Detail of the "WA" cipher stamped on the lower case of the double chest in fig. 3. (Photo, Gavin Ashworth.)

tutional history. John was the author of numerous books and articles including those cited previously in this review, *Long Rifles in North Carolina* (1968), and *The Moravian Potters in North Carolina* (1972), which he also co-authored with Rauschenberg.

As a teacher, John inspired students to enter the museum field, and as a colleague, he shared his research and opinions generously. Perhaps the greatest tribute to John's career will be how *The Furniture of Charleston* inspires future generations to advance the study of the topic he loved so well. For an example, one need only consult pages 102 to 113 of the first volume. Here, the authors illustrate two quintessential Charleston pieces, a mahogany desk-and-bookcase with cypress and a mahogany and mahogany veneer double chest with cypress and white pine secondary woods (see figs. 3 and 4) made between 1750 and 1765. Each bears the cipher "WA" stamped on the bottom of the lower cases. The ciphers are identical, and the authors predict that their discovery will lead to an eventual attribution to the cabinetmaker William Axson (ca. 1739–1800), based on "matching marks" seen on the brickwork at Pompion Hill and St. Stephen's churches, where Axson is known to have worked, and as "he was the only Charleston cabinetmaker with those initials that was active in the 1750s and 1760s" capable of producing such stylish wares. However, Rauschenberg and Bivins conclude that:

> Linking these two pieces to the same shop and thus further linking the other eight or nine pieces in this group to Axson is tempting, but impossible to positively attribute without further research on this topic—research that is impossible for the authors to perform with the discovery of the mark on the double chest coming so close to deadlines for this publication. The marks and their relationship to furniture and cabinetmakers must be left for future researchers to investigate (pp. 102–3).

Which American furniture student is now prepared to accept the authors' challenge? By completing such a comprehensive encyclopedia of Charleston furniture, Brad Rauschenberg and John Bivins have guaranteed that questions such as these will occupy the minds of America's furniture scholars, collectors, and dealers for decades to come.

Robert A. Leath
Colonial Williamsburg Foundation

1. J. Thomas Savage, "The Holmes-Edwards Library Bookacse and the Origins of the German School in Pre-Revolutionary Charleston" in *American Furniture*, edited by Luke Beckerdite (Hanover, N.H.: University Press of New England for the Chipstone Founation, 1997), p.107.

Compiled by
Gerald W. R. Ward

Recent Writing on American Furniture: A Bibliography

▼ THIS YEAR'S LIST includes primarily titles published in 2002 and through late September of 2003. The short title *American Furniture 2002* is used in citations for articles and reviews published in last year's issue of this journal, which is also cited in full under Luke Beckerdite's name.

For their assistance in various ways, I am grateful to Luke Beckerdite, Edward S. Cooke, Jr., Jonathan L. Fairbanks, Steven M. Lash, Milo Naeve, Pat Warner, and Philip Zimmerman.

As always, I would be glad to receive information about titles that have been inadvertently omitted from this or previous lists, as well as information about new publications. Review copies of significant works would also be much appreciated.

Adamson, Glenn. "The Politics of the Caned Chair." In *American Furniture 2002,* 174–206. 39 color and bw illus.

Adamson, Glenn. "A Writer's Block." *Woodwork,* no. 80 (April 2003): 40–41. 1 color illus.

Adamson, Glenn. Review of Jeremy Adamson, *The Furniture of Sam Maloof* and Ursula Ilse-Neuman et al., *The Furniture of Garry Knox Bennett.* In *American Furniture 2002,* 243–50. 1 color and 1 bw illus.

Albert, Gary J. "The Furniture of Charleston, 1680–1820." *The Catalogue of Antiques and Fine Arts* 3, no. 6 (2002): 236–241. Color and bw illus.

Albertson, Karla Klein. "Byrdcliffe Arts Colony." *Antiques and the Arts Weekly* (June 13, 2003): 1, 40–42. 14 bw illus.

Albertson, Karla Klein. "The Incredible Elastic Chairs of Samuel Gragg at Winterthur." *Antiques and the Arts Weekly* (April 4, 2003): 1, 40–41. bw illus.

Alexander, John D. "Riving Wood." *Woodwork,* no. 80 (April 2003): 64–70. Color illus., line drawings.

American Period Furniture 3 (January 2003): 1–75. Numerous bw illus. (This issue of the journal of the Society of American Period Furniture Makers includes a number of construction-related articles, including Arthur K. Peters, "The Goddard-Townsend Shells of Newport: A Construction Monograph.")

Ames, Kenneth L. Review of Wendy A. Cooper, *An American Vision: Henry Francis du Pont's Winterthur Museum.* In *American Furniture 2002,* 256–59.

Antonsen, Lasse B., et al. *Craft Transformed: Program in Artisanry.* Brockton, Mass.: Fuller Museum of Art, 2003. 56 pp.; numerous color illus., checklists. (Includes essays by Jonathan L. Fairbanks, Gail M. Brown, and others.)

Ayres, James. *Domestic Interiors: The British Tradition.* Aylesbury, England: National Trust, 2003.

New Haven: Yale University Press, 2003. 256 pp.; illus.

Bailey, W. N. *Defining Edges: A New Look at Picture Frames.* New York: Harry N. Abrams, 2002. 136 pp.; numerous color and bw illus., glossary, bibliography, index.

Banks, William Nathaniel. "History in Houses: Woodlawn in Ellsworth, Maine." *Antiques* 163, no. 1 (January 2003): 142–49. 15 color illus.

Bates, Elizabeth Bidwell. "An Idea Whose Time Has Come: Virtual Restoration of a Once Glittering Chair." *Maine Antique Digest* 30, no. 12 (December 2002): 8A. 2 bw illus.

Beach, Laura. "*American Furniture*: A Decade of Discoveries." *Antiques and the Arts Weekly* (February 7, 2003): 1, 40–42. bw illus.

Beach, Laura. "Wallace Nutting and the Invention of Old America." *Antiques and the Arts Weekly* (June 27, 2002): 1, 40–41. 15 bw illus.

Beckerdite, Luke, and Alan Miller. "Furniture Fakes from the Chipstone Collection." In *American Furniture 2002,* 54–93. 73 bw illus.

Beckerdite, Luke, ed. *American Furniture 2002.* Milwaukee, Wis.: Chipstone Foundation, 2002. xii + 289 pp.; numerous color and bw illus., bibliography, index. Distributed by the University Press of New England, Hanover, N.H., and London.

Benton, Charlotte, Tim Benton, and Ghislaine Wood, eds. *Art Deco 1910–1939.* London: V&A Publications, 2003. 464 pp.; numerous color and bw illus., bibliography, object list, indexes.

Berlin, Carswell Rush. "'Solid and Permanent Grandeur': The Design Roots of American Classical Furniture." *International Fine Art and Antiques Dealers Show* [catalogue] (New York, 2002): 17–26. Illus.

Binzen, Jonathan. "A Curious Career: David Powell and Leeds Design Workshops." *Woodwork,* no. 75 (June 2002): 64–71. Color illus.

Bivins, John, Jr. "Collection of Essays by John Bivins, Jr.: The Luminary Editorials." *Journal of Early Southern Decorative Arts* 28, no. 1 (summer 2002): 53–156. bw illus.

Blackburn, Roderic H. "Living with Antiques: The Jesse Van Slyke House in Schenectady, New York." *Antiques* 164, no. 2 (August 2003): 70–79. 13 color illus.

Blom, Philipp. *To Have and to Hold: An Intimate History of Collectors and Collecting.* Woodstock, N.Y.: Overlook Press, 2003. xiv + 274 pp.; bw illus., bibliography, index.

[Blunk, J. B.]. Obituary. *American Craft* 62, no. 5 (October/November 2002): 20–21. 1 bw illus.

Bowman, Trina Evarts, and Thomas Andrew Denenberg. "Wallace Nutting, Antiquarian and Entrepreneur." *The Catalogue of Antiques and Fine Art* 4, no. 2 (early summer 2002): 142–46. 7 color and bw illus.

Brown, Ann Eckert. "Painted Parlors: Jacob Maentel's Ornamented Interiors." *Folk Art* 27, no. 3 (fall 2002): 38–45. Color illus.

Brown, Bill. *A Sense of Things: The Object Matter of American Literature.* Chicago: University of Chicago Press, 2003. xii + 245 pp.; 19 bw illus., index.

Bruce, Ian. *The Loving Eye and Skilful Hand: The Keswick School of Industrial Arts.* Carlisle, England: Bookcase, 2001. 152 pp.; numerous bw illus., bibliography. (Re English arts and crafts.)

Brunk, Andrew. "The Claypoole Family Joiners of Philadelphia: Their Legacy and the Context of Their Work." In *American Furniture 2002,* 147–73. 30 color and bw illus.

Burks, Jean M. "The Shelburne Museum: Selections from the 'Collection of Collections.'" *The Catalogue of Antiques and Fine Arts* 3, no. 6 (2002): 266–69. Color illus.

Buskirk, Russell. "Lily of the Valley Inlay." *The Catalogue of Antiques and Fine Arts* 3, no. 6 (2002): 242–43. Color illus.

"Cabinets of Curiosities." *American Craft* 63, no. 3 (June/July 2003): 64–66. 5 color illus.

Carlisle, Nancy. *Cherished Possessions: A New England Legacy.* Boston: Society for the Preservation of New England Antiquities, 2003. 448 pp.; numerous color and bw illus., bibliography, index.

Carlisle, Nancy. "Revolutionary Acts: Selections from the SPNEA Collection." *Antiques* 164, no. 2 (August 2003): 60–69. 11 color and 2 bw illus.

[Cederquist, John]. "Aileen Osborn Webb Awards 2002: . . . John Cederquist, Fellow." *American Craft* 62, no. 5 (October/November 2002): 74. 1 color illus.

The Chair. Worcester, Mass.: Krikorian Gallery, Worcester Center for Crafts, 2002. 44 pp.; color and bw illus.

Chastang, Yannick. *Paintings in Wood: French Marquetry Furniture.* London: Wallace Collection, 2001. 118 pp.; 71 color and bw illus., bibliography.

Chinnici, R. Curt. "Pennsylvania Clouded Limestone: Its Quarrying, Processing, and Use in the Stone Cutting, Furniture, and Architectural Trades." In *American Furniture 2002,* 94–124. 43 color and bw illus.

Clark, Michael, and Jill Thomas-Clark. *Stickley Brothers: The Quest for an American Voice.* Salt Lake City, Utah: Gibbs Smith, 2002. 176 pp.; numerous color and bw illus., bibliography, index.

Clowes, Jody. "Studio Case Furniture: The Inside Story." *American Craft* 62, no. 5 (October/November 2002): 80–83. 8 color illus.

Cohen, Lizabeth. *A Consumer's Republic: The Politics of Mass Consumption in Postwar America.* New York: Alfred A. Knopf, 2003. 567 pp.; 64 bw illus., 3 maps, index.

Congdon-Martin, Douglas, ed. *The Gustav Stickley Photo Archives.* Atglen, Pa.: Schiffer Publishing, 2002. 256 pp.; numerous illus.

Connors, Michael A. "Caribbean Elegance: Exotic Furniture from the English Islands." *The Catalogue of Antiques and Fine Art* 3, no. 2 (autumn 2002): 32–39. Color illus.

Cooke, Edward S., Jr., Gerald W. R. Ward, and Kelly H. L'Ecuyer, with the assistance of Pat Warner. *The Maker's Hand: American Studio Furniture, 1940–1990.* Boston: MFA Publications, 2003. 168 pp.; numerous color and bw illus., appendixes, chronology, bibliography, index.

[Crozat, George B., Collection]. *Houmas House Plantation and Gardens, River Road, Burnside, Louisiana: Historic Property and Entire Contents.* New Orleans: Neal Auction Company, May 17–18, 2003. 60 pp.; numerous color illus. (Auction catalogue for the pioneering collection of Dr. Crozat [1894–1966] including a great deal of Louisiana furniture.)

[Currier Museum of Art]. "Currier Museum to Restore Rare Cupboard." *Antiques and the Arts Weekly* (August 1, 2003): S–30. 1 bw illus.

Curry, David Park. "Impressionism versus the Aesthetic Movement." *Antiques* 162, no. 5 (November 2002): 140–51. 24 color illus.

Danto, Arthur C. "Like a gift for someone you love: The Furniture Art of Judy Kensley McKie." In *Judy Kensley McKie,* 3–7. Boston, Mass.: Gallery NAGA, 2002. 28 pp.; color illus.

Darling, Michael. *Roy McMakin: A Door Meant as Adornment.* Los Angeles: Museum of Contemporary Art, 2003. 97 pp.; color illus.

Denenberg, Thomas Andrew. *Wallace Nutting and the Invention of Old America.* New Haven: Yale University Press in association with the Wadsworth Atheneum Museum of Art, 2003. xi + 228 pp.; numerous color and bw illus., bibliography, index.

Denenberg, Thomas Andrew, and Trina Evarts Bowman. "Wallace Nutting and the Invention of Old America." *Antiques* 163, no. 5 (May 2003): 130–37. 9 color and 4 bw illus.

Dervan, Andrew H. "A Study of Full Size 'Willard Clocks' Manufactured by the Waltham Clock Company." *NAWCC Bulletin* 45, no. 2 (April 2003): 157–68. Numerous bw illus., tables.

"Discoveries." *The Catalogue of Antiques and Fine Art* 3, no. 4 (autumn 2002): 11+. Color illus. (Includes painted blanket chest, dated 1818, from Kent County, Delaware.)

"Discoveries." *The Catalogue of Antiques and Fine Art* 3, no. 6 (2002): 18. (Re corner cupboard, attributed to the "W. H." workshop, Roanoke River Basin, North River Basin, ca. 1785, acquired by the Mint Museum of Art.)

"Discoveries." *The Catalogue of Antiques and Fine Art* 4, no. 2 (early summer 2002): 17. 1 color illus. (Re Wallace Nutting Sudbury cupboard acquired by SPNEA.)

"Discoveries." *The Catalogue of Antiques and Fine Art* 4, no. 3 (summer 2003): 16. 1 color illus. (Re New England high chest of drawers, ca. 1725, acquired by Longfellow's Wayside Inn, Sudbury, Massachusetts.)

Ebert-Schifferer, Sybille, et al. *Deceptions and Illusions: Five Centuries of Trompe l'Oeil Painting.* Washington, D.C.: National Gallery of Art, 2002. 407 pp.; numerous color illus., checklist, bibliography, index. (Includes a work by Wendell Castle.)

Edwards, Julie Eldridge. "The Brick House: The Vermont Country House of Electra Havemeyer Webb." *Antiques* 163, no. 1 (January 2003): 192–201. 10 color and 9 bw illus.

Edwards, Robert. "Furniture Designed at the Byrdcliffe Arts and Crafts Colony." *Antiques* 163, no. 5 (May 2003): 106–15. 20 color and 1 bw illus.

Eliens, Titus M. "Furniture from Batavia and the Cape." *The Cata-*

logue of Antiques and Fine Arts 3, no. 6 (2002): 256–61. Color illus.

Elliott, Bridget, and Janice Helland, eds. *Women Artists and the Decorative Arts, 1880–1935.* Burlington, Vt.: Ashgate, 2002. 246 pp.; illus.

"Exhibition Showcases Work of NH Furniture Masters and Their Students from NH's State Prison." *Antiques and the Arts Weekly* (June 27, 2003): 14.

Fairbanks, Jonathan L. "Sam Maloof, Curator." In *The Chair,* 40–42. Worcester, Mass.: Krikorian Gallery, Worcester Center for Crafts, 2002. 1 bw illus.

Fairbanks, Jonathan L., et al. *Becoming a Nation: Americana from the Diplomatic Reception Rooms, U.S. Department of State.* Washington, D.C.: Trust for Museum Exhibitions; New York: Rizzoli, 2003. 232 pp.; numerous color illus., bibliography, index.

[Farrar-Mansur House Museum]. "Farrar-Mansur House Museum to Display Early Nineteenth Century Chest." *Antiques and the Arts Weekly* (October 4, 2002): 59. 2 bw illus. (Re cherry chest made in Weston, Vermont, by Aaron Miltimore, ca. 1827.)

Favermann, Mark. "Review: Judy Kensley McKie." *American Craft* 63, no. 2 (April/May 2003): 70–71. 3 color illus.

Feigenbaum, Gail, et al. *Jefferson's America and Napoleon's France: An Exhibition for the Louisiana Purchase Bicentennial.* Seattle: New Orleans Museum of Art in association with University of Washington Press, 2003. xvii + 286 pp.; numerous color and bw illus., bibliography, index.

Fletcher, Brigitte. "Trendy Wine Furniture." *The Catalogue of Antiques and Fine Art* 4, no. 2 (early summer 2002): 126–19. 10 color and bw illus.

[Fogg Art Museum]. "Anne and Fred Vogel Make Initial Gift of Early American Furniture to Fogg." *Building Our Future* 11, no. 2 (fall 2002): 7. (Re gift of Essex County, Massachusetts, armchair, 1660–1690, of painted maple and ash.)

[Fogg Art Museum]. "A Lifetime of Pleasure: Passions of Collectors Past and Present Enrich Harvard's Art Museum." *Building Our Future* 11, no. 1 (winter 2002): 4–5. Re promised gift of six pieces of seventeenth-century Massachusetts furniture.)

Follansbee, Peter. "Manuscripts, Marks, and Material Culture: Sources for Understanding the Joiner's Trade in Seventeenth-Century America." *American Furniture 2002,* 125–46. 37 color and bw illus.

Follansbee, Peter. "Seventeenth-Century Carving Techniques." *The Catalogue of Antiques and Fine Art* 4, no. 2 (early summer 2002): 140–41. 14 color illus.

Forsyth, Amy. "Review: Peter Pierobon." *American Craft* 63, no. 3 (June/July 2003): 72–73. 2 color illus.

Forsyth, Amy. "The Trouble with History: Three Case Studies." *Woodwork,* no. 83 (October 2003): 72–76. Color illus.

Friary, Donald R. "Fifty Years of Collecting for Historic Deerfield." [Catalogue of] 43rd *Annual Ellis Antiques Show* (Boston, 2002), 70–82. 14 color illus.

Furniture: Field Guide. Iola, Wis.: Krause Publications, 2002. 512 pp.; 400+ bw illus., line drawings, glossary.

Furniture History 37 (2001): 1–134. Numerous bw illus.

Furniture History 38 (2002): 1–165. Numerous bw illus.

[Furniture Society, The]. *Furniture Matters: A Periodic Forum of The Furniture Society* (October 2002): 1–12; (May 2003): 1–16. bw illus.

[Furniture Society, The]. *Furniture 2003 Program / Furniture Society Directory.* Free Union, Va.: The Furniture Society, 2003. 280 pp.; bw illus.

[Furniture Society, The]. *The Right Stuff: A Juried Exhibition of Upholstered Furniture.* Free Union, Va.: The Furniture Society, 2002. 32 pp.; color illus. (Includes short essays by Andrew H. Glasgow and Bebe Pritam Johnson.)

"Gallery." *Woodwork,* no. 75 (June 2002): 42–49. Color illus. (Re contemporary furniture.)

"Gallery." *Woodwork,* no. 76 (August 2002): 44–49. Color illus. (Re contemporary furniture.)

"Gallery." *Woodwork,* no. 77 (October 2002): 40–45. Color illus. (Re contemporary furniture.)

"Gallery." *Woodwork,* no. 78 (December 2002): 46–53. Color illus. (Re contemporary furniture.)

"Gallery." *Woodwork,* no. 79 (February 2003): 42–48. Color illus. (Re contemporary furniture.)

"Gallery." *Woodwork,* no. 80 (April 2003): 42–48. Color illus. (Re contemporary furniture.)

"Gallery." *Woodwork,* no. 81 (June 2003): 42–50. Color illus. (Re contemporary furniture, turned wooden vessels, and other objects.)

"Gallery." *Woodwork,* no. 82 (August 2003): 42–51. Color illus. (Re contemporary furniture.)

"Gallery." *Woodwork,* no. 83 (October 2003): 44–49. Color illus.

"Gallery." *Woodwork,* no. 84 (December 2003): 37–43. Color illus.

Gibson, Scott. "A Shaker Life." *Woodwork,* no. 82 (August 2003): 22–28. Color illus. (Re contemporary woodworker Christian Becksvoort.)

Gleason, Tara. "The Bayly Suite of Painted Furniture." *The Catalogue of Antiques and Fine Art* 4, no. 1 (spring 2003): 206. Color illus.

Gould, James. "Artisans of the New Forest." *Woodwork,* no. 81 (June 2003): 70–76. Color illus.

Gray, Nina, and Pamela Herrick. "Decoration in the Golden Age: The Frederick W. Vanderbilt Mansion, Hyde Park, New York." *Studies in the Decorative Arts* 10, no. 1 (fall/winter 2002–2003): 98–141. 23 bw illus.

Gronning, Erik. "The History of an Heirloom." *The Catalogue of Antiques and Fine Art* 3, no. 5 (holiday 2002): 150–51. 2 color illus.

Gronning, Erik. "New Haven's Six-Board Chests." *Antiques* 163, no. 5 (May 2003): 116–21. 10 color and 3 bw illus.

Gronning, Erik. "Patria in Vermont." *The Catalogue of Antiques and Fine Art* 4, no. 1 (spring 2003): 38–45. Color illus.

Gustafson, Eleanor H. "Museum Accessions." *Antiques* 163, no. 5 (May 2003): 42. 3 color illus. (Re acquisition of chest of drawers, 1867, attributed to Jeremiah Stahl of Soap Hollow, Pennsylvania, by the Westmoreland Museum of American Art; of a desk-and-bookcase, ca. 1807–1810, by James Dinsmore and Smith Batchelder of Brunswick, Maine, acquired by the Maine State Museum; and a Herter Brothers cabinet of ca. 1879, by the Museum of Fine Arts, Boston.)

Gustafson, Eleanor H., ed. "Collectors' Notes: Thomas Richards, Clockmaker?" *Antiques* 162, no. 4 (October 2002): 46. 1 color illus.

[Hancock Shaker Museum]. "The Hancock Bishopric." *Antiques and the Arts Weekly* (October 11, 2002): 111. 1 bw illus.

Havard, Ralph O., III. "Global Appreciation." *Sotheby's Preview* (January 2003): 126–27.

Hicks, Robert, and Benjamin Hubbard Caldwell, Jr. "A Short History of the Tennessee Sugar Chest." *Antiques* 164, no. 3 (September 2003): 128–33. 13 color illus.

Hofer, Margaret K., and Roberta J. M. Olson. "Highlights: Seat of Empire." *The Catalogue of Antiques and Fine Art* 3, no. 2 (autumn 2002): 29. 2 color illus.

Hofer, Margaret K., and Roberta J. M. Olson. "Napoleon's Fauteuil: From Paris to Point Breeze." *Antiques* 162, no. 4 (October 2002): 140–49. 12 color and 2 bw illus. (See also Patricia Tyson Stroud, "Point Breeze: Joseph Bonaparte's American Retreat" in the same issue.)

Hogbin, Stephen. "Aspects of Structure." *Woodwork*, no. 82 (August 2003): 61–65. Color and bw illus.

Hood, Graham. "State, Dignity, Authority: Four Williamsburg Chairs are Distinctive Expressions of Colonial Sophistication and Culture." *Colonial Williamsburg* 25, no. 1 (spring 2003): 30–35. 7 color illus.

[Hudson River Museum]. "Shaker Crafts and Furniture Focus of Hudson River Museum Show." *Antiques and the Arts Weekly* (June 13, 2003): 16. 1 bw illus.

Jackman, Bob. "Federal and Empire Treasures: The Lighthouse Clocks of Simon Willard at the Willard Museum." *Antiques and the Arts Weekly* (October 4, 2002): 1, 40–43. 27 bw illus.

Jackson, David, and Dane Owen. *Japanese Cabinetry: The Art and Craft of Tansu.* Salt Lake City, Utah: Gibbs Smith, 2002. ix + 256 pp.; numerous color and bw illus., glossary, bibliography, chronology, index.

John Cederquist. New York: Franklin Parrasch Gallery, 2003. Unpaged; color illus. (Includes essay by Eleanor Heartney, "Form Forgets Function: The Perplexing Work of John Cederquist.")

Jones, Robin D. "'Furniture of Plain but Substantial Kind' at the British Governors' Houses in Ceylon, c. 1830–1860." *Studies in the Decorative Arts* 10, no. 1 (fall/winter 2002–2003): 2–34. 12 bw illus.

Judy Kensley McKie. Boston, Mass.: Gallery NAGA, 2002. 28 pp.; color illus.

Kalb, Laurie Beth. "The Chair in Worcester County History, Craft Patronage, and Education." In *The Chair*, 5–12. Worcester, Mass.: Krikorian Gallery, Worcester Center for Crafts, 2002.

Keno, Leslie. "Celebrating Colonial Style." *Sotheby's Preview* (January 2003): 120–21. 1 color illus. (Re Appell collection of American furniture to be sold at auction.)

Keno, Leslie. "Top Form." *Sotheby's Preview* (January 2003): 117. 2 color illus. (Re New York marble-top pier table, ca. 1775.)

Kirtley, Alexandra Alevizatos. "Survival of the Fittest: The Lloyd Family's Furniture Legacy." In *American Furniture 2002*, 2–53. 77 color and bw illus.

Kirtley, Alexandra Alevizatos, Thomas Heller, and Mary McGinn. "Lloyd Family Painted Furniture: Revisited." *The Catalogue of Antiques and Fine Art* 4, no. 1 (spring 2003): 174–77. Color illus.

Landsmark, Ted. "Charleston's Antiques Symposium 2003: A Presenter's View." *Maine Antique Digest* 31, no. 8 (August 2003): 45D. 3 bw illus.

Lane, Joshua W., and Donald P. White. "The Woodworkers of Windsor." *The Catalogue of Antiques and Fine Art* 4, no. 2 (early summer 2002): 135–39. 6 color and bw illus.

Lapansky, Emma Jones, and Anne A. Verplanck, eds. *Quaker Aesthetics: Reflections on a Quaker Ethic in American Design and Consumption.* Philadelphia: University of Pennsylvania Press, 2003. 400 pp.; numerous bw and color illus., glossary, index.

Latta, Steve. "Skin Deep: Three Centuries of Inlay." *Woodwork*, no. 83 (October 2003): 66–71. Color illus.

Lavine, John. "Making the Case for Studio Furniture." *Woodwork*, no. 79 (February 2003): 66–71. 15 color illus.

Lavine, John. "The Stickley Legacy." *Woodwork*, no. 80 (April 2003): 80. 2 color illus., biblio.

L'Ecuyer, Kelly H. "Uplifting the Southern Highlander: Handicrafts at Biltmore Estate Industries." *Winterthur Portfolio* 37, nos. 2/3 (summer/autumn 2002): 123–46. 12 bw illus.

Ledes, Allison Eckardt. "Current and Coming: Decorative Arts of New York." *Antiques* 162, no. 5 (November 2002): 28, 29. 2 color illus. (Re installation of the Wunsch collection at the New York State Museum, Albany.)

Ledes, Allison Eckardt. "Current and Coming: "A First Lady and Furniture." *Antiques* 164, no. 4 (October 2003): 20, 22. 2 color illus.

Ledes, Allison Eckardt. "Current and Coming: French Furniture in Boston." *Antiques* 162, no. 4 (October 2002): 22, 24. 2 color illus.

Ledes, Allison Eckardt. "Current and Coming: New York Neoclassical Furniture." *Antiques* 164, no. 2 (August 2003): 18, 20. 2 color illus.

Ledes, Allison Eckardt. "Design Notes: Conserving a French Furniture Suite." *Antiques* 162, no. 4 (October 2002): 176. 3 color illus.

Lefteri, Chris. *Wood: Materials for Inspirational Design*. Mies, Switzerland: RotoVision, 2003. 160 pp.; color illus., index.

"Lifestyle: A Collector's Collector." *The Catalogue of Antiques and Fine Art* 4, no. 2 (early summer 2002): 32–37. Color illus. (Re collection of Peter Tillou.)

Lindquist, David P., and Caroline C. Warren. *The Big Book of Antique Furniture*. Iola, Wis.: Krause Publications, 2002. 600+ pp.; numerous color and bw illus., index. (Reprint in one volume of three previous works by the authors: *English and Continental Furniture, Colonial Revival Furniture*, and *Victorian Furniture*.)

McCormick, Heather Jane. Review of Anna Tobin D'Ambrosio, *Masterpieces of American Furniture from the Munson-Williams-Proctor Institute*. In *Studies in the Decorative Arts* 10, no. 1 (fall/winter 2002–2003): 171–74.

McMahon, James D., Jr. "The Ninth Wonder of the Age: The John Feister Monumental Apostolic Clock Unveiled." *NAWCC Bulletin* 45, no. 4 (August 2003): 425–35. 18 bw illus., bibliography.

McMahon, Patricia. "Hands On: Peacock Feathers on Gragg Chairs." *The Catalogue of Antiques and Fine Art* 4, no. 3 (summer 2003): 168–69. Color illus.

McPherson, Anne S. "The Charleston Double Chest." *The Catalogue of*

Antiques and Fine Arts 3, no. 6 (2002): 244–47. Color and bw illus.

[Minneapolis Institute of Arts]. "Unified Vision: The Purcell-Cuts House and the Prairie School Collection at the Minneapolis Institute of Arts." *Antiques and the Arts Weekly* (January 31, 2003): 1, 40–43. bw illus.

"Modern Times: Reviving Dunbar . . . Kagan's Lastest . . . ." *Modernism* 6, no. 1 (spring 2003): 27–32. Color and bw illus.

Mones, Richard Alan, and Sir George White. "Museum Focus: The Worshipful Company of Clockmakers." *The Catalogue of Antiques and Fine Art* 4, no. 2 (early summer 2002): 152–54. 3 color illus.

Moser, Thomas, with Brad Lemley. *Thos. Moser: Artistry in Wood*. San Francisco: Chronicle Books, 2002. 192 pp.; numerous color and bw illus.

Mostyn, Thomas. "The Search for Clockmaker Duncan Beard and Casemaker John Javier." *NAWCC Bulletin* 45, no. 3 (June 2003): 315–17. 2 bw illus.

[Munson-Williams-Proctor Institute]. "Heavy Metal: Innovative Victorian Furniture On View at Munson-Williams-Proctor Arts Institute." *Antiques and the Arts Weekly* (November 15, 2002): 49. 5 bw illus.

[Museum of Early Southern Decorative Arts]. "New in the MESDA Collection." *The Luminary: The Newsletter of the Museum of Early Southern Decorative Arts* 23, no. 2 (fall 2002): 6–8, 5 bw illus. (Includes turned great chair from Mecklenburg County, Virginia, 1720–1750.)

Mussey, Robert. "Fact or Inscription?" *Sotheby's Preview* (January 2003): 128–29. 3 color illus. (Re serpentine front, bombé chest of drawers signed "Nathan Bowen 1772" being offered for auction.)

[New-York Historical Society]. "Seat of Empire Opens October 8 at the

New-York Historical Society." *Antiques and the Arts Weekly* (October 4, 2002): 71. 1 bw illus.

"Noteworthy Sales." *The Catalogue of Antiques and Fine Arts* 3, no. 4 (autumn 2002): 16+. Color illus. (Includes painted corner cupboard, New Jersey, ca.1790.)

"Noteworthy Sales." *The Catalogue of Antiques and Fine Arts* 3, no. 6 (2002): 24. (Re Seymour-style tambour desk.)

Nunes, Pater A. "F. J. Gately: Winchester, N.H., Maker of Wooden Clocks." *NAWCC Bulletin* 45, no. 4 (August 2003): 436–38. 9 bw illus.

Nye, John B. A. "Painterly Provenance." *Sotheby's Preview* (May 2003): 116. 1 color illus. (Re Connecticut chest of drawers, ca. 1780, owned by Norman Rockwell.)

Nye, John B. A. "What's in a Name?" *Sotheby's Preview* (January 2003): 122–25. 5 color illus.

Pastiglia Boxes: Hidden Treasures of the Italian Renaissance. Florence: Centro Di, 2002. Unpaged; numerous color and bw illus.

Pierce, Anne. "Exhibition Notes: 'Heavy Metal: Innovative Victorian Furniture,' on View at Munson-Williams-Proctor Art Institute." *Newsletter of the Decorative Arts Society* 11, no. 12 (summer 2003): 7–8. 1 bw illus.

Pierce, Kerry. "How-To in the Corn Belt: The Marc Adams School of Woodworking." *Woodwork*, no. 75 (June 2002): 52–57. Color illus.

[Pierschalla, Michael]. Obituary. *American Craft* 62, no. 5 (October/November 2002): 21. 1 bw illus.

Podmaniczky, Michael. "Hands On: The Elastic Chairs of Samuel Gragg." *The Catalogue of Antiques and Fine Art* 4, no. 3 (summer 2003): 166–67. Color illus.

Podmaniczky, Michael. "The Incredible Elastic Chairs of Samuel Gragg." *Winterthur Magazine* (winter 2002): 14–18. 4 color illus.

Podmaniczky, Michael. "The Incredible Elastic Chairs of Samuel Gragg." *Antiques* 163, no. 5 (May 2003): 138–45. 15 color illus.

Prown, Jonathan, and Katherine Hemple Prown. "The Quiet Canon: Tradition and Exclusion in American Furniture Scholarship." In *American Furniture 2002*, 207–27. 24 color and bw illus.

Ramljak, Suzanne. *Crafting a Legacy: Contemporary American Crafts in the Philadelphia Museum of Art*. Philadelphia: Philadelphia Museum of Art, 2002. 192 pp.; numerous color illus.

Rauschenberg, Bradford L., and John Bivins, Jr. *The Furniture of Charleston, 1680–1820*. 3 vols. Winston-Salem, N.C.: Old Salem, Inc., and the Museum of Early Southern Decorative Arts, 2003. Vol. 1, *Colonial Furniture*. Vol. 2, *Neoclassical Furniture*. Vol. 3, *The Cabinetmakers*. xxxv + 1388 pp., numerous color and bw illus., maps, appendices, bibliography, concordance, index.

Rauschenberg, Bradford L., and John Bivins, Jr. "Robert Walker, Charleston Cabinetmaker." *Antiques* 163, no. 2 (February 2003): 62–69. 9 color and 8 bw illus.

"Recent Acquisitions." *Newsletter of the Decorative Arts Society* 10, no. 3 (fall 2002): 15–18. 8 bw illus. (Includes desk-and-bookcase, ca. 1800, from lower southern Piedmont region, acquired by Georgia Museum of Art; and walnut corner cupboard, ca. 1785, by the "WH" shop of Roanoke River Basin, North Carolina, acquired by the Mint Museum of Art.)

"Recent Acquisitions." *Newsletter of the Decorative Arts Society* 11, no. 12 (summer 2003): 9–11. (Includes references to furniture acquired by Historic Deerfield and the Virginia Museum of Fine Arts.)

Regional Furniture 16 (2002): 1–121. Numerous bw illus. (Includes reprint of *The Glasgow Book of Prices for Manufacturing Cabinet Work*, 1806.)

Regional Furniture Society Newsletter, no. 37 (autumn 2002): 1–16. bw illus.

Rossberg, Anne-Katrin. "The Interiors and Furniture of Dagobert Peche." *Antiques* 162, no. 4 (October 2002): 112–21. 11 color and 4 bw illus. (Re Austrian designer of the early twentieth century.)

Sandberg, Jeni L. "Stanford White's House for Payne Whitney in New York City." *Antiques* 162, no. 4 (October 2002): 122–29. 9 color and 5 bw illus.

[Schaefer, Chris]. "New America." *Antiques and the Arts Weekly* (October 4, 2002): 80. 1 bw illus. (Re exhibition of contemporary furniture by Schaefer at Hudson, New York, gallery.)

Serfaty, Gail F. "Becoming a Nation: Americana from the Diplomatic Reception Rooms." *The Catalogue of Antiques and Fine Art* 4, no. 1 (spring 2003): 188–93. Color illus.

Sheridan, John Grew. "Story Furniture." *Woodwork*, no. 84 (December 2003): 59–63. Color illus.

[Society for the Preservation of New England Antiquities]. "SPNEA Acquires Wallace Nutting Sudbury Cupboard." *Antiques and the Arts Weekly* (October 18, 2002): 8.

Solis-Cohen, Lita. "Long-Awaited Study of Charleston Furniture." *Maine Antique Digest* 31, no. 8 (August 2003): 45B. 1 bw illus.

Solis-Cohen, Lita. "Rare Phyfe Chairs Don't Go Unnoticed." *Maine Antique Digest* 30, no. 12 (December 2002): 9A. 1 bw illus.

Solis-Cohen, Lita. "The Tenth *American Furniture*" (book review). *Maine Antique Digest* 31, no. 3 (March 2003): 24E–25E. 1 bw illus.

Sperling, David A. "The Connecticut Dwarf Tall Clock—Or Is It a Shelf Clock?" *Maine Antique Digest* 31, no. 10 (October 2003): 7B. 10 bw illus., bibliography.

Spriggs, Remi. "Living with Antiques: The Vira Hladun-Goldmann House in New York City." *Antiques* 163, no. 4 (April 2003): 112–19. 13 color illus.

Taragin, Davira S., et al. *The Alliance of Art and Industry: Toledo Designs for a Modern America*. Toledo, Ohio: Toledo Museum of Art, 2002. 235 pp.; numerous color and bw illus., biographies, catalogue, index. Distributed by Hudson Hills Press, New York.

Tarantal, Stephen, Helen W. Drutt English, and Edward S. Cooke, Jr. *Daniel Jackson: Dovetailing History*. Philadelphia: Rosenwald-Wolf Gallery, The University of the Arts, 2003. 64 pp.; color and bw illus., checklist.

Trent, Robert F., and Michael Podmaniczky. "An Early Cupboard Fragment from the Harvard College Joinery Tradition." In *American Furniture 2002*, 228–42. 29 color and bw illus.

Trout, George. "Teaching." *Woodwork*, no. 76 (August 2002): 39–43. Color illus.

Van Cott, Margaret. "Thomas Burling of New York City, Exponent of the New Republic Style." *Furniture History* 37 (2001): 32–50. 14 bw illus., appendix.

[Virginia Museum of Fine Arts]. "VMA Acquires Still Life, Rare Desk." *Antiques and the Arts Weekly* (March 7, 2003): 18. 2 bw illus. (Re acquisition of Newport block-and-shell bureau dressing table, ca. 1765–1770.)

Ward, Gerald W. R. "West Meets East: American Furniture in the Anglo-American Taste at the Museum of Fine Arts, Boston." *Apollo* 157, no. 495 (May 2003): 27–29. 12 color and 1 bw illus.

Ward, Gerald W. R. Review of Clive Edwards, *Encyclopedia of Furniture Materials, Trades, and Techniques*, and Witold Rybczynski, *One Good Turn: A Natural History of the Screwdriver and the Screw*. In *American Furniture 2002*, 250–52.

Ward, Gerald W. R. Review of Ronald L. Hurst and Jonathan Prown, *Southern Furniture, 1680-1830: The Colonial Williamsburg Collection* and Donald C. Peirce, *Art & Enterprise: American Decorative Art, 1825–1917: The Virginia Carroll Crawford Collection*. In *Studies in the Decorative Arts* 10, no. 2 (spring/summer 2003): 143–45.

Ward, Gerald W. R., comp. "Recent Writing on American Furniture: A Bibliography." In *American Furniture 2002*, 260–70.

Watson, Anne. *Mod to Memphis: Design in Colour, 1960s–80s.* Burlington, Vt.: Ashgate, 2003. 80 pp.; 70 color and 21 bw illus.

Widmer, Kemble, II, and Judy Anderson. "Furniture from Marblehead, Massachusetts." *Antiques* 163, no. 5 (May 2003): 96–105. 21 color and 3 bw illus., 2 line drawings.

Wilbur, Frederick. "Blaise Gaston: In the Studio Furniture Tradition." *Woodwork*, no. 79 (February 2003): 22–31. Color illus.

Williams, Bradley J. *The Complete Reference Guide to Cushman Colonial Creations.* Robesonia, Pa.: Brady J. Williams Publishing, 2002. 259 pp.; illus.

[Windsor Historical Society]. "Windsor Historical Society to Open 'Woodworkers of Windsor' Sept. 20." *Antiques and the Arts Weekly* (September 12, 2003): 88. 1 bw illus.

[Windsor Historical Society]. "The Woodworkers of Windsor." *Antiques and the Arts Weekly* (September 5, 2003): 48–49. 3 bw illus.

[Winterthur Museum]. "The Incredible Elastic Chairs of Samuel Gragg." *Decorative Arts Society Newsletter* 11, no. 1 (spring 2003): 7–8. 3 bw illus.

Wood, D. "Body Language: Translating the Furniture of Michael Puryear." *Woodwork*, no. 83 (October 2003): 22–29. Color illus.

Wood, D. "Practical Matter: Contemporary Metal Furniture." *Metalsmith* 23, no. 1 (winter 2003): 42–49. Color and bw illus.

Wood, David F., and Robert Cheney. Review of Paul J. Foley, *Willard's Patent Time Pieces: A History of the Weight-Driven Banjo Clock, 1800–1900.* In *American Furniture 2002*, 252–56.

Wood, Ghislaine. *Essential Art Deco.* London: V&A Publications, 2003.

96 pp.; color and bw illus., timeline, bibliography, index.

Wright, Mary, and Russel Wright. *Guide to Easier Living.* 1950. Reprint. Salt Lake City, Utah: Gibbs Smith, 2003. xiv + 201 pp.; bw illus., line drawings, appendixes.

Zimmerman, Philip D. "Eighteenth-Century Chairs at Stenton." *Antiques* 163, no. 5 (May 2003): 122–29. 7 color and 2 bw illus.

Zimmerman, Philip D. "Mahantongo Blanket Chests." *Antiques* 162, no. 4 (October 2002): 160–69. 10 color illus.

Zimmerman, Philip D. Review of David B. Warren et al., *American Decorative Arts and Paintings in the Bayou Bend Collection.* In *Studies in the Decorative Arts* 10, no. 1 (fall/winter 2002–2003): 168–71.

Zinnkann, Heidrun. *Furniture Woods.* Munich: Prestel, 2002. 94 pp.; color illus., glossary, bibliography.

41; clothes frame, 34; cradles, 58, 89n101; cribs, 59; desk, 229(fig. 21); embroidery frames, 49; footstoves, 71; hand bellows, 68(fig. 24); kitchen tables, 29; Pembroke table, 252(figs.); side chair, 142(fig. 7); tea tables, 102(fig. 9), 117(fig. 31), 119(fig. 35)

Chess set, 75

Chester County (Pennsylvania), tea table, 122(fig. 39)

Chestnut: desk, 121(fig. 38); looms, 51

Chests: double, 282(fig. 3), 283(&fig. 4); low, 61–63(&fig. 22), 90n117; medicine, 68; sea, 63

Cheves, Langdon, 3

Chew, Harriet R., 186n35

Children's furniture, 54–58(&figs. 19, 20): bedsteads, 54–60(&figs.); cradles, 57–58(&fig. 20), 89n101, 89n102, 244–245(&fig. 5), 263, 266n10; cribs, 59; crickets, 58–60, 90n108; little chairs, 56–57; rocking chairs, 56

Children's wagon, 81

Chimney board, 69

Chimneypieces: Benjamin Savage House, 14–16(&figs.); Drayton Hall, 4(fig. 3)

Chipstone Foundation, 279

Chisholm, Archibald, 77

Chopping box, 41

Chopping trough, 85n47

Christian, Charles, 257–262(&figs. 13, 14), 267n17, 269

Chrome yellow, 142(fig. 7)

Church, Uzziel, 48

Church, use of low stools in, 60

Church and Sweet, 67

Churns, 32, 38–39

City Assembly Room and Library, 164(&fig. 36)

Claremont, 149, 150, 181n12, 183n16

Clark, John J., 35

Clark, William, 31

Claus Hufschmit at the Butter (Miller), 39(fig. 10)

Claw tables, 102; illustrations, 125(&fig. 42). *See also* Tilt-top tea tables

Cleaveland, Nathan, 38, 50

Clermont. *See* Claremont

Clinging vine motif, 190n47

Clinton, William Jefferson (Bill), 232

Clock reel, 48

Clocks, 45: cases, 272; Castle, 222, 223(fig. 9); pendulum, 274; shelves for, 61

Closets, kitchen, 30

Clothes frames, 33–34

Clotheshorse, 33–34, 244, 245

Clothespins, 33(&fig. 5)

Codman, John, 77

Coffee mill, 41–42

Coffeepots, 44

Coffins, 264

Cohen, Benjamin, 165, 177

Cole, Solomon, 53, 58

College of the Redwoods, 221

Collins, Stephen, 46, 80

Colonial craftsmanship, as Golden Age, 215, 216

Colonial economy, growth of, 113–114

Columbian Courier and Weekly Miscellany, 243

Colwill, Stiles, 149

Commercial and Farmers Bank, 190n46

Commercialism, of American studio furniture, 221

Common bedstead, 52–53(&fig. 18)

Compass boxes, 68

Comstock, Harold Eugene, 279

Constantine, Thomas, 262, 265, 268n32

Consumerism, 18th-century, 96–97, 130–131, 133n3, 137n45

Contract furniture industry, 277

Cook, Nathan Topping, 74

Cooking vessels, 43–44

Cooper, Wendy, 161

Corinthian capitals, 12(fig. 16), 13, 15

Corner cupboard, 60, 90n110

Cornice, 24

Corotomin, 134n10

Cort, Hendrik De, 186n33

Cost. *See* Prices

The Cottage (Hyde de Neuville), 79(fig. 32)

Cotton, Joseph, 34

Counting house desks, 261

Country houses, Baltimore: identification of, 151–159; painted furniture and, 161; women as head of household, 157–158. *See also* Morris suite

Courtenay, Hercules, 112

Cowdry, Lyman, 74

Cradles, 57–58(&fig. 20), 244–245(&fig. 5), 263, 266n10: woods for, 58, 89n101, 89n102

Craft Horizons, 219

Crafts, commercialization, 56, 226

Craftsman. *See* Artisans

Craftsmanship, 276

Craft Today: Poetry of the Physical, 233

Crage, Robert, 47, 55, 56, 57

Creamware plates, 132(&fig. 52)

Crest rails: Buchanan suite chair, 144(fig. 11); carving, 7(fig. 9); painted, 141(fig. 6), 168(fig. 39); painted medallions, 143(fig. 9), 158(fig. 30), 159(fig. 31), 172(figs.), 173(fig. 43), 176(figs.)

Cribs, 59

Crickets, 58–60, 90n108

Crim, William H., 140(fig. 4), 141

Cripps, William, 123(fig. 40)

Crotch veneers, 262

Crowninshield, Mary Boardman, 175

C-scrolls, 137n42

Cupboards: corner, 60, 90n110; hanging, 60; kitchen, 30–31; milk/cheese, 31

Curled maple: crickets, 59; walking stick, 77(fig. 30)

Curly English sycamore, 222(fig. 8)

Curly koa veneer, clock, 223(fig. 9)

Curly maple: settee, 231(fig. 24); use by Maloof, 231(&fig. 24)

Chipstone Foundation Publications

Order Form

Title	Code	Qty	Price
American Furniture 2002	AF2002	_____	$55
American Furniture 2001	AF2001	_____	$55
Back Issues Available 1994 – 2000	AFback	_____	$55
American Furniture – *2 year subscription*		_____	$100
American Furniture – *3 year subscription*		_____	$145
Ceramics in America 2002	CA2002	_____	$55
Ceramics in America 2001	CA2001	_____	$55
Ceramics in America – *2 year subscription*		_____	$100
Ceramics in America – *3 year subscription*		_____	$145
If These Pots Could Talk	IFTHCL	_____	$75
_____	_____	_____	_____
Shipping		_____	_____

U.S. Shipping $5.00 for first book; $1.25 for each additional book.
Foreign Shipping $6.50 for first book; $2.00 for each additional book.

TOTAL _____

Name _____

Tel _____

Address_____

_____

City State ZIP _____

❏ Check payable to "UPNE"

Credit Card

❏ AMEX ❏ Discover ❏ Mastercard ❏ VISA

CC#_____ Expires _____

Please send to:
University Press of New England
37 Lafayette Street
Lebanon, NH 03766
University.Press@Dartmouth.edu
603/643-7110 • 800/421-1561 FAX 603/643-1540 www.upne.com

www.chipstone.org